Figuring Racism in Medieval Christianity

Figuring Racism in Medieval Christianity

M. LINDSAY KAPLAN

OXFORD
UNIVERSITY PRESS

OXFORD
UNIVERSITY PRESS

Oxford University Press is a department of the University of Oxford. It furthers
the University's objective of excellence in research, scholarship, and education
by publishing worldwide. Oxford is a registered trade mark of Oxford University
Press in the UK and certain other countries.

Published in the United States of America by Oxford University Press
198 Madison Avenue, New York, NY 10016, United States of America.

CIP data is on file at the Library of Congress
ISBN 978–0–19–067824–1

1 3 5 7 9 8 6 4 2

Printed by Sheridan Books, Inc., United States of America

This book is dedicated to my mother, Anne Wingfield Kaplan, and in memory of my other "mothers" Emma Burnside Willis, Doris Bryce Ingram, and Frieda Grunfeld Eisen, whose love, courage, and integrity inspire all I do.

אני יי אלקיכם אשר הוצאתי אתכם מארץ מצרים מהית להם עבדים

(ויקרא כו:יג)

I am HaShem your G-d, who brought you out of the land
of Egypt, that you should not be their slaves.

(LEVITICUS 26:13)

Contents

Illustrations

Acknowledgments

THE PRODUCT OF a Christian-Jewish marriage, I grew up in a predominately African American neighborhood of Philadelphia at an experiential intersection of blacks and Jews, adjacent to but outside of either identity. While each group seemed obviously distinct from the other, there was nevertheless for me an inexplicable space of overlap between the two. This imagined coincidence emerged not simply from the ways in which I noticed blacks and Jews relating to and sometimes identifying with each other, but also the ways in which they were perceived by white Christian US culture. Years later, after I converted to Judaism, I began to explore in my scholarly work representations of Jews and Jewish law in early modernity. I was surprised to find moments of overlap between blacks and Jews in this period as well. Influenced by the formative scholarship of Kim Hall and James Shapiro, I started investigating how early modern formulations of race that shaped views of Africans might also be considered in relation to Jews. Since discourses about black people in this period included Muslims and Africans, as well as, occasionally, Jews, it appeared that both somatic and religious conceptions produced race. This realization raised rather than resolved questions: how, exactly, did religion relate to race; what role did color play in religious identity; and what were the filiations that seemed to connect Jews to Muslims and to Africans in early modern discourses? The research I undertook for my contextual edition of Shakespeare's *Merchant of Venice* indicated the extent to which ideas prior to early modernity continued to shape representations of religion and race in sixteenth- and seventeenth-century England. Thus began my exploration of early and Medieval Christian texts about Jews that contributed to a racist construction of their identity. Once immersed in the study of religious others in medieval Christianity, I discovered the ways in which these earlier discourses coordinated ideas of Jews and Muslims. The rising intolerance toward Islam in the late twentieth and early twenty-first centuries brought into focus the long history of this hostility, one that is imbricated with degrading constructions of Jews and Africans. This study led me far afield from my training in early modern English literature; while I have worked hard to immerse myself in the scholarship of early and patristic Christianity, medieval exegesis, canon law, natural philosophy, art history, and the early history of the trade in enslaved persons, I cannot have covered all these fields as well as I would have wished. I hope the findings of this study compensate for its inevitable inadequacies.

Two chapters in this book appear in very different versions in previous publications. Thanks to the editors of *Philological Quarterly* for permission to use material from "The Jewish Body in Black and White in Medieval and Early Modern England," *Philological Quarterly* 92.1 (2013): 41–65. I am also grateful to be able to include sections from my essay " 'His blood be upon us and upon our children:' Medieval Theology and the Inferior Jewish Body," in *The Cultural Politics of Blood, 1500–1900*, edited by Ralph Bauer, Kim Coles, Zita Nunes, and Carla Peterson, (New York: Palgrave Macmillan, 2015), 107–26, reproduced with permission of Palgrave Macmillan.

The strengths of this book derive in large part from the insights and support of my very smart colleagues and friends. Conversations over the years with my aunt, Ruth Kaplan Goluboff (z'l) and Gisha Linchis Berkowitz (z'l) helped lay the foundations for my thinking about Judaism and race. I thank Patricia Akhimie, Amanda Bailey, Rebecca Boylan, Dympna Callaghan, Adam Cohen, Ashley Cohen, Jeffrey Jerome Cohen, Kim Coles, Michael Collins, Roslyn Daniels, Charles Edelman, Jonathan Elukin, Pam Fox, David Friedenreich, Eva Frojmovic, Keren Hammershlag, Marcia Kupfer, Kathy Levezzo, Sarah McNamer, Rachel and Chip Manekin, Lena Orlin, Gail Kern Paster, John Pfordresher, Amanda Phillips, Michael Ragussis (z'l), Jonathan Ray, Libbie Rifkin, Jason Rosenblatt, Carole Sargeant, Michael Shapiro, Daniel Shore, Efraim Sicher, Christine So, Ellen Spolsky, Debra Strickland, Kathryn Temple, and Dennis Todd. I am particularly indebted to Valerie Traub who continues to inspire my work in countless ways. Extra special thanks to Nathan Hensley and Samantha Pinto for invaluable help in the final stretch! I am very grateful for and indebted to the work done by the Medievalists of Color (http://medievalistsofcolor.com/). Georgetown University and the English Department have also provided invaluable assistance to this project in the form of grants and leaves that made this book possible. I am also deeply grateful to President Barack H. Obama for appointing my husband, Norman Eisen, as ambassador to the Czech

Republic; my time in Prague constituted the best leave of my career. Profound thanks to the staff of the Chief of Mission Residence who relieved me of every quotidian responsibility and gave me time and space to write: Miroslav Černík, Lukáš Stach, Marek Vild, Jakub Tůma, Karel Bína, Dana Škrnová, Jiřina Štědrá, Eva Šilhánková, Iva Gothardová, Martin Severin, Jana Zahradnická, Dagmar Kubová, Václav Kozel, and Karel Sedlak.

Heartfelt thanks go to Cynthia Read at Oxford University Press who advocated for this book at every step of the process. I am also grateful to Aiesha Krause-Lee at OUP for all of her help, Shalini Balakrishnan at Newgen for a smooth production process, and Anne Sanow and Sangeetha Vishwanathan for copyediting the manuscript. *Todah rabah* to Jonathan Boyarin, who disclosed himself as one of the anonymous readers of my manuscript, and provided incalculable assistance in his response.

This book could not have been written without the support of my wonderful family. Thanks to my mother, Anne Wingfield Kaplan, and to my sister Rachel Kaplan, for your confidence and love. I miss my beloved mother-in-law, Frieda Grunfeld Eisen (z'l) and brother-in-law, Steven Eisen (z'l), who encouraged me along the way. To my darling Tamar, thanks for keeping it all in perspective. And, *acharon acharon chaviv*, to my Nachman, who took on the larger share of parenting and household responsibilities, who had faith in my project when mine failed, and whose love is a constant source of *nachat ruach*.

—Rosh Chodesh Adar 5778

Figuring Racism in Medieval Christianity

Introduction

THEOLOGY, INFERIORITY, RACISM

FIGURING RACISM IN Medieval Christianity demonstrates the formative role that the trope of Jewish enslavement, developed in Christian theology, plays in the construction of modern racism. The continuing and necessary contestation of racism—a virulent, multifaceted, and constantly morphing ideology—benefits from examining the various strands in its historical development. Many factors contribute to racism, including recent phenomena; identifying older elements provides an understanding of its larger organizing ideas that may help us better grapple with contemporary manifestations of the problem. I contend that focusing on inferiority as a category of analysis sharpens our understanding of this history as well as our current moment. This study shows how medieval religious discourses give rise to a racist idea of hereditary inferiority, developed through figural interpretations of Cain, Ham, and Ishmael as representing the enslavement of Jews to Christians. Against the older critical commonplace that race does not exist prior to the development of the modern discourses of nationalism and biology, my project contends that this concept of cursed inferiority, developed within medieval Christian theology, produces a racial status that functions like and anticipates modern racism.

In demonstrating how inferiority contributes to the history of racism, my project moves the scholarly conversation beyond the question of whether cultural discourses such as religion can operate like biological ones in the construction of racial identity. The damaging power of race lies in ascribing inferiority to a set of traits and not in the fact of bodily or cultural difference. Furthermore, while modern iterations locate inferiority in skin color or blood, we should not assume that all racism begins with these signs. A study of the processes by which some groups of people are rendered inferior to others helps us understand the history of racism without focusing on a particular set of signs or authorizing discourses.[1] Since the beginning of the modern era, the powerful discourse of biology has provided "evidence" for the "natural" inferiority of one group to another. I argue that for the medieval period the discourse of theology holds the same authorizing power to pronounce hierarchical relations, in this case as reflecting divine will. An analysis of the medieval Christian doctrine of Jewish enslavement, *servitus Judaeorum,* reveals a concept of hereditary inferiority that shapes the emergence of modern racial ideologies.

My project distinguishes itself from other analyses of early forms of racism by placing theological discourses at the center of its analysis. I examine the *servitus Judaeorum,* a concept developed in a range of Christian religious texts that initially adumbrates an inferior spiritual status, but evolves into an enduring cursed enslavement visited upon Jews as a consequence of the crucifixion. The archive for this work includes the Hebrew and Christian scriptures, with particular focus on Paul's citation of the former to produce new, tropological meanings in the latter. His readings of the Genesis narratives of Esau and Hagar simultaneously develop a figural interpretive practice and employ that hermeneutic to construct a servile spiritual status. The Church Fathers adopt and adapt the Pauline concept and practice; Augustine's writings, in particular, sharpen the definition of Jewish servitude and expand its figures to include the characters of Cain and Ham. His readings profoundly influence the understanding of Jews in later Christian exegesis, which reformulates their theological status as denoting perpetual servitude, citing Matthew 27:25, "His blood be upon us and our children" as evidence of its hereditary and enduring nature. The concept of Jewish perpetual servitude, secured by the authorizing warrant of a biblical figure, circulates widely in the medieval period, not only in biblical exegesis but in the texts of canon law, natural philosophy, and medicine, influencing visual representations as well.

The practice of figural interpretation provides the foundation for my analysis of the racial implications of Jewish servitude. Figures employ the divine texts of the Bible to express a prophetic truth about historical events. They serve as evidence of the fulfilment of God's will in the past as well an imperative to realize it in the present and future. Figures also create hierarchy in subordinating the message of the Hebrew Bible to Christian scripture, the former offering mere "shadow" or prefiguration of the truth expressed in the latter. This tiered logic shapes Augustine's figural development of Jewish enslavement on several levels: in reinterpreting texts from the Hebrew Bible in the context of Christian scripture, he develops figures that define Jews as punished with slavery; this slavery functions as a figure or metaphor for the degraded status of the Jews after their expulsion from Israel; and finally, his reading transforms the Jews themselves into figures who, in their adherence to the Law do not prove the veracity of Judaism, but serve as unwitting witnesses to Christian truth.[2] This influential formulation of figural hierarchy moves beyond its scriptural development to help shape the status of Jews in medieval Christendom. Beginning in the thirteenth century, figures of Jewish enslavement enter into the authoritative corpus of canon law through papal rulings. The popes' citation in law of Cain and Hagar as figures of the Jews' ontological inferiority seeks a transformation of society that reflects this hierarchy between Christians and Jews. They thus create a racial status of inherent Jewish subordination, which, in its articulation of divine will, empowers both church and state to enforce that position. The development of this racial construction within the multivalent system of typology enables the reapplication of these figures to similarly justify and subordinate other infidels: Muslims and the pagan inhabitants of Africa.[3] Thus figural logic serves as a prototype of racial thinking in developing authoritative discourses that project signs of essentialized inferiority onto groups to rationalize their oppression and exploitation.

Religion and Race in Premodernity

This study joins the recent trend in medieval and early modern scholarship to argue for the existence of racism in premodernity. Because work on the subject of race is vast and continues to burgeon, I restrict my analysis to a few topics relevant to my argument in order to make a specific contribution to this ongoing debate.[4] First, my research focuses on the development of racism, that is, discriminatory concepts and practices that produce, accompany, or follow the (fictive) idea of race.[5] Second, I focus on inferiority as a primary category of analysis to argue that the creation of a hierarchy in which one group represents itself as superior to another constitutes a necessary element of racism. While this claim might seem an obvious one, many discussions of racism assume inferiority rather than interrogate its structure and function; attending to the tropes and effects of subordinating differentiation helps trace racism's history in drawing a line from medieval forms to contemporary white supremacism. Third,

I examine how the concept of slavery—in particular, a figural status of unfreedom—serves to construct inferiority in premodernity; this analysis contributes to the ongoing examination of the relationship of slavery to racism. Finally, I argue for the importance of analyzing not only religious identity, but also theology, for understanding the history of racism. Many studies consider how discourses outside of religion articulate racial identities for Jews and Muslims, but they do not focus on how theological texts contribute to these constructions. The claim that religious intolerance absolutely differs from pseudo-biological race, while increasingly challenged, still circulates; I demonstrate that a theological notion of cursed inferiority shapes the (il)logic of both religious and pseudo-biological racism.

The ascription of inferiority by one group to another provides a particularly helpful lens for exploring the early history of racism when somatic markers and permanence did not always obtain. For many scholars, the establishment of hierarchy might seem so obvious as to preclude discussion, but attention to its presence reveals it to be a pivotal aspect of racism. Even those who argue that racism does not develop until the modern period cite subordination as one of its distinguishing features; as Kwame Anthony Appiah observes: "Ideas about race could, in principle, have developed without a commitment to the view that some races were superior to others; but they did not. . . . By the middle of the nineteenth century the notion that all races were equal in their capacities was a distinctly minority view" (280). Although he recognizes the presence of relative inequality in the development of race, he does not focus on its function. George Kelsey offers an explanation of this phenomenon:

> Racism erects a system of status by ascription. . . . The racist affirmation of superiority points to a cluster of physical traits and claims that the superiority of a group of persons inheres precisely in that cluster of physical traits. . . . The correlate of this claim is that inferiority is present in all persons who do not share the cluster of physical traits of the favored race. (241)

While his definition notes a preoccupation with physical traits, Kelsey contends that the attribution of relative superiority and inferiority to these characteristics and groups effectually produces racism. In his study of classical antiquity, Benjamin Isaac argues that an analysis of inferiority can help locate premodern racist discourses that do not attach themselves to somatic features. Isaac quotes the work of Robert

Miles, who posits that "any argument which suggests that the human species is composed of discrete groups in order to legitimate inequality between those groups of people" produces racial distinctions, even absent "biological" referents (20). The postulation of relative superiority/inferiority thus constitutes a defining element of racism.[6] As Isaac concludes: "Racism['s] . . . aim is always to prove that the other group is inferior and the racist superior, and that these qualities are permanent and cannot be changed" (22; see also 23, 35, 37). Although Isaac's own analysis of racism defines it as manifesting in physical characteristics understood as immutable, he argues that its aim and essence lie in the ascription of relative inferiority to one group by another. More recently, Bethencourt affirms the centrality of inferiority to racist discourses, although he maintains that racism does not emerge until early modernity. His definition of racism includes religious as well as ethnic others and notes the counterintuitive ascription of subordinating qualities to groups perceived as equal or even superior (7–8). Attention to the development of discourses imputing inferiority enables the identification and analysis of early iterations of racism, which also allows us to follow its trajectories to the present moment.

An early, powerful means of defining and ascribing inferiority that provides an effective model for racist hierarchy can be found in discourses about slavery.[7] Isaac argues for the racist implications of ancient theories of natural slavery beginning with Aristotle's influential writings. This concept "asserts that slaves are different, physically and mentally, from free men through inherited characteristics. . . . The claim that some members of humanity are born to be slaves could be described as the ultimate form of proto-racism" (46; see also 169–224, 248–51). Natural slavery comprises the crucial elements of modern racism in positing that the inferiority of enslaved people inheres in hereditary and unchanging physical, intellectual, and moral qualities. Attention to discourses that ascribe slavery in order to establish inferior status discloses the logic of racism at work.[8] While Aristotle's theory influences some patristic and medieval Christian thought, the idea of natural slavery conflicted with Christian teaching that God created humans equal and free. Slavery results from sin, but since all participate in original sin, this servility does not appear to create a hierarchy. However, the elaboration of Christian freedom through salvation, in contrast to the *servitus Judaeorum,* creates a category of cursed hereditary slavery that subordinates Jews to Christians, thus producing a theological type of inherent inferiority.[9]

The growing scholarship on race in the middle ages productively considers the topic of religious identity from a variety of perspectives. In an early contribution, Yosef Hayim Yerushalmi argues that a racialized religious identity, identical to the modern definition, developed in late medieval Iberian blood purity statutes, which marked the bodies of converts to Christianity as retaining a trace of their inferior Jewish or Muslim status: "the very fact that the consequences of Jewish ancestry, however remote, were considered by so many to be indelible, perpetual and *unalterable*, is already sufficient to indicate the racist mentality at work" (15).[10] But Yerushalmi pressed for a more expansive understanding of the racist implications of medieval religious identity, one that moves beyond locating race in physical features that remain even after conversion. He notes a number of examples—predating the Iberian laws, sometimes by as much as seven centuries—which assume that converts to Christianity preserve some type of Jewish essence (6–7).[11] Although he carefully distinguishes between religious and racial antisemitism, he calls for an investigative study of "latent *racial* anti-Semitism" in medieval Christianity, arguing that "any hostile conception of the Jews which implies that their negative characteristics are permanent must already be considered as essentially, or at least potentially, 'racial' " (19, 21). Yerushalmi makes a strong case for a racist inflection in the formation of non-Christian religious identity and expands racial traits beyond the corporeal, while insisting on permanence as a defining feature of racism.

Étienne Balibar theorizes the call for the study of racism to move beyond somatic traits. Balibar argues that a cultural or neo-racism not only functions like but also replaces somatic racism in our contemporary moment: "*culture can also function like a nature*, and it can in particular function as a way of locking individuals and groups a priori into a genealogy, into a determination that is immutable and intangible in origin" (22). Arguing that the pseudo-biology previously sustaining racist discourse has been discredited, culture now functions to create immutable hierarchical difference. However, this "new" racism that encompasses religious identity—Muslim identity in particular—has, in fact, very old roots in antisemitism, a "culturalist" racism that he claims has "always existed," or emerges at least in the late medieval Spanish state (23–4). As such, it functions as a kind of prototype for nonsomatic racism: "Anti-Semitism is supremely 'differentialist' and in many respects the whole of current differentialist racism may be considered, from the formal point of view, *as a generalized anti-Semitism*" (24).[12] Balibar thus claims that antisemitism provides a model for culturalist racism that attaches to religious identity; however, he locates his analysis within a political state or national context, and argues that theological anti-Judaism is not racist (23–4).

Scholars of premodernity have found Balibar's formulation of a nonsomatic racism particularly productive, but have also emended his ideas in important ways.[13] Ania Loomba's intervention challenges the distinction Balibar and others make between theological anti-Judaism and culturalist racial antisemitism to argue that religion is not a "preracial form of difference" but "has been central to the development of modern forms of racism all across the globe" (2009, 508).[14] A fuller study of the history of racism thus requires that we examine the contribution that constructions of religious identity make to it. Loomba rejects the apparently opposing categories of "cultural" and "scientific" racism to offer a persuasive reformulation of these ideas:

> Balibar's phrase for neoracism—'racism without race'— . . . can reconfuse matters by continuing to equate the term "race" with ideologies of difference that center around color or pseudobiological classifications. As a result, a theological or culture-centered notion of difference becomes a special kind of racism . . . but not racism per se. . . . Early modern histories of difference, by illuminating the centrality of religion and culture to the development of the idea of race, can help us retheorize the idea of racial difference in a much more radical way. (508)

She powerfully concludes that "biology" and "culture" have always been mutually constitutive (509). My project takes up Loomba's call to retheorize racial difference by focusing not simply on religious identity, but on the work that medieval Christian theology performs in the formulation of racist ideas about Jews and Muslims.[15]

Some important recent work on the modern formulation of racism also argues for the centrality of theology in this process. J. Kameron Carter's theoretically rigorous analysis of Kant's contribution to the development of race in the eighteenth century contends that "modernity's racial imagination has its genesis in the theological problem of Christianity's quest to sever itself from its Jewish roots" (4).[16] He situates the Kantian development within a longer historical moment, one that dates back to the fifteenth-century Iberian establishment of the Atlantic trade in enslaved persons; although it is beyond the scope of his project to attend to this earlier period, his suggestion of a medieval theological racialization of Jews provides support for my analysis.[17] Willie James Jennings's perceptive exploration of race in relation to theology, however, does consider the racial implications of Jewish and Muslim convert identity developed in Iberia. He argues that the logic of supersession animates the development of racist thinking in early modernity and "begins with positioning Christian identity fully within European (white) identity and fully outside the identities of Jews and Muslims" (33). The authenticity of conversion is crucial to a process of identity formation which contrasts Christians to Jews and Muslims and produces "an ecclesial logic applicable to the evaluation of all peoples" (33). Jennings derives his argument from an analysis of the *Sumario de las cosas de Japón*, authored by the sixteenth-century Jesuit missionary Alessandro Valignano. In a comparative discussion of the receptivity to salvation of different peoples, he ranks as most hopeless converts from Judaism and Islam: "At the bottom, chained to the deepest suspicion of incapability, are the conversos (or marranos) and moriscos. Valignano locates Africans with these New Christians and Christian Moors as those he strongly doubts capable of gospel life" (34). Religious identity here secures, rather than prevents, the imposition of a racist inferiority in mistrusting the efficacy of conversion. The incapacity of Jews and Muslims to be saved thus provides a model for constructing the imperviousness of Africans that Jennings identifies as racist: "Through a racial calculus, comparative analysis becomes the new inner logic of how one deploys supersessionist thinking" (36).[18] Far from being the test case of a nonracial status, religious identity is increasingly understood by scholars as contributing powerfully to the history of racism.[19]

The growing critical consensus on the centrality of religion for the historical—as well as the contemporary—construction of racism additionally challenges the claim that true racism imagines the inferior status as permanent. Although Yerushalmi and Balibar have respectively argued that biological as well as cultural formations of religious status give rise to an immutable racist identity, scholars have subsequently contended that premodern as well as later racist discourses rely on ideas of both fluidity and fixity.[20] Denise Kimber Buell's account, developed with recourse to the work of Ann Laura Stoler, argues for the necessity of both elements in the construction of race, a concept "to which fixity is *attributed* but that [is] nevertheless malleable" (6–7, author's emphasis). Ascribing fluidity to an identity, according to both Stoler and Buell, makes racist discourses more, not less effective.[21] In her exploration of the circulation of Iberian pure blood discourses, María Elena Martínez demonstrates how these ideas defined religious identity both in terms of fixity and fluidity, nature and culture. The process of certifying *limpieza* drew on conflicting standards of purity of faith and purity of blood: "The two definitions of purity of blood—as descent and practices—created a deep ambiguity in the concept of *limpieza* as a 'natural' condition" (83). This early iteration of racism combined what appear to be contradictory accounts of its etiology, but Martínez, like Buell and Stoler, demonstrate the increased force of this double definition: "This slippage between biology and culture, rather than destabilizing the concept of *limpieza*, made it more powerful . . . [in producing] a discursive flexibility that facilitated the preservation of social hierarchies and structures of inequalities" (84). The interplay of nature and culture works to secure even more effectively hierarchies that position some groups as inferior. Loomba extends the implications of this argument to contend that the supposedly fluid and fixed qualities of religious identity and color in medieval and early modern representations of conversion in effect serve to construct both as permanent.[22] Focusing on the trope of the futile washing of the "Ethiope" used to signify the inefficacy of conversion, she cites an instance in which "black skin is fixed as permanent by comparing it to the 'indurate heart of heretics,' but the comparison in turn anchors the heart of the unbeliever as also unchangeable" (504–5). Thus, some early discourses understand the ostensibly mutable category of religious faith to be equally as durable as physical characteristics.

However, this argument must still answer the counterexamples posed by other medieval texts that represent physical characteristics as susceptible to change through conversion. As many have noted, medieval literature includes representations of black Muslims who become white upon converting to Christianity, suggesting the theological view of the impermanence of both of faith *and* physical characteristics (Hahn, Lampert, Heng, Whitaker). Loomba points out that even in the case of these "successful" Muslim converts, color operates to reinforce the association of blackness with Islam and whiteness to Christianity.[23] Hence the transformation reinscribes religious difference even as it appears to erode it. A similar logic operates in the Christian construction of Jewish identity, albeit largely outside of somatic markers. Even while noting the mutability of Jewish identity in doctrines upholding the efficacy of baptism, Yerushalmi suggests that other Christian theological attitudes simultaneously support the construction of Jewish identity as inherently resistant to change (22). As noted earlier, a number of subsequent studies have provided further evidence, much of it prior to the Iberian example, of the perception of a persisting Jewish identity even after conversion. Although these examples do not constitute a medieval consensus on the inefficacy of conversion in all cases, or even in most, the claim that conversion enables Jews to transform their status from negative to positive suppresses the fact that a convert is no longer a Jew, but a Christian: the condition of a Jew remains a degraded one. Even if some Jews could escape their inherent inferiority through conversion, God's curse nevertheless rendered all Jews, as long as they remained Jews, subordinate to all Christians. Hence conversion actually preserves a racist status for Jews rather than providing an escape in leaving intact the view that understood Jews, qua Jews, as cursed with a hereditary enslavement that rendered them permanently inferior to Christians. This debased Jewish status emerges initially and primarily in the context of medieval Christian theology.

Figuring Racism

Given their importance for an analysis of racism, figures organize the argument of the book. The first chapter identifies the biblical characters from which Jewish servitude is derived, with particular focus on Cain, Ham, and Ishmael. The second and third chapters focus on the ways in which Cain's identification with the cursed primal scene of Jewish abjection, the crucifixion of Jesus, shapes discourses about Jewish bodily function and images that color Jews with dark and demonic colors, literalizing their inferiority as a relegation to the infernal regions through eternal damnation. The last two chapters trace the histories of the figural discourses on Ham and Ishmael to demonstrate how they produce a racial logic of cursed hereditary inferiority subsequently applied to justify the subordination of Muslims and Africans to European Christians.

Chapter 1, "*Servitus Judaeorum*: Biblical Figures, Canon Law, and the Construction of Hereditary Inferiority," draws on Eric Auerbach's influential formulation of figural interpretation to demonstrate its importance for developing the concept of Jewish enslavement. Scholarship on Jewish servitude has largely sought to determine the exact nature of this status in civil law and its effect on medieval Jews.[24] I focus instead on how it gives rise to a status of hereditary inferiority through the interpretation of the Biblical figures of Esau, Hagar/Ishmael, Cain, and Ham as representing Jewish servitude or subjection to Christians. Paul's foundational figural reading of the servile status of Esau and Hagar imagines a lesser spiritual status, relative to the faithful, that likely applies to unbelievers rather than to all Jews. Augustine builds on and diverges from Paul in developing an etiology that identifies these figures as Jews who have been enslaved to Christians as punishment for the rejection and (alleged) crucifixion of Jesus. Furthermore, he views this punishing servitude as not only fulfilled at the time of the deicide, but as continuing to be visited upon contemporary Jews, deprived of dominion in their own land and subject to the power of a Christian Roman empire. His formulation thus includes not only the spiritual but the political consequences of this enslavement. Medieval exegetes draw on Matthew 27:25 as a scriptural proof-text to emphasize the hereditary nature of this cursed inferiority, reformulating Augustine's figures of the *servitus Judaeorum* to the *servitus perpetua*, perpetual servitude. In emphasizing the generational consequences of this condition, these texts develop a racial idea of hereditary enslavement, one that derives its authoritative force from biblical warrant. Papal letters, or decretals, explicitly cite the figures of Cain and Hagar/Ishmael as evidence of Jewish perpetual servitude in directives requiring secular rulers to enforce the subordination of Jews to Christians in a variety of legal and social contexts.[25] These ecclesiastical rulings deploy the racist status of perpetual enslavement to define all Jews as ontologically inferior to all Christians and to justify the temporal realization of this degraded condition in a range of discriminatory laws.

While the papal construction of Jewish servitude created a racial status that could be legally enforced in social and economic contexts, its figural logic also shaped representations of degraded Jewish bodies in medieval texts and images. Although hereditary inferiority initially defines a Jew's position in Christian society absent a corporeal effect, the figure of Cain, marked by God, provides a means by which his subjection could be embodied. Chapter 2, "The Marking of Cain and Embodying Inferiority," explores how medieval Christian theologians, natural philosophers, and physicians employ the marked and cursed figure of Cain in the invention of a divinely inflicted curse of bleeding that functions to humiliate and subordinate Jewish bodies. The context of hereditary inferiority helps clarify critical controversies in the scholarship on the medieval fabrication of a Jewish male bleeding disease. Does this discourse originate in theological or "scientific" contexts? Is the bleeding construed primarily as menstrual, an attempt to feminize Jewish men, or as hemorrhoidal in nature? Some of the earliest accounts of Jewish bleeding evolve in the theological context of the mark of Cain, Jewish guilt for the deicide, and Jewish servitude. My analysis is the first to demonstrate that Jacques de Vitry's account of this disease, articulated in his influential thirteenth-century *Historia Orientalis*, very closely traces the logic of papal decretals referencing Cain and Jewish servitude. Following the objective of legal attempts to enforce Jewish inferiority, the discourse of Jewish bleeding, whether described as menstrual or hemorrhoidal, seeks to embody inferiority by means of demeaning disease. De Vitry introduces a paraphrase from Psalm 77:66 to demonstrate the degradation this malady imposes on Jewish bodies: "And [God] smote his enemies on the hinder parts: he put them to an everlasting reproach." While some subsequent discussions of Jewish bleeding in natural philosophy represent this ailment in humoral, not theological terms, the underlying religious logic returns in later elaborations. This is evident from the citation of scriptural warrants, including Psalm 77 but also Matthew 27, as well as the direct ascription of the disease to God, who inflicts it on contemporary Jews as a continuing punishment for the crucifixion. The theological concept of *servitus Judaeorum* influences the discourses of natural philosophy and medicine to render Jewish bodies as materially inferior through the shaming force of physical infirmity.

Cain's figuration of cursed servitude resulting from the Jews' crime of deicide not only shapes ideas about the punishing malfunction of their bodies, but also influences denigratory representations of their appearance in visual images. Rather than focusing on tropological images of Cain that prefigure the Jews' murder of Abel/Jesus, I analyze depictions of the Passion that materialize the consequences of their enslaving punishment in the Jews' physical attributes. The third chapter, "Making Darkness Visible: The Colors of Subjection in Medieval English Psalter Illuminations," considers how figural inferiority, a result of Jewish deicide, accounts for the representation of dark-skinned Jews in New Testament scenes of the Passion in which Jews betray, accuse, and torture Jesus. These portrayals in thirteenth-century English illustrated psalm collections emerge in the context of a rise in affective piety in the eleventh through fourteenth centuries that, in emphasizing Jesus's suffering, correspondingly exaggerates the cruelty of his enemies. During this period, passion narratives and images increasingly equate Jews with these enemies, and identify them with a range of negatively charged physical characteristics. English psalter illuminations introduce dark-skinned attackers with caricatured "Jewish" markers, such as hats and/or distorted facial features. Scholars have cited the negative patristic association of the dark-skinned "Ethiopian" with sin, hell, and the devil to explain these images. While traditional anti-black discourses are operating here, I argue that attendant associations of the colors black, blue, and gray with death and damnation provide an additional explanatory context. I consider representations of the damned and of devils portrayed in these shades to interpret the earliest images of similarly toned Jews that appear in several psalters produced in early thirteenth-century Oxford. The passion illustrations depict dark Jews as attacking Jesus, whose death secures redemption from the eternal death of damnation. In rejecting and crucifying Jesus the Jews bring upon themselves not only the curse of a servile life, but also the damnation of the soul that leads to everlasting death. The images embody the Jews' spiritual abjection by representing it as dark and infernal: not only hellish, but inferior.

The last two chapters of the book trace the history of the figures of perpetual servitude developed with recourse to the Jews, demonstrating how they create powerful tropes of inferiority that are redeployed to justify the subordination of other peoples. Chapter 4, "Jewish Ham: Developing a Discourse of Hereditary Inferiority," focuses on the curse of slavery imposed by Noah on Ham's offspring and its figuration of the Jews' punishment for the crucifixion. Many scholars demonstrate how the Genesis text serves as a justification for the enslavement of the inhabitants of Africa, but in seeking the origin of the association of Ham with blackness they overlook the formulation of hereditary inferiority that develops initially with regard to Jewish guilt. The identification of Jews with Ham helps explain the scholarly confusion over Noah's cursing of his grandson, Canaan; the imposition of slavery on the offspring figures its perpetual nature, continuing to effect the subordination of contemporary Jews. Jewish Ham also clarifies the otherwise perplexing conflation of Cain and Ham that frequently occurs; since both figures represent the Jews' enslavement as resulting from the crime of deicide, exegetes understand them as essentially exchangeable. I demonstrate the evolution of this idea in Christian biblical commentaries, including the *Glossa Ordinaria*, the definitive medieval commentary on the Bible. I also show its wider popular circulation in medieval visual arts, poetry, and the *Speculum humanae salvationis*, a frequently illustrated text of typology that appears in numerous Latin and vernacular manuscripts and printed editions. The association of Ham with Africa also develops during this period, though largely in discussions of the geographical significance of the Genesis text. In this context, commentators do not consider Noah's curse as applying to African Ham and his offspring. However, the idea of cursed servitude developed with reference

to Jews begins to intersect with considerations of African peoples in medieval exegesis, paving the way for a transfer of hereditary inferiority from
one group to the other. While the association of Jews with Ham survives
into the early modern period, it subsides in the wake of the Reformation
as the imperative to subordinate Jews gives way to intra-Christian enmity.
The figure of Ham as representing a curse of Jewish perpetual slavery is
eclipsed by its more profitable, opportunistic application to the inhabitants
of Africa to justify their enslavement.

The final chapter, "Cain, Ham, and Ishmael: The African Travels of
Perpetual Servitude," demonstrates how these fully developed ideas of
Jewish hereditary inferiority, supported with evidence of Biblical typology,
translate and reattach to Muslims and other inhabitants of Africa. An
analysis of this process revisits the important role played by canon law,
functioning as an early iteration of international law. I consider how the
intersection of the Roman law of slavery with early patristic accounts of
servitude contributes to just war theory's discussion of the enslavement of
captured enemies. The canon law formulation of Jews as the original enemies of Christendom, and the punishment of *servitus Judaeorum*, underlies and ramifies attitudes toward other infidels; ecclesiastical law and just
war theory combine in the law in support of the Crusades. Biblical figures
play a central role in this process, since the figure of Ishmael, applied
from the time of Paul as signifying the Jews, also connotes the peoples
occupying the geographic area of Arabia and, in subsequent associations,
Islam. Anachronistically, popes and canonists begin describing Muslims
as cursed with perpetual servitude for the crime of deicide, thus subjecting
them to the same rationale that secured Jewish subordination to Christians.
Crusader logic also provides the legal justification for the European expansion into Africa, which begins in North African territory frequently
associated with Islam. With the rise of the trade in enslaved Africans, the
figures of Cain and Ham are introduced as justifying examples in travel literature and apologetic treatises. The language of papal bulls transfers the
figural concept of hereditary inferiority through the inclusion of the term
"perpetual servitude" in edicts that not only authorize the Iberian appropriation of African lands, but also license the trade in enslaved peoples by
representing Africans as already inferior enemies of Christendom.

While this analysis focuses on figural and not chattel slavery, it draws
on the racist implications of "natural" slavery, already articulated in the
works of Aristotle. I therefore do not argue for an origin or invention
of racism in medieval Europe, but for a particular articulation of it that

powerfully influences the subsequent history of race. The theological formulation of Jewish servitude incorporated the idea that chattel slavery created a status subordinate to free persons. While not always understood as permanent, the condition served to degrade the person as long as she or he remained a slave. The Augustinian development of enslavement, whether chattel or figural, as resulting from sin, explained the condition as a punishment justly merited by the recipient's transgression. His expansion of servitude to include all Jews, including their descendants, suggested its persisting effects for the group as a whole. However, Augustine offers what he takes to be an empirical account of Jewish enslavement, basing his claims on the fact of the domination of the Christian Roman empire over the Jews. Medieval popes and clerics advanced the racial potential of figural servitude by understanding it as requiring enforcement by the medieval church and state, thus justifying discriminatory temporal practices in order to realize what was already theologically true: Jewish inferiority relative to Christians. Figural servitude articulates a condition of hereditary inferiority, a rationale which defines some humans as lesser than others. I argue that this process—the development in authoritative discourses of an ontologically inferior status—lies at the heart of racism. This category can be articulated as an inherent quality, as requiring legal enforcement, and/or as a physical manifestation. While inferiority also supplies the foundation for other hierarchical systems, such as gender, class, and sexuality, and therefore is not a sufficient element of racism, it is nevertheless necessary to its derogating process.[26]

A study of the *servitus Judaeorum* makes multiple contributions to critical race theory and the history of racism. In its subjugating operation, hereditary permanence, divine warrant, and physical manifestations, perpetual servitude creates a racial status: "a highly malleable category which historically has been deployed to reinforce existing social hierarchies and create new ones" (Loomba 2002, 3). By establishing that religious texts define and implement a status of Jewish hereditary inferiority, I show that theological discourses can produce a racist identity not reliant on the body. A focus on the discursive process by which bodies, and thus peoples, are degraded emphasizes the work racism performs rather than the attributes to which it attaches. Any authorizing narrative that imputes an essentialized inferiority to a group rendering it susceptible to discriminatory practices and violence must be interrogated and challenged as racist. The development and transmission of Jewish hereditary inferiority also reveals the extent to which racial histories are intertwined; once established with respect to one group, racial tropes of inferiority can be easily reassigned to degrade another. Biblical figures' capacity for various ascriptions enables an almost endless reappropriation; because perpetual servitude does not rely on a specific somatic marker, even as it can be easily located in the body, hereditary inferiority can be attributed to diverse categories of people. Jews themselves become a kind of figure for the enemy of the faith, and the subjugation of the Jews extended to others so identified. Hence we find the canon law use of the figure of Hagar/Ishmael to prove Muslim servitude to Christians, the application of perpetual servitude to justify the Crusades against Islam, and the appropriation of the figures of Cain and Ham to denote the inferiority and support the trade of enslaved inhabitants of Africa. Medieval theological discourses about Jews thus create a racial rationale that renders not only them, but through the multivalent capacity of figures, Muslims and Africans as well, subordinate to Christians. This history of theological racism makes legible the ways in which it continues to circulate in contemporary white supremacist discourses that similarly seek to subordinate these groups to whites.

In tracing the development and history of a concept of hereditary servitude in medieval Christian theology, exegesis, and canon law, this project does not delineate the medieval Jewish experience of subjection. Rather, it charts the articulation of an idea that is variously redeployed to imagine the inherent inferiority of Jews, Muslims, and Africans.[27] I follow the lead of other recent work on the history of racism in employing an intellectual history approach to the study of hereditary servitude. As Isaac contends:

> Racism is a phenomenon that can assume many apparently different shapes and forms while preserving a remarkable element of continuity which is undeniable, once it is traced over the centuries. . . . If we recognize only one variety that belongs to a restricted period, we may fail to recognize it as it emerges in an altered guise. (3)

In focusing on inherent inferiority, a particular articulation of a constitutive element of racism, I hope to lend a greater analytical precision to our study of racism's history.[28]

However, the benefits of intellectual history must be counterbalanced by an acknowledgment of their limits and misuse. One potential error would be to extend in a facile manner the claims of this study beyond the period under analysis. I do not trace a continuous line from medieval racializing ideas to the racial antisemitism of Nazi Germany.[29]

Evidence from the early modern period reveals a redirection of religious animus from Jewish to Christian enemies of the faith during the Reformation, an increasing emphasis on somatic markers in racial discourses, as well as the invention of Jewish whiteness in the seventeenth century (Schorsch 2004), thus indicating ruptures in the development of a Jewish racial identity.[30] Focusing on the development of a single idea has the additional disadvantage of precluding consideration of the multiplicity of views that exist during the period under consideration. While I cannot attend to the range of varying attitudes toward Jews, Muslims, and Africans in medieval Christian theology, this project does not argue that the Church is responsible for the development of racism. Christianity is not a monolith; my book traces only one particular strand out of many in medieval Christian discourse.[31] Finally, in arguing for a shared discourse of inferiority that initially shapes the construction of Jewish, Muslim, and African inferiority, I do not make comparisons between its divergent effects in the histories of these three groups. Nevertheless, the benefits of making visible the figural logic applied to these different identities contributes to our understanding of the intersections among them in both the past and present moment.

I

Servitus Judaeorum

BIBLICAL FIGURES, CANON LAW, AND THE CONSTRUCTION OF HEREDITARY INFERIORITY

THE CHRISTIAN CONCEPT of *servitus Judaeorum*, enslavement of the Jews, appears in Scripture, exegesis, theology, canon law, and secular law, although its definitions and effects are multiple and disputed.[1] It emerges in the form of Biblical figures, the interpretation of persons and episodes in the Hebrew Bible as presaging events in Christian history; in this context it signifies a spiritual inferiority. Paul's citation from Genesis of Esau and Ishmael, two older brothers deprived of their primary status and supplanted by their siblings, establishes a hierarchy that links the first-born with bondage and Jewish law and the younger with freedom and faith. In the patristic period, Augustine includes Cain and Ham in these examples to construct and represent a servile status inflicted upon the Jews as a punishment by God for their rejection and (alleged) crucifixion of Jesus. Augustine's invocation of the historical circumstances of the Roman conquest of Israel subtly modifies this punishment from an entirely spiritual condition; in reading the subjection of the Jews in terms of their current domination by the Christian Roman Empire, he focuses on the political consequences of their status. Although the *servitus Judaeorum* does not signify actual enslavement of Jews to Christians, it relegates Jews as a group to a position of inferiority that persists, transferring from one generation to the next. Nevertheless, the social and political implications of the concept remain merely theoretical until the medieval period, when the discourses of medieval ecclesiastical and secular law begin to employ variations on the term in legislation regulating Jewish–Christian relations.

The civil law of the Christian Roman Empire grants Jews the status of citizens roughly on a par with Christians, a position that early Church Councils confirm in ecclesiastical law (Mathisen; Simonsohn vol. 7, 94–5).[2] The view of Jews as spiritually inferior to Christians initially exists in contrast to the two groups' equal legal status, but over time, as theologians emphasize Jewish servitude, it enters into ecclesiastical law. From the ninth to the eleventh century, clerics, notably Agobard, Amulo, Hrabaunus Maurus, and Peter Damian, react to the perceived preferential treatment accorded Jews relative to Christians by arguing vehemently for the degradation of the former. Each theologian cites the *servitus Judaeorum* as a rationale for challenging alleged Jewish superiority and in calling for the subordination of the Jews to Christians (Simonsohn vol. 7, 97). Alexander II introduces the idea of Jewish servitude into legal discourse when the canon law incorporates his eleventh-century letter citing this status to justify projection of Jews (Simonsohn vol. 7, 97–8). A clear articulation of the theological argument for Jewish subordination appears in canon 26 of the Third Lateran Council (1179). One section of the law overturns a practice that has allowed Jews to serve as witnesses against Christians in secular courts while preventing Christians from testifying against Jews:

> And we decree that those who in this matter want to give Jews greater privileges than Christians shall be placed under anathema, for the only fitting condition is that Jews be placed below Christians, and that they be treated kindly by the latter solely because of humanitarian reasons. (Grayzel 1966, 297)

In permitting Jews a privilege not enjoyed by Christians, the civil law courts violate the principle of *servitus Judaeorum*, which moves here from a merely spiritual idea to one that alters the position of Jews in law.[3] However, Pope Innocent III develops the most definitive and influential statements of Jewish slavery in a series of letters promulgated in the first decade of the thirteenth century. He transfers a full theological account of the concept—including Jewish guilt for the death of Jesus and biblical figures supporting this claim—into legal discussions which concern the relative position of Jews and Christians. One of the most stringent of these pronouncements, the 1205 ruling *Etsi Judaeos*, is incorporated into the official codification of canon law produced at Pope Gregory IX's behest in 1234 (Kisch 151).

While most scholars concur that this idea translates from theology and ecclesiastical law to secular legislation, they disagree about its significance for the status of medieval Jews. Many studies focus on the import of this concept within the structure of secular law and politics. Guido Kisch argues that shortly after the canon law codifies the *servitus Judaeorum*, it appears in the form of *servitus camerae* (chamber serfdom) in German civil law, which he sees as ultimately serving to degrade the Jews' status to one of unfreedom by the fifteenth century (Kisch 152, 129–68 passim). Salo Baron also focuses on Germany to consider the development of the idea of "Jewish serfdom" in the context of the conflict between the papacy and the Empire, and in relation to the development of nationalism. He argues that the status of Jews as "serfs of the emperor's Chamber [was] intended to benefit, not humiliate them" (1972b, 307) and "was employed by the medieval rulers when they wished to protect the Jews" (1972a, 320). Langmuir shifts the focus to England and France to challenge the notion that the German notion of "serfdom" applies in other countries. He disputes the use of the term "serf" to approximate the status of medieval Jews; he sees the use of the term "servi" in secular law as a ruler's attempt to assign them a unique status under his or her control and exclusive jurisdiction. He also argues that the *servitus Judeorum* as delineated in theology and canon law differs from the status of Jews in secular law (189–94 passim; see also Watt 1991). More recently, David Abulafia revisits the German development of "cameral servitude" to show its relevance for the status of Jews—and Muslims—in medieval Sicily and Spain; although he views this form of unfreedom as balanced by the honorable connotation of service to a ruler, he concludes that it is ultimately degraded by the theological concept of perpetual servitude (700, 714). Anna Sapir Abulafia considers the broader concept of Jewish service, which includes servitude, and its mixed influence on medieval Christian–Jewish relations (2011, 2013). In his survey of the scholarship, Simonsohn argues that in civil law, "in a strictly legal sense Jews were never defined as serfs, nor was their legal position tantamount to that of serfs. Jews were citizens—albeit with some privileges . . . and subject to restrictions not imposed on other citizens" (Simonsohn vol. 7, 95). The Jews' status as citizens limited the effect of the concept of *servitus Judaeorum* on secular legislation during much of the medieval period.[4]

Similarly, ecclesiastical law affirms that medieval Jews as a people were never reduced to actual slavery. As Johannes of Agnani, a fifteenth-century canonist, writes: "Nor is it true that Jews are slaves in such a way as they could be sold; but whatever there is of law <or> custom, it is not preserved that they can be held like slaves" (*Super quinto decretalium*, qtd. in Pakter 329, my revision of his translation). But this statement raises questions even as it asserts that Jews are not chattel slaves; Johannes implies that law and custom regards them as slaves in a different way. The texts of canon law support this notion, as they repeatedly refer to Jews as slaves. Simonsohn suggests one way of addressing this conundrum:

> The theological concept of Jewish subjugation, inferiority and servitude, while not legal per se, carried weight inside and outside the Church. And although most canon lawyers never declared the Jews to be slaves or serfs in a purely legalistic sense, the terminology employed by the popes and other churchmen makes it very difficult to draw a line between theology and law. (vol. 7, 96)

However, after suggesting that a definition of this status requires us to go beyond the law, he does not develop a methodology for understanding this liminal category that operates between and within theology and law.

I argue that the significance of the *servitus Judaeorum* cannot be determined by focusing on the letter of the law, but rather by understanding its figures. Attention to the texts of papal letters and canon law reveals that they rely on Biblical types established in scripture and exegesis to illustrate the enslavement of the Jews. These proof-texts ostensibly appear as a divine rationale for laws that ensure Christian pre-eminence over Jews, or to chastise rulers who permit the violation of these laws. Once received into the corpus of ecclesiastical law, however, the use of figures evolves from a means of enforcing law to creating a new status: figural slavery.[5] Distinguished from chattel servitude, this innovation aims to impose a condition of inferiority upon Jews relative to Christians, not only in the case of specific laws, but comprehensively. It operates as a doubly figural servitude in employing slavery as a metaphor for the degraded position of the Jews and relying on scriptural figures to provide authoritative proof of this condition. The presentation of this servitude as a divine punishment seeks to create an existential condition that defines all Jews, in all cases and in all places, as subordinated to Christians. Furthermore, in asserting that this penalty, imposed at the time of Jesus's death, continues to affect contemporary Jews, the discourse of figural slavery defines this status as a perpetual servitude. It thereby establishes an ontological state: hereditary inferiority.

While not, strictly speaking, a legal status, hereditary inferiority nevertheless gains power through its articulation and circulation as perpetual servitude in the authoritative texts of papal decretals and canon law. In this context, its impact extends more widely and consistently than formulations articulated in particular types of secular law, insofar as it functioned as international law; as such, it contributed powerfully to "the creation of some of the elemental ideas and institutions that continue to this day to characterize Western societies" (Brundage 1995, 3, 189).[6] The canon law incorporation of the *servitus Judaeorum* produces and authorizes one such elemental idea, a category of inherent subordination that circulated throughout Western Christianity. It moves beyond the spheres of law and theology in its consequences: "In effect . . . the definition of the Jews' status ceased to be a purely Christian theological argument and assumed socio-political connotations. . . . There was hardly an area in which Jews were not discriminated against and degraded politically, socially and economically" (Simonsohn vol. 7, 99, 156). But beyond its impact upon the lived experience of medieval Jews, figural slavery creates an inferior status that anticipates subsequent biological rationales that undergird modern racism. The canon law development of the figural concept of the *servitus Judaeorum* creates a new, racial status of second-class citizenship.

In the following sections, I offer a description and analysis of biblical figures before tracing a chronological evolution of *servitus Judaeorum*. I consider the early articulation of the figures of Esau and Hagar/Ishmael in Paul's letters, as well as Augustine's interpretation of Cain and Ham as signifying the subordination of Judaism and the punishment of the Jews. The next section explores how canon law cites and develops figural representations of Cain and Hagar/Ishmael to formulate the powerful concept of Jewish perpetual servitude—a permanent, persistent condition of servility. While scholars have argued that the internal logic and precedents of medieval canon law demarcate its priorities as clearly separate from the aims of theology, the citation of figures connoting *servitus Judaeorum* by medieval canonists demonstrates its successful translation from theology to law. This oscillation between a spiritual state and a legal status enables the authoritative construction of a racist concept of inherent, hereditary inferiority that redefines as subordinated the ontological status of Jewish people.

The History of Figura *and the* Figura *of History*

A brief explanation of biblical figures will clarify how they function not only in the New Testament and biblical exegesis, but also in the canon law. Eric Auerbach elucidates this interpretive approach as it develops within Christianity, in which the Hebrew Bible "both as a whole and in its most important details, is [understood as] a concrete historical prefiguration of the Gospel" (44).[7] At its most basic level figures set up a reciprocal relationship between two moments in scripture: the first which anticipates and points to the second, and the second which explains the significance of the first. Although this is a theological method of understanding biblical narratives, it operates within historical time and describes material consequences; both figure and fulfillment are understood as actual historical persons and occurrences. A figural interpretation not only construes an incident in the Hebrew Bible as foreshadowing an incident in Christian Scripture, but could also understand the first event as pointing to a future moment beyond the biblical text (53).[8]

In the history of early Christianity, figural interpretations emerge in the texts of the New Testament. The new movement developed within the practice of Judaism, which shapes attitudes toward the Hebrew Bible figure in relation to its fulfillment:[9] "It seems only natural that the new Judaeo-Christians should have looked for prefigurations and confirmations of Jesus in the Old Testament and incorporated the interpretations thus arrived at into the tradition" (50). Jewish followers of Jesus may have assisted in this mode of reading to connect their received scripture with the narrative of his life. Paul, one of the most influential Jewish Christians, makes frequent use of figures in his writings. However, Auerbach argues that Paul's figural practice creates a hierarchy of New Testament antitype over Hebrew Bible type (50–1).[10] The logic of supersession shapes the significance of Hebrew Bible events, rendering them meaningful only in relation to their counterparts in Christian Scripture.[11] The trend continues in the writings of some of the Church Fathers, influenced by a particular classical connotation of *figura* as "the rhetorical image or circumlocution that conceals, transforms, and even deceives" (45). This received tradition serves to emphasize the graded relation between connected events in Hebrew Bible and the New Testament: while the latter represents the truth (*veritas*), the *figura* of the former are merely shadow (*umbra*), an inferior category of significance.[12] I would argue that figural interpretation itself effectually subordinates Judaism to Christianity insofar as it subsumes the Jewish interpretation of the text to a Christian one.[13]

While figural interpretation seeks to convey the spiritual truth of biblical texts, it also explains historical events that are currently transpiring, or will transpire, in the real world. Typology provides not only a method of reading, but organizes one's lived experience in the world. However, contemporary events, while real, are also merely shadows that gesture toward the actual truth to be revealed at the end of days. While humans experience this process chronologically, God understands all figures and truth simultaneously. Thus figures shape the way Christians understand their place in the world, but also serve as guides to transforming that world to bring it in line with divine will. Taken all together, these elements of the figure demonstrate that while reflecting a divine ideal, figures also influence real events in the present and future (72). Furthermore, the logic of supersession, which renders Judaism and Jews subordinate to Christianity and Christians, shapes the reception of the Pauline approach to figures in subsequent theology, exegesis, and even law.

Scriptural and Patristic Figures of Jewish Servitude and Hereditary Guilt

Before analyzing the figures of servitude that Paul develops in his letters, we must first consider in brief the context in which he and the other authors of Christian Scripture lived. While later readers of the New Testament have understood it as representing conflicts between Christians and Jews, in fact the term "Christian" did not exist at the time in which its authors wrote (Fredriksen 2010, xxi–xxii). Jesus and his followers were all Jews and the controversies debated in the gospels represent concerns internal to the practice of Judaism (79–80). These disputes, similar to other internal Jewish arguments of the period, explored "conflicting ideas about the right way to be Jewish" (81). However, in setting forth a defense of their own beliefs, authors of the New Testament articulate anti-Jewish stereotypes to vilify the views of their opponents. In interpreting the texts that follow, we should understand that references to Jews and Jewish Law indicate an opponent or opinion under attack by a Jewish author, with the awareness that that this nice distinction falls away over time (80–1). I pass over contemporary issues at stake in New Testament debates to focus on the strategy of a particular polemical strand: the association of servitude with an adversary's opinion or practice.

Paul's letters in the New Testament articulate the basic elements of what will later evolve into hereditary inferiority, the *servitus Judaeorum*, through figural readings of slavery. Drawing from the text of the Hebrew Bible, he emphasizes the servile nature of the fraternal relations between Jacob and Esau, and Isaac and Ishmael to establish a new hierarchy. While this relationship will be interpreted by medieval exegetes as figuring the subordination of Jews to Christians, Paul's contemporaries would not have understood it this way. Even as the meaning of these figures continues to be debated today, it can plausibly be argued that they contrast two paths, one superior to the other, probably reflecting controversies over the practice of Jewish law amongst non-Jewish members of the Jesus movement.[14] In Romans 9:12 Paul reinterprets the prophecy in Genesis 25:23 that reverses the primogeniture of the brothers Esau and Jacob/Israel, "The elder shall serve the younger."[15] The word "serve" in the original text derives from the Hebrew root עֶבֶד (*eved*), servant or slave; New Testament quotation of Genesis 25 employs the Greek term in the Septuagint derived from δοῦλος (*doúlos*), slave.[16] The Hebrew Bible traces the lineage of Israel from Jacob, for whom they are named; however, Paul reinterprets the text to argue that Gentile believers are also "the children of God," while not all of Abraham's descendants are (Rom. 9:7–8).[17] Paul includes "Israel of the flesh," of whom he is one, among the elect if they have faith: "Even us whom also he hath called, not only of the Jews but also of the Gentiles" (9:24). However, the elder Esau, whomever he might represent, is supplanted by and subjected to the younger (9:30–33).[18]

Paul clarifies the concept of slavery by associating it with the law in his "allegorical" (*allēgoroumena*) reading of the Genesis narrative of Hagar and Sarah (Galatians 4:21–31).[19] In chiding his Gentile audience for their desire to be "under the law," he rereads Genesis to emphasize the alignment the children of the promise with freedom and the children of the flesh with slavery (4:21–3). Paul cites God's confirmation of Sarah's demand that Abraham's younger child, Isaac, be given priority over his first-born, Ishmael, conceived by his servant Hagar: " 'The son of the bondwoman shall not be heir with the son of the freewoman' " (Gal. 4:30, rephrasing of Gen. 21:10). He identifies Ishmael and his mother Hagar with "that Jerusalem which now is"; she is the woman "from mount Sina"—where the law was given—"engendering unto bondage" (Gal. 4:24–5).[20] Sarah and her children, in contrast, figure the "Jerusalem which is above" who is free (4:26). Paul does not create a clear division between free Gentiles and enslaved Jews; all followers of Jesus are free. Nevertheless, the text implies a hierarchy that contrasts and subordinates the enslaved followers of the law to the free followers of Jesus.

While the New Testament sometimes represents servitude positively,[21] some verses also appear to associate an evil articulation of slavery with Jewish Law or the Jews. Paul contrasts a negative servitude in observance of Jewish Law to that of the Spirit: "so that we should serve in newness of spirit, and not in the oldness of the letter" (Rom. 7:6). While Christians also serve (*douleuein*) as slaves in this new life, this is nevertheless a freeing condition: "For the law of the spirit of life, in Christ Jesus, hath delivered me from the law of sin and of death" (Rom 8:2). Clear-cut binaries don't seem to hold, as Paul associates slavery both with the old law and the new dispensation, as well as connecting law both with slavery and freedom, but the texts suggest that negative slavery, sin, and death are linked to Jewish Law, marking it as inferior to the new way preached by Jesus. The Gospel of John describes his Jewish antagonists as slaves to sin and the devil. In response to Jesus's statement that "the truth shall make you free," some of his Jewish followers protest that they have never been slaves (John 8:32–3).[22] Jesus replies that "whosoever committeth sin, is the servant [slave/doulos] of sin" and identifies the Jews not as children of Abraham, but of the devil: "You are of your father the devil, and the desires of your father you will do" (8:34, 44). This passage suggests that Jews are children of the devil and in serving him are enslaved to sin.[23] In sum, these scriptural associations, whatever their original context, create a hierarchy that designates a spiritually inferior status by associating it with slavery.

In addition to but entirely separate from the representation of spiritual servitude, Christian Scripture also suggests the idea of Jewish hereditary guilt.[24] In its account of the trial of Jesus, the Gospel of Matthew sets forth this notion of congenital culpability.[25] When Pilate absolves himself from fault in refusing to order Jesus's crucifixion, the Jews respond: "His blood be upon us and our children" (27:25). Here the Jewish people as a whole seem to take responsibility for Jesus's death, not only implicating themselves, but their children as well. It is important to note that the text does not specify a consequence for this assumption of accountability; they are neither cursed nor subjected by this action. In accepting this hereditary guilt, the Jews do not appear to undergo a permanent alteration in their status, particularly when we keep in mind that forgiveness for sins and ultimate salvation are open to the Jews, as well as to the Gentiles, if they accept Jesus as the son of God. However, this text and its suggestion of an inherited condition will be cited and reinterpreted by later commentators in developing the idea of Jewish inferiority.

The great church father Augustine (354–430 C.E.) produced his influential figural development of the *servitus Judaeorum* in a rich and diverse theological context.[26] One of the traditions that shaped his writings about Jews was a patristic polemic *adversus Judaeos* (against the Jews).[27] While not representing the reality of contemporary relations between actual Christians and Jews, this discourse established a set of negative claims that circulated during the period and influenced subsequent eras.[28] These ideas include the accusation that the Jews killed Jesus; the charge was expanded beyond those present at his death to include other Jews as well (Fredriksen 2010, 82–3). As punishment for this crime, according to the "Christian interpretive imagination," God destroyed the Temple in Jerusalem in 70 C.E. and permitted Hadrian's imposition of Roman rule and worship in Judea, epitomized by his building a pagan city on the ruins of Jerusalem (84).

> In the eyes of gentile Christian theologians . . . [the] diaspora Jewish population had . . . been driven out of Judea by the Romans after 70 c.e. into a punitive, divinely mandated, and long-foretold exile. . . . By interpreting the whole sweep of biblical history from Cain to Caiaphas and beyond as the record of God's anger against the Jews, Christian theologians combined episodes in the Jewish Bible with these more recent disasters of the first and second centuries to produce a mass of mutually reinforcing arguments *adversus Iudaeos*. (85)

These ideas of crime, loss of political autonomy, exile, and dispersion all contribute to Augustine's development of Jewish figural slavery.[29]

However, even if he clearly draws from this antagonistic tradition, Augustine powerfully transforms it to craft a more positive image of the Jews. A number of scholars have argued that Augustine develops a protected and privileged role in Christian society for the Jews as witnesses to the truth of Scripture.[30] Fredriksen and Unterseher contend that Augustine formulates the core of this affirmative concept in the *Contra Faustum*, an anti-pagan polemic (Fredriksen 2010, 350, 260–89; Unterseher 105–42). His extended explanation of the narrative in Genesis 4:1–15 employs the figure of Cain to reinterpret the *adversus Judaeos* accusations. Yes, the Jews, like Cain, are guilty of killing their brother, Jesus, but Cain's marking and expulsion demonstrate not only punishment but protection. God marks the Jews through their continued adherence to their Bible and Law, testifying to its truth. He protects them from being killed or prevented from continuing their observance of the Law. They are dispersed everywhere to spread their testimony, although they misunderstand the Bible's message; what they prove is the truth of Christian interpretation and thus act in the service of, and in servitude to, the Church (Fredriksen 2010, 260–352; Unterseher 105–62).[31]

Although this doctrine advances clearly salutary elements, its figural logic not only subordinates Jewish misunderstanding of their own texts to the "true" Christian interpretation, but also emphasizes the servile role Jews perform for Christianity.[32] An exploration of Augustine's use of figures to illustrate Jewish servitude shows its centrality for his theology of Jews.[33] In *De Civitate Dei* he cites Paul's "allegorical" interpretation of Hagar and Ishmael in Galatians 4:21–31 to figure the Hebrew Bible and the earthly city:

> This method of interpretation, which comes down to us with apostolic authority, opens the way for us to understand the writing of the two covenants, the old and the new. A certain part of the earthly city has been used to make an image of the heavenly city, and since it thus symbolizes not itself but the other, it is in servitude. (15.2, 419)[34]

Jewish Scripture, part of the earthly city, performs a positive function in figuring the heavenly city. However, in so doing, it serves in a form of slavery as a symbol of the heavenly city. This interpretation renders the Hebrew Bible a mere figure, a signifier without inherent meaning that operates only to indicate the signified of Christian truth. Augustine presents the figural status itself and its function as a kind of slavery. *De Civitate Dei* also employs the Romans use of Esau to figure Jewish servitude:

> As to the statement, "the elder shall serve [serviet/will be a slave to] the younger," however, scarcely anyone among us has understood it to mean anything else than that the older people of the Jews should serve [serviturum/be a slave to] the younger Christian people. . . . Christ . . . is lord over his brother, since his people rule the Jews. (Book 16, Chapters 35, 165, and 37, 173)[35]

Significantly, Augustine extends the spiritual hierarchy established by Paul by using it to comment on the present time. The prophecy is, not was, fulfilled; Christ's people rule, in the present tense, over the Jews in the form of the Christian Roman Empire, as established in the *adversus Judaeos* tradition. Spiritual supersession begins to take on political significance in this interpretation.

Augustine moves beyond Paul not only in the entry into history, but also in developing new types from the Hebrew Bible in order to explain the cause of Jewish enslavement. Supersession results not merely from Jewish unbelief, but from crime; slavery serves as a marker of unfaithfulness, but more significantly, punishment. The *Contra Faustum Manichaeum* employs the fratricidal Genesis narrative of Cain and Abel to innovate and explain Jewish subordination.[36]

> The Jews were . . . guilty of unbelief . . . when Christ came. . . .
> If Cain had obeyed God . . . he would have ruled over his sin, in-
> stead of acting as the [slave] of sin in killing his innocent brother.
> So also the Jews, of whom all these things are a figure, if they
> had . . . acknowledged the time of salvation through the pardon
> of sins by grace . . . they would have ruled over sin as long as it
> continued in their mortal body. But now . . . in subjection to sin
> reigning in their mortal body . . . they have . . . been inflamed with
> hatred against [Jesus]. . . . Abel, the younger brother, is killed by
> the elder brother; Christ, the head of the younger people, is killed
> by the elder people of the Jews. (*Contra Faustum Manichaeum*,
> 12.9, 186)[37]

The reference to the younger and elder peoples here recalls Esau's servitude to Jacob, but the dynamic between Jews and Christians is located in a new figure.[38] Metaphors of ruling and subjection present in the Genesis text of the Cain narrative (4:7 "and thou shalt have dominion over [sin]") run through this passage: by disobeying God, Cain is unable to rule over his sin, instead becoming its slave in killing his brother. These ideas resonate strongly with the verses in John, quoted here, which articulate the concept of subordination to sin.[39] The Jews, in failing to recognize Jesus as the messiah, also fail to rule over their sin; in insisting on their own authority rather than submitting to God, they become slaves to sin and kill Jesus.

The *Contra Faustum*'s discussion of Cain draws from formulations of sin and punishment articulated in the *adversus Judaeos* tradition to explain and justify contemporary Jewish political exile and subordination.

> "Groaning and trembling shalt thou be on the earth." (Genesis 4:12) Here no one can fail to see that in every land where the Jews are scattered they mourn for the loss of their kingdom, and are in terrified subjection to the immensely superior number of Christians. . . . So to the end of the seven days of time, the continued preservation of the Jews will be a proof to believing Christians of the subjection merited by those who, in the pride of their kingdom, put the Lord to death. (*Contra Faustum*, 12.12, 187–8)[40]

By glorying in "the pride of their kingdom," their earthly power and authority, and killing Jesus, Jews have been punished by exile from that kingdom and subjection to "the immensely superior number of Christians." Guilt for the crime of killing Jesus devolves not only upon the Jews allegedly implicated at the time of the crucifixion, but also on all Jews, and will extend from that event, through Augustine's day, until the end of days.[41] Augustine clearly identifies even contemporary Jews as guilty of deicide and thus punished with exile and subjection to Christians (Fredriksen 2010, 82–5, 322–23). He develops this idea, also with recourse to the figure of Cain, in his *Ennartiones in Psalmos*. Although conquered by the Romans,

> The Jews nevertheless remain with a mark; nor in such sort conquered have they been, as that by the conquerors they have been swallowed up. Not without reason is there that Cain, on whom . . . God set a mark in order that no one should slay him. . . . These are therefore Jews, they have not been slain, they are necessary to believing nations. . . . Throughout all nations there have been scattered abroad the Jews, witnesses of their own iniquity and our truth. (*Ennartiones in Psalmos* 58:12, part one 21–2 241)[42]

To this day, the Jews remain apart from, rather than absorbed by their rulers. The distinctive mark of Cain figures their separate identity as a people. The persistence of the Jews as a conspicuous, subjected people is part of their divine punishment; they are subordinated both to the Roman Empire and to the truth of Christianity, forced to serve as proof of the latter and their own sin.[43]

The *Contra Faustum* reinforces the idea of Jewish servitude and elaborates upon its hereditary nature by introducing a proof-text that makes direct reference to slavery: Noah's curse on his offspring. In the episode in which he lies drunken and naked, Noah represents Jesus, while the

> middle son [Ham] is the Jewish people, for they neither held the first place with the apostles, nor believed subsequently with the Gentiles. They saw the nakedness of their father, because they consented to Christ's death. . . . And thus they are the [slave] of their brethren. For what else is this nation now but a desk [scriniaria/bookslave][44] for the Christians, bearing the law and the prophets, and testifying to the [manumission] of the Church, so that we honor in the sacrament what they disclose in the letter? (12.23, 190–1)[45]

Although this discussion omits explicit mention of the moment in Genesis when Noah curses Ham's son Canaan with slavery, in identifying Ham with the Jews, Augustine directly links this punishment to the Jews' alleged crucifixion of Jesus. The malediction that Canaan will be a slave of slaves to his brothers ("Chanaan servus servorum erit fratribus suis" [Gen. 9:25]) is expressed in the future tense in the biblical text. This, and the fact that it will affect the offspring of Ham, indicates its hereditary nature.[46] Augustine emphasizes a persisting slave status in employing this narrative, as he does with the figure of Cain, to explain the contemporary servitude of the Jews in witnessing to Christian truth.[47]

Especially when viewed in the context of earlier and contemporary writings, Augustine's account of the Jews and Jewish Law as occupying a privileged place of protection beneficial to Christian society appears strikingly positive. Furthermore, his teachings served to shield Jews from Christian violence for centuries after Augustine lived and wrote (Cohen 1999). However, scholars who have demonstrated the innovative aspect of this valuable Jewish role have downplayed its negative contribution: if Augustine originates the claim that the Jews' continued observance of their Law performs a beneficial service in Christian society, at the same time he creates a new inferior status for the Jews as slaves to the Church. In fact, I would argue that it is precisely because Augustine presents such a favorable view of Jews and Judaism that he must balance it by positing their subordination to Christian truth and freedom through the figure of slavery.[48]

Moreover, the concept of Jewish servitude, far from being a mere corollary to his theology of the Jews, is central to this teaching; of the six elements of the "doctrine of witness" identified by Cohen, it is the *only* idea to appear in all fifteen of Augustine's noteworthy writings on the Jews (1999, 41). Even Paula Fredriksen, whose positive assessment of Augustine's view of Jews is reflected in the subtitle of her recent monograph, *A Christian Defense of Jews and Judaism*, acknowledges that "Augustine's theology, for all its innovative and positive positions, does ultimately subordinate Judaism to Christianity. This is why he uses such terms as 'servant' or 'librarian' or 'bookslave' to describe Judaism's subservient role" (372). In articulating this status, Augustine almost certainly did not adversely affect the position of actual contemporary Jews. Nevertheless, his development of a figure of Jewish slavery influenced subsequent thinking about the role of Jews in Christian society as it migrated from its largely theological context and entered into the discourse of medieval canon law.[49]

Figural Slavery and the Canon Law Formulation of Perpetual Servitude

Before turning to an analysis of biblical figures of Jewish servitude in legal documents, let us first briefly consider the sources, structure, and function of canon law. Canons, the principal type of church law, originate as legislation determined by bishops in church councils, and by local clergy in synods, or regional gatherings. Papal letters or decretals, which typically issue a ruling on a matter, also contribute to the body of canon law, although only the most important opinions are codified. The first authoritative compilation of canon law, Gratian's *Decretum*, appears in the mid-twelfth century; originally titled *Concordia discordantium canonum*, it gathers and attempts to reconcile ecclesiastical laws into a coherent system and serves as a textbook in canon law schools. Teachers at the University of Bologna, one of the earliest law faculties in Europe, develop commentaries on the *Decretem*, becoming known as decretists. As decretists discover gaps or inconsistencies in the law, the popes were called upon to issue rulings, in effect creating new law. Commentators on these papal decretals are referred to as decretalists. Pope Gregory IX ordered the Dominican canonist Raymond of Peñafort to produce an official collection of papal and conciliar law, the *Decretales Gregorii IX*, or *Liber Extra* (1234).[50] As popes and councils continue to promulgate law, subsequent collections appear over the next century: Innocent IV's *Novellae* (New laws), Gregory X's *Novissimae*

(Newest laws), Boniface VIII's *Liber sextus* (Sext or Sixth book of decretals), John XXII's *Constitutiones Clementinae* and *Extravagantes*. The production of these authoritative collections gave rise to commentaries or glosses on the decretals. By the end of the fifteenth century, a compilation of the definitive texts of canon law—Gratian's *Decretum*, the *Liber extra*, the *Sext*, the *Clementine consitutions*, and the *Extravagantes of John XXII*—appear as the *Corpus iuris canonici* (Brundage 1995, 8–59 passim).[51]

The concept of Jewish servitude enters into legal discourse by means of papal decretals, one of the more dynamic and innovative aspects of canon law. Furthermore, since the *servitus Judaeorum* is formulated in Christian scripture and theology by means of biblical examples, it is also not surprising to find popes employing the logic of figures, and the types themselves, when they introduce this status into their letters. Once papal practice establishes this convention, it is taken up and repeated in the texts of conciliar rulings and even infiltrates the arguments of commentators on the canon law. The three figures adduced to illustrate the enslavement of the Jews are Cain, Hagar/Ishmael, and Ham/Canaan. In what follows, I first consider the example of Cain, as I argue that it shapes the earliest decretal on Jewish servitude to Christians, and demonstrate how subsequent popes make use of this figure. I then consider citations of the figure of Hagar/Ishmael. Out of these two figures, Pope Innocent III develops the idea of *servitus perpetua*, perpetual Jewish enslavement; the idea of perpetual servitude pre-exists its association with Jews, but it is first powerfully and systematically applied in a legal context to this group. The remainder of this chapter explores the ramifications of this idea, including its expansion in canon law commentaries to include the figure of Canaan, Ham's offspring. I conclude by demonstrating how perpetual Jewish enslavement produces a racial status of hereditary inferiority.

In a 1063 letter to the bishops of Spain, Pope Alexander II introduces a mild formulation of the idea that Jews occupy a position of servitude relative to Christians. He employs this status in support of the argument that Jews—in contrast to Muslims—are willing to submit themselves to Christians and therefore deserve protection. The letter praises the bishops for shielding Jews from violence threatened by armies mobilized to fight against Muslims. The pope condemns those who

> wanted to kill [the Jews] in their rage, though divine piety might have predestined them to salvation. In this way did the blessed Gregory prohibit some who were inflamed in their wish to destroy

them, denouncing as impious those who wished to destroy people
who were saved (servati) by God's mercy; for since the loss of their
freedom and fatherland they live dispersed in all parts of the world,
condemned to lasting penance (diuturna paenitentia) for the crime
of their fathers in the effusion of the savior's blood. [Dispar nimi-
rum] There is assuredly, a difference between the case of the Jews
and that of the Saracens. It is just to fight those who persecute
Christians and who expel them from their cities and houses, while
these people [Jews] are everywhere ready to serve (ubique parati
sunt servire). (Linder 1997, 452)

Although Alexander does not explicitly mention Cain, his discourse parallels a number of elements explained in Augustine's development of the
figure: the exile, dispersion, and subjugation of the Jews as lasting atone-
ment for the crucifixion. However, the decretal, in line with its aim to
protect Jews, mitigates the punitive elements associated with the patristic
figure of Cain; condemned to penance, not punishment, the Jews may well
repent, convert and attain salvation. Distinguished from Muslims in not
persecuting Christians, Jews nevertheless are tolerated only as subordinates. Alexander's use of the terms *servati* and *servire* may emphasize their
common root in the *servus* or slave as understood in Roman civil law.[52] As
Augustine explains in *De Civitate Dei*:

The origin of the Latin word for "slave" is believed to be derived from
the fact that those who by the law of war might have been put to
death, when preserved (servabantur) by their victors, became slaves
(servi), so named from their preservation (servando). (19.15, 187)[53]

Jews, in Alexander's case, should be protected from destruction, but only
conditionally: insofar as they inhabit a position of servitude (Simonsohn
vol. 7, 12–14, 98; Sapir Abulafia 2011, 139–40). While many papal letters
do not enter into the code of canon law, official compilations include this
decretal under the title *Dispar nimirum* and commentaries frequently cite
it. Although the codified version cuts the preliminary discussion with its
possible allusions to Cain, subsequent canonists adduce this ruling as evidence of Jewish servitude to Christians.

This concept as figured by Cain appears explicitly in the thirteenth-
century decretals of Innocent III. The employment of biblical figures
characterizes much of his writings even before his election to pope,

reflecting his training in the liberal arts and theology while studying at the University of Paris. These faculties focused on the study of the Bible, and patristic texts as a means to understanding it, emphasizing a typological interpretive approach (Moore 9). Furthermore, as Auerbach adumbrated, Innocent applied figural thinking as a lens to understand contemporary events: the successes and failures of Christendom reflected God's favor or punishment for sin (Moore 14–15). In response to the morally indefensible capture of Constantinople by the crusading armies in 1204, Innocent interprets the event positively in a letter to the accompanying clergy by means of a complex reading of Mary Magdalene, John and Peter coming to the empty tomb of Jesus. As he concludes:

> Behold, now, brothers and sons, you can clearly conclude that God has finally fulfilled through you and in us that sacrament which he foresaw from all eternity and presaged in the Gospel. You may understand that God has brought about this mystery through your ministry not like some chance occurrence but as something issuing from his high counsel, so that now there may be one flock and one shepherd. According to his foreknowledge, the creator of times has so arranged all times that when the fullness of the gentiles has entered into the faith, then even all of Israel will be saved. (qtd. in Moore 133)

Here Christian Scripture provides the figure that is fulfilled in the actions of the pope, his clergy and Western Christian crusaders; their actions serve to implement the will of God in the current moment. As head of the Church, Innocent felt a strong responsibility to realize, with the help of all Christians, God's "high counsel" in the world, including the conversion of the remaining gentiles and Jews.

Scholars who have focused primarily on Innocent's rulings on the Jews have tended to interpret them as promoting a particularly harsh view.[54] However, when considered in the context of entire range of concerns in his activist papacy, his writings on Jewish subordination to Christians play only a small role in his larger agenda to bring the world under Christendom and execute God's will. During the length of his papacy, Innocent faced significant challenges and responsibilities, not the least of which was the constant litigation that passed through the papal curia. In addition, he sought to continue the reform of the Church (both with an eye to promoting its independence from secular authorities as well as ensuring the adherence of the clergy to their holy duties); he played an active role in the politics of Italy and the Holy Roman Empire; he preached the reconquest of the Holy Land (launching the Fourth Crusade); and actively battled what he perceived as two substantive threats to Christianity, heresy and Islam (Moore 44). Even a cursory review of the events of his career demonstrates that the Jews were almost surely the least of his many, pressing problems. The vehemence with which he writes aligns with his guiding preoccupation: the pope's responsibility to bring Christendom into line with God's will. As he fights this battle with recalcitrant secular rulers and fellow prelates, as he launches violent crusades, internal and external, against heretics and Muslims, he also responds to complaints of the day that the Jews exercise undue power over Christians. While Jews have a rightful place in the Church, following Augustine's teaching, that position is predicated on their subordination to not only to Christianity, but to Christians. During the twelfth century, Jews flourished in the lands under Christian control, enabling them in various contexts to occupy positions of authority over Christians. In emphasizing their servitude, Innocent seeks to return them to their proper place in the Church. His letters take the form of reprimands both to secular rulers and clerics for allowing Jews to exercise improper power over Christians. Although he, like Alexander II, refers to the *servitus Judaeorum* as a justification for protecting Jews, Innocent reinterprets the concept to signify not merely Jews' acceptance of Christian authority, but as *proof* of their social inferiority, a status that he feels requires reinforcement given its transgression in contemporary Christendom.

The first explicit reference to Cain in a decretal appears in Innocent's 1208 letter chastising the Count of Nevers for favoring Jews by allowing them, contrary to their divinely imposed servitude, to dominate Christians. He complains that amongst other transgressions, princes appoint Jews to practice usury and serve as royal collection agents; when debtors default, Jews seize their real estate, thereby depriving the church and poor of tithe payments that Christians are required to pay on landed property. In order to redress the scandal of Jews oppressing Christians, the letter includes an extended discussion of Cain's punishment to remind the Count of the proper place of the former people in relation to the latter:

> The Lord made Cain a wanderer and a fugitive over the earth, but
> set a mark upon him, making his head to shake, lest any finding
> him should slay him. Thus the Jews, against whom the blood of

Jesus Christ calls out, although they ought not be killed, lest the
Christian people forget the Divine Law, yet as wanderers ought
they to remain on the earth, until their [face] be filled with shame
and they seek the name of Jesus Christ, the Lord. That is why blasphemers of the Christian name ought not to be aided by Christian
princes to oppress the servants of the Lord, but ought rather to be
forced into the servitude of which they made themselves deserving
when they raised sacrilegious hands against Him Who had come to
confer true liberty upon them, thus calling down His blood upon
themselves and upon their children. . . . You are not afraid to show
favor to those who dared to nail to the Cross the only-begotten Son
of God, and to this moment have not ceased to blaspheme [against
Him]. (Grayzel 1966, 127–29)

Cain, punished with exile and physically marked to prevent others from
murdering him, figures the Jews, guilty of Jesus' death, yet protected from
retributive execution in order to provide witness to the truth of Scripture.[55]
While Innocent mentions the protective doctrine of witness, he emphasizes Augustine's notion of Jewish subjection, explained with recourse to
an ascribed servitude by which Cain was punished; preserved from death,
Jews now serve as slaves. For Innocent, this rebuking imposition of inferiority ought to humiliate the Jews into conversion; he cites Psalm 82:17,
"Fill their faces with shame; and they shall seek thy name, O Lord," to
prove his point.[56] He introduces the question of servitude in reproving the
improper suppression of the superior servants of the Lord (Rom 1:1) by the
Jews, who must be subordinated into the slavery to which they sentenced
themselves in killing Jesus. Jesus's sacrifice freed believers from sin and
death; the Jews, in rejecting Jesus, remain in the servitude of original sin,
and by crucifying him deserve an additional penalty of enslavement. This
punishment afflicts not only the perpetrators of the crucifixion, but, following the verse from Matthew, their children as well. Innocent describes
contemporary Jews as if they themselves nailed Jesus to the cross; to aid
them is to assist in the deicide. His citation of individual verses to support
his claims, in addition to the analogy of Cain, also functions like figures
which require fulfillment through the recognition of the Jews' crime and
the imposition upon them of a humiliating punishment—slavery—in the
current moment.

Innocent's complaint of Jewish dominance over Christians, illustrated with the corrective figures of Cain and the verses from Matthew

and Psalms, serves as a precedent for later popes who also seek to identify Jews as inferiors and relegate them to their proper place. Clement IV
(1265–1268) makes use of Cain in a letter (1265–1266) condemning the
preference of Jews over Christians in Poland:

> The Jewish people sinned terribly; therefore it was made unstable
> [Lam. 1:8], like the fratricide Cain . . .a vagabond and fugitive on the
> earth. . . . They impiously killed [Jesus] . . . damnably calling his
> blood to be on them and their children [Matt. 27:25]. Whence, since
> their dispersion until now . . . enough humaneness is accorded to
> their inhumanity if they are too few to be killed by all who come
> upon them, so the law of God be not eternally forgotten, but at last
> the remnant shall be saved. They are however, as damned slaves
> pressed to the deserved yoke of servitude (ut servi dampnati iugo
> servitutis merito comprimendi), to see if strong vexation will in-
> struct their understanding and when their faces will be full of
> shame, they will be compelled to seek the name of the Lord [Ps.
> 82:17]. (Grayzel 1989, 110–11, my translation)

Clement opens his letter with a paraphrase of Lamentations, the prophet
Jeremiah's account of the destruction of the first Temple and the subsequent exile and captivity of the Jews.[57] In equating this experience to that
of Cain (following Augustine's explanation of this type), he provides historical precedent for the Roman destruction of the second Temple and
prefigures contemporary Jewish servitude; he replaces "Jerusalem" in the
biblical verse with "Jewish people" who still feel the effects of their sin.
The fratricidal Jews, like Cain, suffer exile for crucifying their brother; although preserved from death, they are subjected to slavery, iterating the
doctrine of subordinated witness. Innocent's influence clearly appears
here, with the inclusion of paraphrases from Matthew and Psalms and
following his word choice "comprimi servitute, qua se dignos merito red-
diderunt" (Grayzel 1966, 126, see also 114 for the use of the term *iugo*,
discussed later).[58]

While Cain provides a useful figure for Jewish guilt and expulsion, the
Genesis text does not mention slavery as the punishment for fratricide.
Although Augustine describes Cain as figuring Jewish servitude, the authoritative Pauline account in Galatians more explicitly introduces relative
positions of freedom and servitude. Innocent introduces into his decretals
the example of Hagar, the slave woman (*ancilla*) and Sarah, the free woman

(*libera*) to exhort the proper ordering of Jews in relation to Christians. He employs the figure strategically, either to reinforce the hierarchy of Christian over inferior Jew, or to castigate secular rulers and clergy for permitting a blasphemous inversion in which free people serve slaves.[59] Writing in 1205, Innocent complains to the King of France that he and other princes violate divine will by allowing Jews to dominate Christians:[60]

> Though it does not displease God, but is even acceptable to Him, that the Jewish Dispersion should live and serve (serviat) under Catholic Kings and Christian princes until such a time as their remnant shall be saved . . . nevertheless, such [Princes] are exceedingly offensive to the sight of the Divine Majesty who prefer the sons of the crucifiers, against whom to this day the blood cries to the Father's ears, to the heirs of the Crucified Christ, and who prefer the Jewish slavery (servitutem) to the freedom (libertati) of those whom the Son freed, as though the son of a [slave woman/ancill{a}e filius] could and ought to be an heir along with the son of the free woman (filio liber[a]e). (Grayzel 1966, 104–7)

Jews may be tolerated as long as they serve under Christian rulers, but cannot, as sons of deicides, be favored above Christians without exceeding offense to God. While he is not directly named, Cain lurks in this text as well in the echo of Genesis 4:10: "the voice of thy brother's blood crieth to me [God] from the earth."[61] The cry of blood against the Jews "to this day" also recalls Matthew 27:25, emphasizing their continuing culpability; it anticipates and justifies their contemporary enslaving punishment. These proof-texts of Jewish servitude and hereditary guilt add weight to the quotation of Galatians; the contrast between the children of the *ancilla* with those of the *libera* emphasizes and explains the juxtaposition of Jewish slavery to Christian freedom. Together, these references combine to recall and assert the subordination of Jews to their Christian superiors.[62]

Innocent's concern for the correct hierarchy of Christian over Jew is evidenced in this same letter in a fascinating digression on the social status of Jesus. The pope complains about Jews deriding Jesus's antecedents:[63]

> [Jews] publicly insult Christians by saying that they [Christians] believe in a peasant (rusticum) who had been hung by the Jewish people. Indeed, we do not doubt that He was hung for us, since He carried our sins in his body on the cross, but we do not admit that

He was a peasant either in manners or in race. Forsooth, they themselves cannot deny that physically He was descended from priestly
and royal stock, and that His manners were distinguished and
proper. . . . Wherefore, lest through them the name of God be blas-
phemed, and Christian liberty (libertas) become less than Jewish
[slavery/servitus], we warn . . . that you restrain the Jews from their
presumptions. (Grayzel 1966, 106–9)

The letter energetically argues that scripture vouches for Jesus' elevated
origins, denies that he derives from inferior, peasant stock, and adds that
his manners were noble and honorable (mores ejus praeclari fuerunt, et
honesti). Since Christians believe Jesus to be both the son of God and
God incarnate, it would seem unnecessary to insist on the nobility of his
human lineage. That the pope felt obligated to respond to such a charge
betrays no little anxiety about the need to preserve the pre-eminence of
Christians over Jews. In reverting to the admonition to ensure the proper
ordering of Christian freedom over Jewish slavery, the pope demonstrates
his compulsion to battle this threat at all levels.[64]

Innocent powerfully synthesizes these tropes and references in a subsequent letter to articulate a concept of *perpetual* servitude as punishment
visited upon the Jews. However, since this idea predates the pope's deployment of it, a consideration of the history of its prior contexts is necessary
to clarify the ramifications of its important thirteenth-century appropriation. The *Conferences* of John Cassian (c. 360–c. 435) contain an early appearance of the term "perpetual servitude" ascribed to a certain author.[65]
Expounding on Romans 7:14, "we know that the law is spiritual, but I am
carnal, sold under sin," Cassian explains that original sin effected the sale
of humankind into servitude:

Do I ask what and whose sin this is? It is certainly Adam's, by whose
transgression . . . we were sold; . . . he delivered all his offspring,
now led astray, to the yoke of perpetual slavery (jugo perpetuae servitutis addixit). . . . Abandoning his natural freedom, he chose to
surrender himself in perpetual slavery to him from whom he had
obtained the deadly price of the forbidden fruit. Constrained from
then on by this condition, he . . . subjected the whole line of his
posterity to the same perpetual servitude in which he had become
enslaved. For what else can a marriage between slaves beget than
slaves? (Cassian, *Conferences* 23.12.1–2, 802)[66]

Although Adam was born in a state of freedom, in taking the fruit from the serpent he sold himself and his progeny, putting them under the yoke of perpetual slavery. Having become slaves themselves, Adam and Eve can only give birth to slaves; thus their servitude and that of their children extends perpetually. However, this perpetuity has a conclusion in the salvation offered to believers through Jesus' sacrifice: "For it was right that his offspring should remain under the ancient conditions . . . until by the price of His own blood the grace of the Lord redeemed them from their original chains and set them free in the primeval state of liberty" (802). Jesus redeems Adam's offspring from slavery through the payment of his blood and returns them to their original freedom. This is the spiritual liberty enjoyed by faithful Christians.

The concept of perpetual servitude also appears in exegesis on Noah and his cursing of Ham's offspring. St. Maximus, Bishop of Turin (c. 380–465) offers an early example of the term in his sermon interpreting Noah as a figure for Jesus: "Likewise, Noah, a farmer, signified Christ when he planted his vine; and fell asleep drunk with wine, lay uncovered in his tent; and awaking from sleep, imposing a curse of perpetual servitude upon his son for not concealing [Noah's] shame" (*Patrologia Latina Online* vol. 57 col. 596A–B, my translation).[67] In his interpretation of these events in Genesis, Maximus neither names nor explains the figural significance of the son upon whom perpetual servitude is imposed. Procopius of Gaza, a sixth-century exegete, explicitly connects the Jews with Ham to explain their hereditary slavery in his *Commentary on Genesis*:[68]

> Noah was naked in his own house: so Christ was crucified by the Jews. Ham is the type of the Jewish people, who mocked Christ hanging from the cross; . . . In truth Christ assigned the Jews to perpetual servitude. (*Commentarii in Genesin, Patrologiæ Græcæ* vol. 87a IX col. 306–7, my translation)[69]

He identifies the Jews as crucifying and mocking Jesus, who as a consequence, imposed a sentence of eternal slavery upon them. Procopius also considers this penalty in the historical context of the Persian/Babylonian and Roman subjugations of the Jews. Haymo, Bishop of Halberstat (d. 853), also uses the term in his exposition of Hosea 1:6–7, in which a child named "Without Mercy" anticipates God's employment of the Romans to punish the Jews for the crucifixion: "at the coming of God . . . they called down the blood of the seed of God: 'His blood be upon us and upon our children.' And since they acted *without mercy*, they were delivered to the Romans, and damned to their perpetual servitude and delivered to oblivion" (*Enarratio in Duodecim Prophetas Minores, In Osee Prophetam. Patrologia Latina*, vol. 117 1, col. 14D, my translation and emphasis). Incorporating the proof-text of Jewish guilt from Matthew, Haymo suggests that the prophecy of Hosea, rightly understood, is fulfilled by the Roman conquest resulting in the Jews' damnation to permanent slavery.

The Jews' subjection to perpetual slavery in rejecting salvation and incurring guilt for the crucifixion moves from patristic and medieval biblical commentary into the discourse of canon law with Innocent's inclusion of the phrase in his influential decretal, *Etsi Judeos* (1205).[70] The letter admonishing French prelates responds to reports that Jews force Christian nursemaids to expel their breast milk into latrines if the latter have recently taken the Eucharist. This constitutes not only an insult to the Christian faith, but a violation of the law prohibiting Jews from employing Christian domestic servants. Condemning practices that allow Jews to dominate the Christians, Innocent argues that the perpetual servitude of the former requires their subordination to the latter.

> While Christian piety accepts the Jews who, by their own guilt, are consigned to *perpetual servitude* (quos propria culpa submisit perpetue servituti) because they crucified the Lord, . . . We, therefore, asked . . . the . . . King of France, . . . Duke of Burgundy, and the Countess of Troyes, so to restrain the excesses of the Jews that they shall not dare raise their neck, bowed under *the yoke of perpetual slavery* (perpetue servitutis jugo submissam) against the reverence of the Christian Faith; more rigidly forbid them to have any nurses nor other kinds of Christian servants in the future, lest the children of a free woman should be slaves to the children of a slave; (ne filii libere filiis famulentur ancille) but, that rather as slaves rejected by God, in whose death they wickedly conspired, they shall, by the effect of this very action, recognize themselves as the slaves of those whom Christ's death set free at the same time that it enslaved them. . . . henceforth the perfidious Jews should not in any other way dare grow insolent, [but under servile fear, they should always show the shame of their guilt and venerate the honor of the Christian faith / sed sub timore servili pretendant semper verecundiam culpe sue, ac revereantur

honorem fidei Christian{a}e:] (Grayzel 1966, 115–17, my transl in
[]; emphasis mine)

The Latin version of the text opens with the condemnation of the Jews to
eternal slavery as a result of their own crimes; in spite of their sin Christian
piety tolerates them, but only insofar as they remain subordinate. Because
of the Jews' more recent transgressions, which in effect flout this divinely
imposed subjugated status, Christian rulers must force them into permanent submission. The yoke of servitude, expressing the universal condition of original sin in John Cassian's discussion, appears here to figure a
specifically Jewish penalty. Although God has ordained the Jews' subordination, disobedient Christians permit them to inhabit a higher position.
Innocent brings in Galatians to protest the sacrilegious inversion of free
persons serving as slaves to slaves and uses the proof-text to exhort the
Jews to recognize themselves as slaves rejected by God. He emphasizes
the impious paradox of Jews refusing their inferiority, explaining that in
killing Jesus, the Jews enslaved themselves at the moment his sacrifice
freed the faithful from the servitude of original sin. Although addressing
a Christian audience, Innocent aspires to a transformation from the sinful
reality into a divinely ruled future in which guilt, shame and servile fear
will inculcate in Jews a realization of their enslavement to Christians.

Once introduced by Innocent's decretal to explain and reinforce the
observance of ecclesiastical law, the concept of perpetual servitude appears
in other papal letters. Honorius III seemingly offers papal protection in a
1220 letter written to Isaac Benveniste, the Jewish physician to the King of
Aragon. However, even while the pope expresses hope that Christian piety
and care might prompt the nonbeliever's conversion, Honorius mentions
the punitive debasement of the Jews:

> The Apostolic Throne, the pious Mother, in her love of piety at times
> extends the breasts of charity . . . to the strangers whom . . . she tries
> to bring forth into the Faith, so that . . . they might be adopted as
> her children. . . . Therefore, although the perfidy of the Jews, con-
> demned as it is to perpetual slavery because of the cry by which they
> wickedly called down the blood of Christ upon themselves and their
> children, has rendered itself unworthy of being replenished by the
> breasts of her consolation; nevertheless, since . . . you beg for our
> protection and help, we . . . grant to you the shield of our protection.
> (Grayzel 1966, 153–55)

This offer, ostensibly of benevolent care, comes at the price of humiliating abjection.[71] While mentioning conversion, it does not focus on the potential freedom this change might confer, but rather paradoxically, on the intractable nature of Jewish guilt and enslavement, secured with the reference to Matthew. The theme of Christian mercy and tolerance in the face of Jewish ingratitude and contempt similarly animates Gregory IX's April 1233 complaint to German prelates that Jews are holding public office, forcibly circumcising their Christian slaves and committing other transgressions of canon law. Gregory mentions the yoke of perpetual slavery twice in this text and echoes the language of Innocent's previous letters, emphasizing the concern that unfree Jews are dominating free Christians.[72] He includes virtually identical phrases in a letter written a month later (May 1233) to the Archbishop of Compostella, in which he condemns Jewish insolence and their flouting of numerous canons by holding public office, employing Christian servants, practicing usury and failing to wear clothing that would distinguish them from Christians. The opening sentence repeats verbatim Innocent's phrase in the first line of *Etsi Judaeos*: "quos propria culpa submisit perpetue servituti," and the passage rehearses earlier points that the Jews should acknowledge their sin and submit themselves to the yoke of servitude; as in the previous letter, Gregory iterates the phrase "perpetual slavery" (Grayzel 1966, 205–7).[73]

However, the influence of *Etsi Judaeos* extends well beyond its quotation in other individual papal letters, insofar as it was selected for inclusion into the body of canon law and thus serves as precedent for subsequent legal commentaries and decisions. Innocent promulgates the first official collection of decretals in his *Compilatio tertia* (1209) (Brundage 1995, 195; Pakter 136); the inclusion of *Etsi Judaeos* in this compilation ensures its wide dissemination.[74] Gregory IX's definitive dectretal collection, the *Decretales* or *Liber Extra* (1234), also retains it, where it became part of established canon law, the *Corpus iuris canonici*. This collection also serves as the text book for the study of canon law and becomes the basis for consequent commentary (Czerwinski 26–7).[75]

Thus *Etsi* imported into canon law a concept that heretofore largely addressed the spiritual status of Jews in relation to Christians. In so doing, the idea of Jewish inferiority, understood as permanent and hereditary, took on a legal reality that enabled its enforcement. One important consequence of *Etsi* was the application of this hierarchy to a variety of Christian–Jewish relations; for example, the rationale of Jewish inferiority enabled canon law to extend the prohibition of Jews employing free Christians as domestic servants to include all Christian servants.[76] In addressing this question, Innocent contributes to an already very large body of law on the question of Jews owning or employing Christians.[77] Pakter notes the odd incongruity that the bulk of medieval law on Jews concerned their owning slaves in spite of the fact that this did not reflect actual practice. "The interest in these texts for canonists was that the prospect of servitude to Jews played on the fears and pride of Christians. As a result, canonical concern in this area was all out of proportion to historical realities" (84).[78]

While a number of thirteenth-century canonists disapprove of Jews exercising authority over Christians through employment, *Etsi* provides a new rationale for prohibiting this practice: "The doctrine of Jewish servility [served] as grounds to bar Jews from hiring Christians. . . . Innocent aggressively propounded the idea that Jews were not only theologically, but socially inferior. . . . He objected to serving Jews on the basis of their social status" (Pakter 134–5).[79] Innocent translates a theological idea into a legal principle that would enable the enforcement of Jewish subordination and bring social reality in line with their inherent status. The excessive canonical preoccupation with Jews owning Christian slaves reflects the extent of this theological concern.

Once introduced into ecclesiastical law through the inclusion of *Etsi* into the canon, Jewish enslavement enters into the discussion of legal commentators; one area in which this occurs is the question of owning Jewish slaves. In a discussion on the laws prohibiting Jews from holding Christian slaves (c. 1215), Johannes Teutonicus raises the question of whether Christians could acquire Jewish slaves: "However, can it be that a Christian is able to buy a Jewish slave? Yes, provided that (the master) does not live with that (slave)" (Czerwinski 124, my translation).[80] When addressing this question raised by Johannes, Raymond of Peñafort brings both *Dispar nimirum* and *Etsi Iudaeos* into the discussion in his *Summa de casibus* (c. 1225):[81]

> Regarding a Christian, can it be that he may buy or have a Jewish or pagan slave? Certainly, [cites *Dispar* and *Etsi Judaeos*] where it is said that Jews are slaves of the Christians. He therefore ought not to live with that [Jewish slave] so that he might have intimacy with him. If however, that [Jewish slave] would wish to become a Christian, he is permitted; nor ought the master to prohibit, nor can he: for the call of the Holy Spirit unbinds all chains. (Czerwinski 126 n. 68, my translation).[82]

Whereas Johannes simply permits the ownership of Jews as slaves, Raymond offers legal justification for this arrangement; he uses both *Dispar* and *Etsi* to prove that Jews are already slaves of Christians, and can therefore be legally purchased by the latter.[83] They can be enslaved not by the rules of property law, but by virtue of the divine punishment inflicted upon them for the death of Jesus. Therefore, conversion, not the legal process of manumission, dissolves this sentence of servitude.[84] Geoffrey of Trani (d. 1245), in his *Summa super titulis decretalium*, a treatise on the Gregory IX's *Decretals*, similarly analyzes the question of owning Jewish slaves:

> Is it possible that a Christian could buy a pagan or Jewish slave? I respond yes, [cites *Etsi iudaeos* and *Dispar*] but he may not keep the Jew with him in his household. . . . But if he [the Jewish slave] would wish to make himself a Christian, he [the owner] neither can nor should prohibit [this]. Because where there is the spirit, there is liberty. (Czerwinski 128 n. 70, my translation)[85]

Geoffrey's question initially applies to Jews and pagans, probably referencing Muslims (Pakter 114; Kedar 209–10; Czerwinski 37; Freidenreich 2011, 43; Tolan 2002, 105–34). However, he focuses on the case of the Jewish slave in his response; while the commentator does not specify that the slave is a Jew in the case of conversion, the inference is clear, since the law permits Christians to own as slaves pagan converts to Christianity. Both Raymond and Geoffrey were eminent and influential thirteenth-century canonists with close ties to the papacy. Both demonstrate, if only hypothetically, an interpretation of *Etsi* that seems to reduce Jews to the status of chattel slaves and equate Judaism with slavery. However, their opinions also reveal the tension between *Etsi* and established law: if Jews are already slaves, why would Christians need to purchase them? If a Jew's conversion to Christianity would free him or her from slavery, why would this principle not apply to all Christian slaves? These examples demonstrate the construction of an exceptional Jewish status: Jews are not actually chattel slaves, but are in some way predisposed to enslavement. This status renders them always already inferior to, and therefore capable of, domination by Christians.

Another area in which *Etsi* contributes to the formulation of Jewish hereditary inferiority arises in canon law discussions on the question of the forced baptism of Jewish children. A brief consideration of the history of

the Church's position on converting Jews will clarify subsequent developments in the debate regarding their children. Gregory I originally establishes the general protection of Jews from forced conversion in a 591 letter
to the Bishop of Massilia (Marseille). Having heard from Jewish travel-
ers that their coreligionists in the area were "led to the baptismal font by
force rather than through preaching," the pope forbids the practice (Linder
419). He iterates this point even more strongly in his decretal *Qui Sincera*
(602), addressed to the Bishop of Naples. Christians who use suasion to
attempt to convert aliens, including Jews, act for the sake of God; those
who employ "harshness (asperitatibus)" thwart God's will and might instead drive them away.[86] However, the Visigoth rulers of the late sixth
century, by means of secular legislation, ordered the state-wide conversion of the Jews; this resulted in many involuntary conversions. In the
context of responding to those Jews who unwillingly converted and then
apostatized, the Fourth Council of Toledo (633) promulgated a number
of decrees, including canons 59 and 61 that clearly refer to Jewish converts to Christianity who subsequently reverted.[87] The intermediate canon,
number 60, states that the children of Jews should be separated from their
parents in order to be raised by devout Christians. No mention is made of
needing to convert the children, which implies that the children had already been converted in the general order; this canon has been understood
as referring to baptized parents who revert to Judaism as is the case in the
previous and following canons (Linder 487–89; Pakter 315). Subsequently,
ninth-century French advocates for the forced conversion of Jewish children cite Toledo IV's canon 60 out of context in formulating the similar
law, Canon 73, in the Council of Meaux-Paris (845–46); they interpret the
plain meaning of the seventh-century law as referring to Jewish parents,
not lapsed converts from Judaism. Ultimately, the king refused to ratify
Canon 73 and later canonists specify that the Toledan Canon 60 refers to
already baptized children of lapsed Jewish converts, therefore nullifying
its ability to serve as a precedent for forced conversion of Jewish children
(Pakter 316).

A new legal precedent enters this debate in the mid-thirteenth century,
when arguments cite the enslavement of the Jews in support of involuntary baptism, arguing that this status renders Jewish parents powerless
over their children. In a commentary on Raymond of Peñafort's *Summa
de Casibus* (c. early 1240s), William of Rennes writes in favor of seizing
and baptizing Jewish children against the will of their parents in (Goering
419–22).[88] As a theologian learned in canon law, William brings in both

legal and biblical proofs of Jewish servitude to support his case. His discussion begins with a quotation of the term *asperitatibus* [with harshness] that Gregory rejects in his decretal *Qui Sincera*:

"With harshness": But is it possible that [secular rulers] can carry off [the Jews'] children to be baptized? . . . But if truly the Jews are slaves to the masters, as I believe—[offers as citations] *Etsi Iudaeos . . .* and *Dispar*, and Genesis 9 "Cursed be Canaan, slave of slaves he will be to his brothers"—I believe that Princes, of whom the Jews are slaves, are able to carry off their little children without any injury; since they, just as slaves, do not have power over their children. And just as these Princes are able, against the parents' wishes, to give to others or to sell into servitude the same little children, like his own slaves, so they [the Princes] can offer them [the Jews' children] to baptism; and in this they would be right; provided that, nevertheless, they do it not on account of compelling the parents to the faith by this means but on account of saving the children through the sacrament of the faith. (qtd. in Pakter, 322 n. 295, my translation)[89]

Like his fellow Dominican, Raymond of Peñafort, William cites the canonical precedents of *Etsi* and *Dispar* as proving Jewish servitude; in further support of this idea, he introduces the figure of Noah's curse upon Ham's son Canaan.[90] These texts substantiate the argument that Jews are slaves to Christian secular rulers, who have power over the bodies and offspring of the former.

William's argument conferring dominion over Jews to secular rulers enjoyed a wide reception not only in its inclusion in the manuscripts of Raymond's influential *Summa*, but also in its repetition, sometimes verbatim, in subsequent texts. Vincent de Beauvais (d. 1264), another Dominican theologian, incorporated a virtually identical redaction of this view in the widely circulated *Speculum doctrinale* (Pakter 323–24 n. 297). However, William's opinion profoundly influenced legal debate in the commentaries of a number of canon lawyers who reproduced his references to *Etsi* and *Dispar*. Guido de Basio (d. 1313), Archdeacon of Bologna as well as archchancellor and professor of law at the renowned University of Bologna, iterated William's argument in his widely circulated *Rosarium*, a commentary on Gratian's *Decretum* (Brundage 1995, 212–13, Pakter 327). Like William, Guido begins with a reference to the prohibition of using "harshness" included in *Qui Sincera*, in addition to citing *Etsi* and

Dispar (Pakter 327 n. 306). Johannes Andreae (c. 1270–1348), Professor of Decretals and the canon law faculty chair in the *Decretum* at the University of Bologna, authors, among other influential works, a commentary on the *Decretals* titled the *Novella*. He cites Guido de Baysio without arguing against him and includes the references to *Etsi* and *Dispar* (Brundage 1995, 58–59, 216–17; Pakter 328). Francesco Zabarella (1360–1417), in his *In Clementinarum volumen commentaria*, considers the question in terms of both Jews and Muslims; he cites *Dispar* and Guido de Baysio, arguing similarly: "And thus these same infidels do not have power over their children, because they are slaves, and so against their will, the princes are able to carry away and sell their children. Therefore even more so in this do they deserve to be baptized."[91] John of Imola (d. 1436), in his *Super Clementinis . . . co[m]mentaria*, follows Zabarella, and quotes both *Dispar* and *Etsi* (128 r). These arguments in favor of forced conversion continue to circulate into the sixteenth century, through a treatise authored by Ulrich Zasius, a student of canon law before becoming chair of civil law at the University of Freiburg (Rowan 4). In his *De Iudaeis Quaestiones tres* (1508), Zasius draws on arguments from de Baysio, Andreae, and Imola to argue in favor of baptizing Jewish children; he affirms that Jews are slaves (Rowan 14).[92] Some of the most eminent teachers and authors of influential canon law commentaries rely on the status of *servitus Judaeorum* to support their arguments that princes have the power to convert Jewish children against the will of their parents. *Etsi* provides a legal basis for the degradation of the Jews to a status of inherent inferiority in regard to the state whereby, like slaves, they could not even claim dominion over their own children.

Opposing voices counter the notion that the divine consignment of Jews to perpetual servitude renders them actual slaves to secular rulers. The practical implications of this view do not receive official support: Innocent IV clearly opposes it, as demonstrated in a letter sent to the King of Navarre in 1246 commanding him to "do all in your power to prevent any violence from being committed against [the Jews] in the matter of baptizing their children, for this should be a voluntary offering, not a forced one" (Grayzel 1966, 261; Pakter 322). Furthermore, the pope instructs the king "to defend the free [Jews] and theirs [i.e., their children] with their property (ipsos eorumque liberos cum bonis suis . . . defensos)" and to prevent the forced baptism of Jewish children (Grayzel 1966, 260–61, my translation). By identifying the Jews as free, he rejects the assumption that the ruler's power might nullify their rights over their own children and their property.[93] He makes a more forceful statement of Jewish freedom under law in a 1247 letter to the Archbishop of Vienne, again complaining, among other things, of the involuntary baptism of Jewish children: "their free children, born from a free mother in freedom, they forced to be baptized against their wills and against custom" (Grayzel 1966, 262–63, my translation). The use of three forms of the term *liber* shows deliberate emphasis of the free status of the Jews.[94] Additionally, a number of canon lawyers follow this view in discussions of the involuntary conversion of Jewish children. For example, Hostiensis (1190~1200–1271), the cardinal-bishop of Ostia and one of the most eminent canonists of the period, completely ignores the concept of Jewish servitude in considering the question of converting Jewish children in his *Decretalium commentaria*. He omits references to *Etsi* and *Dispar*, and argues instead on the basis of Roman law that Jews, as citizens whose marriages are legitimate, have power over their children (Brundage 1995, 214; Pakter 325–26).[95] Panormitanus (1386–1446), in his *Commentaria super decretalium libris*, summarizes (without reference to *Dispar* or *Etsi*) the arguments of Guido de Baysio and William of Rennes only to contradict them: "I doubt this [theory of servitude] greatly, because strictly and properly speaking [Jews] are not our slaves, indeed coerced servitude cannot be exacted from them" (qtd. in Pakter, 328–29). Johannes of Agnani (1376–1457) offers a wide-ranging exploration of the question in his *Super quinto decretalium*, quoting both canonists and theologians. He cites Panormitanus and offers a concurring view: "Nor is it true that Jews are slaves in such a way as they could be sold; but whatever there is of law <or> custom, it is not preserved that they can be held like slaves" (Pakter 329, my revision of his translation).

Although canonists from the thirteenth century onward agree that Jews occupy a position of inferiority relative to Christians, they do not regard Jews as chattel slaves in the eyes of the law:

> For lawyers, the implications of such a theory were too manifold, including questions of Jewish "slaves" right to acquire, transfer and manumit property and the master's responsibility for his "slaves" [sic] contracts and torts. Few jurists were reckless enough to completely rewrite medieval Jewry law on this basis. (Pakter 323)

Pakter argues that theologians, not canonists, promoted and circulated this concept (323–30). However, this distinction does not hold, since the thirteenth-century debate on the baptism of Jewish children begins with a theologian, William of Rennes, commenting on a legal text and using law,

in addition to scripture, to support his claims. In addition, the legal formulation of *servitus Judaeorum*, articulated so powerfully in *Etsi*, appears in
the theological writings of Thomas Aquinas. His 1270 consideration of the
question "Whether the children of Jews and other unbelievers ought to be
baptized against their parents' will?" affirms the servitude of the Jews; he
iterates this opinion in his *Summa Theologiae*:[96]

> Besides, the children of slaves are themselves slaves and in the
> power of their masters. Now the Jews are slaves of kings and princes,
> who therefore have the power of doing what they will with Jewish
> children. Consequently no injustice would be done in having them
> baptized even though the parents were unwilling. (II.2.10.12.3, 75)

In line with the preceding views of theologians and canonists, Thomas
understands the Jews as slaves to secular rulers: "Jews are the slaves of
princes by civil bondage [*servitute*]" (II.2.10.12, reply to objection 3, 79).
However, he also argues earlier in the *Summa* that the Church has dominion over the Jews, who are classed among "infidels who are [subjected
to/ subiiciuntur] the temporal [subjection/subiectione] of the Church and
her members. . . . Since such Jews are themselves [slaves/servi] of the
Church, she can dispose of their possessions" (II.2.10.10, reply to objection
1, 71; emended translation). Somewhat counterintuitively, secular rulers,
theoretically, can effect the baptism of Jewish children while the Church
can dispose of the Jews' possessions. Nevertheless, Aquinas concludes
that in spite of the Jews' servitude, rulers cannot force the conversion of
their children because it has never been the custom of the Church to do
so.[97] Aquinas also considers Jewish servitude in his *De regimine Iudaeorum*
(1270–1271), a letter written to the Duchess of Brabant opining on the legality of exacting taxes from the Jews. He explains that "as the *laws* say, the
Jews, deservedly (merito) by their sin, have been and are enslaved to perpetual slavery, and so the rulers of the land may take their [the Jews'] things
as their [the rulers'] own."[98] In responding to a legal question Aquinas
cites law, not scripture, in support of the servile status of the Jews with
regard to secular rulers. Although he does not give an explicit citation,
his diction generally follows the opening sentence of *Etsi Judaeos*: "Iudaei
merito culpae suae sint vel essent perpetuae servituti addicti"/"Etsi Iudeos
quos propria culpa submisit perpetue servituti."[99] Instead of bringing in
scriptural evidence to support the notion of *servitus Judaeorum*, the leading

theologian of the medieval period cites law to show the Jews' subjection to secular rulers.[100]

While canonists ultimately rely on other legal principles to reject the involuntary baptism of Jewish children, they do not definitively reject the status of *servitus Judaeorum*. Pakter errs in evaluating the concept literally when determining its efficacy in ecclesiastical law. The canonists never argue for exploiting the full consequences of enslaving the Jews; rather, they explore its figural implications: How and when can the Jews' inherent inferiority be enforced in law so that they acknowledge their sin and convert to Christianity? The legal element of *Etsi* serves as a means for implementing theological and social objectives, as Pakter himself states:

> Inequality was no longer just a theological condition, it was a goal. Jews . . . were to feel their isolation and humiliation. . . . They were social outcasts to be scorned. . . . In the thirteenth century . . . the papacy [was] no longer content to declare Jewish inferiority; they did everything possible to give this idea practical effect. (Pakter 136, 140)[101]

The decretal invokes divine and papal authority to create a new social order, one which attempts to fulfill the theological truth of an inherently inferior and permanent Jewish status. Pakter notes canon law's "universal acceptance of the concept of Jewish servitude"; he offers as evidence not only to Gregory IX's vigorous pursuit of Innocent's attacks on Jewish status, but the reception of this concept as a commonplace by Hostiensis. While the influential canonist ignores the implications of the *servitus Judaeorum* in his opinion on involuntary baptism, elsewhere in his commentary on canon law, he cites both *Etsi Iudaeos* and *Dispar nimirum* to support his claim that "although Jews are truly enemies to our faith, they are nevertheless our slaves, and are tolerated and defended by us" (qtd. in Pakter, 137 n. 186, my translation). Christian toleration is predicated upon all Jews inhabiting a position of relative subordination. Although writing as a canon lawyer, Hostiensis describes the Jews as a people already in a state of perpetual subjection.

The positioning of Jews under the jurisdiction of Church and State in a status inferior to that of Christians is accomplished by the fifteenth century in Western Europe. Simonsohn notes the gradual disappearance of the term Jewish perpetual servitude from the language of papal documents:

By the end of the thirteenth century, the popes ceased to refer to
Jewish servitude. None of the most repressive Bulls of later popes,
such as *Etsi doctoris gentium* of Benedict XIII and *Super gregem
Dominicum* and *Ad reprimendos* of Popes Eugenius IV, Nicholas V
and Calixtus III, respectively, contained the phrase. It is difficult to
determine why the popes stopped using the term, since the secular
authorities continued to do so. (101)

He concludes that "the term Jewish servitude . . . had become so self-
evident that by the end of the Middle Ages it needed no further repetition"
(101–2). Strictly speaking, this is not true. Pope Paul IV's 1555 bull *Cum
nimis*, which establishes the Jewish ghetto in papal lands, opens with the
rationale of Jewish servitude.

> It is absurd and improper that Jews—whose own guilt has consigned
> them to perpetual servitude—under the pretext that Christian piety
> receives them and tolerates their presence, should be ingrates to
> Christians, so that they attempt to exchange the servitude they owe to
> Christians for dominion over them; [lists examples of Jewish actions
> in contempt of Christianity: e.g., they live close Christians, flout
> requirements to dress distinctively, employ Christian servants]. . . .
> Considering that the Roman Church tolerates the Jews in testimony
> of the true Christian faith and to the end that they, led by the piety
> and kindness of the Apostolic See, should at length recognize their
> errors, . . . they should recognize through experience that they have
> been made slaves while Christians have been made free through Jesus
> Christ . . . and that it is iniquitous that the children of the free woman
> should serve the children of the [slave-woman]. (Stow 294–95)

Paul IV's text follows the language and the ideas expressed by Innocent
III in *Etsi* 350 years earlier,[102] from the ascription of perpetual servitude
to the citation of Galatians. However, this is the exception that proves the
rule. The Papal States are one of the few places in early modern Western
Europe where Jews are permitted to live, thus the continued need to enforce Jewish inferiority here. Elsewhere, the successful implementation
of figural servitude with regard to Jewish status obviated the use of the
term. Expulsion, forced conversion and internal exile in ghettos all demonstrate the extent to which their inferiority eroded the Jews' status as
citizens (Pakter 330).[103]

Constructing Racial Hereditary Inferiority

Even if the *servitus Judaeorum* does not consign Jews to chattel slavery, figural slavery—like Aristotle's natural slave—nevertheless renders all Jews,
as long as they remain Jews, permanently and innately subordinated. It
could also be argued that Jews are only relatively, not absolutely inferior, insofar as they are subjected to Christians; however, in a dominant Christian
society, this status relegates Jews to a permanent status of inferiority, particularly given Christianity's universal goals. Additionally, as early as the
twelfth century, the idea circulated that as a result of the crucifixion, Jews
were slaves to all peoples, not just Christians.[104] Taken together, the congenital and hence persisting quality of Jewish identity paired with its subordinate status, produce an ontological condition of hereditary inferiority.
Although the law enables the enforcement of the *servitus Judaeorum*, the
papal formulation does not so much articulate a legal status as describe
the already servile condition of the Jews, confirmed by divine authority.

However, divine warrant and legal force supply only part of the power
of hereditary inferiority. The figural representation of this condition intensifies its influence and significance, as Auerbach explains in his analysis
of the importance of the figural method:

> Figural interpretation, or to put it more completely, the figural
> view of history was widespread and deeply influential up to the
> Middle Ages, and beyond. . . . [A] systematic treatment of the sub-
> ject . . . strikes me as indispensable for an understanding of the
> mixture of spirituality and sense of reality which characterizes the
> European Middle Ages. . . . [The figural method] provides the medi-
> eval interpretation of history with its general foundation and often
> enters into the medieval view of everyday reality. (60–61)

For medieval Christians, figures not only communicate eternal, divine truth and have real historical consequences, but they also powerfully encompass and shape the social understanding of lived experience.
Additionally, as demonstrated earlier, contained in the origin and structure
of the biblical figure, and informing its hermeneutics, is the doctrine of supersession, the doctrine which effectually subordinates Jewish Scripture,
law, interpretations, and people to their Christian counterparts. The centrality of fulfillment—that is, the realization of the figure—indicates
the aspirational aspect of this interpretive practice; while contemporary

events can be interpreted as fulfilling biblical types, the former can also function as figures in need of future consummation. If the total subordination of Jews has not yet taken place, this is the result of sin and in no way prevents the ultimate accomplishment of this element of divine will. This sacred truth nevertheless requires the effort of the church and its members to implement not only through the attempt to internalize a sense within Jews of their own inferiority, but in the production of a shared Christian idea of Jewish existence. Theology, figural method, and law combine here to produce an episteme, an authoritative organizing knowledge structure.

The articulation in law of the figural representation of the *servitus Judaeorum* constitutes a racist construction of Jewish identity. It provides a clear etiology of Jewish inferiority. It ascribes this condition to all Jews as a group. It presents this status as inherent and hereditary. It applies across gender and class difference. It is formulated in the most profoundly authoritative set of medieval discourses. It produces a range of organized discriminatory procedures. While the legal development of Jewish hereditary inferiority does not carry a somatic marker, the influence of figural slavery shapes accounts of Jewish physical distinctiveness in thirteenth and fourteenth century treatises on geography, medicine, and natural philosophy. As I demonstrate in chapters 2 and 3, this strategy, in its attempts to materialize Jewish inferiority and make that inferiority visible, can be understood as the logical consequence of legal maneuvers to subordinate Jews. Finally, as I argue in chapter 5, the application of figural slavery to Muslims and inhabitants of Africa demonstrates its capacity for promiscuous reappropriation.

2

The Mark of Cain and Embodying Inferiority

*After the death of Christ all Jewish men, like women,
suffer menstruation.*[1]

THE IDEA THAT Jewish men possess a physical function distinct from that of Christians develops in a range of medieval discourses—astrological, geographical, polemical, historical, theological, natural philosophical, and medical.[2] Drawing on discussions that emerge earlier in both Christian and non-Christian contexts, the authors and translators who contribute to the construction of a Jewish bleeding illness produce their texts in the period of the twelfth to the fourteenth centuries. In two excellent studies of this phenomenon, Peter Biller identifies and surveys a wide range of texts that associate melancholy and bleeding, melancholy and Jews, and Jews with bleeding. While he concedes that that religious writings offer some of the earliest descriptions of Jewish bleeding, Biller seeks to isolate and make visible "scientific" explanations, usually occluded by religious texts, to get at "common assumptions and prejudices about Jews" (2001, 153). Biller accepts the modernity of "race" and the claim that medieval religious vocabulary is "not 'racial'" (1992, 187); however, in focusing on explanations that supply "natural" causes for Jewish difference, he implicitly suggests that proto-racial ideas should be sought in the discourses of medicine and natural philosophy. Willis Johnson's learned contribution to the question of Jewish bleeding focuses less on race than gender in arguing that early accounts specify anal, not menstrual, bleeding and therefore do not represent an attempt to feminize Jewish men. He situates his analysis within the theological tradition and warns against projecting modern assumptions on medieval discourses of the Jewish body (293–95). Irven Resnick makes the important discovery of Jacques de Vitry's early thirteenth-century description of Jewish bleeding as menstrual; he locates this condition in a theological tradition that presents menses as a curse imposed upon both women and Jews (2000, 248). His subsequent book expansively examines a range of medieval discourses on the Jewish body, in which:

> Jews will be consistently depicted with physical deformities and associated with disease and illnesses that somehow reflect a persistent sinful state, seeing that they remain throughout their lives subject to original sin and its consequences, which Christians overcome through the sacrament of baptism. (2012, 33)

While Resnick acknowledges the workings of theology in texts of medicine and natural philosophy, his project focuses more on "scientific" texts and less on exploring how theology shapes constructions of the body.

In addition to medical and natural philosophy texts, religious polemic also contributes to the fantasy of Jewish bleeding. Alexandra Cuffel carefully documents an assortment of repulsive accusations circulating among and between Christians, Jews, and Muslims in the late antique and medieval periods that employ disgust to solidify communal identity and establish barriers between faiths (7). Given the already charged and contested significance of the flesh and carnality in Jewish–Christian theological debates, these polemicists frequently focus on the body and its functions. Drawing on the scholarship of Mary Douglas and W. I. Miller, Cuffel argues that

> beliefs and rules concerning the body's products reflect the social structures and tensions in a given culture. . . . Accusations of disease and contagion are frequently moralized and then used as tools to control individuals or groups perceived as threatening. Seen in this light, reference to impure corpses, blood, excreta, and disease in late antique and medieval polemic were expressions of anxiety about maintaining the hierarchy and divisions between rival religious communities. (5–6)

The centrality of menstruation and excretion in Christian depictions of diseased Jewish bodily functions quite likely developed as responses to Jewish charges that associated menstrual impurity and feces with Mary and Jesus (117–96). Cuffel's book demonstrates how theological debates in the form of polemical accusations shaped medieval medical discourses on Jewish bleeding.[3]

I build upon and contribute to this research in demonstrating the influence and importance of the theological concept of hereditary servitude in the formation of a Jewish corporeal difference. As indicated above, a number of different discourses contribute to the construction of the Jew's body as suffering a distinct ailment. However, I argue that the most influential of these is Jacques de Vitry's theologically inflected *Historia Orientalis* (c. 1219–1221), which explains that their enslavement, imposed when the Jews allegedly killed Jesus, renders them and their offspring weak, feminized, and suffering a monthly bleeding dysfunction. His quotation of figural verses from Matthew and Psalms as well as the example of Cain, employed as proof-texts for the Jewish disability of periodic anal bleeding, suggest the influence of Innocent III's decretals on Jewish servitude. His text circulated widely, appeared in an early vernacular translation, and enjoyed particular favor among Dominicans. When the analysis of this Jewish body function, explained as hemorrhoids, initially enters into the discourses of natural philosophy and medicine, it does so via a Dominican author, Albert the Great, albeit absent theological references. However, classical and early medieval accounts of the etiology of hemorrhoids make no mention of Jews. Thus the idea evolves first in a theological context, which then influences its consideration in scientific texts. Yet these early naturalized explanations fail to establish a clear distinction between Jewish and Christian bodily function. Strikingly, subsequent medical texts begin citing the theological cause, alongside humoral and dietary ones, to establish a differentiating basis for Jewish bleeding. These scientific discussions reintroduce proof-texts from Matthew and Psalms adduced in theological accounts to indicate the punitive and humiliating nature of this condition. Whether describing the bleeding as hemorrhoidal or menstrual, the authors draw on theological warrants to demonstrate the humiliation and punitive subordination the disease inflicts on Jewish bodies.

This chapter begins with a brief overview of the classical understanding of the humoral system and the functioning of the human body. The medical discussion of hemorrhoids, associated with melancholy and menstruation, makes no mention of Jews, but provides theories and vocabulary later taken up in the medieval innovation of Jewish bleeding. The initial articulation of a divine, hereditary bleeding affliction marking and shaming Jewish bodies emerges instead in theologically informed texts, which subsequently influence and borrow from discourses of medicine and natural philosophy. I demonstrate how the combination of these religious

and medical writings serves, in effect, the goals of papal decretals by articulating an embodiment of the theological, legal, and social status of Jewish
inherent inferiority. The deployment of biblical figures confirms this hereditary condition as well as the illness that realizes its subservience in a
physical manifestation. An analysis of this theological discourse, modu-
lated through the vocabulary of natural philosophy, enables us to trace
the translation of inherent inferiority to an embodied, natural condition, a
movement from a racial status to a racialized body.

Melancholy and Hemorroidal Bleeding in the Classical Tradition

The humoral system accounting for bodily function and dysfunction that
dominates medieval medical theory and practice developed initially in classical Greece. The doctrine correlates the cosmic elements air, fire, earth,
and water with the respective qualities of cold, hot, dry, wet. These proper-
ties correspond to and combine in fluids supposedly found in the human
body: blood, characterized as warm and moist; yellow bile, warm and dry;
black bile, cold and dry; and phlegm, cold and wet.[4] The humors thus constituted by the mixture of the elements and qualities were understood to
function as dominant influences shaping living beings. Termed *crasis* in
Greek texts and *complexio* in later Latin translations, humoral temperament or complexion was used to explain the structure of all corporeal life,
including that of plants and animals (Siraisi, 101–2). Individual humans
obtained a distinct, unique complexion at conception, which continued
throughout one's life, albeit altered by diet, geography, the seasons, age,
and of course illness.[5] Complexion was thought to account not only for
physical characteristics but personality types as well.[6]

Of the four humors, black bile is anomalous in its association with
illness and malevolence.[7] Only melancholy is used as a noun to name an
ailment as well as a humor; authors most frequently associate it with disease.[8] In his second-century c.e. work *On Melancholy*, the physician Rufus
of Epheus distinguishes between two causes of melancholy complexions: one acquired through diet, and one resulting from a person's natural
humoral make-up (Klibansky et al. 48–51). The question of whether an
excess of melancholy is temperamental or caused by diet determines to
some extent whether it is a pathology or not, and remains of interest to
scientific and medical writers through the medieval period.

Melancholy's identification as the black bile also carried malign associations with night and evil, as Galen, the great second-century synthesizer of Greek medicine, opines: "Just as outward darkness fills nearly all men with fear, unless they are very brave or very enlightened, so the dark colour of black bile generates fear, in that it darkens the seat of reason" (qtd. in Klibansky et al. 15–16, n. 44). This correlation may have contributed to another distinguishing feature of melancholy illness: it could present both mental and physical symptoms (14). The earliest consideration of melancholy, Hippocrates's *Aphorisms*, notes its psychological signs:[9] "Fear or depression that is prolonged means melancholia" (VI.xxiii.185). These two emotions become consistently associated with melancholy, whether understood as a temperament or an illness. Galen affirms this view in his *De Locis Affectis*: "Hippocrates was right in summing up all melancholy symptoms in the two following: Fear and Depression" (qtd. in Klibansky et al. 14).[10]

In addition to associating psychological states of sadness and fear with melancholy, the medical writings of the classical Greek corpus link a predominance of this humor with hemorrhoids. Hippocrates's *Aphorisms* offers an early articulation of this connection. His pronouncement on hemorrhoids occurs in the context of opinions about how the flow of various body fluids helps to resolve an ailment, which may shed light on the text's meaning:[11]

X. When the head aches and the pain is very severe, a flow of pus, water or blood, by the nostrils, ears or mouth, cures the trouble.
XI. Hemorrhoids supervening on melancholic or kidney affections are a good sign. . . .
XIV. In the case of a patient suffering from dropsy, a flow of water by the veins into the belly removes the dropsy. (VI.x–xiv.183).

These three proximate points explain how the body's excretion of excess fluids, by various means, serves to heal specific ailments. While the text offers no direct statement indicating what "a good sign" means, the context suggests that when an abundance of melancholy operates like a disease, the onset of hemorrhoids relieves the condition by expelling blood and excess humors out of the body.[12] Thus the text does not present hemorrhoids here as a disease that needs treatment, but a good sign that enables a process by which the body can rid itself of harmful substances.

Medieval Muslim authors with access to the Greek tradition rely on and transform its association of melancholy with hemorrhoids. Avicenna, the influential early eleventh-century c.e. Muslim physician, alters the nature of the relationship in viewing hemorrhoids not as a cure for the excess of melancholy humor but as a disease caused by it. In his opinion, diet affects the increase of black bile, which results in bleeding hemorrhoids. The ingestion of gross or dense foods and foods difficult to digest, such as cheese, salted meat, and eggplants, produces a surplus of black bile. He recommends avoiding foods that increase the production of melancholy as a remedy for the disease this excess occasioned (Biller 2001, 139–40; 1992, 194–95). Thus he identifies diet as both the cause and the cure for the emergence of hemorrhoids.

The association of hemorrhoids and melancholy circulates in Western Christian texts as well. Bartholomeus Anglicus considers this nexus in his encyclopedia, *De rerum proprietatibus* (c. 1240):

> Hemorrhoids are five veins that extend out of the anus, from which come various passions, namely swelling/flatulence, retention, bleeding. Sometimes, moreover, by the force of nature, superfluities are transmitted to these parts, and the veins being broken, the body is freed from diverse diseases. But if the blood-flow is excessive, various sufferings occur. When, truly, they are retained because of custom, many great illnesses follow, such as dropsy, tuberculosis, madness, melancholy, and others. (my translation 337 Book 7, chapter 54)[13]

Hemorrhoidal bleeding again serves a healing function, in most cases, in allowing for the discharge of noxious substances. However, both immoderate and suppressed blood-flow threatens a patient's health by bringing on a variety of conditions, including melancholy. It is not clear whether the condition of melancholy is meant here, or the excess of melancholy humor, but as the latter leads to the former, we need not press this point too far. Bartholomew, like Galen, iterates Hippocrates's basic point that anal bleeding relieves an excess of the black humor.

Other authors writing on hemorrhoidal bleeding compare it to that of menstruation. As Johnson points out, "medical theorists, from Galen (130–99) to Arnold of Villanova (1240–1311), described menstrual and haemorrhoidal bleeding as interchangeable" (288). The medical textbook *Breviarium*, attributed to Arnold, cites Galen in support of this association:[14]

> Many men are purged [of bad humors] via [hemorrhoidal veins]
> (just as women are by their menses) and preserved from diverse
> illnesses when they flow in the appropriate amount. . . . Every flow
> of blood, as Galen said, is unhealthy, except for a moderate flow
> of blood from haemorrhoids, nosebleeds, and menses. (qtd. in
> Johnson 289)

Here the function of the bleeding establishes the point of comparison;
expelling a moderate amount of blood enables the body to rid itself of
harmful humors. Albert the Great (d. 1280), in a discussion of the health
benefits of bleeding, describes hemorrhoidal bleeding as menstrual:

> In [a case of weak digestion] there will be a discharge of the men-
> strual blood which flows sometimes from the openings of the anal
> veins and which are called the hemorrhoids. It flows the same way
> as menstrual blood except that it is a flow of natural blood and the
> hemorrhoids are an unnatural flow. (qtd. in Resnick 2000, 254)

Albert opines that hemorrhoids do not follow a natural, monthly cycle,
as in the case of menses, but other authors disagree on this point. In his
late twelfth-century *Practica maior*, the physician Roger de Baron states
that just as women experience menstruation once a month, so some men
suffer a hemorrhoidal flow once a month (Resnick 2012, 182, Roger de
Baron, tr. 1, cap. 42, fol. 216v). Similarly, Theodorich Borgognoni states in
his *Chirurgia* (c. 1267):

> Now the flow of this sort [bleeding hemorrhoids] is in men: some-
> times it is normal, such as the flow of menses in women, whence
> like a woman they menstruate every month. But some only four
> times a year, and some once a year. (qtd. in Resnick 2012, 204 n 116)

While not all texts on hemorrhoids analogize them with menstruation,
enough influential authors do connect the two types of bleeding either
in terms of its function or timing to ensure a wide circulation of this
connection.[15]

Taken altogether, these texts associate the melancholy humor with illness, malevolence, fear, and sadness. They specify certain foods as increasing its production, and identify its excessive presence in the blood as
causing bleeding hemorrhoids. Several authors liken hemorrhoidal and

menstrual bleeding, noting that the former can also follow a monthly pattern. Although black bile possesses sinister qualities that could threaten good health, it is nevertheless a natural substance produced in all human bodies. Similarly, while some theological and medical discussions understand menstrual periods as a divinely imposed curse and connect this blood with disease, these negative associations are absent in the comparison of menstruation and hemorrhoids considered above (Resnick 2000 244–48, 254–55; 2013 114–16). All of these elements will reappear in medical and natural philosophical accounts of Jewish bleeding, but to find the development of this infirmity, we must first turn to a range of theologically inflected explanations.[16]

Jewish Melancholy and Bleeding in Christian Theology

The notion that God inflicted a physical mark or debility on Jews as punishment for the crime of killing Jesus emerges in a variety of exegetical contexts; Judas's betrayal of Jesus provides an influential example. One interpretive tradition proposes that this punishment takes the form of anal bleeding. As Willis Johnson has argued, early accounts of the death of Judas help form the theological basis for later ideas about this distinctive Jewish bodily function (276). The description of Judas's suicide by hanging in Acts 1.18–19 notes a subsequent hemorrhage: "And hanged, his middle burst and all of his guts poured out" (qtd. in Johnson, 276). Early Christian writers characterize this unspecified intestinal eruption as an effluence of blood and guts exiting from his anus (Johnson, 276). Subsequent authors interpret similarly humiliating appearances of viscera as evidence of a Judas-like punishment of non-Jewish betrayers of the faith. In the early sixth century *De Actibus Apostolorum*, Arator's condemnation of the Arian heresy makes this connection explicit: "Unlucky Arius . . . tumbled down with his bowels poured out . . . and in dying bore a common death with Judas, who, hanging by his neck, died emptied of his entrails" (qtd. in Johnson 277–78). Other accounts of Arius's death explain that the intestines were extruded from the anus (277–78).[17]

The idea that Jews experience a regular flow of blood from the anus develops in the context of the first English accusation of ritual murder. This twelfth-century fiction accused Jews of kidnapping and crucifying a young Christian boy in a mocking reenactment of the death of Jesus.[18] The *Life and Passion of St. William of Norwich* (c. 1149–1155) by Thomas of

Monmouth makes the case for the boy's martyrdom by emphasizing its similarities with the death of Jesus, as the title of the text makes clear.[19] He explains the supposed logic of this atrocity, purportedly confided to him by Theobald, a mysterious monk and convert from Judaism:

> He verily told us that in the ancient writings of his fathers it was written that the Jews, without the shedding of human blood, could neither obtain their freedom, nor could they ever return to their fatherland. Hence it was laid down by them in ancient times that every year they must sacrifice a Christian in some part of the world to the Most High God in scorn and contempt of Christ, that so they might avenge their sufferings on Him; inasmuch as it was because of Christ's death that they had been shut out from their own country, and were in exile as slaves in a foreign land. (Thomas 93–4)

Jewish servitude, resulting from the crucifixion, provides the explanatory lens through which to understand contemporary Jewish crimes against Christians. Thomas presents an inversion of Augustine's account, told, as it were, from perspective of Jewish vengeance. In retaliation for and as a means of undoing their exile and slavery, Jews must sacrifice a Christian to God each year. In the account of William's ritual murder, the perpetrators of this crime are punished by divine vengeance, just as were the Jews who crucified Jesus (97–9). However, the guilty include a Christian, Sheriff John of Chesney, whom Thomas presents as "openly [opposing] the Christian law" in protecting the Jews against the charge of murdering William (111). As a result, a mysterious ailment afflicts the sheriff: "[From his behind drops of blood began to flow.] And so clearly was the vengeance of God shown in this case that he might in very truth say with the Jews 'Let the innocent blood be upon us and upon our children'" (111, with my emendation).[20] Thomas supports his claim with a paraphrase of Matthew 27:25, the verse employed to indicate the hereditary nature of the enslaving punishment inflicted on the Jews for the crucifixion of Jesus; it will also provide a common proof-text for subsequent allegations of Jewish bleeding.[21] Here, John, behaving in a Jewish, Judas-like manner, becomes like one of the Jews who crucified Jesus; the sheriff consequently suffers from the ailment of anal bleeding. We see the further elaboration of a Jewish disease, though at this stage, as in the case with Judas's punishment applying to heretics, it does not exclusively affect Jews.[22]

However, henceforward, theological texts that treat this periodic bleeding identify it as a malady suffered only by Jews. A later twelfth-century treatise on this condition does not present it as a divinely imposed punishment nor explicitly cite a biblical proof-text for support. However, it does refer to a universal Jewish servitude and service to the Bible, theological ideas articulated by Augustine, who explains this subordination as retribution for the crucifixion. The anonymous Christian author of the *Tractatus de locis et statu sancte terre ierosolimitane*, a late twelfth-century survey of peoples and places in the Holy land, begins with the Jews in his description of non-Christians living in Jerusalem: "Of whom Jews are the first, an obstinate people, more unwarlike than women, slaves everywhere, each month suffering a flow of blood, they are slaves to the Old Testament to the letter, and they have the Hebrew alphabet" (qtd. in Biller 2001, 158, transl. mine).[23] In this early contribution to travel literature, the distinguishing characteristics of the Jews include the fact of their inferior status, a concept elaborated in theological discourses. Even their stubbornness, a sign of resistance, suggests that they are wrong to hold out and ought to submit. However, their distaste for war paradoxically signals their inherent submissiveness; they are weaker than the "weaker sex," subordinated wherever they live, and slaves to the letter of the Hebrew Bible, akin to Augustine's "bookslaves." The monthly bleeding that they experience functions like menstruation, reinforcing the claim that Jews as a people occupy the subservient status of women.

Subsequent iterations situate the analysis of this periodic Jewish bleeding in explicitly theological contexts and explain it in terms of divine punishment in retribution for the death of Jesus. In one of his exempla, or sermon stories, Caesarius of Heisterbach (d. 1240) states that Jews living in an unnamed English city experience a flow of blood once a year.[24] "[I]n the night of the sixth day, which precedes Easter . . . the Jews are said to labour under a sickness called a bloody flux, with which they are so much occupied, that they can scarcely pay attention to anything else at that time" (*Dialogue*, II.xxiii. vol. 1, 102).[25] While the author does not specify the location of the bleeding in the body, the timing of this infirmity coincides with the evening of Good Friday, the day on which the crucifixion is commemorated, thus linking this illness of the Jews with the death of Jesus.

A powerful articulation that incorporates these varying trends appears in Jacques de Vitry's *Historia Orientalis* (c. 1219–1221), the first of three proposed books of the larger *Historia Hierosolimintana Abbreviata*.[26] The *Historia Orientalis* is a chronicle of the history of Jerusalem during the crusades. As a preacher against heresy and in support of crusade, Jacques actively engaged with these two important concerns of the papacy; he would certainly have been familiar with papal views.[27] A brief digression demonstrating the striking echoes of Innocent III in the *Historia* establishes the context in which Jacques develops his account of Jewish bleeding. The chapter of the *Historia* that describes this ailment contains additional allegations against the Jews that resonate with concerns Innocent voices in his letters. Jacques describes the status of contemporary Jews living among Muslims and Christians:

> The Saracens among whom they dwell hate and despise them more than the Christians; for whereas the abominable avarice of Christian Prince tolerates them for the sake of worldly profit, allows them to hold Christian men in bondage (Christiana mancipia), and suffers Christians to be plundered by them by their intolerable usury, among the Saracens they work with their own hands at the vilest and roughest trades, they are the serfs and slaves of the infidels, and are only suffered to dwell among them in the lowest station of life. (1896, 87)

Innocent similarly notes the comparatively favorable treatment the Jews receive at the hands of Christians as opposed to Muslims. In the influential decretal *Etsi Judaeos* (1205), he observes that Christian piety "permits them to dwell in the Christian midst, although, because of their perfidy, even the Saracens who persecute the Catholic faith and do not believe in the Christ whom the Jews crucified, cannot tolerate the Jews" (Grayzel 1966, 115). While Innocent here notes the benevolent motives of Christians tolerating Jews in their midst, Jacques focuses on base ones. Both, however, forbid Jews from placing Christians in a position of servitude; Jacques condemns secular rulers for permitting Jews to holding Christians as slaves,[28] noting the contrast of Muslims who ensure that Jews occupy their proper inferior status. Christian princes, motivated by greed, fail to enforce this subordination, a claim paralleled by the pope in a 1208 letter that criticizes their susceptibility to bribes: "certain nobles and princes and their ministers, with their eye to the Jewish gifts . . . had corrupted their hearts" (Grayzel 1966, 129). In the same letter, he also reprimands these authorities for encouraging rather than prohibiting Jews from taking interest on loans.[29] While Innocent similarly calls for the preservation of the Jews from violence, he tempers his statement with the condition that Jews not oppress

Christians nor be assisted in this by Christian rulers: "although they ought not to be killed . . . blasphemers of the Christian name ought not to be aided by Christian princes to oppress the servants of the Lord" (127). He incorporates the Augustinian formula which offers protection on the condition of Jewish subordination to Christians.

The concerns that Jacques raises about Jews corrupting Christian princes, exercising deplorable authority over Christians, and practicing illicit usury all reflect papal apprehensions about Europe, not the Holy Land, the ostensible subject of this book. Like Innocent, Jacques definitively establishes the hereditary inferiority of Jews by deploying theological proof-texts, which he supplements, as I will show, with somatic and historical evidence. The remainder of the discussion of the Jews treats the condition in which their remnant should be preserved until the final days when they shall be saved. Jacques surveys the history of the Jews' repeated subordination to other nations as punishment for their offenses against God, noting that in previous instances they were freed. The Jews' crucifixion of Jesus resulted in a subjection that has not been revoked. The proof-texts selected do not emphasize Jesus's forgiveness, but his vengeance that will "reward" and "repay" the Jews by punishing their actions. Jacques's postponement of the salvation of the Jews to the last days effectively renders Jews permanent slaves; "this last captivity" will endure to the end of the world (1896, 88–9). The divinely imposed perpetual servitude of the Jews provides the context in which the text develops and represents the embodied manifestation of this punishment.

The *Historia's* account of Jewish bleeding appears within a survey of Jews and derivative sects who inhabit the Holy Land (Biller 2001, 142). However, in a shift from an ethnological to a theological description of the Jews, Jacques turns away from local communities to the diaspora:

Also, all of those Jews whose fathers called out: "His blood [be] upon us and upon our children," [Matt. 27:25] they are dispersed generally through the whole world and in all winds, they are slaves everywhere, everywhere tributaries, and their strength, as Isaiah the prophet said, is turned into ashes. [paraphrase Is. 1:31] Indeed, they have become unwarlike and weak like women. Whence, it is said, they suffer a flow of blood each month. God smote them on their bottoms and put them in eternal shame. [Ps. 77:66] Indeed after they killed Abel, their true brother, they became rovers and fugitives on the earth [Gen. 4:12]; just as Cain was cursed, having a trembling head, that is, a terrified heart, fearing day and night, not believing his life. (qtd. in Biller 2001, 158, transl. mine)[30]

He identifies the Jews by their guilt for the death of Jesus, citing the verse from Matthew, which results in their universal dispersal and enslavement. The *Historia* appears to follow closely the *Tractatus*, which described the Jews as unwarlike as women, enslaved and suffering a monthly flow of blood; whereas the earlier text merely lists these characteristics, Jacques organizes them into an explanation. Furthermore, he consistently cites scriptural evidence in support of his claims; these function like figures insofar as they predict their fulfillment in the contemporary condition of Jews. Relying on a paraphrase of Isaiah 1:31, the *Historia* suggests that their servitude has transformed the Jews' strength to ashes. They are now unwarlike and weak like women, from which cause, *unde*, they experience periodic bleeding.[31] Like Caesarius, he signals that he is passing along the claims of others, "ut dicitur" (Biller 2001, 142). However, Jacques introduces a new proof-text for Jewish bleeding, Psalm 77:66: "And he smote his enemies on the hinder parts: he put them to an everlasting reproach [Et percussit inimicos suos in posteriora, opprobrium sempiternum dedit illis]" (78:66 in modern Bibles).[32] The punishment effectively embodies the spiritual and political degradation already inflicted upon the Jews as a result of the deicide. Citing the murder of Abel as a figure for Jews crucifying Jesus, Jacques equates Cain's curse with the debilities God threatens to inflict upon the Jews in Deuteronomy 27–28. Thus a trembling head, previously associated with Cain, now enters the list of physical manifestations included in God's malediction of the Jews: "the Lord will give thee a fearful heart. . . . Thou shalt fear night and day, neither shalt thou trust thy life" (Deut 28:65–6).[33] The *Historia* draws on a number of prophetic verses to expand Augustine's use of Cain as a figure for the Jews, increasing the consequences of their hereditary punishment to include the physical symptoms of humiliating bleeding and trembling along with the psychological state of fear.

With the exception of the bleeding illness likely contributed by the *Tractatus*, many of the references in the *Historia* appear in the letters of Innocent III.[34] The 1208 letter to the Count of Nevers paraphrases Genesis 4:14–15, in describing Cain as "vagus et profugus super terram" and identifying the sign imposed by God as "tremorem capitis," statements that Jacques follows closely. The papal letter also cites Matthew as evidence of the Jews' hereditary guilt resulting from the crucifixion and their subsequent dispersion and subjection to slavery, continuing to this day. Innocent paraphrases Psalms 82:17, "Fill their faces with shame; and they shall seek thy name, O Lord," to argue that Christians must enforce this subordination to induce an acknowledgment among the Jews of their own humiliation. Jacques selects a different Psalm verse, one that proves the debility of regular anal bleeding, but similarly emphasizes the degradation intended in God's punishment. Although Jacques's description galvanizes an influential explanation of Jewish disease, he does so in the service of developing and advancing the theology of Jewish servitude.

The *Historia* enjoyed a wide circulation and reception, judging from the large number of surviving manuscripts; we can trace its influence on later discussions of this Jewish ailment in other theological texts, particularly in a Dominican context.[35] The Dominican cardinal, Hugh of St. Cher (d. 1263), in his commentary on the Psalms, alludes to anal bleeding with reference to the verse proffered by Jacques, 77:66:

> He smote his enemies in their posteriors, [he set them in everlasting shame] . . . It was their *everlasting shame* because such an infirmity was most vile [vilis]. And some say that the Jews bear this shame, that in vengeance for the passion of the Lord they suffer a flux of blood. And that is why they are so pale. (qtd. in Johnson, 281).[36]

Noting that he is passing on the claims of others, he emphasizes the degrading, *vilis*, nature of this illness, which serves to punish the Jews for their alleged deicide. The verse from Matthew is thus implied here, but the illness is extended to all Jews, not just those who called down Jesus's blood on themselves and their children. While the frequency of the bleeding is not specified, its physical consequence—paleness—is emphasized as a Jewish somatic characteristic.[37] Another Dominican, Thomas of Cantimpré (c. 1200/1201–1270/1272), in his text on contemporary miracles, restricts this bleeding to Good Friday (like Caesarius), and directly references the crucifixion and the verse from Matthew:[38]

> It is known from the holy Gospels that when Pilate washed his hands and said "I am clean of the blood of this just man" the impious Jews cried out: "His blood is on us and on our children" (Matt. 27:25). . . . it is seen to mean that because of the curse of the ancestors a vein of villainy runs in the children up to the present, by

means of a defect of their blood. And by this inconvenient flow, the impious progeny are incurably afflicted, until such time as the sinner, repenting, acknowledges the blood of Christ and is healed. (qtd. in Johnson, 288)[39]

It is not clear if all Jews suffer this affliction, or only the descendants of those who cried out against Jesus. Thomas does not specify the physical location of the bleeding, but represents the infirmity as a hereditary curse that marks the blood with criminal sin. The Dominican Rudolph of Shlettstadt (c. 1302) includes a description of Jewish bleeding in his collection of historical anecdotes: "I heard from a Jew that certain Jews— descended from those who cried out before Pilate at the time of Christ's passion 'his blood be on us and on our children' (Matt. 27:25)—flow every month with blood and often suffer dysentery" (qtd. in Johnson, 290). Johnson notes the mixing of medical and theological discourses in this account. In his thirteenth-century lexicography, the Dominican Joannes Balbus (d. 1298) also notes this humiliating Jewish condition: "God smote the Jews in their posteriors and set them in everlasting shame [Ps 77:66] for every year on Good Friday they emit blood from their posteriors" (qtd. in Johnson, 291). He follows Jacques's use of a figural proof-text to note the location of the bleeding, but relies on the same tradition Caesarius relates in specifying an annual occurrence. While all of these accounts vary somewhat from each other, together they contribute to a theological discourse in which Jewish responsibility for the crucifixion results in a humiliating embodied punishment.

Jewish Bleeding in Medieval Natural Philosophy and Medicine

The theological construction of Jewish bleeding develops before its articulation in the texts of medieval medicine and natural philosophy. In effect, theological assumptions influence scientific discourses to create a new understanding of Jewish bodily function.[40] The first purely scientific explanation of this Jewish condition appears in the Albert the Great's lectures on Aristotle's De Animalibus, given in 1258 (Biller 1992, 196). Biller offers two possible sources for Albert's account: Caesarius's redaction, which was compiled slightly earlier in the same Rhineland vicinity in which Albert lived; and Jacques's version, whose work circulated widely among

Dominicans. Albert delivered his opinion on Jewish bleeding in his capacity as lector at the Dominican convent of Heiligenkreuz (Biller 1992, 196; 2001, 143).[41] Included in this discussion, and absent from Aristotle's, is an account of Jewish bleeding:

> Haemorrhoids are caused by a superfluity of gross blood, because when such blood abounds in the body, it descends below . . . and then frequently one or two veins are ruptured, and then the blood flows . . . Whence this happens mostly to those who live off gross and salted food, such as the Jews, [and this happens thus] according to nature. (qtd. in Biller 1992, 196)[42]

Following discussions in classical texts on hemorrhoids, Albert describes how excess blood in the body results in this bleeding, though he makes no explicit mention of melancholy here. Drawing on Avicenna's analysis, this account identifies diet as the etiology of the disease; this is not specifically a "Jewish" ailment, but one that afflicts any people like them who ingest heavy, salty food. In a text of natural philosophy, the author logically focuses on the "physical" causes of hemorrhoids.[43] This consideration of bleeding does not distinguish Jewish bodies from Christian ones; Jews appear as one example, among others, of people who fall into this category. Nevertheless, the specific mention of Jews at all—superfluous in a text which has already provided a general explanation for cause of this disorder—indicates that Albert has in mind a discourse of bleeding associated particularly with the Jews. By presenting it in a naturalized version, he translates a theological construct into a scientific discussion.

Subsequent to Albert's lectures, university faculties took up the question of the particularity of Jewish bodies. This issue appears in a quodlibet, an intellectual exercise carried out in medieval universities, in which a series of propositions were debated on a range of topics in theology and natural philosophy; the latter were considered in the faculty of arts or medicine (Biller 1992, 188–89). An early fourteenth-century debate by the faculty of arts at the University of Paris investigated the causes of Jewish bleeding:[44]

> It was asked whether Jews suffer a flux of blood . . . [First response] no because Christians and some Jews are of the same complexion. . . . [Second response]: the opposite appears in truth,

because for the most part, these lechers suffer a flux of blood. . . .
Jews have a flux of blood of the haemorrhoids, and the first cause
of this, is that doctors say that a flux of blood is caused by gross
indigested blood which nature purges. This abounds more in the
Jews because for the most part they are melancholics . . . Jews naturally withdraw themselves from society and from being connected
with others, as is patent, therefore they are melancholics. Item,
they are pallid, therefore they are of melancholic complexion. Item,
they are naturally timid, and these three are the contingent prop-
erties of melancholics, as Hippocrates says. But he who is melancholic has a lot of melancholic blood, and manifestly must have a
flux of blood, but Jews are of this sort. [Cites Jews' alleged diet of
roast foods and abstinence from wine, as well as their reluctance to
blood-letting as other reasons for this flow of blood.] (qtd. in Biller
1992, 192–93)[45]

Although only natural explanations are again given for Jewish bleeding
and classical texts provide the basis for much of the reasoning, neither
the received humoral tradition nor empirical evidence supports these
claims. A number of the symptoms of this infirmity appear in theological
texts: regular anal bleeding; pallor, as alleged by Hugh of St. Cher; and fear,
as stated by Jacques de Vitry. While the theological explanation is omitted
here, it supplies the rationale for the idea of Jewish physiological difference.[46] The text homes in on the question of Jewish variance that Albert
leaves unexplored. The author first proposes that Jews and Christians possess the same complexion, but rejects this position on the basis that Jews
suffer a flow of blood, implying that they do not share a complexion with
Christians. The flow of blood is identified as hemorrhoidal and associated with the melancholy humor, identified as a Jewish complexion. The
qualities of melancholics here attributed to Jews—shunning society, fear,
and pallor—are commonly found in classical medical and natural philosophy texts, which, however, omit any reference to Jews. In this quodlibet
they are identified as "natural" conditions of Jews. Dietary factors identified in Avicenna's and Albert's works are also brought in to explain the
excess of melancholy in Jews. The debate concludes with the statement
that some Christians also suffer a flux of blood, but explains vaguely that
"they have some aids whereby they repel" it (193). This discussion attempts
to identify and explain the natural causes of a distinct Jewish bleeding,
but the humoral evidence considered ultimately fails to distinguish Jews

from Christians in somatic terms. This scientific discourse alone does not formulate the necessary concepts to construct the distinct and inferior Jewish body.

However, subsequent texts considering Jewish bleeding in a scientific context explicitly adduce its theological rationale in order to establish a clear somatic difference between Christians and Jews. Here we see a combining of exegetical and medical ideas on the subject, demonstrating that the divine is at work in the natural realm. A later commentary on the late thirteenth- or early fourteenth-century *De secretis mulierum*, a medical treatise often ascribed to Albert, introduces, in the context of a discussion on menstruation, a theological explanation for Jewish bleeding.[47] The commentator initially contrasts three types of "menses":

> According to some, menses is understood in three ways. The first way is natural menses, such as the menstrual periods of women. The second is supernatural, as the Jews experience. The third way is against nature, for example certain Christians of melancholy disposition bleed through the anus and not through the penis. (qtd. in Lemay, 71).

Jewish bleeding is distinguished here not by physiological causes, but by an unspecified supernatural one. It is not clear whether the author thinks Jews bleed through the penis, in contrast to the Christian example that follows. In a subsequent passage, the author returns to this notion in response to a question and answer in the main text: "whether the menses flow out through the anus with solid waste, or through the vulva . . . To this I reply that the menses flow through the vulva in the form of crude, thin blood" (qtd. in Lemay 73). Commentary B adds:

> This . . . question is perfectly appropriate to ask because men who have dysentery experience a flow of blood from the abdomen which resembles the menstrual flow, and this dysenteric bleeding is suffered by both men and women. Melancholic males generate a good deal of black bile which is directed to the spleen, and then to the spine. From there it descends to other veins located around the last intestine which are called hemorrhoids. After these veins are filled they are purged of the bile by this flow, which if it is moderate, is beneficial. This is found in Jews more than in others, for their natures are more melancholic, although it is said that they have this

flow because of a miracle of God, and there is no doubt that this is true. (73–4)

After distinguishing between dysentery and menses, the commentator proceeds to consider yet another bleeding of the posterior, hemorrhoids. The physical description of the development of hemorrhoids follows Albert in part, but omits discussion of diet and focuses instead on the susceptibility of men possessing a melancholy complexion, following Avicenna's view. Jews initially seem to differ only in quantity, not quality, from Christian melancholics. However, their condition is given a supernatural etiology, a miracle of God. Jews experience this condition more than others, but the distinct cause differentiates their bodies from Christian ones. While the author does not provide a reason for this miracle, its citation augments the scientific discussion with recourse to theology to secure Jewish bodily difference.

Other texts considering Jewish bleeding in scientific terms address and expand upon its theological origin in articulating the reason for this condition. Bernard of Gordon, a member of the medical faculty of the University of Montpellier, cites both natural and supernatural causes in his early fourteenth-century *Lilium medicinae*:

Note . . . that Jews for the most part suffer a flux of haemorrhoids for three reasons. Generally they are in [a state of] idleness, and for this reason superfluities of melancholy are gathered. Secondly, they are generally in [a state of] fear and anxiety, and for this reason melancholic blood is multiplied, according to this (dictum) of Hippocrates: "Fear and timidity, if they have had a lot of time [to work], bring about melancholic humor." Thirdly, this [occurs] because of divine punishment {according to (Psalms 77:66): "And he struck them in the bottom of the back; he put them to an everlasting reproach"}. (qtd. in Biller 1992, 198, the final section in brackets is my rendering of the Latin which Biller leaves untranslated.)[48]

The use of limiting terms here—"for the most part" and "generally"— suggests that this infirmity afflicts many, but perhaps not all Jews. These restrictions apply to the first two reasons which cite the conditions of idleness and fear considered in natural philosophy and medical texts on the subject of excess black bile. However, the third reason offers no qualification, and appears to provide the explanatory cause: Jewish idleness and fear are a result of divine punishment. Bernard cites, with slight emendation, the familiar proof-text from Psalms 77:66 introduced by Jacques to demonstrate the fulfilment of this figure in the diseased bodies of contemporary Jews. These statements present what is in fact a suppressed tautology: religious ideas conjure a chimerical Jewish difference that is here initially articulated in terms of cultural and "biological" phenomena, which in turn are explained and proven by biblical warrant. This construction functions both as a projection onto and a lens for reading Jewish bodies as rendered inferior through the punishment and its attendant shame. While the natural causes may not secure Jewish physical difference and debility, the theological basis effects a clear, hierarchical distinction between Christian and Jew.

The *Omnes homines*, an anonymous text probably contemporary with Gordon's *Lililium* and the Paris quodlibet, synthesizes many of the discussions considered here.[49] Like the quodlibit, it situates Jewish difference within a general discussion of human, implicitly Christian and male, bodily function.

> First, why do some men suffer a flow of hemorrhoids? It should be answered that such are melancholic, because they are cold, therefore also much melancholy will be generated in them, which first is sent to the spleen, to the primary seat of melancholy and, because of its abundance cannot be retained there and therefore it is expelled to the spine where the aforementioned five veins which terminate in the neck are [located]. And when these veins are very full with melancholy blood, then those veins open by force of nature and that blood exits once a month as it flows once monthly in women, and such men by such a flow are preserved from severe diseases, such as dropsy, leprosy, and the like. (Pseudo-Aristotle 38; my translation)[50]

In answering the question of the causes of bleeding hemorrhoids, the text repeats the explanations given by Bartholomew, Albert, and the commentary on the *De secretis*: they afflict men dominated by cold who produce excessive black bile, which must be expelled from the body in order to prevent worse illnesses. Similar to the opinion of the commentator of *De secretis*, and in contrast to Albert, the timing of hemorrhoidal bleeding occurs monthly, as with menstrual bleeding. This general account thus follows closely earlier scientific discussions of Jewish bleeding; however, when the author turns to a consideration of Jews, he strongly emphasizes the distinguishing theological origins of their illness:

> Why do Jews indiscriminately suffer this flux? One should reply first of all theologically, because at the time of Christ's passion they cried out, "Let his blood {be upon us and upon our children." For that reason it says in Psalms: "He struck them in the bottom of their backs"} One should reply in another way, and more according to nature, that the Jews eat . . . cold foods . . . [and] from these meats melancholic blood is generated, which is purged through the flux of haemorrhoids. The second natural reason is that . . . because the Jews are not in work or motion nor in converse with men, and also because they are in great fear because we avenge the passion of Christ our redeemer—all these things produce coldness and impede digestion. For this reason much melancholic blood is generated in them, which is expelled or purged in them at the menstrual time. (qtd. in Biller 1992, 199; {} brackets include text Biller leaves untranslated).[51]

The consideration of the Jewish form of the disease opens with the query why Jews similarly (*indifferenter*) suffer from this illness. The author immediately dismisses the specter of their parity with Christians, however, with the introduction of the primary cause establishing Jewish difference: the crucifixion. Instead of offering this reason last, as Bernard of Gordon does, the *Omnes* text affirms: "one should first reply to this question theologically." It cites the two most salient proof-texts supplied by Jacques, Matthew 27, and Psalm 77, to explain the source of Jewish bleeding.[52]

Omnes homines proceeds to distinguish between theological and natural reasons for the Jewish illness, citing in the latter category diet, lack of movement, isolation and fear. However, the religious rationale returns at the conclusion of this list with an indication of the origin of this fear: Christians seeking to revenge the passion of Jesus. A form of the word *ulciscor*, to avenge or punish, which appeared in the theological answer offered by Bernard (*ulcione divina*), occurs in the list of "natural" causes. Here we see a synthesis of most of the texts considered earlier: divine punishment for the death of Jesus in the form of anal bleeding, the generation of melancholy blood—explained as a result of fear of Christian revenge—and the association with menses. Again, the Jewish body is characterized by its abjection: subject to humiliating bleeding as specified in the Psalms text, likened to the menstruating female body, and cowed in fear of Christian violence. While natural causes for Jewish bleeding are offered, theology nevertheless provides the divine origin of this condition that constructs and secures the Jews' bodily inferiority.[53]

The desideratum, articulated in Innocent's letters, that the Jews' social status be diminished to match their ontological condition of inferiors, underlies the discourses positing a humiliating embodied punishment for Jewish guilt. The logic of biblical proof-texts that authorizes pronouncements of Jewish servitude in papal decretals also operates in Jacques de Vitry's influential formulation of Jewish bleeding. The example of Cain, which establishes enslavement as punishment for the Jews' sin of deicide, usefully includes the divine imposition of a mark, a means by which this status can be materialized in the body. The verse from Matthew demonstrates the hereditary nature of this affliction while the verse from Psalms specifies its location and function: a degrading blood flow that manifests servitude. Together these texts operate as figures, demonstrating their fulfillment in contemporary Jewish physical infirmity, itself a sign of the hereditary inferiority of the Jews. The earliest medical and natural philosophical discussions of Jewish physical function suppress this religious origin insofar as their authors seek to offer scientific explanations for the condition. However, the theological basis cannot be disputed, given the absence in classical medical texts of a specifically distinct Jewish illness. The creative employment of the classical medical tradition to account for Jewish bleeding in terms of black bile, fear and bleeding show how these ideas are applied and repurposed to aid a theological agenda: to materialize Jewish inferiority in a degrading feminine or humiliating illness. The religious rationale, suppressed in early scientific accounts, re-enters in later discussions to distinguish Jews definitively from and prove them inferior to Christians.

Alexandra Cuffel has persuasively argued that scientific discourses on Jewish bleeding develop within and respond to intra-theological debates. On the one hand, the medieval reception of classical medical knowledge helps "lay the groundwork for a powerful corporeal religious polemic" (Cuffel, 87). On the other hand, theological doctrines also helped to shape this burgeoning knowledge of the functions, and dysfunctions, of the human body, particularly when that human belonged to an opposing faith:

Behind the careful scientific arguments based on theories of diet and humoral imbalance was a long tradition of religious polemic based on scatology, impurity, blood lust, and expectations of divine vengeance. . . . Thus even when a text did not directly invoke religious exegetical traditions of the other as struck by God, these views were still current enough that readers would have invariably recalled tales of cursed Jews . . . as they read or heard medical explanations of why their religious enemies were more sickly than they. The cumulative effect of the merging of religious polemic and medical theory was doubly to 'damn' the targeted group. (156–57)

By incorporating theological teachings with received classical learning in medicine and natural philosophy, medieval scholars created a powerful authoritative discourse. It served to naturalize by embodying Jewish inferiority as a means of asserting a proper religious hierarchy currently being thwarted in contemporary Christendom:

In the context of medical polemic between thirteen-century Christians and Jews, Christians presentations of Jews as sickly may be seen as an expression of feeling threatened and resorting to extreme measures to reassert the "correct" societal and religious order. . . . That the Jews' sicknesses made them like women or servants symbolically rectified the hierarchy that Christians perceived was violated by Jewish economic power and royal and ecclesiastical protection. (158, 182)

Whether articulated in medical treatises or bible commentaries, the discourse of Jewish bleeding attempts, like the papal directives that provide its inspiration, to remedy the improper inversion of relations between Christians and Jews by manifesting Jewish inferiority.

The combined discourses of theology and natural philosophy provide indisputable evidence for the abjected Jewish body at a time when both ecclesiastical and secular authorities struggled with the challenges of implementing Jewish subordination. The notion of Jewish bleeding offers an ideal solution: the disease itself functioned, in its embarrassing menstrual/ hemorrhoidal form, to demean Jews. Although virtually undetectable, its divine origin secured its reality. Located in the body, this affliction reveals less concern about visibility than about embodying a servitude not properly enforced in social contexts. Jews ought to feel the humiliation of their punishment and acknowledge their subordination to Christians and Christianity.[54] Furthermore, the scientific explanation of the infirmity serves to naturalize it, thereby ramifying its authoritative truth. The case of Jewish bleeding supports Loomba's claim that the exploration of premodern racism should attend to religious and cultural constructs insofar as they provide the basis for imagining biological, corporeal difference (2009, 508–9). The concept of Jewish servitude establishes a racist ontological status for Jews in conceiving them as inherently inferior to Christians. While this form of racism does not initially attach itself to bodily markers, we can trace its influence on somatic discourses that seek to realize a subordinated Jewish status. Chapter 3 continues the exploration of this racializing impulse in analyzing the attempt to develop a mark of *discernible* inferiority: visual representations of dark-skinned Jews that appear in Passion scenes illuminating thirteenth-century English Psalm collections.

3

Making Darkness Visible

THE COLORS OF SUBJECTION IN MEDIEVAL
ENGLISH PSALTER ILLUMINATIONS

AS DEMONSTRATED IN chapter 2, even though the development of racial Jewish inferiority does not depend upon physical attributes, it nevertheless easily translates to and shapes scientific discourses of the Jewish body. Cain, punished and yet marked with a protective sign by God, provides a particularly generative figure for imagining the material consequences of Jewish crime. Peter of Cluny ingeniously combines the preserving and punitive elements of Cain's fate to figure Jewish servitude as a kind of living death. In an 1146 letter to King Louis VII supporting the Crusade, he writes:

> Indeed, God does not wish [them] to be utterly killed, not entirely destroyed, but to be preserved in a life worse than death, for the greater torture and greater disgrace, like the fratricide Cain. . . . Thus has the most just severity of God done with regard to the damned and damnable Jews, from the very time of the passion and death of Christ, and continuously to the accomplishment of the end of this world. Who are slaves, wretches, afraid, groaning and refugees on the earth since they shed the blood of Christ, certainly their brother according to the flesh. (*Letters* 1: 328–29, my translation)[1]

Even while invoking Augustine's protective teaching regarding the Jews, Peter explains that God's sentence of enslavement has consigned them not only to a life worse than death, but to eternal damnation, stretching from the time of the crucifixion until the end of time.[2] His account resonates with early Christian textual traditions that imagined sin as effecting a death during life and drew on the condition of slavery to represent the suffering of the damned in hell (Bernstein, 55–61, 82–7, 99–134). In the *Moralia in Job*, Gregory I formulates the phrase "inner death" to describe a sinful state in which the living experience the torments of hell (57–9). Furthermore, Peter's description of the Jews' punishment in terms of slavery, torture, and humiliation reflects accounts of hell that draw on degrading, physical torments associated with the chastisement of enslaved persons to envision the condition of the damned (Bernstein, 99–134).[3]

In the thirteenth century, the concern of popes and councils to subordinate Jews so as to prevent them from exercising wrongful authority over Christians finds an intensified visual analogue in images of the blasphemous tormenting of Jesus during the Passion. One striking example of this occurs in medieval English psalter illustrations of the life and death of Jesus that portray his attackers as Jews with dark skin. These images participate in a larger iconographic convention, emerging in the twelfth and thirteenth centuries, that represents Jews with distorted features signifying evil.[4] Scholars have understood the denigrating portrayals of the Jews' unredeemed status as deriving from classical and early Christian traditions in which blackness and African peoples represent sin and the demonic.[5] While portrayals of dark skin certainly participate in anti-black conventions, I argue that they also rely on associations of dark colors with death, hell, and damnation. Although the psalter images do not directly represent Cain, they nevertheless draw on views like Peter's to make visible the consequences of deicide. Theological ideas of slavery and inner death correlated with darkness and the experience of hell pains during life provide an important context for understanding the convention in which internal torment colors the skin of the Jews as they commit their heinous crime. Situated in a series of illuminations demonstrating Christian truth and venerating Jesus, Jews are shown as violently rejecting both. In so doing they turn away from salvation and consign themselves not only to a cursed servitude during life, but also to the death of the soul that leads to enslaving torments of perpetual damnation. These images thus materialize the spiritual basis of inferiority by representing it as dark, servile, and infernal: not only hellish, but literally "underneath."[6]

This chapter begins with a consideration of the theological importance of the psalm collection and its illustrations, with particular focus on medieval developments. In this period, the textual and visual representations of the Passion acquired new significance that influenced the types of images artists created for inclusion in psalters. The choice to represent Jews with dark skin in images of the Passion requires us to explore meanings attendant upon dark colors in late antiquity and early Christianity. Scholars have noted clear associations between sin, evil, and the demonic with blackness in texts and images that often ascribe these negative connotations to Ethiopian, or African, bodies and peoples. However, other implications attached to these colors, including death, illness, injury, and damnation, which may also contribute to our understanding of these portrayals. The early and medieval Christian conceptualization of second or inner death as delineating the status of the eternally damned, in addition to ideas of hell that imagined the torments of the damned in terms of punishments reserved for slaves provide additional contexts for my analysis of two early instances of dark Jews in English psalter manuscripts.

Medieval Psalter Illuminations of the Passion

In order to analyze the significance of these particular images of dark tormentors, we must first understand the Christological significance of the context in which they appear: medieval English illuminated psalters. Manuscript collections of the 150 psalms contained in the Hebrew Bible enjoyed the widest circulation and readership of any of the books of Scripture in this period (Lobrichon, 535; van Liere, 29–31; Brown, 3). As with the other texts of the Hebrew Bible, the Psalms were reinterpreted in the light of Christian revelation. The New Testament and early Christian commentaries understood the Psalms as prefiguring the coming of Jesus; exegetes emphasized his status as descendant of David, considered the author of most of these songs, as well as a type of Jesus. Thus the Psalms functioned as prophetic evidence for Jesus as messiah (Dyer, 65). Beginning in the eighth century, artists illuminated English psalters with a variety of pictures, especially portrayals of David, the Psalms' author and the precursor of Jesus; "but it was above all the Christological interpretation of the Psalms themselves which dominated the embellishment of Psalters in the high Middle Ages" (Kauffmann 2003, 106, 112). English psalter illuminations were among the first to extend an image of the Crucifixion into a series of pictures of the life of Jesus; over time particular psalms were associated with specific events in the Gospel narratives (112, 117).

The psalter served as prayer book from early Christian communities until the fourteenth century.[7] The use of psalms for private prayer moved from the monastery to the laity, stimulated in part by the increase in literacy in the eighth and ninth centuries. "The Psalms. . . were perceived to be the property of lay Christians in a way that the rest of the Scriptures were not" insofar as it was the only reading in church that a lay person could recite and the one book of the Bible to which they were regularly permitted access (Holladay, 178). From the eleventh century onward, changes in the nature and meaning of private prayer attendant upon the rise of affective piety influenced the use and content of the psalters. Beginning with St. Anselm's *Prayers and Meditations* (c. 1070) and continuing with the Franciscans' preaching and writing directed to the laity, Christians were increasingly encouraged to identify with Christ's humanity and develop empathy for the suffering he experienced during the crucifixion and the ordeals that led up to it (Kauffmann 2003, 118, 166, 170; McNamer; Fulton).[8] Thus the Passion figured as a central event in prompts to prayer.

The practice of affective devotion stressed as another strategy the importance of sight in the process of identifying with Jesus's suffering by encouraging the development of graphic mental images. The faithful were exhorted to visualize the scene of anguish, as in Anselm's first prayer to Jesus: "Why could you not bear to see the nails violate the hands and feet of your Creator? Why did you not see with horror the blood that passed out of the side of your Redeemer?" (qtd. in Kauffmann 2003, 118). As Kauffmann explains:

> Images played a large part in this devotion and their importance in arousing emotion was repeatedly emphasized at the time. Both St Bonaventure and St Thomas Aquinas expounded the view that images excite the emotions "which are more effectively aroused by things seen than by things heard." . . . In the thirteenth century . . . this stress on the power of images to excite empathy became commonplace and applicable both to the ordinary devotee and, in heightened form, to the visionary mystic. (2003, 170).

The function of psalter as book of private prayer, its interpretation as a Christological text and the convention of incorporating portrayals of scenes from Jesus's life rendered it a perfect vehicle for the advancement of affective spirituality; consequently, psalter illustrations increasingly reflect the larger devotional context in their focus on Jesus's suffering.

These developments in spirituality stimulated an influential genre of Passion narratives beginning in the twelfth century (Bestul, 1, 36). While these texts employ a variety of strategies to stimulate compassion for the suffering of Jesus, one of the most effective was the emphasis on the cruelty of his tormentors, increasingly identified as the Jews. A consideration of the literature of affective piety sheds light on the more negative view of Jews it articulated. As Thomas Bestul convincingly argues:

> One result of this new piety . . .[is] the increased attention paid to those who were perceived to be Christ's enemies during his life on earth, namely the Jews. The heightened devotion to the Passion with its greater attention to the physical sufferings of Christ, had as its by-product an inevitable attention to the perpetrators of the torments, showing them to be exceptionally cruel or depraved as a means of increasing the emotional response of readers to their reality. (71)

This development parallels a shift in the theological understanding of the Jews' culpability for the crucifixion. Prior to the eleventh century, the consensus among exegetes viewed the Jews as acting without knowledge of Jesus's status as God when calling for his execution; while still judged guilty, the Jews' ignorance somewhat mitigated their crime. However, beginning in the twelfth century, this idea gradually gave way to an interpretation that the Jews acted with malice and full knowledge of their crime (Cohen, 1983). Although the New Testament narrative and early medieval exegetical treatises divided responsibility for Jesus's torments between the Jews and the gentiles, with the former acting in the earlier persecutions while the latter carried out the subsequent tortures and the final execution, by the thirteenth century the passion narratives increasingly represent the Jews as the central or sole agents of the events prior to and including the crucifixion (Bestul, 70–71). Besides shifting culpability to the Jews, these accounts also elaborate upon scriptural descriptions of their acts:

> The treatises of the late twelfth and early thirteenth centuries extend this "Jewish" part of the Passion, from the betrayal of Judas through the release of Barabbas, by expanding the gospel account through fuller and more detailed descriptions of these events and by throwing emphasis on the fact of Jewish participation in them. (Bestul, 71)

The emphasis on the centrality of Jewish culpability in the verbal narratives resulted in their description "in realistic, though highly exaggerated terms, as the physical embodiments of malice, instead of abstract symbols of human sinfulness" (Bestul, 72).[9]

The Passion narratives, in emphasizing Jewish menace, also address the emerging problem of enforcing Jewish servitude. The texts tap into anxieties over the reversal of the proper hierarchical relationship between Christians and Jews. As Bestul explains, Ekbert of Schonau's influential twelfth-century Passion treatise, the *Stimulus amoris*

> expresses as well as provokes the greatest fear of all: it relates a story in which the subordinate relationship of Jew to Christian is inverted, in which Jews have power and authority over a Christian, in which the social boundaries between Christian and Jew are violated, in which it is a Christian, and not a Jew who is subjected to degradation and stigmatization. . . . Within the generic confines of a devotional treatise, Ekbert creates a way of regarding Jews as a horrifying threat, thereby implicitly legitimating the need for strict policies to control them, to keep them in that state of servitude which, as the Popes beginning with Innocent III repeatedly proclaimed, they deserved because they were the murderers of Christ. . . . The treatment of the Jews in the thirteenth century Passion narratives can be viewed largely as continuations and extensions of rhetorical strategies and methods definitively instituted in his *Stimulus amoris.* (90)

In staging the sacrilegious violence posed to Jesus himself, the narrative casts the Jews as deserving of subordination, thereby contributing to increasing calls to enforce their servitude. However, in emphasizing their vicious actions, it also depicts them as already degraded.

As with the devotional narrative texts during this period, psalter images depicting scenes from the life and death of Jesus also accentuate Jewish violence by expanding their role in the representations of Jesus's torment. Blumenkranz carefully documents a trend across a wide range of thirteenth-century depictions of the Passion to demonstrate how they consistently contradict the evidence of the New Testament in transforming the agents of Jesus's suffering from gentiles to Jews. The Roman actors in the latter part of the Passion—Pilate, the flagellators, those who crown Jesus with thorns, as well as the lance- and sponge-bearers—are translated into Jews in portrayals from the latter part of the century (96–104; Kauffmann 2003, 175).[10] This focus on the role of the Jews increasingly emphasizes their status as enemies of Christianity and Christians. Thus, the psalter as a prayer book that advances a supersessionist interpretation of the psalms and illustrates these texts with images of Jewish menace establishes the powerfully negative frame for understanding figures with dark skin included in these contexts.

Medieval Connotations of Darkness

A considerable body of scholarship documents the long-standing association of the color black with negative values.[11] Ancient cultures linked blackness with night, the earth, the underground world, and death; while not initially understood as malign, the color acquired more malevolent connotations in classical antiquity, which also attached themselves to persons with dark skin (Pastoureau, 30, 35; Hunter, 141). These ideas appear in early Christian writings as well, which connect not only blackness with death, sin, and damnation, but also reference Ethiopians to describe the appearance of demons and devils. Although patristic authors sometimes employ the colors of black and white metaphorically to describe the sinful or repentant soul, others identify Ethiopian people as essentially evil and demonic (Courtès; Goldenberg 2009).

Medieval images include a wide range of visual representations of figures with dark skin. I focus here on English psalters illustrated with images of antagonistic Jews in scenes from the Passion narrative; at least fifteen medieval psalm collections include these depictions. The earliest of these, two manuscripts produced in Oxford in the first decade of the thirteenth century, present the Jewish enemies of Jesus with variously colored skin.[12] Several possible influences account for the evolution of this convention. Patristic traditions associating the "African" with sin and the demonic intersect with anti-Jewish discourses and may contribute to these representations of Jews.[13] However, I'd like to explore the wider medieval context of meanings attached to blackness and related dark colors to assist in the reading of Jews portrayed with dark complexions.

As noted earlier, blackness accrued a range of negative connotations from the period of antiquity onward. As Michel Pastoureau explains in his history of the color black, these associations intensify in visual representations during the medieval period:

> In the West, beginning in the eleventh century, black became the diabolical color par excellence. . . . Of course, the darkness of hell justifies the dark or black qualities of those who resided there, who came

and went there, but it does not explain everything. . . .Whatever the case, before and after the year 1000 and for many centuries, black was constantly called upon to adorn the body or clothes of all those maintaining relationships of dependence or affinity with the devil. (52)

However, artists employed more than one color to represent the devil and his allies:

It was not just a matter of black, but involved all dark colors: brown, gray, purple, and even blue. . . . Dark blue was often considered and perceived as equivalent to black, a semi-black or sub-black, used notably for painting hell and demons. (52)

We must therefore consider not only the ways in which black, but a range of dark colors, confers meaning in visual as well as verbal representations.[14]

The visual association of black with blue that registers in the language used to describe the complexion of Ethiopians or Africans conveys meanings in addition to evil and the demonic.[15] The Middle English and Latin terms used to describe an array of dark skin colors also characterize the appearance of the ill and the dead. Kathleen Ann Kelly notes that the "Middle English. . . word blo (bla, bloe, ble), meaning 'dark blue,' 'blue-black,' 'leaden-coloured,' 'livid,' came into English from Old Norse blár" and may also be linked to the German term for lead, "blei." The Middle English "blo" corresponds to the Latin term lividus, which similarly denotes black and blue and leaden colors (Kelly, 41).[16] Bartholomew Anglicus's thirteenth-century encyclopedia, De proprietatibus rerum, devotes two chapters to explain the significance of the color livid:

Livid color is produced. . . in things having gross and cold humor. . . . Lead, [which] is naturally white, however . . . appears livid. . . . Whence livid color signifies the dominance of cold. Therefore the color livid in urine is the sign of the extinction of natural heat and death of the animal. (Book 19, Chapter 19, 1156, my translation)[17]

Bartholomew links lividness to lead, which can appear both white and gray-dark, hence accounting for the combination of apparently opposing colors. Dominated by cold, the color also signifies the suppression of natural heat, an element necessary to life. As Bartholomew elaborates:

Therefore the color livid is evil in living bodies, for it signals either the dominance of cold that extinguishes natural heat and begins to kill life; or an excess of melancholy blood, that damages entirely the color and surface of the skin; or anguish of heart, that recalls the heat of the blood to the interior, as is seen in an envious person; or when an injury from a fall or blow corrupts the blood under the skin, as appears in beatings. . . (Book 19, Chapter 20, 1156–57, my translation)[18]

Lividness represents variously that which is life-threatening, the melancholy humor, envy, or bruising, among other possibilities. The fact that melancholy comprises the elements of cold and dry renders it, at some level, antithetical to life, which requires heat and moisture to exist.[19] Kelly makes a similar point about the harmful, if not lethal, connotations of "blo":

The expression "black and blue" (in the sense of colouring due to cold or to bruising) was, in Middle English, *black and bla*. . . . "[D]iscoloration" of the skin was a sign of ill-health and, sometimes, madness. . . . Curry notes. . . that "the livid, ghastly pallor of dying or dead bodies is described by the adjectives pale, wan, blue and black" in Middle English. (41, 46)[20]

Black, blue, and livid represent the color of ill, bruised, or otherwise injured skin, as well as the color of insanity and death.

Hence, in addition to the anti-black attitudes attached to Ethiopians, we should also consider the extent to which dark colors signifying death and damnation shape representations of sin and hell. In his discussion of depictions of dark devils, Devisse cites what he understands as an early example of this convention that appears in a ninth-century illustrated manuscript of the Apocalypse of St. John (Revelations) (2010a, 56).[21] The image depicts a figure in profile with deep bluish-gray, or livid, skin, wavy dark hair, and a white headband (Fig. 3.1). A chain encircling his neck and hands binds him to a horned snake, also portrayed in profile. Both figures appear to vomit flames. Henri Omont identifies the dark human figure as "the devil, whose nude corpse is painted in blue and whose long greenish hair is gathered in a red band" (my translation 81). However, the image that directly precedes this one in this manuscript shows an angel with a headband in the process of binding the human figure to the snake (Fig. 3.2).

In this rendering, the artist depicts the human with light skin and without a headband. It seems clear that both images represent the same figures, human and serpent, and that the complexion of the former transforms from light in the first portrayal to dark in the second. Further examination of the Apocalypse context that these figures illustrate clarifies the significance of this shift in color.

As Devisse explains, and the accompanying caption indicates, the creator of this manuscript placed this illumination in a section of the Apocalypse or Book of Revelations that discusses "the second death (Apoc. 20:9, 11, 14–15, 21:8)" (2010a, 245, n. 275). While all humans succumb to death as a result of their having eaten of the tree of knowledge (Gen 2:17), the Book of Revelations intimates that there awaits for infidels a subsequent death in the torments of hell: "But the fearful, and unbelieving, and the abominable, and murderers, and whoremongers, and sorcerers, and idolaters, and all liars, they shall have their portion in the pool burning with fire and brimstone, which is the second death" (21:8). In *De Civitate Dei*, Augustine offers a complex account of the various stages of death that can conclude in the second death.[22] When the soul leaves the decayed body, the whole person dies, but those who die in a state of sin, as described in Revelations, experience the second death: "from the abuse of free will has come the linked sequence of our disaster, by which the human race is conducted through an uninterrupted succession of miseries from that original depravity... all the way to the catastrophe of the second death that has no end." Those not "freed by grace" are subject to an eternal, punishing afterlife (*Civitate Dei* 13.14, 181).

The Apocalypse manuscript illustration of this phenomenon includes images and captions drawn from John's text. The first of the images, in which the human figure is represented with light skin, bears the caption: "When the angel of the Lord bound the devil, the old serpent, and that false prophet with him, who made signs before him, and sent them into the abyss and enclosed them and set a sign on him until a thousand years are completed" (36r Fig. 3.2, my translation).[23] The text provides a pastiche of phrases from Revelations 20:1–3, which describe the angel binding, casting and sealing the devil serpent in the abyss, and Revelations 19:20: "And the beast was taken, and with him the false prophet, who wrought signs before him. . . . These two were cast alive into the pool of fire, burning with brimstone."[24] Thus the human figure portrays the false prophet whom the angel binds to the devil serpent. The subsequent image of this pair represents the "second death," which is situated below a portrayal of Jesus, nimbed and seated on a brown throne (Fig. 3.1). The caption for the lower image rests below Jesus's throne; it explains "this is the second death: this is the lake of fire and brimstone where the devil is sent and the damned" (37 r, paraphrase of Rev 20:9–10 or 14).[25] The caption suggests that the dark figure chained to the snake represents a deceased sinner, condemned to a second death beyond salvation. He is not a black demon, since the serpent here represents the devil, but a damned, permanently dead soul. His infernal blue/gray complexion denotes not only the death of the body, but of the soul as well. He inhabits an inferior position below a majestic Jesus seated on his throne; the chains that bind the sinner and the devil provide a visual metonym for their enslaved status.

Early Christian discussions of hell emphasize darkness in their descriptions of its location and the condition of its inhabitants. In its portrayal of infernal torments, the apocryphal *Apocalypse of Paul* (late 4th–early 5th c. C.E.) notes the absence of light: "There was no light in that place, but darkness and sadness and gloom" (qtd. in Bernstein, 107). In his commentary on Job, Gregory I employs the idea of the obscurity of hell to describe the interiority of the sinner. The biblical text represents the end of life as a journey "to a land that is dark and covered with the mist of death/ A land of misery and darkness" (10:21–2). Interpreting these lines as describing hell, Gregory explains that "misery" indicates the pain that torments the external body of those whose internal "darkness," or blindness, separates them from the true light of God (Bernstein, 57; Gregory 9.64.96, ll 1–4).[26] Origen similarly employs metaphors of darkness to explain that the interior gloom of the sinful in this life will manifest itself on the body at the end of days:

> the sinful who loved the darkness of error and the night of ignorance in this life, after the resurrection will be clothed in dark and black bodies, so that the same mist of ignorance which in this world took possession of their interior mind, in the future will appear through the garment of their exterior body. (*Peri Archon* II.10.8 *Patrologiæ Græcæa* vol. 11, my translation)[27]

These texts create a rich complex of association with darkness that includes the appearance of hell, death, sin, blindness and resurrected bodies.

Gregory's *Moralia in Job* elaborates on the idea of darkness as a punishing blindness to develop his concept of "inner death," corresponding to the Revelations' notion of "second death." In his formulation, outer death separates the body from the soul while inner death separates the soul from God (Bernstein, 58). Drawing on the idea of the interior torment of blindness suffered in hell, he imagines inner death as afflicting the unrepentant sinner during her life:

> The blindness or stubbornness that prevents respect for divine directives or repentance for violating them in life, is a future hell pain already suffered here. Hell then grasps the living person's heart and thereby begins to separate the soul from God and introduces hell's torments during one's life. Hell's foothold in the living person's soul is inner death. (Bernstein, 59)[28]

Hence, the blindness of the sinner figured by the gloom of hell results in an interior death of the soul experienced as a living postmortem pain. Isidore iterates Gregory's idea of the punishment of the mind and the body, in this world as well as the next; he emphasizes the perpetual nature of the damned sinner's punishment. (*Sententiae* 2.26.3; Bernstein 84, n. 49). He similarly describes a doubled penalty in the afterlife: "The punishment of the damned in Gehenna is twofold: *tristitia* [sadness] burns the mind, and fire burns the body" (Bernstein 84). While both Gregory and Isidore delineate the suffering of the sinful in this life, they also note the affliction of the flesh after death. If the flesh is burned in hell, as Isidore explains, it might contribute to portrayals of the damned with dark, burned skin. The associations of darkness in hell, derived initially from the text of Job, develop connotations of sinful blindness, inner death, and hell-pains during one's life as well as the afterlife.

In addition to themes of darkness, the Early Christian representations of hell's torments correlate with servitude, insofar as they derive in part from penalties exclusive to slaves in Greek and Roman law. The Athenian Decree of Scamandrius established the connection between servitude and torture by exempting citizens from that punishment (Bernstein, 113). A ruling from the Twelve Tables (c. 450 B.C.E.), the earliest Roman code of law, similarly affirmed that slaves could be punished more severely than free men (114). These punishments included hanging, burning, being beaten while carrying a yoke, and crucifixion. Since public shaming also accompanied this type of penalty, torture and humiliation characterized the chastisement reserved for slaves in this period (116). Christian visionary literature drew from these punishments in representing the torments of hell. In doing so, they established an equivalency between the damned and slaves.[29]

The inferior status of the slave, as we have seen in the writings of Augustine, provided a model for thinking about the subordination of religious others:

> The liability of slaves to physical punishment corresponds also to their otherness in religion. Just as wrong belief determined one's liability to torture in the afterlife, it also determined one's liability to slavery here and now. . . . Thus religious differences came to provide a rationale for damnation, the ultimate othering. In addition, lifetime suffering, including torture, imposed on slaves strongly influences images of post-mortem retribution. Therefore, wrong religion made one liable to both enslavement here on earth and damnation in the otherworld. (Bernstein, 130)

While the late antique and early Christian development of ideas about hell do not include Jews, Muslims, and heretics among the damned, these groups begin to appear in subsequent periods, not only in literary texts but also in visual representation, including manuscript illumination (Bernstein, 358).

This collection of Christian views connecting darkness with death, hell, blindness, torture, servitude, and inner death—the experience of infernal torment during life—provide a context for reading the images of dark-skinned Jews included in scenes from the Passion of Jesus. Corresponding to Peter's description of the "damned and damnable" Jews as sentenced, at the time of the Crucifixion, to a life worse than death, psalter portrayals make this status visible. In rejecting and torturing Jesus, the Jews consign themselves to eternal death, the servitude of sin, and servile, humiliating, eternal torture. Their dark complexion suggests the color of the dead, their interior blindness, their experience of a living hell, and the marks of burning and beating inflicted by infernal torment on their bodies.

An examination of the medieval English palette of hell will help us read the images of dark Jews. The extensively illustrated Munich Psalter (c. 1200–1210), produced just prior to psalters representing dark Jews and in the same thirteenth-century Oxford milieu, offers a possible influence in its portrayal of hell. The psalter's representation of the life, death, and resurrection of Jesus includes an illumination of the twelve torments of hell, which colors the devils in shades of blue, gray, and brown (Fig. 3.3).

The artist organizes his subject by means of a golden grid that divides the scenes into four rows of three compartments portraying dead bodies entering hell and suffering torture at the hands of various devils. He depicts the background of each section in alternating shades of black and gray, establishing the darkness of hell. The demons possess animalistic features such as paws, claws, beaks, fur, and fangs; some have flame-red tongues and eyes. They torment the damned with a variety of tortures, all of which include hellfire. In the top right illustration, two demons force the damned into the gaping, fanged mouths of two larger devils; of these latter two, the devil on the left is painted a beautiful deep blue, with lighter blue and black accent lines. The bottom left-hand image, directly diagonal from this one, contains another bluish hellmouth, muted to a livid hue with gray, brown, and black accents overlaying the blue. The illumination portrays the other tormenting devils in shades of reddish brown or livid blue-gray, with black used as an outline to distinguish their features. While these colors certainly participate in the negative association of Ethiopians with devils, they also connote death, torment, and damnation.

Materializing Slavery in the Dark Jewish Enemies of Jesus

Some of the earliest portrayals of Jews with dark skin appear in two illuminated psalm collections produced in Oxford: the Royal and Arundel Psalters, dating from the first decade of the thirteenth century.[30] In the images of the betrayal and the trial, the Royal Psalter offers a mixed representation that distinguishes between repentant Jews and those who seek Jesus's death. The latter appear as hostile figures with distorted features and brown skin, the former with symmetrical features and white skin, however, as we shall see, the color symbolism does not yet offer a clear binary (Fig. 3.4, fol 5v).[31] The illustration follows the Gospel narratives in which Judas, paid by the chief priests and officers of the Temple, comes with a crowd to betray Jesus.[32] The arrestors in the betrayal scene stand in a group on the right of Jesus; their faces and hands are brown, their hair either darker brown or red (Fig. 3.4, top image). Two of the arrestors have flame-like or spiky hair or beards. To the left of Jesus, Peter strikes off the ear of the high priest's servant, Malchus (John 18:10), also depicted with brown skin and red hair; the grimacing servant shakes an admonishing finger at Peter. These colors and shapes echo brown demons and the pointy red flames of hell in the Munich psalter.[33] Portrayed in profile with gaping mouths and other distorted features, they participate in a developing convention for the negative representation of Jews.[34] The arrestors hold a large black sword, an axe, and a lantern, as indicated in John's description of them carrying "lanterns and torches and weapons" (John 18:3). In Luke's account, Jesus asks: "Are ye come out, as it were against a thief, with swords and clubs?/When I was daily with you in the temple, you did not stretch forth your hands against me: but this is your hour, and the power of darkness" (Luke 22:52–3). The dark skin of the arrestors may be suggested by "the power of darkness," akin to the brown demons presented in the Munich Psalter. The Jews' complexion clearly identifies them as agents of the devil; but as servants to sin and the devil, their darkness may also signify their deathly, damned, servile status.

The images of the mocking and scourging of Jesus similarly depict his attackers with brown skin and dark brown or red hair (Fig. 3.4 lower register, Fig. 3.5 upper register); in subjecting Jesus to humiliation and torture, the Jews appear to degrade his divine status to a servile one. Three brown-skinned antagonists, two with red hair, stand on either side of Jesus, striking his face and ridiculing him, illustrating the trial before Caiaphas: "And some began to spit on him, and to cover his face, and to buffet him, and to say unto him: Prophesy: and the servants struck him with the palms of their hands" (Mark 14: 65).[35] The distorted features and coloring of all three tormentors link them to the arrestors in the upper register of this image, but they have progressed from merely threatening Jesus to directly taunting and physically attacking him. This assault intensifies on the facing page, in which two brown tormentors flog Jesus with a scourge (Fig. 3.5, upper register).[36] Jesus, nude except for his halo and a loincloth, stands behind a pole to which he is bound. Blood courses down his left arm and chest, revealing both the extent of his suffering and the humiliating violence inflicted upon him. Nevertheless, from behind his pillar, Jesus serenely responds to his right-hand assailant with a compassionate gaze. His scourgers hold their weapons aloft, ready to continue the whipping. In both images, even as they subject Jesus to servile torment, the attackers' dark complexion marks them, in rejecting Christian salvation, as experiencing inner death and consigning themselves to the enslaving torture of eternal damnation.

However, the use of white complexions in the image does not establish a clear contrast to the evil of the dark Jews. All of the figures represented in these two images, with the possible exception of Pilate who might be one of the judges, are Jews; the artist distinguishes Jesus and his disciples by portraying them with white skin and halos. Judas, clad in white, appears as a lovely, almost feminine, youth whose complexion is even lighter than the brunette, bearded Jesus he embraces (Fig 3.4). Notice, though, that Judas lacks a halo and his red hair connects him visually with the dark antagonists. His complexion here suggests the falsity of hyper-whiteness belying an interior evil, akin to the "scribes and Pharisees, hypocrites. . . like to whited sepulchres, which outwardly appear to men beautiful, but within are full of dead men's bones, and of all filthiness" (Matt. 23:27). Counterintuitively, Judas's whiteness may signal his interior death, just as the dark skin of the tormenters does.

Nevertheless, the Royal Psalter ultimately stabilizes the color binary in juxtaposing the dark antagonists to the light complected judges and Judas in the representation of his death. In a conflated image of the trials of Jesus before the high priest Caiaphas, Pilate, or Herod (Luke 22–3), two judges sit to the left of Jesus in apparent consultation (Fig. 3.4, lower register). The red-headed judge gestures toward Jesus, while the brunette points back to his fellow magistrate; although they share the hair color of the antagonists of Jesus, their skin is white and their features are regular. This suggested conversation may visualize Luke's account: "And Herod and Pilate were made friends, that same day; for before they were enemies one to another" (Luke 23:12). Herod and Pilate reach an accord here about Jesus's innocence (23:14–15); the image seems to indicate this through the gestures of the judges. Although Pilate ultimately gives in to the wishes of the crowd who call for Jesus to be crucified, he and Herod do not here instigate the violence. The "Christian" features of the judges reflect their relative lack of culpability in this scene, in contrast to the dark, distorted appearance of the brutal attackers of Jesus.

This clear-cut color binary continues in the illustration of Judas's repentance and suicide that includes only white-skinned figures (Fig. 3.5, bottom register). Judas appears here as older than the youth of the betrayal, with longer hair and a beard; his forehead is creased with sorrow. His right hand drops the coins received as payment from the chief priests (Luke 22:2–6; Matt. 26:14–16, 27:1–10). Matthew's account describes him as having a change of heart; Judas turns his back on the priests as he returns their money, facing toward an image in which he hangs himself from a tree (27:3–5).[37] Judas's whiteness here, unlike the seductively deceptive whiteness in the betrayal, might reflect his repentance and his refusal to participate in the crucifixion. His contrition saves him from the torments of inner death that anticipate the described punishments of the

FIGURE 3.1 The devil and the damned condemned to the second death.

Bibliothèque nationale de France. Bibliothèque municipale de Valenciennes, MS.99 fol 37r.

FIGURE 3.2 The angel of the Lord binds the false prophet and the devil.
Bibliothèque nationale de France. Bibliothèque municipale de Valenciennes, MS.99
fol 36r.

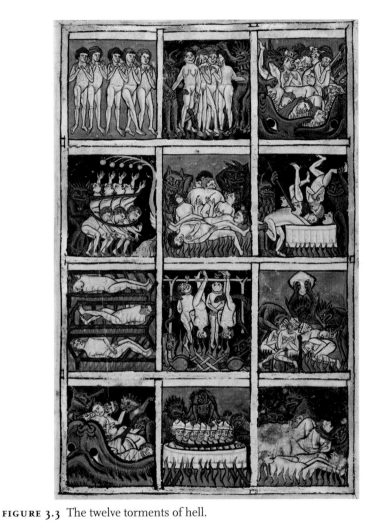

FIGURE 3.3 The twelve torments of hell.
Bayerische Staatsbibliothek München, Clm 835, Munich Psalter fol 30v,
urn: nbn:de:bvb:12-bsb00012920-3.

FIGURE 3.4 Upper register: Judas, accompanied by a crowd of dark arrestors, betrays Jesus. Lower register: Three dark tormentors mock and hit Jesus in the trial before Caiaphas and Pilate or Herod.

© The British Library Board. MS Royal I D X fol 5v.

FIGURE 3.5 Upper register: two tormentors scourge Jesus. Lower register: Judas repents his betrayal and hangs himself.

© The British Library Board. MS Royal I D X fol 6r.

FIGURE 3.6 Upper register: Judas, accompanied by a crowd of dark arrestors, betrays Jesus. Lower register: Two tormentors mock and hit Jesus in a trial before dark judges.

© The British Library Board. MS Arundel 157 fol 9v.

FIGURE 3.7 Upper register: Judas repents his betrayal and hangs himself. Lower register: Two tormentors scourge Jesus.

© The British Library Board. MS Arundel 157 fol 10r.

FIGURE 3.8 A Jewish convert to Christianity converts and heals a blinded Jew.
© The British Library Board. Add MS 49999 fol 63r.

FIGURE 3.9 A blind Jew refuses conversion and healing.
© The British Library Board. Add MS 49999 fol 63v.

damned in hell.³⁸ Matthew's text suggests that the priests also undergo some pangs of conscience in their handling of the returned money.³⁹ The image depicts the priests discussing what to do with the money; although the figure on the far left is portrayed with slightly distorted features, réd hair, and a beard, all three have white skin. The image suggest the priests, following Matthew's account, recognize the money as tainted by blood; like Judas, they show a modicum of remorse that preserves them from the inner death and servile torment signaled in the dark, menacing features of the arrestors and the mockers in the scenes of the betrayal and trial.⁴⁰

While the Arundel Psalter shares many compositional elements with the Royal Psalter, it differs in offering a more consistent representation of Jews with dark skin. The image of the Betrayal (Fig. 3.6) portrays all of the arrestors with pale gray or livid faces and hands. As in the Royal Psalter, the arrestors inhabit the left side of the image; several have dark red hair, distorted features, or profile portrayal. Judas appears with white skin and occupies the same position in both psalters, but the Arundel artist portrays him in profile as a more threatening older, bearded man with dark red hair that matches that of some arrestors. On the same page in the lower register, as in the Royal psalter, the artist again conflates the trial before various Jewish authorities into one scene. To the right of Jesus, the women admonishing Peter and the mockers all appear with pale gray/ tan skin; the latter have lighter complexions and less threatening facial expressions than their counterparts in the Royal. However, the Arundel artist enhances the menace of the authorities by increasing their number and presenting them in profile, with distorted features, dark red hair and dark beards. One raises an admonishing hand and points a red-tipped finger at Jesus. All have livid faces and hands, strongly aligning them with the dark arrestors who appear in the opposing corner of the upper register; the effect is to situate Jesus within a more intimidating environment.⁴¹ Even as the Jewish antagonists threaten Jesus in these images, their light brown and pale gray complexions give them the appearance of the dead and the damned.

The increased hostility in the atmosphere of the Arundel images continues into the next scene where the suicide of Judas and the scourging of Jesus are inverted from their placement in the Royal psalter (Fig. 3.7). The Arundel artist presents Judas's suicide in the upper register, and alters the representation of the Jewish authorities by increasing their number and depicting them all with livid faces and hands. Unlike the priests of the Royal images, this group shows no signs of internal debate; all of the dark figures face Judas while the foremost priest shakes a chastising finger at him, as if in disapproval of his expression of remorse. The image of the flagellation in the lower register continues the dark representation of Jesus's Jewish enemies with livid skin and red hair; the tormentors display distorted features and vicious expressions. The torso of figure to the right of Jesus twists in a grotesque, almost tortured pose. The artist does mitigate the representation of Jesus's wounds, which appear here as small red dots rather than wounds emitting a copious flow of blood. Nevertheless, the effect of the Royal Psalter's rendering of Jews with both light and dark skin serves to reduce their culpability, especially in its choice to conclude the page with an image of Jewish remorse. In Arundel, the scenes begin with the threat of Jewish violence and conclude with the Jews realizing it on the body of Jesus. The consistent representation of Jews with livid skin indicates their rejection of the salvation offered by Jesus, resulting in their inner death, damnation, and enslaving torment.

A consideration of one final image of a dark Jew will help to sharpen the significance of the colors used in the Arundel, Royal, and subsequent medieval English psalters. A series of illuminated initials from a book of hours produced in Oxford (c. 1240) illustrates events from the lives of both Jesus and Mary,[42] including an episode in which Jews assault the Virgin's funeral bier. This story essentially reprises the Jews' role as enemy of Jesus in their plot to destroy Mary's body.[43] In attempting to assail Mary's bier, the Jews are miraculously afflicted; one attacker's hand becomes affixed to the bier, and is ripped from his body, while the other Jews are blinded. St. Peter converts and heals the first assailant, restoring the hand, and directs him to convert and heal the blinded Jews. While the new Christian successfully converts some Jews, he fails to convince others.[44] In the book of hours, the last two images illustrating this story represent these successful and failed conversions; in the first, a light-skinned new Christian converts and heals a similarly complected Jew by the miraculous means of the Virgin's funeral pall (Fig. 3.8).[45] However, in the last image, the white new Christian fails in his attempt to convert and heal a Jew (Fig. 3.9). A caption written in Anglo-Norman at the top of the page explains: "G[iu] ne veut croire romeint avegle" (Jew not wanting to believe remains blind).[46] The Jew expresses his resistance by averting his head and stretching out his hand in a sign of refusal. His skin is colored dark brown and his eyes are closed. These features signal his continued blindness: he literally remains in the dark.[47] The image brings to mind Gregory's idea of the blindness as a sign of inner death and its accompanying experience of hell's torment in life. Alternatively, the figure's closed eyes and dark hue give him the appearance of a corpse. All readings offer the same message: in his blind refusal of Christian salvation, the Jew damns himself to eternal death.

These images of variously colored Jews in English psalter illuminations can be situated in the larger context of developments in medieval society. In her recent wide-ranging analysis of medieval anti-Jewish iconography, Sara Lipton describes a "new intensity" in Christian perceptions of their world. One way in which it manifests itself is "in a new desire to regulate peoples' appearances and mark peoples' identities. . . and in the use of art to clarify and highlight moral and spiritual correspondences" (2014 166). This impulse to understand and properly organize society includes strategies of marking Jews in a way that realized their subordination. The Fourth Lateran Council (1215), convened by Innocent III, included canon 68, which required Jews and Muslims to wear distinctive clothing. Although the ruling offered as its rationale the need to separate Christians from other faith groups, it required only Jews (and Muslims) to wear distinctive clothing, thus establishing asymmetrical and hierarchical identities (Grayzel 1966, 67, 309).[48] As Lipton observes,

> New signs, too, were devised to make Jews' appearances project their desired state of subjection. . . . The imposition of the Jewish badge . . . attempted to restore social and moral clarity, to reestablish a correlation between identity and outward aspect. . . . Perhaps the most graphic, and ultimately the most powerful, of all the means by which the church tried simultaneously to caution against confusion and model heavenly hierarchy was art. (2014, 164–65)

Hence, the larger forces that sought to impose order in the social realm also operate in the sphere of visual representation.[49]

One such new sign of subjection was the creation of a set of stereotyped attributes used to depict Jews, which Lipton situates within the growing interest in the natural world and human body that emerges in first part of the thirteenth century:[50] "In a growing number of artworks, the range of features assigned iniquitous Jews was condensed into one fairly narrowly construed and easily recognizable Gothic 'Jewish' face, . . . [whose] features alone could serve to signify 'Jewishness'" (2014, 173).[51] In attempting to explain the function of this artistic construction, Lipton queries whether, in response to ecclesiastical complaints about Jewish indistinguishability from Christians, "the assigning of fixed facial features to Jews [was] merely a new way to express and address this problem, enrolling the innovative language of artistic naturalism to outwardly embody invisible spiritual flaws?" (2014, 175).[52] Parallel to this visual development is the exploration of the nature of the Jewish complexion in natural philosophy, medicine and other discourses. As noted in chapter 2, several authors ascribe a pallid complexion to Jews as a result of their bleeding disease.[53] In a much discussed anecdote, the English chronicler Orderic Vitalis describes a descendent of converts from Judaism as "nigrum et pallidum . . . magis Judaeo vel Agareno quam Christiano similem" [black and pallid, more like a Jew or Muslim than a Christian] (qtd. in Stroll 167, n. 44).[54] As suggested in the color descriptors discussed above, blackness and pallor can co-exist in a single complexion, and this combination seems to be a defining quality of Jewish and Muslim appearance, in contrast to that of Christians.

Lipton concludes her discussion of the invention of the Jewish caricature by considering the effect of these images on the elite and royal audience for whom they were produced:

> It was their duty as Christian rulers to strive to make the visible world approximate as nearly as possible the City of God. And the Gothic Jew's face showed them the way, in directing their attention toward a visible population ripe for correction or punishment. . . . Viewers thus came to be trained to look to Jews' bodies and faces for confirmation of their difference. . . . When authorities gazed on the sign of the "Jew's face," they saw a figure whom, above all others, they *could* and *should* identify, mark, and control. (2014, 197–98)

I would take this argument one step further to suggest that some of the derogatory images of Jews represent them as subordinates whose status must be realized through ecclesiastical and secular enforcement in order to move toward the ideal City of God. Hence, as Lipton points out, art does not necessarily simply reflect reality, but it can influence and alter the status quo: "Anti-Jewish imagery was a significant factor in the *creation* of the attitudes and conditions it is often held to reflect" (Lipton 2014, 10). In fact, the first Oxford psalters that represent Jews with dark skin actually predate and thus anticipate the innovations Lipton considers. Furthermore, the dark colors in the psalter images do not simply reflect attitudes about the actual complexions of Jews; the preponderance of medieval visual images prior to the thirteenth century represents Jews and Christians as virtually identical. Additionally, the laws requiring the former to wear distinguishing attire indicate that the two groups shared a common appearance. Rather, the discourses on Jewish appearances as well as developments in their visual representation instead reveal attempts to construct and impose an innovative meaning upon Jews. I argue that the psalters produced in the Oxford context employ a varied palette of colors associated with death to create a new understanding of Jewish inferiority. This invention appears in the precise context of Jesus's Passion, in which the Jews who torture and murder Jesus condemn themselves to death even as Jesus conquers it and offers salvation to the faithful.[55] In rejecting Jesus, Jews consign themselves to a differently imagined cursed subordination: the abjection of eternal damnation.

In the early thirteenth century, papal and conciliar rulings drew on figures of Jewish servitude to condemn emphatically the impious exercise of authority by Jews over Christians. The psalter illuminations of the Passion scenes explicitly illustrate this blasphemy in representing Jews as enemies of the faith who physically attack the body of Jesus. In subjecting him to humiliating violence, the Jews appear to reduce Jesus to a servile status; the images of flogging, carrying the cross, and crucifixion all reference punishing tortures initially imposed exclusively upon enslaved persons (Bernstein, 115–16, 122).[56] Although these illustrations ostensibly depict the Jews tormenting and ultimately killing Jesus, both Christian doctrine and the scenes that follow teach that Jesus, by enduring death, defeats it. At the moment of Jesus's suffering and death, dark-skinned Jews attest rather to their own demise and damnation. Original sin condemns all humanity to death, but Jesus's sacrifice redeems the faithful to eternal life.[57] The Jews, in their blind rejection of Jesus as the Messiah, cut themselves off from forgiveness and life. They give themselves over not only to cursed servitude in this world, but also to everlasting darkness, damnation, and death in the next. Augustine explains that this fate awaits all infidels in the afterlife who, like the Jews, reject salvation: "the catastrophe of the second death that has no end" (*Civitate Dei* 13.14, 181). Ultimately representing Jesus's triumph, these depictions visualize the popes' call for Jews to be forced into their proper servile position in Christian society. The dark Jews who reject Jesus in these portrayals embody the consequences of sin, servitude and eternal death.

The use of dark colors to depict the Jewish enemies of Jesus certainly draws from negative associations that are also applied to Africans.

Nevertheless, even though degrading portrayals of Africans appear in colors associated with demons, death, and damnation, not all uses of these colors have Africans as their primary target. Dark-skinned Jews appearing in English psalter illuminations employ colors connoting a range of negative associations: death and damnation provide the most salient resonances in images of the Passion that ultimately illustrate Jesus conquering death even as Jews succumb to it. The psalter portrayals depict a point of Christian doctrine regarding the lasting effects of death as a result of original sin and the power of grace to grant liberty and life. Jews, in rejecting Jesus as the Messiah, cut themselves off from forgiveness, freedom, and life and give themselves over to death, damnation, and the perpetual servitude of hell's torments.[58] Though they can convert and be whitened, those who refuse salvation through faith in Jesus remain dark and, in essence, dead. The Jews' coloring indicates their experience of the punishments of hell during their lives. As a people relegated to hell—that is, the lower world, and its humiliating torture—dark Jews proclaim their status as infernal inferiors. Even while artists draw on color symbolism formulated with recourse to denigrations of Africans to represent demonic, damned Jews, these images contribute new meanings to that destructive tradition.

4

Jewish Ham

DEVELOPING A DISCOURSE OF
HEREDITARY INFERIORITY

SCHOLARS HAVE EXTENSIVELY debated the role played by the Genesis
account of Noah's curse of Ham's offspring in the development and per-
petuation of the enslavement of African peoples and the history of racism.
Many of these studies include consideration of the theological antecedents
that link the curse of slavery articulated in the biblical text to black skin,
a connection absent from the original Hebrew.[1] Central points of con-
tention include attempts to locate within Jewish, Christian, and Muslim
traditions the origin of the notion of Ham as black, the role played by
the idea of Ham's curse in the Atlantic trade in enslaved persons and the
contribution this biblical story made to the development of race. Largely
missing from this discussion is a systematic consideration of role played
by the association of Ham with the *servitus Judaeorum* in patristic and medieval Christian writings. There is good reason for this: whatever influence Noah's curse's had on the history of slavery, the figure's association
with Jews was not accompanied by their subjection to chattel servitude.
Furthermore, in rightly focusing on the centrality of blackness in the development of Noah's curse, analyses of racism and American slavery have
tended to consider as attendant, rather than separate, the history of the
other important element of his punishment: hereditary slavery.

While the Genesis text already articulates the cursed enslavement of
Ham's offspring, early Christian exegetes elaborate on the causes and consequences of this servitude to explain God's institution of slavery, both generally and specifically with regard to the Jews. In this chapter, I begin with
Augustine's analysis of the Ham narrative to explain all human slavery as

punishment for sin, as well the servitude of the Jews. Other patristic and medieval commentaries similarly equate Ham with the Jews, emphasizing the hereditary nature of the curse; although Ham transgressed, the malediction of servitude afflicts his offspring Canaan. The familiar verse from Matthew appears in these discussions as a proof-text for the original crime and the punishment of the progeny of its perpetrators. This identification of Ham with the Jews continues to circulate widely in later medieval popular culture. At the same time the Jewish connection is solidified, exegetes also begin to identify Ham geographically; sometimes the same author interprets Ham's offspring as enslaved Jews and more neutrally as inhabitants of Africa. The emergence of this African–Jewish imaginary from a theological nexus also appears in a thirteenth-century visual rendition of the biblical genealogy of Ham that places Jews and Africans among his offspring. While early modern exegesis continues to circulate Ham's identification with Jews, it also de-emphasizes this association just as the deployment of African Ham gains traction. This accounts in part for the omission of Jewish Ham in analyses of the trade in enslaved Africans and the history of racism. However, an examination of the curse of Ham as a figure for the Jews helps identify and trace the important concept of perpetual servitude, a necessary element in the development of the status of the African as similarly cursed with hereditary inferiority, one that undergirds both the trade in enslaved persons and the ideology of racism.

Figural Ham

Augustine develops his theory of the origin of slavery in *De Civitate Dei* (c. 411–426) with recourse to the Genesis account of Noah's cursing of Canaan, the son of Ham.[2] He opens with a discussion of the pronouncement in Genesis 1:26 that humans should have dominion over all the animals. From this he deduces that God

> did not wish a rational creature, made in his own image, to have dominion save over irrational creatures: not man over man, but man over the beasts. So it was that the first just men were established as shepherds of flocks, rather than as kings of men, so that even so God might indirectly point out what is required by the principle of gradation among his creatures, and what the guilt of sinners demands; for of course it is understood that the condition of slavery is justly imposed on the sinner. Wherefore we do not read of a slave

anywhere in the Scriptures until the just man Noah branded his
son's sin with this word; so he earned this name by his fault, not by
nature. [gives etymology of slave] . . .

The prime cause of slavery, then, is sin, so that man was put
under man in a state of bondage. . . . But by nature, in which God
first created man, no man is the slave either of another man or of
sin. Yet slavery as a punishment is also ordained by that law which
bids us to preserve the natural order and forbids us to disturb it; for
if nothing had been done contrary to that law, there would have been
nothing requiring the check of punishment by slavery. (*Civitate Dei*
19. 15, 187–89)

Prior to the advent of sin, God did not intend for humans to rule over
each other, establishing an original equality between all people. Animals,
understood as irrational creatures, thus occupy a lower status that permits their domination by superior humans. Sin introduces hierarchy into
human relationships; slavery serves as a punishment that subjects sinners
to the status of the irrational animal and thus delivers them into the power
of another human being. Although one would expect Augustine to locate
the effects of sin on human autonomy in the moment of the fall, he instead relies here on Noah's curse.[3] As he explains, the term "slave" does
not appear in the biblical text until Noah uses it to brand his son's sin.
The introduction of the institution of slavery at this later point in human
history provides support for his argument that God created humans free
from sin: thus, there are no natural slaves and slavery is not a part of the
natural order.[4]

A consideration of the verses in Genesis describing this curse alerts us
to a number of interpretive cruxes that Augustine and subsequent commentators will attempt to settle.

And Noe, a husbandman, began to till the ground, and planted a
vineyard. And drinking of the wine was made drunk, and was uncovered in his tent. Which when Ham the father of Chanaan had
seen, to wit, that his father's nakedness was uncovered, he told it to
his two brethren without. But Sem and Japheth put a cloak upon
their shoulders, and going backward, covered the nakedness of
their father: and their faces were turned away, and they saw not their
father's nakedness. And Noe awaking from the wine, when he had
learned what his younger son had done to him, He said: Cursed be

Chanaan, a [slave] of [slaves] shall he be unto his brethren. And he said: Blessed be the Lord God of Sem, be Chanaan his [slave]. May God enlarge Japheth, and may he dwell in the tents of Sem, and Chanaan be his [slave]. (Genesis 9:20–27)

One of the first questions the text raises is how to interpret the Hebrew term עבד (*eved*), rendered in Latin as *servus,* used to denote Canaan's cursed status; in both languages it can be translated as either "slave" or "servant." That Augustine uses this episode and this term to identify it as the origin of slavery indicates that "slave" offers the more apt definition for our discussion.[5] The text offers support for this reading in its intensification Canaan's inferior status, prophesying that he will be a "slave of slaves" and twice repeating the prediction of his servitude to his brothers. The text poses another conundrum in that Noah curses his apparently innocent grandson Canaan, rather than the actual sinner, with the punishment of servitude. Contrary to the evidence of the text, Augustine states that Noah "branded the sin of his son with this name." While he offers other interpretations for this text that address this question elsewhere, here his primary concern lies with establishing the origin of slavery rather than the object of the malediction.[6]

However, this is not Augustine's only or even his first analysis of the curse of slavery articulated in Genesis 9. We have already briefly considered the text of the *Contra Faustum* (c. 398–399), in which he identifies Ham, in addition to Cain, as a figure predicting the enslavement of the Jews. It might be argued that the reading of Jewish slavery lays the groundwork for the later analysis of slavery in *Civitate Dei*.[7] In the *Contra Faustum,* this discussion takes place in the context of explaining the figures for Jesus in the Hebrew Bible in an effort to prove to Faustus that the prophets predicted Jesus's coming. Several paragraphs after the account of Abel as a type for Jesus, Augustine interprets Genesis 9 to prove that Noah is another such type:[8]

Again, the sufferings of Christ from His own nation are evidently denoted by Noah being drunk with the wine of the vineyard he planted, and his being uncovered in his tent. . . . Moreover, the two sons, the eldest and the youngest, carrying the garment backwards, are a figure of the two peoples, and the sacrament of the past and completed passions of the Lord. They do not see the nakedness of their father, because they do not consent to Christ's death; and yet they honor it with a covering, as knowing whence they were born. The middle son is the Jewish people, for they neither held the first place with the apostles, nor believed subsequently with the Gentiles. They saw the nakedness of their father, because they consented to Christ's death; and they told it to their brethren outside, for what was hidden in the prophets was disclosed by the Jews. And thus they are the [slaves] of their brethren. For what else is this nation now but a [bookslave] for the Christians, bearing the law and the prophets, and testifying to the [manumission] of the Church, so that we honor in the sacrament what they disclose in the letter? (12.23, 190–91)

Because he focuses on exegesis here, Augustine offers a much more detailed analysis of the episode. He opens by emphasizing the Jews' role in the crucifixion: "the sufferings of Christ from His own nation are evidently denoted by Noah"; Jesus is a member of the people of Israel. All three brothers are accounted for in this construal: Shem, the eldest, stands for the apostles, Jesus's Jewish followers, and Japhet, the youngest, represents the Gentile adherents. Augustine recasts the Pauline elder/ younger dichotomy by identifying the former not as superseded, but as Jews who believed in Jesus. However, he also identifies Ham, the middle son, with the Jews. The text establishes a distinction here: they are the Jewish people who consented in Jesus's death. These Jews consequently serve as text-bearers, proving the authenticity of the Hebrew scripture employed in the defense of Christian doctrine; the metaphor of the bookslave implies not only the Jews' supersession, but their servitude to Christian masters. Noah's curse of Canaan is fulfilled implicitly in the case of contemporary Jews, the figure of Ham's offspring, who are now slaves to their brethren, believing Christians, into which both Shem and Japhet have been subsumed.[9]

Augustine's expansion of the episode of Noah's drunkenness from a figure for Jesus to an explanation and justification of contemporary Jewish servitude influences many subsequent interpretations of the text. As noted in chapter 1, Procopius of Gaza's commentary on Genesis also includes an exploration of the typological meaning of Noah's nakedness and the curse of servitude.

Now to dwell on a little allegory. Noah the farmer planted and prepared the most beautiful vines, namely his people in Christ. Noah

first drank from the vine, so Christ, of whom he was a type, suffered. Noah was drunk, so Christ's passion was completed. Noah
was naked in his own house: so Christ was crucified by the Jews.
Ham is the type of the Jewish people, who mocked Christ hanging
from the cross; . . . . In truth Christ assigned the Jews to perpetual
servitude, saying "All who sin, are slaves to sin. But the slave
does not remain in the house forever. If therefore the Son shall
release you from servitude into liberty, you are free." [John 8:34–
6] . . . "And let Canaan be his slave," etc. Do you see if the prophetic
speech of Noah resonates at all? In truth, Madian, that is, Mede,
son of Japheth, took possession of the very beautiful tabernacle and
building of Shem; one may know Media, of which Persia is not a
small part. By this passage the Roman Empire could be predicted,
which invaded the tabernacle of Shem and Canaan. So the oracle of
Noah, which speaks in the way of blessing, ends in a curse. In that
the Jews were slaves to the Persians and the Romans, and Canaan
still is subject to slavery.

(*Commentarii in Genesin, Patrologiae Graecae* 87a IX cols 306–7,
my translation)[10]

We see the reinforcement of the idea of Noah as a type for Jesus, and more
focus on explaining the elements of the Genesis narrative. Here the vineyard takes on significance as symbolizing Jesus's followers, while drinking
and drunkenness are glossed separately. Procopius makes explicit the
equation between Noah's house and the Jewish people; Jesus was crucified by his own people, the Jews. He reinforces the notion of Ham as a
figure of the Jews and interprets Noah's curse as Jesus assigning the Jews
not only to servitude, but to perpetual slavery. While he seems to mitigate
this curse with the quotation from John, which states that Jesus can free
the Jews from their slavery, his subsequent discussion does not contemplate this final conversion. Instead, Procopius focuses on the continued
enslavement of the Jews in history. He interprets the name of Japhet's
son Madai to signify the Medes or Persians, by which he probably means
the Babylonians who conquered Israel, effected the destruction of the first
Temple, and enforced the exile of a significant number of Jews.[11] The text
identifies the Temple as belonging to Shem, the forefather of the Jews
according to biblical genealogy. This invasion and subjection prefigures
that inflicted subsequently by the Roman Empire on the Temple of Shem
and Canaan. Procopius assumes a supersessionary logic here: before the

advent of Jesus, the Jews are the descendants of Shem, who built both the first and second Temples. After the crucifixion, Shem's line represents the Jews who believed in Jesus and in effect became Christians, while the unbelieving Jews are placed among the descendants of the cursed Canaan and subject to slavery. The second Temple destroyed by the Romans pertained both to the line of Shem and Canaan, since it pre- and post-dated the crucifixion. Thus Noah's prophecy resonates through time in its fulfilment both prior to and following Jesus's death. The Jews' identity as slaves is established through prophecy even before they allegedly participate in the crime of the crucifixion and continues to Procopius's own time: "Canaan still is subject to slavery."

The ideas cumulatively set forth by Augustine and Procopius—the identification of Ham with the Jews and Noah's cursing of Canaan and his offspring into slavery—find a full and coherent synthesis in Isidore of Seville's (7th c.) commentary on Genesis 9 in the *Mysticorum Expositiones Sacramentorum Seu Quaestiones In Vetus Testamentum*. He establishes Noah as a figure for Jesus and then lists the elements in the biblical narrative, succinctly pairing them with their figurative counterparts:

> Now, truly, that one who after the flood was drunk from the vine he planted is Noah, and was uncovered in his own house, to whom does he not appear to be a figure of Christ? Who was made drunk, while he suffered; was naked, while he was crucified; in his own house, that is, among his people, and among his household members, certainly, the Jews. (*Mysticorum, Patrologia Latina* vol. 83 8 col 235A–B, my translation)[12]

Isidore equates Noah's drunkenness and nudity with Jesus's suffering and human vulnerability during the crucifixion and identifies Noah's house as Jesus's people, the Jews. His discussion of Ham borrows, if not quotes directly from Augustine's discussions:

> Which nakedness, that is, the suffering of Christ, Ham seeing, he derided, and the Jews, seeing the death of Christ, mocked. Moreover Ham, the middle brother, he is the impious people of the Jews (for that reason the middle, because it neither held the primacy of the apostles, nor last believed among the nations), he saw the nakedness of the father, because [the Jewish people] agreed to the death of the Lord Saviour. Afterward, he publicly

reported this to his brothers. Through him, of course, is made manifest, and published in a certain way, all that was in the secret prophecy. And for that reason he was made a slave to his brothers. For what else indeed is this same nation today, but a bookslave for the Christians, bearing the law and prophets and testifying to the manumission of the Church, so that we can honor in the sacrament what they disclose in the letter? (*Mysticorum, Patrologia Latina* vol. 83 8 cols. 235C–236A, my translation, with reliance on my translation of Augustine)[13]

Ham's viewing of his father's nakedness becomes the Jews' mocking of the crucifixion, an idea Procopius set forth, but the explanation of the middle brother as belonging neither to the Apostles nor the believing gentiles and as a slave to both, follows Augustine's explanation in the *Contra Faustum*.[14]

Up to this point, Isidore's commentary comprises an organized restating of views expressed variously by Augustine and Procopius. However, in the following section, which iterates the view of Ham and Canaan as the Jews, he brings in a clarifying proof-text not adduced by either commentary.

Also with respect to which, Ham sinning, his offspring were damned, it signifies insofar as the reprobates here indeed offend, but in the coming generation, that is, in the future, they receive the sentence of condemnation. And in the same way the mob of Jews, who crucified the Lord, even now transmit the penalty of their damnation to their children. For they said: His blood be upon us and upon our children (Matt. 27:25). (*Patrologia Latina,* vol. 83 8 col. 237A, my translation)[15]

Procopius articulated the idea, implicit in Augustine, that the enslavement of Canaan, Ham's descendant, foreshadows the enslavement of the Jews after the crucifixion. Here Isidore quotes Matthew 27:25 to explain how the curse passed from the Jews who participated in the crucifixion, as represented by Ham, to their offspring, as represented by Canaan. This curse condemns him as a slave to his brothers—or their descendants—which holds true up to the contemporary moment: "For what else indeed is this same nation today, but a bookslave for the Christians, bearing the law and prophets and testifying to the manumission of the Church?" The familiar verse from Matthew operates in this context to solve definitively the crux of Ham sinning while Canaan is cursed: it demonstrates the effect of the curse in the current subordinated status of the Jews, while also accounting for its transmission from their sinning forefathers.[16]

Isidore's formulation appears to influence the writings of Bede (8th c.), who repeats his ideas about Jewish servitude and its transmission to subsequent generations.[17] The analysis of Genesis in his *In Pentateuchum Commentarii* repeats many of Isidore's points, sometimes word for word. However, he elides Canaan from the biblical text, replacing him with his father Ham, even when appearing to quote scripture:

> By the younger son the people of the Jews is denoted. Cursed be Ham: seems to prefigure the vengeance on the Jews. It is said moreover that Ham would be a slave to Shem and Japhet; through which is understood the wicked portion of the Jews would be bowing to the good portion of the Jews and the people of the Gentiles. In truth, Ham is the people of the Jews, Shem is the good portion of the people of the Jews, and Japhet, the people of the Gentiles. (*Expositio In Primum Librum Mosis, Patrologia Latina* vol. 91 9 col. 228A, my translation)[18]

The text iterates the direct identification of Ham with the Jews, but in transferring Canaan's punishment to his father, Bede reinforces the idea that the Jews have been made slaves to Shem and Japhet. He expands on Isidore's language to describe Ham as representing "the evil portion of the Jews" who embody their subservience to the "good" Jews and Gentiles by bowing to them. While he imagines the existence of good Jews, he clearly subsumes this group into the larger community of believing Christians. This becomes evident in another lightly emended statement borrowed from Isidore and Augustine:

> Blessed be the Lord God of Shem; Ham will be his slave. For what else is the people of the Jews, but a slave of the Christian people, bearing the law and the prophets, so that we may honor through the sacraments which they announce through the letter. (*Patrologia Latina* vol. 91 9 col. 228C, my translation)[19]

The good Jews disappear into the category of "Christian people," leaving only wicked Jews behind. He also replaces the term *scriniaria* (book desk or bookslave) with *servus*, making explicit the idea in Augustine's metaphor. Furthermore, Bede understands Ham's enslavement to his brother

Shem as effectively reducing the Jewish people to slaves of the Christians. Neither Isidore nor Augustine state this so directly, but convey the idea with pronouns while hewing to the typological language of the text: "they are the [slaves] of their brethren" or "he was made a slave to his brothers" (Augustine *Contra Faustum*, Isisdore *Quaestiones*). Bede also repeats the hereditary nature of this condition:

> Although Ham was in the wrong, his posterity was damned, because the reprobates offend in the present circumstances, but they receive the condemnation in the future. And in fact the Jews transmitted the condemnation to the coming generations, saying: "His blood be on us and on our children." (*Patrologia Latina* vol. 91 9 col. 228D, my translation)

Bede's phrasing emphasizes the position of servitude inhabited by contemporary Jews, which he reinforces by repeating Isidore's point about Ham's children being punished in his stead and quotation of Matthew 27:25.[20]

Isidore's far-reaching influence also registers in the writings of Rabanus Maurus (d. 856), who similarly identifies Ham as a figure for the Jews.[21] In his *Commentariorum in Genesim* (c. 819, as dated in the *Patrologia Latina*) he names many of his sources, which include both Augustine and Isidore. He quotes verbatim from Isidore's *Quaestiones In Vetus Testamentum*, choosing the two passages discussed earlier which emphasize the Jews' subjection to Christians and the hereditary curse. In the first, he reprises the idea that the prophecy predicting enslavement to Ham's brothers has been fulfilled in the servitude of the Jews, who are now the archive keeper and book bearer/slave of the Christians.[22] In the second, he repeats the allegory which uses Matthew 27 to explain how Canaan's punishment for Ham's crime figures the Jews who condemned their descendants at the time of the crucifixion.[23]

The interpretations developed by Augustine and Isidore were widely adapted. According to Longland, "Once the idea of the allegory took root, it was repeated and added to in the writings of every commentator" (53). One such commentary, the *Allegoriae in Vetus Testamentum* by Richard of St. Victor (d. 1173), synthesizes the idea of Jewish hereditary servitude quite forcefully:[24]

> Unhappy Ham signifies the faithless Jewish people who derided [Jesus]. . . . Wherefore Chanaan the son of Ham is punished with a

curse, and thus so will the descendants of the Jews be damned [be-
cause of the curse of the Jews. And Chanaan son of Ham becomes
a slave of slaves, because the unbelieving successors of the Jews
are slaves of Christians, insofar as Christians are slaves to Christ,
whom to serve is to reign. The curse of Canaan, the son of Ham,
is the damnation and the scattering of the Jewish nation.] (partially
qtd. in Longland, 54, with my translation in brackets)[25]

The punishment of Canaan for his father's transgression again figures
the children of the Jews whose sin brought about an intergenerational
curse. Richard does not cite Matthew 27:25, but conveys his point effectively nonetheless. Richard explains Noah's curse that Canaan will be a
slave of slaves by identifying the Jews as slaves to Christians, who in turn
are slaves to Jesus. However, Christian servitude paradoxically constitutes
a type of domination: to serve Jesus is to reign, as it were, over the Jews.
To illustrate the subjection of the Jews, Richard cites their damnation and
dispersal from their land, perhaps intimating Cain's figuring of Jewish
servitude and exile.

I adduce one last piece of evidence to indicate the authoritative weight
of the association of the Ham narrative with Jews and hereditary subjection: the *Glossa Ordinaria*, the definitive edition of the Latin Bible that included marginal and interlinear commentaries and circulated throughout
Europe in numerous manuscript copies beginning in the mid-twelfth century (Lesley Smith, 1). In the *Glossa*, the text of Isidore's interpretation of
the enslavement of the Jews, relying on Augustine's view, surrounds the
verses from Genesis relating the curse of Canaan.[26] Additionally, the editors intersperse between the lines of the biblical verses quotations from
patristic commentaries as glosses on particular words. The lines relevant
to Ham and Canaan are quoted here with the corresponding notes included in brackets:

Ham [Because he assented to the death of Christ. The middle
brother, that is, the Jewish people, who neither held the primacy of
the apostles, nor last believed among the nations. Israel according
to the flesh.] (*Genesis . . . cum glossa* Gen 9:22, 40r image 83)[27]

As we have seen in previous interpretations, the text identifies Ham with
those who agreed to the crucifixion of Jesus: Israel of the flesh, the Jews,
in contrast to Israel of the spirit, the Christians.[28] The interlinear gloss

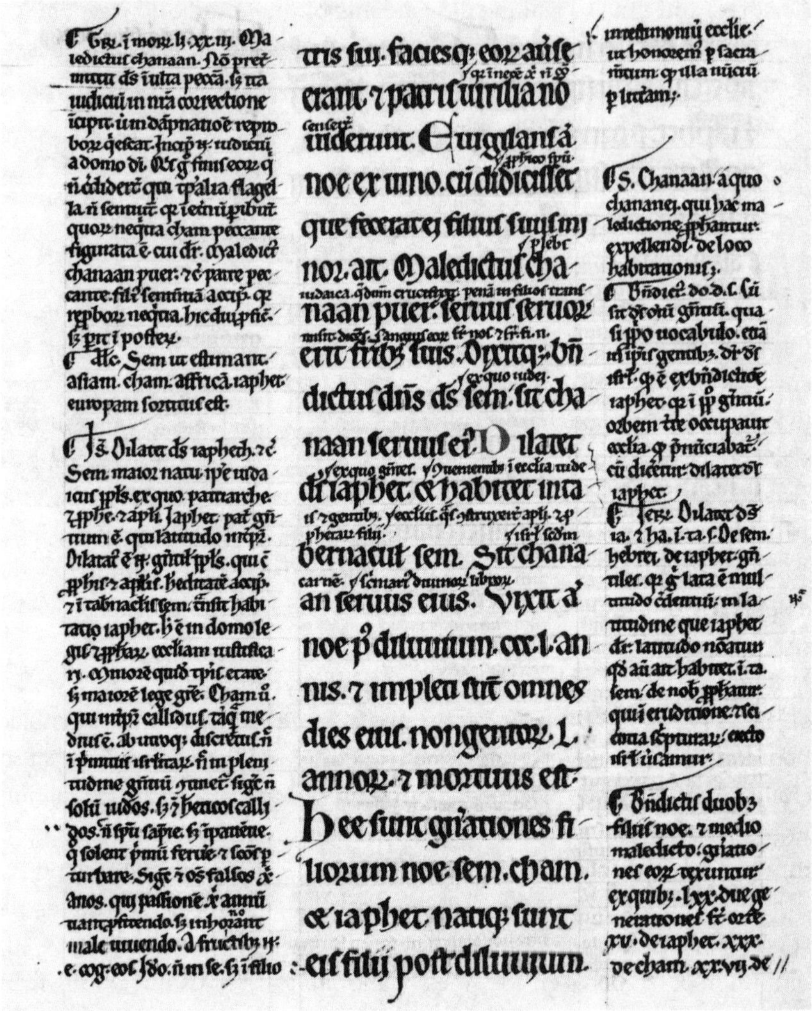

FIGURE 4.1 Page from the *Glossa Ordinaria* that includes the text of Genesis 9:24–29 and accompanying commentaries.

Bayerische Staatsbibliothek München, Clm 14132, *Genesis et Exodus cum glossa ordinaria* fol 40v, urn: nbn:de:bvb:12-bsb00034372-2.

also repeats previous exegetes who distinguish the Jewish people from the Apostles and the Gentiles who believe in Jesus (Figure 4.1).

> Noe . . . said: Cursed be Chanaan, the child, a slave of slaves shall
> he be unto his brethren. [The Jewish mob, who, while it crucified

Christ transferred punishment to the children, saying: His blood be on us and on our children,] And he said: Blessed be the Lord God of Sem, [from whom are the Jews] let Chanaan be his slave. May God enlarge Japheth, [From whom are the Gentiles] and may he dwell [the Jews and Gentiles coming together in the Church] in the tents of Sem, [the churches which the apostles, children of the Prophets, constructed] and let Chanaan be his slave [Israel according to the flesh. Book-slave of divine books]. (40v, image 84, my translation; gloss in brackets)[29]

The text explains Noah's cursing of Canaan with the reason synthesized by Isidore, linking it, by means of Matthew 27:25, to the Jews who called down punishment on their children at the time of the crucifixion. Here, as in Isidore and elsewhere, they are "Plebs Iudaica," which I have translated as "mob," and which carries the sense of lower class Jews. This idea reinforces the notion of Jewish inferiority in contrast to the status of Jesus's supporters, both the Jewish apostles and the Gentiles. While the gloss indicates that the Jews descended from Shem, as the biblical text makes clear, these are not the "Plebs Iudaica," but the foreparents of Israel who antedate Jesus and constitute his own ancestors and those of the apostles. This text adds a word to the Vulgate version in describing Canaan as *puer*: while this term can simply emphasize that he is the child of Ham, it also denotes a servant. It thus conveys the sense of hereditary inferiority: Canaan represents the offspring of Jewish deicides who have been cursed with subjection to their Christian brothers. Additionally, the presentation of two groups of Jews again serves to reinforce the hierarchy of Christians over Jews, as Shem and Japhet merge together into the Christian Ecclesia. The tents of Shem that Japhet inhabits figure the churches built by the noble line of prophets, parents of the apostles; Christians now occupy these sanctuaries. Following Augustine's formulation, the Jews serve as bookslaves, a sign of their subordination to Christian interpretation and power. The identification of Ham with the enslavement of the Jews is literally written into the margins and text of the Bible itself.

Given its centuries-long articulation culminating and circulating in the authoritative *Glossa Ordinaria*, the association of Ham with the Jews not surprisingly appears widely through figural representations in visual and popular culture. The *Pictor in Carmine*, a collection of biblical types and antitypes for use by artists, provides an important and similarly influential example (James, 141).[30] The anonymous author, deploring the contemporary state of church decoration, compiled these examples from the Bible, along with brief explanations, to provide artists with more suitable topics for contemplation by worshippers (142). The text thus presents a convenient interpretive system for artists and viewers to understand the prophetic significance of events narrated in the Hebrew Bible.[31] These images would have provided worshippers with an influential visual rendering of Scriptural texts to which only a few would otherwise have had direct access. The manuscript consists of a preface in which the author explains his purpose, a list of titles of antitypes and their various types, and finally explanatory couplets, between two and six in number, for each type. For the antitype *Crucifigitur Christus* (Christ is crucified) seventeen types are listed, including: "Cain occidit Abel fratrum suum in agro" [Cain kills Abel, his brother, in the field] (161). In the chapter titled "Deridetur in cruce pendens a principibus sacerdotum" [Hanging on the cross, he is mocked by the high priests], the text lists four types, including "Cham deridet pudenda patris sui detecta et nunciat duobus fratribus suis" [Ham mocks the exposed genitals of his father and announces it to his two brothers] (162). While other types are included, both antitypes link their types to Jewish crimes—Cain as figuring the Jews who participated in the crucifixion, Ham as a type for the Jewish priests who mocked Jesus on the cross.

The link between Ham and the Jews appears in English visual art even prior to the writing of the earliest manuscript of the *Pictor in Carmine*.[32] The late twelfth-century ivory crucifix, the Bury St. Edmunds or Cloisters Cross, includes the following inscription on the long side of the upright piece: CHAM RIDET DVM NVDA VIDET PVDIBUNDA PARENTIS + JVDEI RISERE DEI PENAM MOR[IENTIS] (Ham laughs when he sees the father's naked genitals + The Jews laughed at the pain of God dying) (Parker and Little, 52). Here the Ham narrative from Genesis provides the caption for the image of the crucified Jesus. As Parker and Little note, this verse is written in upper-case letters, making it and its partner verse the most legible of the cross's inscriptions.[33] Taken together, these verses "declare that even though the Jews mocked the dying Christ, through him Death and Synagogue are defeated" (56). The dominant message of this image declares the victory of Jesus over his Jewish adversaries, and the supersession of Judaism by Christianity. Once again, the motif of Ham mocking Noah's nakedness provides the vehicle for expounding the tenor of Jewish subjection to Christianity.

While the impact of this one cross might have been limited in scope, the verse connecting Ham and the Jews evidently circulated through a number of different texts in the twelfth and thirteenth centuries.[34] In her research on this couplet and its origins, Sabrina Longland has discovered that variants appeared in manuscripts in England, France, and Austria. A very similar version of the distich appears as a marginal notation to a passage discussing Noah and Ham in a manuscript of Peter Comestor's *Historica Scholastica*, a condensed history of the Hebrew Bible. Although the provenance of the manuscript is unknown, Longland assumes the scribe is not the author of this "versiculus" and suggests that the couplet was "apparently known in literary circles by that time" (Longland, 54). Another rendering appears in the standard version of a sermon in the *Sermones Dominicales* by the thirteenth-century English author Odo of Cheriton. Longland has found nine examples of this verse in copies of Odo's sermons, four of which were produced in England (55, 67). In addition, she has found similar versions of the couplet in four verse collections: two thirteenth-century compilations of Latin verses produced in France, a fourteenth-century Austrian manuscript containing verses, and a fourteenth-century Welsh manuscript of a biblical poem, in which the couplet appears in a marginal note (61–3, 64, 66).

The association of Ham with the Jews would have reached an even wider audience in the circulation of numerous copies of the *Speculum Humanae Salvationis*, an anonymous fourteenth-century text that uses figures from the Hebrew Bible, often represented in illustrations, to explain the fall and redemption of humankind.[35] It considers Christian history beginning with the narratives in Genesis and concluding with the Seven Joys of the Virgin. Of the work's forty-five chapters, forty deal with the Passion of Jesus and the life of Mary; each of these includes one antitype from Christian Scripture and three types from the Hebrew Bible (Scott, 178–79). The text provided typological explanations of sin and salvation, drawing from motifs set out in existing Bible commentaries, that the clergy could make use of in sermons. However, the *Speculum* is clearly also intended for lay use, given its translation into the vernacular and its inclusion of images, through which the illiterate could have access to the Bible. Thus it enables a wide dispersion of typological representations, including the use of Ham to figure the Jews in both verbal and visual forms, to almost every level of medieval society (Wilson and Wilson, 24).

The copies of the *Speculum* that include illuminations typically present an image of the mocking of Jesus with illustrations of three other types, one of which is Ham viewing Noah's nakedness. The Wilsons note that all copies of the *Speculum* produced up to the fifteenth century "followed the precise numerical pattern of the original manuscript and the subjects and iconography of its miniatures." The sequence of these subjects is "identical" across the various texts (10). Thus, the association of Ham with the Jews' mocking of Jesus was firmly established and widely circulated in these popular texts. In this interpretation of the typological significance of Ham's action, the moment of the Jews' mocking shifts from the crucifixion, as indicated in patristic exegesis, to the trial before Caiaphas.[36] The anti-type of the mocking appears in Matthew 26:67, Mark 14:65, and Luke 22:63–4; in all accounts, the Jewish chief priests, elders, and scribes attack and ridicule Jesus when he appears before the high priest Caiaphas: "Then did they spit in his face, and buffeted him: and others struck his face with the palms of their hands,/Saying: Prophesy unto us, O Christ, who is he that struck thee?" (Matt. 26:67–8).[37]

In an image from the earliest English illustrated manuscript of the *Speculum* (c. 1330–1340) Jesus sits, with his hands crossed, between two groups of two men who mock and attack him (Figure 4.2).[38] The text of the rubricated caption, "Christus fuit uelatus consputus et colaphizatus" [Jesus was veiled, spit upon and beaten], combines elements of the gospel accounts. The text from Luke, written in smaller red letters, appears next to each group of attackers: "prophetiza quis est qui te percussit [Prophesy: who is it that struck thee?]" (22:64). Two Jews, with covered heads, stand in the foreground of the image while holding a transparent veil before Jesus's eyes; he looks directly at the attacker on the left who lifts his hand as if to strike. This figure, presented in denigrating profile, has an elongated nose and a distorted eye. The two rear attackers who lift their hands against Jesus' halo are portrayed with a variety of grotesque features associated with Jews, including balding, grimacing mouths, distorted eyes and noses, and a derogatory winged headdress (Mellinkoff, 1985).

Participating in the pattern that organizes all versions of the *Speculum*, the Sloane manuscript presents images of three types after the antitype. The obverse of the page representing the mocking depicts the figure of Hur kneeling in the midst of a group of Jews who restrain, spit upon, strike, kick, and pull his hair; a figure in the background holds a sheathed sword whose point rests on Hur's leg.[39] The rubricated title explains: "Hur, the husband of Miriam is suffocated by the Jews' spit [Hur uir Marie sputis iudeo{rum} suffocat{ur}]" (Figure 4.3). The image depicts four of the attackers or onlookers with uncovered heads and regular features, in frontal or three-quarter portrayal. One background figure on the left wears a soft, folded hood, while opposite him a bare-headed figure appears in

FIGURE 4.2 The Jews veil and beat Jesus.
© The British Library Board. MS Sloane 346 fol. 5r.

profile, with a distorted mouth, nose and eye. Next to Hur stands a Jew portrayed in profile with a distorted eye and nose, wearing a soft folded cap. He simultaneously kicks, strikes, and spits upon Hur, represented by two thin lines of ink issuing from his mouth. The facing page represents Ham pointing at Noah, asleep on the ground with his uncovered genitals graphically depicted. His two brothers stand alongside, covering their eyes with their right hands, while lifting their robes to cover Noah with their left hands. No distortion appears in the features of any figure. The title, resonating with the couplet on the Cloister's cross, emphasizes that Ham mocks, not merely reports (as Genesis 9:22 states), Noah's nakedness: "Ham derides Noah, his father [Cam deridet patrem suum Noe]" (Figure 4.4). The fourth and final image in this set depicts a scene from Judges; in this rendering, a group of Philistines surround Samson, while some pull his hair (see Judges 16:21–5). The title explains, "The Philistines blind and deride Samson [Philistei excecauerunt sampsonem

FIGURE 4.3 The Jews spit upon Hur, the husband of Miriam.
© The British Library Board. MS Sloane 346 fol. 5v.

et deriserunt]" (Figure 4.5). The three figural images depict and emphasize the derision, violence, and contempt that the Jews direct toward Jesus
in the initial image derived from the Gospel accounts. The repetition and
wide circulation of these fixed patterns would have reinforced the association of Ham with the Jewish enemies of Jesus.[40]

Geographical Ham

While the reading of Ham as a figure for the Jews circulated widely in
the medieval period, commentators also offered other interpretations,
some of which attended to the geographical significance of the Bible's
postdiluvian organization of peoples and lands following the episode of
Noah's curse. In these readings, Ham is primarily associated with the
continent of Africa; as David Aaron comments, "One need only take into
account the genealogies of Genesis 10 to recognize that the biblical text
establishes (some) African peoples as the descendants of Ham" (723).[41] As
Benjamin Braude has noted, the Bible does not associate Ham exclusively

FIGURE 4.4 Ham mocks the nudity of the sleeping Noah while Shem and Japhet hide their eyes.

© The British Library Board. MS Sloane 346 fol. 6r.

with Africa; his progeny also settle in areas that we would now identify as the Middle East (108–11).[42] Writing in the first century, Flavius Josephus follows and elaborates on the biblical distribution of lands to the three sons; as Braude explains, "in effect, [his] designations were that Japhet was Eurasian, Ham Afrasian and Shem Asian" (111). By the end of the eighth century, Alcuin situates each son of Noah's in a separate and particular body of land (Braude, 112–13): "How is the world divided by the sons and grandsons of Noah? As is reckoned, Shem obtained Asia, Ham, Africa, Japhet, Europe" (Alcuin, 95, my translation).[43] While various commentators follow the biblical and Josephan tradition of more complex ascriptions, all situate some portion of Ham's heirs in Africa.

Strikingly, the same authors who develop the most influential and negative association of Ham with cursed, subjected Jews also advance a reading of Ham as the father of African peoples. These latter accounts emphasize Ham's geographical significance rather than advance a moral or allegorical

FIGURE 4.5 The Philistines deride and blind Samson.
© The British Library Board. MS Sloane 346 fol. 6v.

interpretation, even when discussing prophecy. In his *Etymologies*, Isidore includes an explanation of Ham's name in his discussion of people whose names have prophetic significance:

> Cham (i.e. Ham) means "warm," and he was so named as a presaging of his future, for his posterity possessed that part of the land which is warmer because the sun is near. Hence still today Egypt, in the Egyptian language, is called Kam. . . . Canaan the son of Ham is translated "their movement"—and what is this other than "their action"?—for because of the "motion" of his father Ham, that is, because of his action, he was cursed (Genesis 9:25). (2006 VII. vi. 17. 162–63)[44]

We recognize these etymological references from Augustine's discussion, but they are presented here without theological implications. Here the definition of the Hebrew term *cham* meaning warm reveals that Ham's offspring will live in the warm climate of Africa, and is linked in this context with the language of Egypt. While Isidore also glosses Canaan's name, and mentions his curse in relation to Ham, he does not allude to blackness, Jews or servitude.[45] Isidore returns to Ham in his discussion of the names of nations:

> There were four sons of Ham, from whom sprang the following nations. Cush, from whom the Ethiopians were begotten. Mesraim (i.e. Egypt), from whom the Egyptians are said to have risen. Put, from whom came the Libyans—whence the river of Mauretania is called Put still today, and the whole region around it is called Puthensis. Finally Canaan, from whom descended the Africans and the Phoenicians and the ten tribes of Canaanites. . . . There were eleven sons of Canaan, from whom descended the ten tribes of Canaanites, whose land the Jews occupied when the Canaanites were expelled. . . . These are the nations from the stock of Ham, which extend across the whole southern region from Sidon to the Gaditanian Strait (i.e. the Straits of Cadiz). (2006 IX.ii.10–25, p 193)[46]

Influenced by Josephus's account, Isidore locates Ham's sons in the land that descends from the southern edge of the Mediterranean, encompassing modern day Morocco to the west, Lebanon to the east and the vaguely situated Ethiopia. Although he identifies Africans as among the eleven descendants of Canaan, ten of these tribes are associated with the land of Canaan, and the eleventh is not clearly associated with Africa or Phoenicia.[47] While he departs from Josephus in placing some, though not all Africans, in the line of Canaan, he makes no mention of the curse or servitude in this context.

In Book Three of his *Hexaemeron, sive libri quatuor in principium genesis, usque ad nativitatem isaac et electionem ismaelis*, Bede, like Isidore, considers Ham in terms of his geographical location. He opens his discussion of Genesis 10 with an allegorical reading of the significance of the text's ordering of the names of Noah's sons to indicate the gentile supersession of the Jews. However, Shem and not Ham figures the Jews here, following the lineage established in the biblical genealogy. Bede iterates the established tradition of associating each son with a particular area:

> Moreover, the sons of the sons of Noah who are mentioned are believed to come forth as the ancestors of each of the separate tribes who thus divided the world among themselves, so that Shem, the eldest son

occupied Asia, Ham, the second, Africa, Japheth, the last, Europe; so to this extent that, because Asia is the greater situation of lands than Europe or Lybia, the family of Ham and Japhet likewise possess some portion in Asia. (*Patrologia Latina* vol. 91 3col 115b, my translation)[48]

He offers a terse account of the distribution of the world, focusing on the three sons of Noah rather than their progeny and attendant locations. He associates Shem with Asia, Ham with Africa (which he seems to equate or interchange with Lybia), and Europe with Japhet. However, perhaps influenced by the more complex account offered by Isidore, he acknowledges that the peoples and the lands did not divide evenly, reinforcing Braude's claim of an Afrasian Ham. Nevertheless, of the three brothers, only Ham and his descendants are associated with Africa.

Rabanus Maurus similarly conveys the association of Ham with Africa, but he does so in his exegetical *Commentariorum in Genesim*, in the section just subsequent to the passage in which he summarizes Augustine's and Isidore's interpretations of Ham as a figure for cursed Jewish servitude. In describing Ham's African descendents, he relies here on Isidore's discussion in the *Etymologies*.

Also the sons of Ham: Cush, and Mitzraim and Canaan, and Put. To this day, Ethiopia is called Cush by the Hebrews, Egyptians, Mitzraim, Libya, Put—whence the river of Mauritania is still called Put, and the surrounding region Putensis. Many writers, both Greek and Latin, are witnesses of this thing. Why moreover, the ancient name of Libya remained in one great part of the climate, and the remaining land called Africa, this is not the place or time [to explain]. Hereafter, Canaan occupied the land which the Jews thereafter took possession of, expelling the Canaanites. (*Patrologia Latina* vol. 107 9 col. 527C, my translation)[49]

He follows the Bible and other subsequent authors in situating Ham's sons in various locations in Africa and the Middle East. Canaan, far from being a figure for the Jews, appears here as the forefather of the Canaanites, who will be ousted by Israel. Rabanus ponders the question of the names associated with various territories in Africa, drawing on terms absent from the Bible but present in classical texts. Although he follows the trend of previous commentators in treating Ham's Jewish and African associations separately, he differs in considering the two formulations in the same text and in close proximity to each other.

Rabanus returns to a discussion of both constructions of Ham in a later text, his *De universo libri viginti duo* (c. 844, as dated in the *Patrologia Latina*), in a section that derives some of its content from Isidore's *Etymologies*. He restates Isidore's more neutral assessment of Ham but also includes allegorical readings that reference the Jews:

> Ham means "warm." And he was so named as a presaging of his future. For his posterity possessed that part of the land which is warmer because the sun is near. Hence still today Egypt, in the language of the Egyptians, is called Ham. This indicates the image of the Jews, who mock Christ's body and death. . . . Therefore, the second origin of the world grew in these three sons of Noah, that the three parts of the world would be filled up by the three generations. Hereafter, Shem, in his sons, occupied Asia, Ham Libya and Japhet, Europe. In whom is revealed, furthermore, the Church of Christ would be propagated by the faith of the Holy Trinity. (*Patrologia Latina* vol. 111 2.1, col. 34C–34D, my translation)[50]

Here Rabanus links Ham to North Africa, associating him with Egypt and Libya. However, in the midst of this geographical discussion, Rabanus abruptly shifts to a discussion of the Jews' mocking of Jesus. The author makes no attempt to explain how the meaning of Ham's name, or its association with the name of Egypt, indicates the image of the Jews. While other portions of this text also combine allegorical and geographical interpretations, it usually provides a rationale for linking the two interpretive frames. For example, Rabanus sees the number three in the example of the three sons repopulating the world as foreshadowing the Trinity propagating the Church. Although he articulates an analogy in this instance, he fails to offer one in the equation of Ham with the Jews. The effect, however, serves to create an association, albeit unexplained, between the inhabitants of North Africa and the Jews.

In the very next section of *De universo*, Rabanus not only mentions the Jews' enmity, but considers their punishment in his subsequent discussion of the significance of Canaan's name:

> Canaan, the son of Ham, can be interpreted as "their movement." With respect to which, what else is this but their work? Namely, for the movement of the father, that is, for his [the father's] work he [the son] was cursed. Wherefore, cast out of his seat, he abandoned the land of his possession to the sons of his brothers, indicating the

posterity of the Jews, who in the passion of the Lord received the sentence of damnation, proclaiming: His blood be upon us and upon our children (27 Mt). On account of which, as it were, the ungrateful were expelled from their country by the Romans in retribution of the blood of Christ, and they devoted it to the place of the holy Church, in which the true worship of the one God continues for ever. (*Patrologia Latina* vol. 111 2.1, col. 34D–35A, my translation)[51]

He relies upon Isidore's appropriation of the *Civitate Dei* (16.2), in which Augustine uses the etymologies of the names of Ham and Canaan to describe the actions of heretics, instead of the Jews. In the *Etymologies*, Isidore omits this reference to heresy, but in the biblical commentaries both he and Rabanus reproduce the same interpretation. However, here Rabanus recasts Augustine's commentary, and his own appropriation of it, applying it exclusively to the Jews. In the original version, Ham's name is glossed to mean "their movement," that is, of the heretics, which is interpreted in turn to mean "their works." Ham's action brings about the curse upon the son; here the movement denotes the expulsion of Canaan from his land and its subsequent possession by his brothers. Rabanus reads this as figuring the children of the Jews who were condemned when their parents called out in Matthew 27:25. As a consequence of receiving this curse, the Jews and their descendants were expelled by the Romans from the land of Israel, which was subsequently dedicated to the Christian church. By excluding heretics, this reading strengthens the identification of Ham with the Jews and their supersession by the Christians. While slavery is not emphasized here, the expulsion of the Jews from Israel renders them stateless and abject, as emphasized in Augustine's discussions of the figure of Cain considered earlier. Notably, the strong articulation of the Jews' malediction, figured through Ham and Canaan, directly follows the discussion of Ham as the founder of Africa.

While most treatments of Ham, including the synthesis of views expressed by the *Glossa Ordinaria*, present separate accounts of his identification with Jews and with Africa, both ideas received wide circulation and were available for comparison or conflation. Juxtapositions such as the one Rabanus makes are rare, but do occur. A parchment roll produced in Soest, Germany (c. 1230), representing a genealogy of Jesus in text and image, offers an interesting example (Figure 4.6).[52] The accompanying text next to the name "Cham" explains that Noah, being mocked by him, cursed the offspring of one of Ham's children. The image represents the

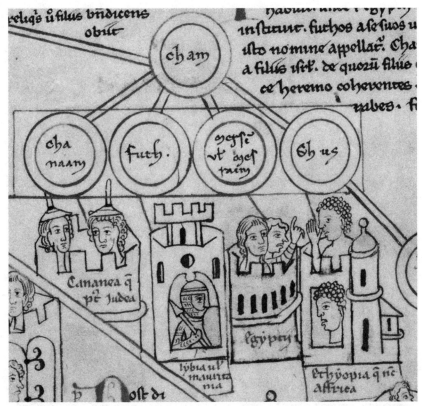

FIGURE 4.6 Rotulus representing the genealogy of Jesus; detail showing off-spring of Cham (Ham).

bpk Bildagentur / Staatsbibliothek zu Berlin / Art Resource, NY Ms.lat.fol.141 Rotulus.

names of four descendants of Ham along with their depictions in sepa-rate towers that represent their lands. Reading from right to left, in the order the Bible presents them, Chus appears first. Two figures with tightly curled hair appear in this building, underneath which is written "Ethiopia which is now Africa [Ethyopia q n Affrica]." Both figures face the next castle representing Egypt; two Egyptians face one African as if in some dis-pute. The third tower, Put or Fut, representing Lybia or Mauritania, houses a single man, dressed in armor holding a sword and shield; we might read him as a Muslim solider. Finally, the tower of Chanaan, explains in its caption that it is part of Judea. The accompanying text explains that "Chanaam inhabited the land from which they were expelled by the chil-dren of Israel [Chanaam t[er]ram inhabitavit de qua eiecti su[n]t a filiis Isr[ae]l]." However, the two men representing Chanaan's descendants wear the iconic "Jewish hat": a conical hat with a single long stem at the top. Visualizing the typology suggested first by Procopius, the two men here simultaneously portray the Canaanites expelled from Israel by the Jews and the Jews themselves, cursed and expelled from the land by God. Although the depiction places both Jews and Africans as descendants of Ham, Jews inhabit the position of the cursed children of Canaan.

Jewish Ham in Early Modernity

Even in the medieval period when ideas about Ham as cursed Jewish slave or inhabitant of Africa circulated widely, no logic clearly connected the two interpretations sufficiently to go beyond an occasional tenuous link. Furthermore, the early modern period brought about a number of changes that influenced the meaning of Jews in Christian theology and diminished their association with Ham. By the sixteenth century, with a few exceptions, most of Western Europe had exiled or forced the conversion its Jewish inhabitants. At the same time, a new religious enemy emerged to displace the Jews: the proponents of the Reformation or the supporters of the Catholic Church, depending on one's confession. As religious polemic in the period focused on attacking Christian opponents, the status of Jew as enemy of the faith subsided. Medieval accusations formally directed against Jews, such as colluding with the devil, embodying the Antichrist, relying on outmoded ceremony, and so on, now targeted Catholics in a Protestant context.[53] In England, as Achsah Guibbory has argued, Protestants increasingly identified with Jews and cite Jewish examples as a means of authorizing the newly emergent national religion. Additionally, and perhaps most importantly, new Protestant approaches to Bible interpretation reduced the dominance of typological approaches, resulting in more literal, rather than figural, interpretations of Ham.[54]

While the identification of Ham with the Jews as the enemies of Jesus does not completely disappear from early modern English texts, this connection is literally marginalized. Richard Day's illustrated collection, *Christian prayers and meditations* (1569), includes images in the borders surrounding the prayers; among other pictures contained in the book are scenes from the life of Jesus, paired with two figural episodes from the Hebrew Bible, running along the outer, long margin of each page.[55] The image of the Jews mocking a blindfolded Jesus appears in the middle of the right margin next to one of the prayers; it is framed above and below with the text from Matthew 26:67–9 describing the scene (Figure 4.7). At the top of the margin sits an illustration of the sleeping Noah being mocked

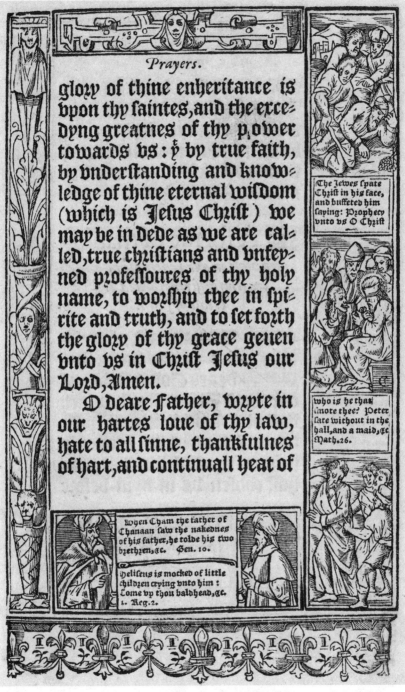

Prayers.

glory of thine enheritance is vpon thy saintes, and the excedyng greatnes of thy power towards vs : ý by true faith, by vnderstanding and knowledge of thine eternal wisdom (which is Jesus Christ) we may be in dede as we are called, true christians and vnfeyned professoures of thy holy name, to worship thee in spirite and truth, and to set forth the glory of thy grace geuen vnto vs in Christ Jesus our Lord, Amen.

O deare father, wryte in our hartes loue of thy law, hate to all sinne, thankfulnes of hart, and continuall heat of

The Jewes spate Christ in his face, and buffeted him saying: Prophecy vnto vs O Christ

who is he that smote thee? Peter sate without in the hall, and a maid, &c. Math.26.

Wyen Cham the father of Chanaan saw the nakednes of his father, he tolde his two brethren, &c. Gen. 10.

Heliseus is mocked of little children crying vnto him : Come vp thou baldhead, &c. 1. Reg. 2.

FIGURE 4.7 Ham mocks Noah, upper right hand-image, as figure for Jews mocking Jesus, middle right-hand image. Richard Day's *Christian prayers and meditations* (1569), RB 60973, fol diir.

by Ham, who points at his father's genitals and smiles while his brothers cover their father. The depiction in the lower portion of the margin shows boys mocking the prophet Elisha. A box at the center bottom of the page contains representations of the prophets who reported these events; they point at the biblical texts of their prophecies explaining the figures. The upper portion of the box quotes from Genesis 9:22 in which Ham saw Noah's nakedness and reported it to his brothers, the lower section recounts the boys mocking Elisha with the cry of "bald head" in 2 Kings.[56] The three episodes share the theme of mocking and clearly link Ham's derision of his father with the Jews' ridicule of Jesus.[57] While the body of the text does not relate directly to the pictures, anyone using the book through its five editions (1569, 1578, 1581, 1590, and 1608) would have been exposed to the figural linking of Ham with the Jews.[58]

The typological association of the Jews with Ham and Noah's curse occasionally appears in other early modern texts. For example, Alexander Ross, a Church of England clergyman and chaplain to Charles I, includes it in two of his treatises, *An exposition on the fourteene first chapters of Genesis* (1626) and *Three decads of diuine meditations* (1630), both of which offer typological interpretations.[59] In the first text, in a discussion of Genesis 9, Ross poses and answers the question "Wherein was Noah the tipe of Christ?" He offers list of parallels, including:

> Noah was mocked by his owne sonne, and so was Christ by his owne people the Iewes: . . . Noah awoke from his sleepe, and so did Christ from his graue: . . . Cham was cursed for scorning his Father, and the Iewes are yet accursed for killing their Sauiour. (1626, 69–70, images 104–5)

The list includes a number of interpretations from patristic commentaries, including the identification of Ham with the Jews in their mocking of Jesus and in their cursed status, which extends to the present day. Similarly, the *Three decads* includes a poem, "Noahs Drunkennesse," which first describes the events in Genesis, then explains their figural significance:

> . . . thē[n] Cham
> Vncouer'd in the Tent his Fathers shame,
> Noah perceiued that he was made naked:
> And cursed Cham as soone as he awaked.
> . . .
> When sin had spoyl'd the world, God sent his Son

To plant vnto himselfe a Church, which done,
He dranke the red wine of his Fathers wrath,
Then sleep'd, & on the crosse gaue vp his breath.
The Iewes, his wicked Sons, did laugh and scorne,
To see his body naked, wounded, torne. (1630, 3, image 5)

While Ross establishes again the ridicule that links Ham's actions to those of the Jews, he deploys both of these episodes as figures for God's correction of the Church of England and rejection of the Catholic Church.[60] Even in rehearsing the crimes of the Jews, the text passes over them to focus on more pressing internal religious concerns. The Jews as Ham no longer figure themselves in post-Reformation England, but serve as a figure for Christian transgression.

However, even the few texts that link Ham to the Jews omit the curse of servitude that organized the earlier exegetical discussion. The concept of a servile Jewish status does persist, but it draws upon the medieval development of figure of Cain who is sometimes coordinated or conflated with Ham.[61]. As noted in chapter 1, this correlation already appears in Augustine's discussion in the *Contra Faustum*; although he employs both Ham and Cain to represent Jewish servitude, he does not forge an explicit connection between the figures. Subsequent authors do make implicit or even explicit connections between the two, however initially without mention of the Jews. A Middle Irish historical treatise on the Six Ages of the world explains that, owing to his perversity, Ham is "the Cain of the people after the Flood" (John Block Friedman, 99). Furthermore, the medieval spelling of Ham as Cham could easily be confused with the name Cain, as the three lines in the "m" could be viewed as "in" (100). In an account of human history beginning with Adam, Ranulf Higden's *Polycronicon* (1482) explains that "cayn . . . is comunely callyd caym" (Book 2, chapter 4 p lxxvi, image 96).[62] The late fifteenth century seems to be a time of confusion regarding these two characters, as Gui de Roye substitutes Cain for Ham in his handling of the Emperor Constantine's interpretation of Noah's nakedness:

yf I sawe a preste synne I shold couere hym wyth my mantel to thende that noo persone shold see hym ne knowe hys synne for the sklandre and deshonour that myght happen thys is ayenst them that dyscoueren the synnes of theyr faders goostly. as dyd the euyl Cayn whyche dyscouered hys fader Noe for to see his membres naturel. For whyche case hys fader made hym bonde to hys bretheren and alle hys lygne. & fro thenne forthon began seruytude as witnesseth scripture. (Dır, image 25)

This follows a patristic tradition of reading Ham's sin as one against the clergy, but strikingly, de Roye identifies Cain as the sinner who humiliated his father, misidentified here as Noah. Following Augustine's logic that understands the Ham episode as explaining the origin of slavery, here Cain and his entire lineage are bound to his brothers in hereditary "seruytude."

This correspondence between Ham and Cain already available through medieval figural associations may facilitate the shift in the identification with Jews from the former to the latter in early modernity. The revived use of Cain as a figure for the Jews appears across a range of religious and secular texts, sometimes absent reference to servitude. A number of authors employ Cain to exemplify the exiled and dispersed status of contemporary Jews. In his *History of the World* (1614/ 1617), Walter Raleigh brings in the example of the Jews in the midst of his analysis of Cain as a wanderer:

> Cyrillus saith, that Cain and Abel were figures of Christ, and of the Iewes; and that as Cain, after that he had slaine Abel vniustly, had thenceforth no certayne abiding in the world: so the Iewes, after they had crucified the Sonne of God, became Runnegates: and it is true, that the Iewes had neuer since any certayne Estate, Commonweale, or Prince of their owne vpon the earth. (72, image 81)

Although he does not claim the Jews are enslaved, his source uses Cain to explain that they are punished with expulsion, and since then live as fugitives, prevented from ruling themselves in their own land. John Boys, in a treatise explicating the use of scripture in the English liturgy, brings in the trail of blood motif, citing Cain and the Jews, to explore the question of hereditary punishment:

> The children of such as murthered the Prophets, as the Iewes were the sons of Cain, in slaying the righteous Abels. If Cain and all the bloudy Iewes as well after as vnder the Law, make the same generation, vnited in fact and faction, it is in God very good iustice that all the righteous bloud shed from the foundation of the world should be required of this generation. (89, image 47)[63]

The author emphasizes the hereditary nature of Cain's punishment in his indictment of the Jews' crimes against the prophets as well as Jesus. George Wither's translation of and commentary upon the Psalms closely follows Augustine's exegesis, which links Cain particularly to Psalm 59. Whither explains that the Psalm

> cheefly propheciefd the Iewes dogged crueltie to Christ, & that they should be preserved to wander in a vagabond Condition (as wee see at this day) for an example to others &c. . . . According to thy promises thou hast . . .scattred the Iewes (with a Cain-like marke preventing their vtter extirpation) that so, their vagabond life may be a perpetuall memoriall, both of their crueltie, & of our Saviou[r]s Passion. (108–10, images 64–5)

The elements of preservation and continuing dispersion as punishment for crime that Augustine employed through the figure of Cain continues to describe the status of contemporary Jews.[64] Other theological discussions iterate these ideas; Edward Kellet's *Miscellanies of divinitie* (1635) considers Cain, Jews, and hereditary punishment in an elaboration on the trail of blood motif (120–21), while Henry Robinson cites the mark of Cain as protecting Jews from forced conversion in his 1644 polemic on liberty of conscience (17–18). However, many of these cases employ the example of Jewish punishment to make a polemical point regarding intra-Christian conflict. Nevertheless, early modern texts occasionally cite Cain to iterate the idea of Jews as cursed with hereditary servitude as a consequence of their deicidal crime. Samuel Purchas spells out the medieval theological discussion of the Jews, traced in chapter 1, albeit situated within a historical narrative:

> After that imprecation of theirs, His bloud bee on vs and on our children . . . when they . . . crucified the Lord . . . then came the wrath of God on them . . . , and they became a trauelling Nation indeed, trauelling now aboue 1500 yeeres. . . . And euer since. . . [they] haue liued (if such slauery and basenesse be a life) like Cain, wandring ouer the World, branded with Shame and Scorne. . . so that they are strangers where they dwell. (67, image 52)

Citing the proof-text from Matthew, Purchas explains that the Jews, like Cain, have been punished with exile for their crime, but includes their status as slaves as well, an element drawn from the Ham narrative. In his *De republica anglorum* (1583), an overview of English society, law, and institutions, Thomas Smith includes a chapter on bondage that considers Jewish slavery:

> For the lawe of Iewes is well ynough knowen, & at this day so farre as I can learne, amongst all people Iewes be holden as it were in a common seruitude, and haue no rule nor dominion as their own prophesies doe tell that they should not haue after that Christ. . . was of them refused. (119, image 58)

Although he omits mention of Cain or Ham, he cites their antitype in explaining that the rejection of Jesus has resulted in the Jews' enslavement.[65] Hardly a pressing issue in sixteenth-century England, where Jews were not officially permitted to live, Smith nevertheless touches on the law of their enslavement, which he presents as well known.[66] Given the numerous editions of *De republica*, the idea of Jews as cursed with slavery would have circulated widely in early modern England.[67]

The development in patristic and medieval exegesis of the Jews as figured in the cursed enslavement of Ham's offspring helped establish and disseminate an idea of hereditary inferiority. While the idea of Jewish slavery, absent its figural justification, continues to circulate in early modernity, the altered status and significance of Jews no longer require its former enforcement. However, the concept proved increasingly useful for the justification of both the emerging Atlantic trade in enslaved peoples and the racist construction of African peoples. While the Jews' experience of servitude under medieval canon law was in no way commensurate with that of the chattel slavery forced upon Africans, the theological idea of a cursed status that rendered a people as a whole subject to the power of Christians contributed to the racialization of both groups. Although this idea emerges in theological discourses, the status of perpetual servitude only gains power when it enters into ecclesiastical law, as we saw in chapter 1. There exegetical figures support the canon law development of the Jews' special status. Chapter 5 traces the elaboration of this concept with recourse to Hagar and Ishmael in canon law, which enables the inclusion not only of Muslims but other inhabitants of Africa into the category of enemies of the faith who can be battled and enslaved in the course of a just war.

5

Cain, Ham, and Ishmael

THE AFRICAN TRAVELS OF PERPETUAL SERVITUDE

AS THE INCREASING marginalization and eradication of Jews from Western Europe gradually resolves the pressing problem of their proper position in medieval Christian society, the concepts of subordination developed to distinguish and suppress them are repurposed to assert the hereditary inferiority of other groups. One of the earliest figures of Jewish servitude, Paul's reading of Hagar/Ishmael and Sarah/Isaac as signifying the spiritual bondage of unbelievers relative to the faithful, has a double history.[1] Like Ham, Ishmael's literal significance links him geographically to nations other than the Jews; in this instance, to Arabic peoples and subsequently to Muslims. With the advent of Islam and Muslim military prominence, Christian exegetical and legal discourses take up this identification with Ishmael, but fuse it with figural readings developed with regard to Jews, resulting in a representation of Muslims as enemies of Christ who also must be subordinated to Christians. The application of this status to Muslims takes on legal connotations in the context of just war theory that underlies the Crusades; as belligerents promoting a cause deemed unjust against Christians, Muslims taken captive during battle can be reduced to slavery. The construction of Jewish servitude through the figures of both Ishmael and Ham helps sanction and strengthen the legitimacy of Muslim servitude. The identification of the Muslim sphere of influence with Northern Africa subsequently facilitates the translation of these figural discourses of enmity and servitude to black Africans in the Iberian appropriation of African lands and in the fifteenth- and sixteenth-century establishment of the trade in enslaved people. Early justifications of the enslavement of Africans employ the tropes of Ham and Cain, often merged into a single figure, to explain the divine basis for their servitude. The congruence of these two characters, forged in the long history of discourses on Jewish servitude, also functions to transfer the notion of hereditary inferiority to Africans.

Figuring Jewish and Muslim Slavery in Canon Law

Depending on the perspective taken, medieval Christians saw Jews and Muslims as distinctly different groups, as versions of the other, or somewhere between these two poles.[2] Judaism's role in the formation of Christianity would seem to make relations between these two faith groups unique, particularly with regard to the Jews' alleged actions in the crucifixion and the resulting punishments of exile and servitude inflicted upon them. Because Islam developed after Christianity, Muslims could not logically be seen as partaking of the Jewish guilt of deicide and enslaving punishment. In additional contrast to the Jews, Muslims possessed their own lands and armies that could, and did, pose a threat to Christian claims of spiritual and territorial superiority. As noted in chapter 1, Pope Alexander II effactually registers this difference in his decretal *Dispar nimirum*, a ruling that enters into the authoritative compilation of canon law. In this letter, he explicitly distinguishes Jews from Muslims: "There is, assuredly, a difference between the case of the Jews and that of the Saracens. It is just to fight those who persecute Christians and who expel them from their cities and houses, while these people [Jews] are everywhere ready to serve" (Linder, 452). The heading to this canon draws a conclusion from this difference: "We ought not to persecute Jews, but Muslims" (C.23 c.8 c.11 *Corpus Juris Canonici*, my translation).[3] Muslims deserve to be persecuted because they challenge the autonomy of Christians in their own lands.[4] In contrast, the Jews' willing subordination to Christian rule ensures their toleration.

However, subsequent commentators on this canon understood the distinction as situational and not absolute; it is based on the *actions* of Jews and Muslims, and not on some inherent difference between them. Alanus Anglicus, writing at the turn of the twelfth century, explains that Jews are not persecuted because they are everywhere slaves to Christians; if Muslims are also willing to serve, they would not be killed (Herde 365, n. 19). Other canonists agree that if Muslims lived as peaceful subjects of Christian rulers, they should be tolerated, like the Jews (Herde, 365–66). Another late twelfth-century author even reverses the equation: "If the Jews . . . should ever occupy Christian territory and expel the population, they were to be given the same treatment as the aggressive Saracens" (Herde, 367). The acceptance of, or resistance to, Christian rule determines how Jews and Muslims should be treated under law; these opinions focus on the political realities of relating to hostile or subordinated aliens. As Zacour explains, "One might think that in the medieval West the distinction between Jews and Muslims must have been clear. Yet it was often not necessary to treat them separately" (16). He cites the opinion in the *Summa Parisiensis*, composed around the same time that Alexander promulgated *Dispar*:

> What is said here regarding the Jews can be in a similar way understood regarding the Saracens. . . Whether Saracens or Jews, as long as they are rebellious, we must attack them. After we have truly subjugated them, we must neither kill them nor compel them to the faith. (qtd. in Zacour 16, n. 54)

Written before Innocent's formulation of inherent Jewish inferiority, this view suggests that infidel servility is not innate, but volitional: it could be either accepted or rejected by the infidel. The author even seems to include Muslims in the doctrine of protection initially developed by Augustine with regard to Jews.[5] On the other hand, all of these opinions assume that the proper, if not natural, status of the infidel is one subordinated to Christians, thus supporting legal and theological justifications to attack resistant infidels and subjugate compliant ones.[6]

Thus in some respects, canonists read Muslims though the lens of ecclesiastical law governing relations between Christians and Jews. Beginning in the late twelfth century, many collections of medieval canon law organized regulations on Muslims and Jews under the same rubric, often in relation to heretics, pagans, and infidels (Cohen 1999, 158, 162; Czerwinski, 36–9; Herde, 362–63; Freidenreich 2011, 41–3). For example, the notion that Jews must occupy a subservient position relative to Christians extends to Muslims in laws governing the practice of slavery and the employment of servants. As noted in chapter 1, canon law registers an inordinate concern that inferior Jews will exercise power over Christians, particularly in the sphere of domestic service or servitude. The Third Lateran Council (1179) includes Muslims in its canon titled "Regarding Jews and that Christians not be made their slaves" (*de Iudeis et ne Christiani mancipia eorum fiant*). As Czerwinski points out, this heading is based on the similarly titled Roman law in Justinian's Code: "No heretic, or pagan or Jew should have, or possess or circumcise a Christian"; subsequent decretal collections repeated this title (my translation, qtd. in Czerwinski 38, n. 25).[7] The expansion of this law to include Muslims, who did not exist at the time of the Roman Code, is facilitated in part by the fact that some canonists employ the term "pagan" to refer to Muslims and that circumcision is a required part of conversion both to Judaism and Islam (Kedar, 209–10; Pakter, 114; Czerwinski, 37; Freidenreich 2011, 43, 54–55; Tolan 2002, 105–34). The body of the Lateran canon states:

> Jews and Saracens shall not be permitted to have Christian slaves in their homes, [orders that Christian testimony against Jews be accepted just as Jewish testimony of Christians is accepted] and we decree that those who in this matter want to give Jews greater privileges than Christians shall be placed under anathema, for the only fitting condition is that Jews be placed below Christians, and that they be treated kindly by the latter solely because of humanitarian reasons. If moreover, with God's inspiration, anyone become a convert to Christianity, he shall under no condition be deprived of his property. For converts ought to be in better circumstances (melioris conditionis) than they had been before accepting the Faith. (Grayzel 1966, 297)

The inherent superiority of Christians, relative not only to Jews but also to Muslims, governs these rulings that seek to prevent infidels from rising out of their proper place below the faithful. Subsequent councils and popes express outrage over Muslims, in addition to Jews, exercising authority over Christians in public office, owning Christian slaves, and enjoying a *melior conditio* in relation to Christians.[8]

However, even when Muslims willingly live as subjects to Christian rulers, this socio-political subordination would still seem to differ from that of Jews. Jewish hereditary inferiority, while it has secular applications, derives from a spiritual state. It is justified by a theological explanation based on the events described in the New Testament that would seem to be inapplicable to Muslims, whose religion postdates the advent of Christianity. Nevertheless, theologians and canonists strikingly apply the same figures of spiritual servitude to Muslims as they do to Jews.

In order to understand this process, we must first consider the origins of the Muslim people as explained in the received tradition of medieval Christianity.

The book of Genesis again provides the starting point for this genealogy in its account of the birth of Ishmael, the son of Abraham and his servant Hagar (Gen. 16:11–12). Jewish, Christian, and Muslim sources all view Ishmael as the progenitor of the inhabitants of the Arabian Peninsula and of the founders of Islam. In his *Jewish Antiquities*, which draws on the book of Genesis, Josephus identifies Ishmael as the father of the "Arabian nation."[9] Church Fathers follow this connection. Eusebius ascribes the name Σαρακηνοί (*Sarakenoi*) to the descendants of Ishmael in a number of his works. Jerome takes up this connection in his writings, including a commentary on the prophetic book Ezekiel: "Ishmaelites and Agarites, who are now called Saracens, falsely assume for themselves the name of Sarah, that is, the freeborn mistress, from whom they would seem to be born."[10] While the etymology of "Saracen" is disputed, Jerome provides an influential explanation of the name: the Saracens are in fact the offspring of Hagar through Ishmael.[11] They should rightfully, then, be called Agarites, from Hagar; however, in wishing to hide the fact that they derive from the enslaved woman, Saracens call themselves by a name that falsely suggests their descent from Sarah, the free woman.

Other authors follow Jerome's lead in disputing the connection between Saracens and Abraham's wife Sarah. Isidore discusses the people associated with Ishmael in two places in his *Eytmologies* (c. 615–630).

A son of Abraham was Ishmael, from whom arose the Ishmaelites, who are now called, with corruption of the name, Saracens, as if they descended from Sarah, and the Agarenes, from Agar (i.e. Hagar). (IX.ii.6, 192)

The Saracens are so called either because they claim to be descendants of Sarah or, as the pagans say, because they are of Syrian origin, as if the word were Syriginae. They live in a very large deserted region. They are also Ishmaelites, as the Book of Genesis teaches us, because they sprang from Ishmael. They are also named Kedar, from the son of Ishmael, and Agarines, from the name Agar (i.e. Hagar). As we have said, they are called Saracens from an alteration of their name, because they are proud to be descendants of Sarah. (IX.ii.57, 195)

These accounts again establish a link between Ishmael and the present-day people called Saracens, and posits their desire to be known as the descendants of Sarah rather than Hagar. William of Auvergne, thirteenth-century Bishop of Paris (d. 1249), continues this tradition in his *De fide et legibus*, in a chapter "proposing to destroy and subvert the delusion of Muslim law" (49, my translation).[12] He identifies the "Ishmaelites" as

> Arab and Saracen peoples, but they falsely usurp to themselves the name of Saracen from Sarah, just as if they were sons of Sarah through Ishmael, when indeed there is no blood relation, but they have only grafted themselves to Sarah as can be read in Genesis 16. . . . However, truly they are Hagarenes, because they descended from Hagar through Ishmael. (chapter 18 50r, my translation)[13]

He shifts the identification from its previous geographical designation to one of religion; the Saracens, descendants of Hagar through Ishmael, do not simply represent a region, but followers of Islam.

As the exegetical association of Muslims with the "slave woman" Hagar takes on the figural connotation of servitude, initially developed with regard to Jews, the legal discourses make use of this connection. The legal status of the unbeliever as a slave subjected to Christians, transfers from Jews to Muslims, in spite of the apparent theological obstacles. In fact, given the use of Ishmael as a figure for both Muslims and Jews, the Christian exegetical tradition actually facilitates their comparison in law. Bernard of Pavia (d. 1213) brings the figure of Hagar as Muslim into the discourse of canon law in his *Summa Decretalium*, a late twelfth-century commentary on his own compilation of decretals: "Truly, they are called Saracens, who accept neither the old or the new testament, who do not wish to call themselves Hagarenes, from Hagar, Abraham's slave girl, from whom was their origin, but rather from Sarah, his wife and a free woman, they call themselves Saracens" (my translation; qtd. in Czerwinski, 38–9 n. 27). The slave status developed in this type to explain Jewish subordination to Christians is connected here with Islam, but without further elaboration on its consequences. A decade or so later, Innocent III includes Muslims in the context of 1205 letter in which he reprimands the King of Castile regarding his preferential treatment of Jews at the expense of Christians:

> [So that, with the Synagogue ascending, the Church diminishes and the slave woman is put before the free woman {et libere preponatur

ancilla}] . . . Therefore, . . . lest you seem to be decreasing the freedom
of the Church and to be exalting the Synagogue and the Mosque, and
lest you seem to be working against the Church, . . . we urge . . . that
you yourself correct the above-mentioned faults. (Grayzel 1966, 112–
13, and my translation in brackets)

While he does not directly equate the *ancilla* to Muslims with recourse to
the genealogy of Hagar and Ishmael, nevertheless the Mosque joins the
Synagogue as a faith group whose proper place is one of inferiority and
enslavement, relative to the Church. The logic of inferiority that governs
the treatment of the Jews in thirteenth-century canon law here expands to
include another infidel group, the Muslims.

By the middle of the thirteenth century, however, the authoritative canonist Hostiensis merges the two readings of Galatians—Ishmael as Jew,
Ishmael as Muslim—in his *Summa Aurea*, an exposition on the titles of
decretals (1253) (Brundage 1995, 214). Under the rubric *De Iudaeis, Saracenis
& eorum servis*, he first treats the Jews. In the section on how Jews should be
tolerated, he restates the language, included in the *Decretals*, of Innocent
III's *Etsi* on Jewish servitude and Christian forbearance: "Granted therefore that their own sin subjected the Jews to slavery, nevertheless Christian
piety tolerates them" (Liber V. col 1518. 3b).[14] In the original decretal, the
pope includes the figure of the slave and free woman to justify the prohibition forbidding Jews from employing Christian domestic servants: "lest
the children of a free woman should be slaves to the children of a slave;
[ne filii libere filiis famulentur ancille]" (Grayzel 1966, 114–17). Hostiensis
does not include the figure in this section, but he introduces the texts of
Genesis and Galatians in the next, which considers Muslims:

Regarding Sarracens. . . And why they are so named: from Sara,
wife of Abraham, they wish to be named . . . but they were not born
nor have their origin from her. On the contrary, from Hagar, the
slave of Sara; Hagarenes or Hagariens, as it were, they should pref-
erably be called. . . . Hence appositely we are called the children of
Sara, who was the legitimate woman, because in Sara the Church
was established and therefore Pagans or Jews ought not to have
under them Christians, nor children of the free woman Sara, (that
is, Christian children) be placed to serve outside of the Catholic
faith. Of the slave woman, see Hagar, . . . *Etsi Iudaeos*. (Liber V. col
1523. 2, my translation)[15]

Although he appears to have switched topics in treating Muslims here, in fact Hostiensis derives the reference to Hagar and Sarah from Innocent's *Etsi Judaeis*. He thus conflates Muslims and Jews as the children of the slave woman, Hagar, in contrast to Christians, the children of the free woman, Sarah who symbolizes the Church. Pagans, by which he means Muslims here, ought not to have Christians serve them, again with reference to the inappropriateness of the children of the free woman serving children of the slave woman. A decade later, Pope Urban IV also articulates the notion of a servitude shared both by Muslims and Jews. He raises this issue, as Innocent and Hostiensis did, in the context of Jews and Muslims reportedly exercising authority over Christians: "It is neither convenient nor honest that these same Jews and Muslims, whose proper guilt submitted them to perpetual servitude [quos propria culpa submisit perpetue servituti], should exercise strength of power in regard to Christians" (Grayzel 1989, 79, my translation).[16] Although Urban does not explicitly cite Galatians, he quotes verbatim from *Etsi*, which relies on the proof-text to explain the impropriety of slaves ruling over Christians. Although chronologically impossible, Muslims are condemned to slavery, like the Jews, by their own proper guilt, the term used by Innocent and Hostiensis to refer to participation in the crucifixion of Jesus. Perpetual servitude, a condition previously applied to Jews, now similarly describes the status of Muslims.[17]

The legal application of Jewish servitude to Muslims also operates by means of the figure of Ham. The *Quaestiones* of Stephen Bonnier (d. 1298), quoted in commentaries on canon law by Francesco Zabarella (d. 1417) and John of Imola (d. 1436), explain Jewish servitude with recourse to the figure of Ham; they argue that this subjection applies to Muslims as well as Jews (Rowan, 18; see also Patker, 321–30). The reference emerges in a discussion of whether the children of Jews can be baptized as Christians against the will of their parents; while the Church had a long-standing tradition of forbidding this practice, the question was debated in the medieval period, and turned, in part, on the status of Jews as slaves (Rowan, 9–15 and see discussion in chapter 1). "Stephen argued that Jewish servitude was grounded in the condemnation of Ham in Genesis 9, where it is declared that he and his progeny should serve his brothers. This was taken by Stephen to apply both to the Jews and the Saracens" (Rowan, 18).[18] Although Stephen's commentary has not survived, his views are cited by Zabarella and John of Imola in their discussion of this subject under the general heading

"De Iudeis & Saracenis." In his *In Clementinarum volumen commentaria*, Zabarella asks "Whether princes were able to carry off the little children of Muslims and to cause them to be baptized?" (169r). He remarks that according to Stephen, the answer is yes,

> for Jews and Muslims are slaves, Genesis 9 "Cursed be Ham, a slave he will be to his brothers." And thus these same infidels do not have power over their children, because they are slaves, and so against their will, the princes are able to carry away and sell their children. Therefore even more so in this do they deserve to be baptized. (169v)

Although he only asks about the status of Muslim children, he locates the dilemma in the context of a legal and exegetical tradition first developed with regard to Jews. However, he asserts that the curse of Ham applies to both Jews and Muslims, rendering them, and perhaps all infidels, slaves whose children can be sold or baptized by their rulers. In his *Super Clementinis . . . co[m]mentaria*, John of Imola similarly cites Stephen's opinion, noting some argue that

> because Jews and Muslims are the true slaves of the Christians, Genesis 9 [25] "Cursed be Ham: may Canaan be a slave to his brothers" . . . therefore the former are the slaves of the latter, thus they can sell them against the parents will and thus cause them to be baptized against the parents will, because they do not hold power over them (128r).

Both commentators cite Genesis as proof of the true servitude of both Jews and Muslims to Christians, nullifying the parents' power over their children, and rendering them liable to be sold or converted to Christianity.[19]

The shared condition of Muslims and Jews as slaves to Christians, secured with recourse to the narrative of Sarah and her servant Hagar, receives extensive treatment in the early fourteenth-century writings of Oldradus de Ponte (d. 1337), an advocate in the papal court in Avignon (Zacour, ix, 6–9). In his collected concilia, legal opinions solicited for various cases, Oldradus includes a number of rulings on questions about Muslims and Jews.[20] In Concilium 72 on the question of "whether a war against the Saracens of Spain is licit," he draws evidence from both the Genesis and Galatians representations of the mistress and her servant (Zacour, 46):

Sarah signifies the Holy Catholic Church, the handmaiden Hagar, the accursed sect of Muhammad which took its origins from her. Therefore, the Holy Church, symbolized by Sarah, may use that accursed handmaiden as the blessed Sarah had used her, by beating her. She may use her as her Lord commands, by driving her out and depriving her children of inheritance and possession, that they not share with the free children. For since they are the offspring of a slave woman, and are therefore themselves slaves (for the children follow the womb)—indeed, slaves reproved by the Lord—they are not legally competent to hold rights of jurisdiction, lordship or honor. (qtd. in Zacour, 51–2)

In identifying Sarah as the Church, Oldradus follows Galatians, which explains: "that Jerusalem, which is above, is free: which is our mother" (Gal. 4:26). However, as he shifts from Sarah to Hagar, he also shifts from Paul's to Bernard of Pavia's interpretation of Genesis: the handmaiden here stands for Islam. In the Genesis text (which Oldradus quotes just prior to this excerpt), Abraham gives his wife power over Hagar: "thy handmaid is in thy own hand," which she employs: "Sarai afflicted her, she ran away" (Gen. 16:6). Subsequently, Sarah commands Abraham to "Cast out this bondwoman, and her son" and God confirms her demand (21:10–12). Just as Sarah was able to afflict and evict her slave, Hagar, so Christians should be able to wage war against and eject Muslims, their spiritual inferiors, from Spain. This theological inferiority has secular legal consequences; Oldradus applies Roman law on slaves to explain that Muslims, as descendants of the slave Hagar, are also slaves, and thus incapable of rule and ownership. The servitude of Muslims is explained by the fact that they are born of a slave, a principle in Roman law. However, their status as slaves to Christians only obtains within the logic of Galatians, in which the Jews are slaves in relation to Christians. Oldradus provides the proof of slavery in his reference to Innocent's letter, *Etsi*, that Jews are "slaves reproved by the Lord"; however, the canonist suppresses the Jewish identity of these slaves, replacing it with a Muslim one.

Strikingly, Oldradus also applies the figure of Hagar to the Jews in questions about whether a Christian prince can expel Jews and Muslims from his kingdom and confiscate their property (Zacour, 54). In Consilium 87, he opines that Jews should be tolerated, but in certain circumstances he indicates that they could be evicted and deprived of their goods:

This seems to be true where danger or scandal threatens Christians. For when they abuse our grace the ungrateful deserve to lose their privilege. This becomes clear in the case of churches that are burdened because Jews do not pay tithes on their possessions. Therefore lords who possessed land ought to have been compelled to rent their fields to such as would pay the tithes. All this seems clearly prefigured in that slave woman [Hagar] from whom they descend since, because she conducted herself haughtily and ungratefully to the free woman [Sarah], who signifies the church, she was expelled. For it was said, "Expel the slave woman and her son." (56–7)

Although the reply here only refers to Jews, it is probable that Oldradus assumes the case applies to Muslims as well, since the question he answers pertains to both. His use of the figure of Hagar operates as a sign that he may be referring to both groups, given the exegetical and theological traditions that read her as a figure for Jews and Muslims. The Genesis narrative further supports his judgment of the matter in providing a proof-text to justify the expulsion of infidels, since Abraham obeyed Sarah's command to eject the slave woman and her son. The answer to this question pivots on Hagar's status as slave; when they challenge or threaten Christians, Jews and Muslims do not perform their divinely imposed subservience, and thus can be driven out. We return to the logic set out in Alexander II's *Dispar nimirum*, which allows for coexistence with infidels as long as they are subordinates to Christians. Toleration of both Jews and Muslims will be withdrawn not only in the case where they pose a military threat, but even in an instance when they fail to pay tithes to the Church, represented here as resistant and unservile behavior.[21] The plastic definition of proper subjection gives Christian authorities extensive latitude over the bodies and goods of their infidel populations.

Oldradus again alludes to Hagar in another opinion on the legality of expelling Jews and Muslims. Consilium 62 advances a more conciliatory position, in apparent contradiction to number 87, contending that "without a legitimate reason a prince cannot expel peaceful Jews, Saracens and other pagans from his lands" (264). This opinion emphasizes not only the constraints that the law places on a ruler's actions—he may not act without a legitimate reason—but also the kindness and innocence required of Christian kings:

> Mercy is due to . . .a tributary slave, that he not be expelled.
> Princes are required to show love to the respectful and the obe-
> dient, to do nothing from a wish to injure, but to do everything
> from loving care—to do nothing brutally or inhumanely . . . for
> the same reason that we ought not to despoil peaceful Jews,
> pagans and Saracens of their goods, we ought not to deprive them
> of home and birthplace. What they possess, they possess by the
> law of nations, whether things or places, or else they possess by
> legal title, and so by right according to human, not divine justice,
> as Innocent clearly holds. And that they cannot be expelled, ex-
> cept they be persecutors, is well supported according to the con-
> trary alternative. . . . Hagar, the mother of the Agarenes, and her
> son Ishmael, father of the Agarenes, were expelled by Sarah be-
> cause she [Hagar] persecuted her mistress and he [Ishmael] his
> brother Isaac. . . . Therefore where the Agarenes abide humbly
> and do not deceive simple Christians to follow the cult of their
> vile Muhammad they are not therefore to be expelled but are to
> be accepted. (63–4)

The explanation depends on the rights and limitations of a tributary slave;
in exchange for his obedience, he must be allowed to reside in a ruler's
territory.[22] Oldradus applies the status of the slave to explain the position
of Jews, pagans and Muslims, to whom property rights in goods and dwell-
ings are accorded as long as they do not act as "persecutors" or prosely-
tizers. He cites Hagar here as a counterexample; she persecuted Sarah,
therefore she was expelled. In contrast, Muslims who submit themselves
to their Christian superiors may be tolerated. Consilia 62 and 87 therefore coincide, insofar as they predicate the rights of infidels on their performing their subordination.

Servitude and Just War

In considering questions of the infidel's status with regard to war and servitude in Consilium 72, Oldradus enters into a centuries-old conversation
in which slavery was understood as a potential consequence of combat.
Aristotle originates the phrase "just war" in the first book of his Politics to
describe conflicts between Greeks and "barbarians," as Frederick Russell
explains:

War was a natural form of acquisition, and since some men by their virtue, equated with justice, deserved to extend their rule over less worthy men, wars by which they enslaved others were naturally just. Men should only resort to war to prevent their own enslavement, that is, in self-defense, or to obtain an empire for the benefit of the governed or to enslave those non-Hellenes deserving of slavery. (3–4)

The justification of enslaving non-Greeks was based on the assumption of the inherent inferiority of captives to their conquerors. In an earlier section of the *Politics*, Aristotle establishes this idea of deserved slavery: "It is clear, then, that some men are by nature free, and others slaves, and that for these latter slavery is both expedient and right" (qtd. in Muldoon 2005, 73; see Garnsey's discussion of Aristotle's theory, 107–27). Roman law differs from Aristotle's view insofar as it assumed that human law, not the natural order, created servitude, but reinforces the connection between war and slavery with recourse to etymology:

(2) Slaves *(servi)* are so called because commanders generally sell the people they capture and thereby save *(servare)* them instead of killing them.
(3) The word for property in slaves (mancipia) is derived from the fact that they are captured from the enemy by force of arms (manu capiantur). (*Digest* 1.5: "On the Status of Persons"; 4: Florentinus, from *Institutes*, book 9, qtd. in Wiedemann 13)

The authoritative and influential *Digest* of Justinian defines the slave and his status as property in terms of the outcome of combat.

Roman law expanded Aristotle's view by defining in what circumstances justice rendered a war legitimate, which in turn determined who constituted the enemy liable to servitude. Modeled on the civil law redress, just war was waged to recover damages and punish transgressions (Russell, 4–5). The declaration of a just war nullified the rights of enemies, and justified the acquisition of their land, goods, and persons. As in the case of Aristotle, enemies were equated with "barbarians"; the Twelve Tables, the earliest written legislation of ancient Roman law, employed the terms *hostis* (enemy) and *peregrinus* (stranger) interchangeably (Russell, 7).[23] Ulpian, the third-century Roman jurist, conflated two categories in his definition of enemies: those against whom Rome had declared war, and criminals who were considered a type of public enemy. In grouping them together, foreigners in effect became felons. Medieval commentators on Roman law drew from its codes enforcing religious orthodoxy to expand the category of *hostis* to include pagans and heretics:

> Azo [fl 1150–1230] consider[ed] pagans subject to the penalties established for heretics, and mentioned the Saracens as contemporary examples of infidelity and idolatry. . . He assimilated together all those who deviated from orthodoxy, such as heretics, Jews, pagans, and infidels, and held them liable to punishment on account of their beliefs rather than for any acts of rapine. (Russell, 51).

While the Romanists did not consider religious persecution in relation to the laws of war, the definition of religious others as enemies rendered them susceptible to the negative legal consequences of just battle (Russell, 51).

Augustine synthesizes Roman law with examples drawn from Scripture to formulate his influential Christian definition of just war. Although caused by sin, wars also serve as a means for God to punish criminal and sinful transgressions. A just war could only be initiated by a legitimate authority, not a private person. Augustine defines legitimate combat as one which avenges injuries (*ulciscuntur iniurias*). Russell explains how his definition builds upon and extends the Roman concept:

> Just war. . . not only avenged the violation of existing legal rights but also avenged the moral order injured by the sins of the guilty party. . . . As sins as well as crimes, seen in the context of a broadened concept of justice whereby not only illegal but immoral or sacrilegious acts were punishable, the transgressions were both a crime against the law and a sin against righteousness. Augustine's notion of justice included respect for divine rights;. . . any violation of God's laws, and, by easy extension, any violation of Christian doctrine, could be seen as an injustice warranting unlimited violent punishment. Augustine's emphasis on *ulciscuntur iniurias* . . .when coupled with his analysis of *iustitia* paved the way for later justifications of holy wars and crusades that punished all manner of wickedness and vice. (Russell, 16, 18–20).

Augustine's concept of just war as redressing spiritual as well as temporal wrongs could be deployed to punish the sins of heresy and unbelief.

Although he does not specifically apply his formulation of just war to his justification of religious persecution, in both doctrines he argues that secular force could be used against enemies of the faith, such as heretics (Russell, 23).

Medieval canon law elaborates the concept of religious just war against enemies of the faith and defines the power necessary to authorize it. In the eleventh and twelfth centuries canonists stipulate that the pope, and not a temporal ruler, possesses the legitimate authority required to declare a just war. The papacy thus has the power to declare a new type of war that combines the idea of holy war, represented in the Hebrew Bible as one authorized by God, and Augustine's just war:

> The most significant contribution of this period was the synthesis of the crusade out of the holy war and the just war. . . . Now the crusade had become a specifically medieval juridical institution unrelated to more usual notions of public warfare and defense of the *patria*. The holy war of the medieval Church was also a just war, in view of the religious foundations of Augustine's just war. (Russell, 38)

Redefining holy war as just war enabled the canonists to apply Roman laws of *justum bellum* to the waging of religious battle and its consequences.

Slavery is once such consequence for enemies conquered in a just war. Medieval canon lawyers harmonize the Roman law definition of servitude with biblical teachings. Under the *ius naturale*, or natural law, slavery does not exist; it is a product of the *ius gentium*, the law of nations. This idea of slavery as a social construct accords with Augustine's teaching, which holds that humans are born free, but servitude emerges as punishment for sinning against God's will (chapter 4, Muldoon 2005, 74–5).[24] However, Roman law codes sometimes imply that the law of nations is common to all; this suggests it can operate like natural law. Medieval lawyers argue that slavery resulting from war, while not natural, could be considered as such in certain circumstances. Because God's law in the Bible is consonant with natural law, persons who violate the latter are also guilty of transgressing the former and thus, by natural law, could be deserving of enslavement. Furthermore, this accords with Augustine's view of slavery as resulting from transgression: "Given their sins, it was reasonable and legitimate to reduce those taken in a war against the infidel to slavery and, provided it had the Church's sanction, a war of conquest waged against them might even be said to be naturally just" (Keen, 13). However, while the law of nature or nations permits enslaving infidels, in wars between Christian adversaries, victors customarily demanded ransom rather than reduce their captive coreligionists to servitude (Keen, 70, 156–57; Muldoon 2005, 76).

Thus the canon law on servitude resulting from war concerns itself primarily with the enslavement of non-Christians.[25] According to the law's definition, the crusades in the Holy Land and the reconquest of Spain both constitute just wars that legitimize the transformation of infidel captives into slaves.[26] In his thirteenth-century commentary on Innocent III's decretal *Quod super his*, Innocent IV touches on the question of slavery in the context of his consideration of the pope's right to authorize the invasion of lands possessed by infidels (Muldoon 2005, 78–9). He contends that the pope and his followers cannot lawfully deprive "sovereignty or jurisdiction" from non-Christians in their own countries (Muldoon 1977, 191). However,

> the pope who is the vicar of Jesus Christ has power not only over Christians but also over all infidels, for Christ had power over all men. . . Elsewhere He said, "Feed My sheep." Both infidels and the faithful belong to Christ's flock by virtue of their creation, although the infidels do not belong to the sheepfold of the Church, and so it seems from the aforementioned, that the pope has jurisdiction over all men and power over them in law but not in fact, so that through this power which the pope possesses I believe that if a gentile, who has no law except the law of nature [to guide him], does something contrary to the law of nature, the pope can lawfully punish him. . . . Also, the pope can judge the Jews if they violate the law of the Gospel in moral matters if their leaders do not punish them. . . . The pope can order infidels to admit preachers of the Gospel in the lands that they administer, for every rational creature is made for the worship of God. . . . If infidels prohibit preachers from preaching, they sin and so they ought to be punished. In all the aforementioned cases and in all others where it is licit for the pope to command those things, if the infidels do not obey, they ought to be compelled by the secular arm and war may be declared against them by the pope and not by anyone else. (qtd. in Muldoon 1977, 191–92)

Innocent's extends the pope's *de jure* jurisdiction and power to include non-Christians, and authorizes him to punish infidels who violate natural law. He assimilates natural law to divine law here to argue that if Jews violate the moral laws of the Gospel and their leaders fail to punish them, the pope can determine judgment. Infidels have the right to administer their own lands, but they must permit missionaries to enter and preach the Gospel, presumably in accord with natural law. Non-Christians who prevent the work of missionaries commit a sin and become liable to punishment by the Church. In instances when unbelievers reject his command, the pope may declare a just war against them, which would make them potentially susceptible to enslavement upon capture (Muldoon 2005, 78).

While not immediately evident, the logic of Jewish subjection lurks in Innocent's analysis. In his commentary, Innocent cites his own letter of 1244 to the King of France, *Impia Judeorum perfidia*, which condemns the Talmud as containing blasphemy against Christianity and iterates Pope Gregory IX's order that all copies be burned (Muldoon 1979, 30; Grayzel 1966, 250–53). He argues that the Jews' study of the Talmud constitutes a rejection of the Bible and a sin against the Christian faith that the pope must punish. This illustrates the point being made in the commentary on *Quod super his*, that the pope may judge the Jews when they sin against the Gospel. Somewhat anomalously, in the same 1244 letter, he also condemns as an "insult to the Christian Faith" the employment of Christian women to nurse Jewish children. He emphasizes that Jews should not employ any Christian servants, "lest the children of the free-born serve the children of the maid-servants, [ne filii libere filiis famulentur ancille] but, since they were condemned to slavery by the Lord for whose death they sinfully plotted, they shall recognize themselves, as a result of this act, as slaves of those whom the death of Christ set free while condemning them to slavery" (Grayzel 1966, 253). Innocent clearly iterates his citation of Galatians 4 in his contrast of the children of the slave woman with that of the free and the liberty that Jesus secured for the latter. The study of the Talmud and the subjection of Christians to the service of Jews both wrongly invert the proper relation of slave to free, unbelief to true faith, and thus contravene the teaching of the Gospels.[27] A synthesis of the two transgressions cited by Innocent implies both that the pope has the authority to punish infidel sinners and that their sin has already reduced them to servitude; in effect, the pope may enforce what is already an inherent condition of subjection.

The subjection of Jews to Christians serves as a precedent to argue for the proper subordination of infidels to the faithful in the course of the thirteenth century. As James Muldoon observes, "Christian relations with the Jew provided the model for relations between Christians and infidels within Europe"; the pope's ability to exercise power over non-Christians derives from his claim to be able to punish Jews (Muldoon 1979, 28, 30).[28] In his letter *De regimine Iudaeorum*, Thomas Aquinas explains "as the laws say, the Jews, deservedly [merito] by their sin, have been and are enslaved to perpetual slavery, and so the rulers of the land may take their [the Jews'] things as their [the rulers'] own" (art.: 1, resp. ad argumentum, numerus: 727, linea: 5, pag. 249, my translation).[29] The spiritual slavery of the Jews has legal consequences here, as they deserve, by their sin, to lose control over their property. In the *Summa Theologica*, Aquinas takes up the larger question of whether unbelievers are permitted authority or dominion over the faithful with recourse to the example of the Jews. While he concedes that Divine law does not abrogate the human law permitting infidels to have dominion over Christians, "Nevertheless this right of dominion or authority can be justly done away with by the sentence or ordination of the Church who has the authority of God: since unbelievers in virtue [merito] of their unbelief deserve to forfeit their power over the faithful who are converted into children of God" (II 2ae Q x Art.10 Reply to Obj 1). He follows with the example of the Jews, classed "among those unbelievers who are [subjected to the subjection/subiectione subiiciuntur], even in temporal matters, [of] the Church and her members . . . because since those Jews themselves are [slaves/servi] to the Church, she can dispose of their possessions" (II 2ae Q x Art.10 Reply to Obj 1, my emendations in brackets). Because the Jews are slaves to the Church, they are subject to its authority. The application of this idea to unbelievers in the context of just war reveals a suppressed tautology: sin subordinates infidels, rendering them liable to the judgment of the Church, who then has the power to punish them through the declaration of just war and enslavement.

Perpetual Servitude in Africa

The canon law discussions of the Church's authority over infidel lands and persons influenced later debates on the legality of the acquisition of the territories and bodies of African unbelievers.[30] In the early fifteenth century, King Duarte of Portugal (r. 1433–1438) asked Pope Eugenius IV for permission to expand control over islands held by infidels in the Canaries; only the pope, who has authority over infidels, could deputize secular rulers to act on his behalf. The king based his request on the grounds that the Portuguese would occupy these lands for the purpose of converting the non-Christian inhabitants (Muldoon 1976, 468–71). A contemporary summary of the king's request puts it more in terms of war than conversion and misrepresents the Canarians as Muslim: "A certain Catholic prince or King who recognizes no superior wishes to wage war against the Saracens" (Muldoon 1976, 472). Eugenius consulted two canon lawyers to answer this question; both rely on the opinion of Innocent IV to address the issues of the legitimate *dominium* (rule) of infidels and the grounds upon which Christians could deprive them of it. Although the inhabitants of the Canaries are pagans, both canonists assume they are Muslim, which enables the lawyers to draw from existing opinions regarding infidels, developed with recourse to Jews and Muslims, and papal authority.

One of the lawyers, Antonio Roselli, followed Innocent's discussion of papal power as stated in the commentary to *Quod super his*, to explain how the "Saracen" Canarians are subject to the pope. Roselli iterates Innocent's claim that because all people are subject to God's divine power, therefore His representative, the pope, has authority over non-Christians in addition to his role as shepherd over Christ's flock (Muldoon 1979, 127; 1976, 475). Roselli initially draws, as Innocent does, on Psalm 8:8, to argue that although gentiles and pagans are not sheep of the Church, they are nevertheless Christ's sheep by virtue of creation. In his paraphrase of Scripture he asserts "All, indeed, were subject to Christ, sheep and cows and all the cattle of the field."[31] Relying on the Psalm text, however, he alters this initial statement that all peoples are sheep, to draw a distinction between the faithful and unbelievers. He explains that the sheep represent Christians, while the cows and cattle signify "Saracens who, devoid of reason, just as beasts, worship idols, scorning the true God. Even if these in this way were not commended to the shepherd Peter by Jesus, they are therefore nevertheless subjected to divine rule and power beneath the feet of Peter" (my translation, qtd. in Muldoon 1976, 475).[32] While the proof-text serves to show the similarity between sheep and cattle, insofar as both are subject to divine law as adjudicated by the pope, Roselli employs it to create a hierarchy between the two groups. In distinguishing between the Christian sheep and the Muslim cattle, the sheep are preferred to the bestial cattle, which lack reason. He may be recalling discourses like Peter of Cluny's that identify the mentality of both Jews and Muslims as both bovine and senseless (Cohen 1999, 254–70 passim, especially 259, 268). Perhaps also hearkening to Augustine's view that humans were not created to be subjected to each other, but intended by God only to rule over irrational animals, Roselli represents the Muslims as deserving of subordination. He draws on the Latin text of the Psalm, omitted in his paraphrase, "you have placed all (the animals) under his feet (Omnia subjecisti sub pedibus ejus)" to claim that non-Christians have not been favorably commended to, but placed or subjected under, the feet of Peter, the first pope.

Having established, relative to Christians, the greater subjection of Muslims to papal authority, Roselli employs a figurative reading of Abraham, Sarah, and Hagar to reinforce infidel subordination. He may again be following the lead of Innocent IV who also mentions this allegory in the letter, *Impia Judeorum perfidia*, to which the pope briefly refers in his commentary on the question of papal authority over infidels.

> But by Sarah is signified the holy mother Church, and by Hagar the slave woman is signified, that cursed slave woman in whom is signified the sect of Muhammad that trace from her the origin. . . . And therefore, the holy church that I said is signified through Sarah, even if it has legal authority over this slave woman and pagan sect, they certainly cannot be compelled but encouraged to the faith. (qtd. in Muldoon 1976, 475 n. 33, my translation)[33]

Roselli appears to balance his harsh characterization of Islam, derived from the slave woman, with the protection of Muslims' religious freedom in prohibiting forced conversions; they must instead be encouraged to convert. However, he restates Innocent's point that if pagans prohibit missionaries from preaching the faith, then the pope has authority to declare war upon them for violating divine law. Captives taken in such a just war could thus be legally enslaved. While Roselli takes the relatively more tolerant view that infidels have, in theory, a right to possess their own lands and worship in their own way, in practice the prevention of missionizing proved a fairly easy condition to meet in order to justify enslaving infidels and expropriating their lands. In emphasizing the notion that Muslims derive from a slave woman, Roselli implies not only their subordination to papal authority but also their already servile status.

In submitting his request, King Duarte, and the rulers who followed him, sought to secure papal permission to claim control over land and thus establish the primacy of the Portuguese right to seize the Canary Islands against competing Spanish claims (Muldoon 1979, 133–34). However, in requesting consent from the pope to wage a just war, Duarte implicitly obtained the right to capture and enslave the enemy.[34] Although a trade in

enslaved Africans pre-existed the Iberian expansion, it was this legal foundation that justified the European entry into this market (Phillips, 114–27).
As Saunders explains,

> Roman and canon law, the Bible and the Aristotelian corpus all
> permitted slavery and . . .provided a traditional sanction for the
> means employed to acquire slaves: by the end of the Middle Ages
> most commentators on Roman and canon law were agreed that the
> appropriate authorities in any country, Christian or infidel, could
> reduce prisoners of war and criminals to slavery; that children of
> slaves were slaves themselves; and that slaves could be bought and
> sold like chattels. Both slavery and the slave-trade could thus be
> defended by recourse to authority. (35)[35]

Thus "warlike raids," similar to those previously employed to enslave
Muslims, provided the initial means by which the Portuguese acquired
enslaved Africans (Saunders, 4–5). In the early 1440s Duarte's brother,
Prince Henry, asked Pope Eugenius IV to designate his incursions into
West Africa as a crusade, thereby according it the status of a just war and
permitting the capture of slaves (Saunders, 37). The pope granted this request in the bull *Illius qui*, which characterizes Henry's undertaking as
seeking "the ruin and expulsion of the Saracens and also enemies of the
name of Christianity and . . . that the Catholic faith be increased" (Jordão
and Barreto vol. 1, 21, my translation).[36] However, the bull does not give
explicit permission to enslave, even though Henry's representative on this
mission did enslave his captives.

A decade later, King Alfonso asked the pope to confirm the right of the
Portuguese to reduce the enemy to slavery; Pope Nicholas V accorded the
king his wish in the bull *Dum Diversas* issued in Rome on June 18, 1452
(Saunders, 37). The bull opens with the pope's concern over the threat
posed by the enemies of Christianity and his desire that they be repressed
and subjugated to the Christian religion. The text situates Alfonso's en-
treaty of papal support in this context, describing his undertaking as
motivated by a "pious and Christian desire to subjugate the enemies of
Christ, that is the Saracens, and . . .to reduce [them], by means of a strong
hand, to the faith of Christ" (Jordão and Barreto vol. 1, 22, my translation).
Alfonso requires the pope's authority to declare a just war, a conflict properly fought against enemies of the faith, in order, ostensibly, to strengthen
and expand Christianity. However, waging a just war also enables the

Portuguese legally to capture and enslave their alleged combatants. The pope explicitly permits this request:

> By Apostolic authority uninterrupted to the present we concede to you the full and free power, that the Saracens and pagans and other infidels and all enemies of Christ whatsoever, and wheresoever established, the kingdoms, dukedoms, royal courts, principalities and other realms, lands, places, villages, fortresses and whatever other possessions, movable and immovable goods, . . . might be invaded, conquered, plundered, and subjugated, and their persons reduced to perpetual slavery, besides the kingdoms, dukedoms, royal courts, principalities and other realms, possessions and goods of this kind, be brought and made over to you and your successors, and also be converted forever to your use and advantage and the same successors' the kings of Portugal. (Jordão and Barreto vol. 1, 22, my translation)[37]

The pope apparently understood that the West Africans might not be Muslims; he provides an expanded category of enemies of Christ to include not only "Saracens" but "Pagans" and "other infidels." By including Muslims, the text provides an established type of an enemy of Christ against whom a just war could be waged, and then extends the definition to other pagans and infidels. In addition to permitting the Portuguese to appropriate the lands and goods of the Africans, the pope authorizes them to "subjugate . . . and to lead their persons in perpetual servitude." While the legal structure here derives from Roman law, the theological basis by which the enemy is defined and the terminology for the captivity derive ultimately from the example of the Jews, the original enemies of Christ whose sin subjected them to perpetual servitude.

Although just war theory provided the initial legal rationale for reducing Africans to slavery, the method of military attack as a means to gain enslaved people was only employed for a few years in the early 1440s. A peaceful trade in enslaved peoples was already established by 1452 when the pope promulgates *Dum Diversas*; however, this bull authorizes the enslavement of Africans as part of a just war. Hence, the Portuguese sought to establish trade as an alternate option (Saunders, 4–5, 37–8). A different obstacle appears here: trade with the infidel had been prohibited since the times of the crusades in order to prevent Christians, motivated more by profit than faith, from providing materiel and other necessities that could advantage the Church's Muslim adversaries. Alfonso returned to the pope in the mid-1450s asking for permission to trade with non-Christians on the grounds that the profits could support crusading armies and bring about conversions of Africans to Christianity (Saunders, 37–8). In the bull *Romanus Pontifex* (1455 [o.s. 1454]), Nicholas V grants this appeal, noting that the enslavement of people through trade had already taken place and deeming it licit: "Many Guineans and other black [people], taken by force, and also some by exchange of unprohibited goods, or by other legitimate contract of sale,. . . have become converted to the Catholic faith in large numbers" (Jordão and Barreto, 1.32, my translation).[38] While some enslaved Africans were captured in war, others were purchased or acquired through barter of permitted goods—that is, commodities that were not, under the laws developed during the crusades, considered capable of strengthening the military might of the enemy. The promised conversion of enslaved peoples was already being realized and provided evidence for Alfonso's claims. However, in this same bull, the pope explicitly reaffirms right to subjugate the inhabitants of the land articulated in *Dum Diversas* (Maxwell, 53):

> With respect to our other letters to the formerly named King Alfonso, we had fully and freely allowed the ability, among other things, that any Saracens, and Pagans, and other enemies of Christ and wherever located, and also the kingdoms, dukedoms, principalities, dominions, possessions—both movable and immovable goods— whatsoever held or possessed by them, to be invaded, conquered, assaulted, vanquished, and subjugated, and their persons reduced to perpetual servitude. (Jordão and Barreto, 1.32, my translation)[39]

Thus both warfare and purchase establish valid means of obtaining slaves. However, ultimately war provided the legal foundation for the sale of slaves, as the Portuguese assumed (often without evidence) that the people they purchased from African and Muslim traders had been legitimately acquired in war (Saunders, 46). Subsequent bulls incorporated the text of previous edicts; thus in 1456, when Pope Calixtus III confirmed these grants to the Kings of Portugal in the bull *Inter caetera*, he included the identical text from *Romanus Pontifex*.[40] *Aeterni Regis*, promulgated by Pope Sixtus IV in 1481, renews the previous grants made by Nicholas V to Alfonso and Prince Henry; article 5 reiterates the directive that "Saracens, pagans and other enemies of Christ . . .be invaded, conquered, expunged,

vanquished, and subjugated, and their persons reduced to perpetual servitude" (Jordão and Barreto vol. 1, 48). In his 1514 bull *Praecelsae devotionis*,
Leo X includes the original text of *Dum Diversas*, *Romanus Pontifex* and
Aeterni Regis; hence he repeats *three times* the article calling for the reduction of the enemies of Christ to perpetual servitude.[41]

Although the rationale of just war and the focus on Muslims as susceptible to servitude continues in the papal justifications, in practice the trade
in enslaved peoples transformed from a military enterprise for captur-
ing Muslims into a commercial venture in which black Africans were the
main commodity. The enslaved population in Portugal reflects this new
reality: "By the 1550s blacks appear to have displaced Moors [i.e., Muslims]
as the principal ethnic group among the slaves who then constituted up
to 10 per cent of the population of Lisbon and other towns" (Saunders, xi).
The primacy of "Saracens" in other discourses relating to the Portuguese
trade subsides as the enslavement of black Africans replaces that of North
African Muslims. One context in which this appears is in the very terms
used. The earlier equation of Muslim with an enslaved person registers in
the meaning of the Portuguese term "mouro," which signifies "Muslim"
or "slave." The escalation of the African trade and the resulting decrease
in enslaved Muslims in the Iberian context results in an increasing association of blackness, rather than Islam, with servitude. The imprecision of
the word "mouros" gives rise to refinements: "mouros fourros" indicate
free Muslims, "mouros negros" signify enslaved Africans. New expressions also develop; hence the appearance of the more generalized word
"escravo" (derived, like the English word "slave" from Slav) and its variations:[42] "escravos pretos" or "negros" for enslaved black Africans, "escravos
mouros" or "brancos" for enslaved Muslims or whites (Saunders, xiii).

The new practice of purchasing enslaved people requires a new rationale; although just war provides the legal foundation for the trade,
explanations justifying African, as opposed to Muslim, servitude become
necessary.[43] The shift from enslaved Muslim to African, however, does not
produce entirely original justifications; rather older discourses accounting
for servitude are repurposed to rationalize the of enslaving the latter. The
idea of sin as the source of servitude, articulated effectively by Augustine
in his analysis of the origin of slavery with recourse to Ham, appears in
late medieval and early modern explanations of African slavery.

> While slavery's immediate causes were war or trade, many think-
> ers subscribed to the Augustinian doctrine that its ultimate cause

lay in the divine punishment of sin. Alvarus Pelagius [1280–1352], for instance, held that "servitude was introduced after sin and on account of sin" so as to provide a way to order an imperfect world. (Saunders, 38)

However, the model developed with recourse to Jewish slavery, in which a people are cursed with hereditary servitude as punishment for an ancient sin, and not a contemporary transgression, provides the basis for the justifications of the enslavement of Africans.

The application of the figure of Ham to explain contemporary Jewish and Muslim slavery developed not only in canon law, but also in medieval histories to explain the servitude of Africans. While the concept of Ham's slavery emerges through an account of Jewish subordination with recourse to other figures of servitude, its subsequent value appears in its application in other contexts to different peoples. The Jewish element of this servitude disappears in these new contexts, leaving Muslims and Africans as the inheritors of Ham's curse. The association of Ham with Africa established in the Bible and Josephus's *Jewish Antiquities* tends to be treated in early medieval commentaries separate from discussions of the advent of slavery and the allegorical identification of Ham with the Jews. However, by the thirteenth century, commentaries treating Ham's geographical location begin to incorporate his associations with servitude. The *General Estoria*, a universal history commissioned by Alfonso X, King of Castile (1252–1284), cites Josephus as a source in chapter 29 titled "Whence comes the principal enmity of the sons of Jafet and of those of Cam." The author begins with the Genesis story to explain how Noah cursed Ham "in his children and their offspring and in his curse gave them for slaves to Shem and Japhet" (Alfonso, 90, my translation).[44] The three brothers signify three religious faiths: Jews from the line of Shem, Christians from Shem and Japhet, and Muslims from Ham. "And the Muslims [moros] come principally from Ham, who populated Africa. . . who by the false preaching of Muhammed converted to Muslims" (91, my translation).[45] Thus Ham and his offspring represent both Muslims and Africans, who have been cursed with servitude to the offspring of Shem and Japhet. Focusing primarily on the enmity between Christians and Muslims, the text explains: "Thus it is that the Moors that be, are all from Ham, and if we wished to fight with them by battle or by any force and take of them and make them our slaves, then we would not by that be doing a sin, nor a wrong nor an error" (91, my translation).[46] Based on the authority of the biblical story and possibly of just war theory, Christians can legitimately wage war against Muslims and enslave them; Ham represents the African Muslim as already cursed for his sin with hereditary servitude that renders him inferior and thus susceptible to war and captivity.

While the *General Estoria* places Ham in Africa, his descendants, the "moros," are identified as Muslims; his offspring are afflicted with servitude, but the text makes no mention of blackness as a curse or sign of slavery. However, by the beginning of the fifteenth century, accounts of Ham increasingly represent him as cursed with blackness as well as bondage, reflecting the shift in the Portuguese trade from Muslim to black African servitude. In his *Chronicle of the Discovery and Conquest of Guinea*, Gomes Eanes de Zurara gives an account of the exploration and appropriation of the western African coast under the auspices of Prince Henry.[47] His discussion clearly distinguishes between "negros" and "mouros," and correlates the former, not the latter, with slavery.

> And here you must note that these blacks (negros) were Moors [moros, indicating Muslims] like the others, though their slaves, in accordance with ancient custom, which I believe to have been because of the curse which, after the Deluge, Noah laid upon his son, Cain (Caym) cursing him in this way:—that his race [geeraçõ, generation, offspring] should be subject to all the other races (geeraçoões) of the world. And from his race these are descended. (1896, 54; 1978, 77)

Zurara characterizes the servitude of black Africans to all other peoples as an ancient custom, derived, he surmises, from Noah's curse upon his son's offspring. Servitude, not blackness, is the result of the curse, but it serves to subjugate Cain's black descendants. The English translation renders "Caym" as "Cain," but the name more properly signals a conflation of the two names, Ham and Cain.[48] The association of servitude with Cain makes no sense without knowledge of the exegetical identification of Cain's crime and cursed mark with Jewish slavery that can be analogized with Ham's figuration of hereditary Jewish servitude; Augustine described the curse of slavery imposed upon the Jews with recourse to readings of both Cain and Ham in the same chapter of the *Contra Faustum*.[49] Thus Jewish subjection prefigures African subjection in the citing of Cain/Ham as an explanation for hereditary slavery; Ham's sin results not in his own personal slavery, but that of his descendants.

An explicit pairing of Cain and Ham as explanation for hereditary African servitude appears in Alonso de Sandoval's seventeenth-century *Un tratado sobre la escalvitud* in his chapter on "The nature of Ethiopians, commonly called blacks." As the title implies, he focuses here on the skin color of Africans and considers a number of possible causes for it, including climate, before considering biblical explanations:

> One could infer, not without some basis, that the black skin of the Ethiopians not only comes from the curse Noah put on his son Ham but also is an innate or intrinsic part of how God created them, so that in this extreme heat, the sons engendered were left this color, as a sign that they descend from a man who mocked his father, to punish his daring. Thus the Ethiopians descend from Ham, the first servant and slave that there ever was in the world, whose punishment darkened the skin of his sons and descendants. (2008, 20)

In addition to positing climatic influence, Sandoval asserts that Noah curses Ham's children with black skin to punish his son for disobedience.[50] He then identifies Ham as the first slave, the forefather of the Ethiopians; his punishment resulted in darkening the skin of his descendants, but their status in relationship to slavery remains unclear. Strikingly, the author then cites an alternative explanation for Ethiopian blackness and servitude—the example of Cain, who is not cursed with slavery in the biblical text:

> Others have a very different theory, one I agree with. . . .[It] says that Adam cursed his son Cain for the shamelessness he showed in treating Adam with so little reverence, that Cain lost his nobility and even his personal freedom and became a slave, along with all of his children. This was the first servitude in world history. Although Cain was of light-skinned lineage, he was born dark. Thus blacks are also born as slaves, because God paints the sons of bad parents with a dark brush. (2008, 20–1)

The climate theory argument drops out here, leaving only an apocryphal biblical explanation for the appearance of Africans. In imagining a conflict between Adam and Cain, an event absent from Genesis,[51] Sandoval appears to be thinking of the Ham story and exegetical interpretations of his unfilial behavior toward his father. This episode, which includes the curse of hereditary slavery, provides the rationale for the claim that the son's disobedience results not only in his enslavement, but also that of his descendants. In another departure from the biblical text, Sandoval claims that Cain was born with dark skin, although this would seem to antedate his offence and the punishing curse of servitude. He somewhat illogically concludes that blacks are servile as a result of the original sin of filial impiety. In doing so he represents blacks as "naturally" or inherently enslaved at birth as a result of God's curse. While Sandoval makes no mention of the Jews in this discussion, the figural development of their perpetual servitude provides the logic that identifies both Ham and Cain as the first slave in the world. Although he offers multiple explanations of blackness, Sandoval relies on a suppressed exegetical genealogy of Jewish bondage to construct African hereditary servitude.

If the inherent and hereditary enslavement of Africans results from sin, salvation through conversion to Christianity should provide the solution to this cursed status. From the very beginning of the fifteenth-century exploration of the Africa and the Atlantic islands, the Portuguese were motivated by the crusading spirit of the just war against the infidel along with its corollary, the conversion of the infidel. In requesting permission of the pope to conquer the Canary Islands, King Duarte included the plea that he be allowed "to continue the important task of converting the Canarians to Christianity. The work of conversion was, according to the Portuguese king, the fundamental reason for Portuguese activity in the Canaries" (Muldoon 1979, 121). This rationale continues to be articulated in into the next century: "By the sixteenth century the paramount justification of the slave-trade was that enslavement was an effective method of bringing blacks to a knowledge of Christianity" (Saunders, 40). The ascendance of the rationale of conversion would seem to put a definitive end to the just war basis for enslaving Africans. Under the laws of just war as practiced in Europe, Christians did not enslave captive fellow-Christians, but rather held them for ransom (Keen 70, n. 35, qtd. in Muldoon 2005, 76).

However, slaves, once baptized, remained slaves. Canon lawyers explored the question of the baptism of the infidel.

The general practice of medieval European slavery was that Christians were not to be enslaved, and that Christian prisoners should be ransomed rather than sold into slavery. But what of non-Christians who were enslaved and then sold to Christian masters and who then accepted baptism? Would the acceptance of baptism automatically free such a slave? The importance of this issue is obvious; if baptism automatically secured manumission, slaves would be likely to seek it and slave owners would lose both the slave's labor and the financial investment that it involved. The canon lawyers' solution to this dilemma was that while it was good to free slaves who chose to become Christians, this emancipation was not required because their status as slaves preceded their baptism. (Muldoon 2005, 76–7)

Thus slave-owners were careful to purchase people as pagans, subject to captivity by the laws of just war, and then effect their conversion.[52] The desire to increase the number of the faithful was subordinated to, but also compatible with, the motivation to profit from the acquisition and sale of enslaved people. Since Scripture affirmed the legitimacy of slavery, both as a metaphor for a spiritual status in relation to God as well as a legal and economic institution, early modern Christian doctrine posed no immediate theological objection. Rather, tradition taught the value of Christians owing unbelieving slaves—and emphasized the danger of Jews and Muslims employing Christian servants or slaves—insofar as the power of the master could influence the conversion of the servile. Aquinas sets out this logic in consideration of the obverse: "Whether unbelievers may have authority or dominion over the faithful?"

> For subjects are easily influenced by their superiors to comply with their commands, unless the subjects are of great virtue: moreover unbelievers hold the faith in contempt, if they see the faithful fall away. . . . And so the Church altogether forbids unbelievers to acquire dominion over believers, or to have authority over them in any capacity whatever. (*Summa Theologica*, Second Part of the Second Part, Question 10. Article 10)

Although he defends the ability of infidels to exercise dominion in some cases in this Article, Aquinas strongly suggests the value to the faith of Christians exercising dominion over unbelievers. If just war theory militated against the acquisition of enslaved Christians, theological principles supported the enslavement of infidels for conversionary purposes and supported their continued subservient status after they had joined the faith.

However, the justifications for the trade in enslaved Africans do not rely only on the spiritual benefits of Christian conversion outweighing the temporal hardships of servitude. A rationale that establishes the inherent and *sustained* inferiority of Africans is needed in order to naturalize their enslavement. Once converted and civilized through contact with European culture, what ensured the continued captivity of enslaved Africans? As Saunders explains:

> The charge of bestiality could be employed only to justify the en-
> slavement of people in Africa, not the continued servitude of blacks
> living in a civilized manner in Portugal. Once they had forgone bes-
> tial conduct, they remained slaves by convention alone, that is, as
> a result of *Dum Diversas*, which allowed the Portuguese to enslave
> West Africans in perpetuity. (40)

The legal language of the papal documents allows not only the enslavement of captives, following the rules of just war, but also the enduring subjection that derives from theological discourses. The idea of an eternal, deserved subordination helps construct the hereditary inferiority of Africans. Although ostensibly contrary to Christian teachings, this concept gained acceptance in the guise of a hereditary sinful servitude resulting from a divinely imposed punishment. The origins of perpetual servitude in figurative readings of Jewish cursed servility appear in the types of proofs adduced in popular analyses of African slavery. In citing the examples of Cain and Ham, sometimes simultaneously, and the continuing effects of their punishment on the status of their descendants, these accounts clearly draw from existing models developed to subordinate Jews.[53] As a central justification for slavery, these theological discourses had enduring effects:

> The form taken by relations between black Africans and white
> Portuguese in the fifteenth and sixteenth centuries was, with some
> modifications and exceptions, that which was to prevail throughout
> the Atlantic world until the nineteenth century, and we still suffer
> from its consequences today. The salient features of this system of
> relations were the Atlantic slave-trade and the relegation of black
> people to servitude or positions of inferior status in countries ruled
> by whites. (Saunders, xi)

The deployment of these correlated discourses of perpetual servitude at the founding of the trade in enslaved Africans shaped subsequent formulations of slavery and race.

A number of different factors contributed to justifications for and the practice of the European trade in enslaved Africans. What has been overlooked in many other studies on this topic is the extent to which Jewish servitude influenced both legal and popular understandings of a cursed, hereditary—and thus perpetual—slavery of Africans. The creative practice of figural interpretation enables a correlation of several biblical characters—Cain, Ham, and Ishmael—into a theory of hereditary servitude that can be transferred and applied to various peoples. Although Roman law provides the justification for the enslaving of an enemy, the definition of the enemy, his or her predisposition for servitude and the notion of the permanence of this subordination all arise from ecclesiastical efforts to subordinate Jews to Christians. The doctrine of just war in effect provides a vehicle for transferring an established concept of hereditary servitude from Jewish and Muslim enemies of Christendom to African pagans. While the inapplicability of the just war rationale renders it increasingly irrelevant as the acquisition of enslaved people occurs less by battle than through trade, the idea of perpetual slavery that it helped to transmit undergoes transformations to ensure its continued relevance.

Coda

IN FOCUSING ON a medieval theological discourse of figural slavery, this book demonstrates the racist force of the construction of inferior identities for Jews, Muslims, and Africans. The historical consequences of this construction vary widely between and among these groups, such that they occupy complexly different positions in Western society today. Nevertheless, the recent rise in nationalism and white supremacism both in the United States and Europe can be understood in part with recourse to the medieval linkages between the three groups. White supremacists and the alt-right have expressly drawn on medieval tropes and phrases to fabricate a notion of originary medieval Christian whiteness that they aspire to recreate in the contemporary moment. These groups are, on the one hand, constructing a fictional middle ages in their own image, ignoring or suppressing evidence for the ethnic, cultural, and religious diversity of the period. On the other hand, however, they rightly recognize a strand of racial intolerance that developed during the medieval period and still contributes to contemporary racisms. While no apparent rationale organizes white supremacists' animus against blacks, Muslims, and Jews, the history of the ideology of white supremacy can be traced back to medieval Western Europe, when the concept of Christian superiority, often coded as white, emerged and constructed itself against an infidel inferiority that included and conflated Jews, Muslims, and Africans.

The complexity, mutability, and motility of racism requires that its study pursue multiple foci, approaches, and methodologies. Important ongoing work attends to somatic markers, especially blackness, and ethnicity, as well as its intersections with gender, class, and sexuality. In addition, scholars are increasingly identifying the ways in which constructions of religious identity function as racist. This book supplements, rather than contends with, other recent work on premodern racism and religion. *Figuring Racism in Medieval Christianity* contributes a few crucial points to this critical conversation in focusing specifically on and privileging theological discourse. I demonstrate the constitutive force of hereditary inferiority for racism and isolate within medieval Christian theological discourses a concept of Jewish perpetual slavery that creates this status. By exploring the ways in which this racist concept circulates, we can chart its infiltration of legal discourses to provide divine justification for instituting discriminatory practices against Jews and Muslims as well as for the perpetration of chattel slavery in Africa. While the racist formulation of ontological inferiority develops within theology, it easily attaches to the body by migrating into medieval somatic discourses and materializing in visual images. The multivalent possibilities of figural meaning also enable the translation of hereditary inferiority from one group to another. All of these strategies provide us with important information about how racism functions. I hope that this analysis attunes future study not only to identify the various constructions of inherent inferiority, but also to challenge, dismantle, and reject the discourses and practices that instantiate racism.

Notes

INTRODUCTION

1. Many studies of medieval race privilege modern racism's focus on the body; while this approach produces important work, it tends to obscure the racist content of nonsomatic constructions of religious identity. Isaac's analysis of race in classical antiquity considers ethnic and somatic discourses as well as the religious identity of Jews, but argues that the mutability of faith nullifies the possibility of Jewish race in that period. The collection that he coedited with Eliav-Feldon and Ziegler includes essays on religious identity, but the introduction emphasizes the importance of somatic discourses and permanence for the construction of race. Akbari similarly focuses on the body in her discussion of how discourses on climate and geography shape medieval ideas of Muslims and Jews. The *JMEMS* special issue "Race and Ethnicity in the Middle Ages," edited by Thomas Hahn, includes essays that theorize medieval race in terms of ethnicity, color, and religious identity, but Jews are largely overlooked. Lomperis and Jordan (2001) argue for the importance of analyzing medieval constructions of Jewish race, but do not undertake this study themselves. Lampert's essay (2004a) addresses the question of medieval racial constructions of Jews but focuses on how color marks Muslim identity; her book (2004b) considers Jewish racial identity largely in the early modern literary context. Ramey focuses primarily on color, which she sees as intersecting with religious as well as other identities. Whitaker analyzes the productive intersection of religious identity and color, but distinguishes between racial and religious identities on the basis of their im/mutability as marked on the body (2009). Resnick provides an extensive consideration of the racial implications of a range of medieval scientific and medical discourses that distinctively identify the Jewish body (2000, 2012). My work overlaps with that of Krummel, in her consideration of figures and visual representations of Jews, but her account of racism also focuses on the body. See also Green. The medieval reception of Pliny's texts on the monstrous races provides another important discourse for thinking about

race; while the work that explores the racial implications of the monstrous focus primarily on the body, some scholars also attend to the ways in which religious discourses incorporate these ideas. John Block Friedman's *The Monstrous Races in Medieval Art and Thought* lays the groundwork for this line of thinking, although he does not theorize race. See the important work of Strickland (2003 and 2012); Joan-Pau Rubiés (2009, 379–415); Jeffrey Jerome Cohen (1999, 1–61; 2003 and 2006); Bildhauer and Mills (2003, 97–112); and Mittman (2006, 11–26).

2. I rely here on Jeremy Cohen's full and careful explanation of Augustine's "doctrine of witness" (1999, 23–71).

3. While a number of scholars have noted overlapping identities or "imaginaries" between and among these groups, they do so primarily in the context of modernity. Harrison-Kahan employs the term "imaginary" in her exploration of Black-Jewish identity in twentieth-century American literature; she surveys the considerable field of scholarship that explores the intersection of African American and Jewish identities. Other representative work on the intersecting identities of blacks and Jews include that of Gilman (1991); Shell; Karp; Parfitt; Bruder and Parfitt; Schorsch (2004); Kaye/Kantrowitz; Anna Deavere Smith; Lerner and West; and Lester. Anidjar's work on Jews and Arabs as occupying the same category, Semites, similarly registers the history of a Muslim–Jewish imaginary (2003, 2008); see also Majid; Arjana; Akbari; and Burton. For orientalism and the Jews see Trubowitz; Brunotte et al.; Kalmar and Penslar; and Librett, who also considers the figural. While medieval and early modern scholarship has already undertaken a consideration of the black–Muslim imaginary in literary and visual representations, more work needs to be done on this construct of coordinated as well as conflated identities. The scholarship on this question is too large to cover, but some important studies includes Hahn; Heng; Lampert (2004a); Loomba; Whitaker; Ramey; Patton; Strickland; Monteira Arias; Hall (2007); and Bartels. For other significant work, not always focused on the question of racism, that studies the ways in which discourses developed around one group are projected onto another, see Jonathan Boyarin; Burton; Matar; Loomba (2002); Fuchs; and Schorsch (2009).

4. Some important work on medieval race and religion includes: Akbari; Anidjar (2014); Altschul; Bale (2006, 2011); Hahn; Whitaker (2009, 2013, 2015); Lavezzo (2010, 2013, 2016); Bassett and Lloyd; Beckett; Blurton and Johnson; Calkin; Cawsey; Jeffrey Cohen (2001, 2008, 2013a & b); Dagenais and Greer; de Weever; Eliav-Feldon, Isaac, and Ziegler; Epstein; Frakes; Frojmovic and Karkov; Goldenberg (1999, 2003, 2009); Heng (2003, 2007, 2011a & b, 2015a & b); Keita (2006, 2011); Kim; Kinoshita; Kruger; Krummel; Lampert (2004a & b); Loomba (2002, 2007, 2009); Michaelis and Yekani; Mirrer; Nadhiri; and Thomas. I was unable to consult Geraldine Heng's most recent book, *The Invention of Race in the European Middle Ages*, before my manuscript went to press. This is a very partial list; the scholarship on medieval race that considers the topic from other perspectives

is beyond the purview of this book. I am grateful to the Medievalists of Color group for the ongoing labor of compiling a bibliography on this subject; it can be accessed through the blog "In the Middle" at http://www.inthemedievalmiddle.com/2017/06/morevoices-citation-inclusion-and.html, *Postmedieval: A Journal of Medieval Cultural Studies* (2017), 8, 500–31, https://doi.org/10.1057/s41280-017-0072-0, and at http://medievalistsofcolor.com/.

5. Eliav-Feldon et al. make the case for focusing on racism not race: "If we want to understand the history of racism we must concentrate on the question of how one group saw another. Also, we discuss *racism*, not race" (6). I also follow their view, shared by numerous others writing on the subject, that "race" is an imagined category without biological basis: "There is no conceptual basis for race except racism" (7–8, quoting Hirschman, 2004: 385–421, 401). See also Isaac (16ff) and Nirenberg (2009, 235–36). Loomba makes a similar point that includes an important word of caution: "To say that race is socially constructed is not to imply that it is a delusion; 'false' as they may be, ideas about race have nevertheless had very real effects on people's lives" (2002, 2–4). See also Heng's definition: "*Race is a structural relationship for the articulation and management of human differences, rather than a substantive content*" (2011a, 268).

6. Isaac cites definitions of racism and racialism that emphasize the importance of relative superiority for their meaning (21–2).

7. For considerations of slavery in the texts of classical antiquity and early Christianity, absent a discussion of race, see Garnsey's *Ideas of Slavery from Aristotle to Augustine* and Glancy's *Slavery in Early Christianity*.

8. Relevant to this discussion is Patterson's analysis of chattel slavery as effecting "social death," a profoundly abjected form of inferiority. As Sweet points out, scholars have debated the extent to which modern chattel slavery contributed to racism (Sweet 1997, 143). David Brion Davis agrees with Sweet that the answer is complex, but that ideas of slavery probably did contribute to racism (1997, 16). Bartels cautions against viewing slavery as contributing to racism in the early modern English context (1997, 47). See also Akhimie's note on this issue: "For a discussion of the justifications for the slave trade or the effects of its reduction of bodies to chattel as the crucial catalyst for changes in the concept of race, see for example MacDonald, *Women and Race*, 3–4, 7; Floyd-Wilson, *English Ethnicity and Race*, 6, 18–19; Iyengar, *Shades of Difference*, 14; and Chapman, *Anti-Black Racism*, 3" (2018, 37, n. 13).

9. Muldoon notes the reception of Aristotle's natural slave theory in medieval Christian thought, but argues that "the general medieval conception of slavery was that slavery was not a consequence of biological inferiority, but rather a result of the fall of man and a consequence of sin" (2005, 74). See also David Brion Davis's discussion, cited by Muldoon (1966, 88–98). Pagden traces elements of Aristotle's natural slave theory in early modern discourses of empire, but concludes that race plays no part in these ideologies (2009, 312).

10. Studies of the medieval period have largely supported Yerushalmi's view that a racist construction of Jewish and Muslim religious identity located in the body develops in Iberia in the latter part of this era. Nirenberg offers a fine-grained analysis of medieval Iberian discourses by focusing on the term "race" and the development of pure blood laws. Martínez persuasively demonstrates the extent to which the Iberian categories of pure blood, developed with regard to Jewish and Muslim religious identity, profoundly shape racial "caste" when redeployed in the New World. See also Fredrickson (31, 33); Bethencourt (61); Burk; Martínez et al.; Mariscal; Root; Friedman (1987); and Hess.

11. A number of studies, some focusing on locales and periods prior to late medieval Iberia, have provided further evidence of the persistence of Jewish or Muslim identity even after conversion, including Stroll; Stacey (1992); Elukin (especially 1994, 174–252, but see also 1997 and 2001); Havercamp; Heng (2011a & b); Jordan (2001); Kruger (2006); Loomba (2009, 503–6); Nirenberg (2004 and 2009); Tartakoff; Resnick (2012, 2013b); and Ziegler.

12. Balibar develops his theory in response to European anti-Arab and anti-Muslim sentiment already prevalent in the late 1980s and early 1990s (24). I will consider, as other scholars have also noted, the imbrication of Jews and Muslims in racist discourses that already exist in medieval Christianity. While Balibar's analysis offers support for my discussion of early racism, I differ from his view on Jewish inferiority. As he argues:

> In anti-Semitism, the theme of the inferiority of the Jew is, as we know, much less important than that of his irreducible otherness. Chamberlain even indulges at times in referring to the "superiority" of the Jews, in matters of intellect, commerce or sense of community, making them all the more "dangerous." And the Nazi enterprise frequently admits that it is an enterprise of *reduction* of the Jews to "subhuman status" rather than a consequence of any *de facto* subhumanity: this is indeed why its object cannot remain mere slavery, but must become extermination. (28, n. 8)

> I understand premodern engagement of the problem of Jewish inferiority in Christian theology as similarly activated by a perception of improper Jewish superiority relative to Christians; Jews must be forced into a position of subordination in their social, political, and economic dealings with Christians precisely because this subjection matches their inherent spiritual subjection to Christians. See also Bethencourt (7–8) as well as Yerushalmi's point that racist ideologies, like the purity of blood statutes, emerge as a means of reinforcing the subordination of converts who were gaining access to privileges previously accorded to Christians but prohibited to Jews in both the Iberian and German contexts (10–12, 18).

13. Lampert critiques Balibar's use of antisemitism as a prototype for culturalist racism, arguing, based on the work of Southern and Cohen, that "Medieval

Christianity's encounter with Islam was not simply an echo or a generalization of Christian encounters with Jews; rather, it played a crucial role in shaping the history of anti-Semitism" (Lampert 2004a, 399). This claim is not supported by scholarship on canon law attitudes toward Jews and Muslims, as I explore in chapters 1, 3, and 5. However, she makes a strong case for considering early iterations of race in medieval literary representations of Muslims to help us understand contemporary racism (410).

14. Other scholars argue for foregrounding the place of religious identity and theology in analyses of the history of race. Buell demonstrates that an ethno-racial identity based on religion emerges within early Christian communities; however, she does not focus on racism or the body, but on race as a category of self-definition that comprises both fluid and fixed elements. The special issue of the *William and Mary Quarterly*, Vol. 54, No. 1 (Jan. 1997), *Constructing Race*, called for the examination of the "religious dimensions of racism and racist dimensions of religion" (5); essays by Blackburn and Sweet included in the volume consider variously ways in which theology contributes to emerging racist ideas. Lampert takes theology into consideration in her analysis of Jewish difference, but considers Jewish race primarily in the early modern context of Shakespeare's *Merchant of Venice* (2004b). Heng's expansive work contends that racism ascribes immutable, essentialized differences, somatic and/or cultural, to create hierarchies. She argues for the importance of religion, "the paramount source of authority in the Middle Ages," in this process and notes that theological difference functions both "socioculturally and biopolitically"; while her analysis centers on Christian self-definition, she privileges the political theology of the Christian state, rather than theology per se (2011a, 267–68). Kruger makes an invaluable contribution to this conversation through an intersectional exploration of race in medieval Europe, inflected through deconstruction and psychoanalytic theory, to explore the formation of Christian identity in terms of religion, gender, and sexuality, focusing on Jews, but also considering Muslims and heretics. Jonathan Boyarin's important work on how "the troubling instability of Jewish difference shaped both Christian Europeans' self-image and their reactions to those they encountered in the course of exploration and conquest" aligns with the work of Heng and Kruger (2009, 1). His analysis anticipates my project in exploring how Christian constructions of Jewish identity inflected ideas about Muslim and Native American identities. However, neither racism nor inferiority is central to his analysis. Martínez does focus on race in her analysis of the same period; she demonstrates how constructions of Jewish and Muslim identity in the pure blood laws informed the formation of the caste system in Mexico.

15. Loomba includes medieval texts in her exploration of the history of religion as a racial category (2007).

16. He analyzes the process as a sequential one in which race first emerges, followed by racism:

This severance was carried out in two distinct but integrated steps. First, Jews were cast as a race group in contrast to Western Christians, who with the important assistance of the discourses of Christian theology and philosophy, were also subtly and simultaneously cast as a race group. . . . Second, having racialized Jews as a people of the Orient and thus Judaism as a "religion" of the East, Jews were then deemed inferior to Christians of the Occident or the West. Hence, the racial imagination (the first step) proved as well to be a racist imagination of white supremacy (the second step). Within the gulf enacted between Christianity and the Jews, the racial, which proves to be a racist, imagination was forged. (4)

His work resonates with Buell's discussion of the self-formation of early Christian racial identity, although he attends to the necessary work inferiority performs in the support of racism.

17. As he explains:

The Kantian racial-cosmopolitical vision, which was also a theological vision predicated on the extirpation of Jewish flesh, is . . . only the discursive maturing of the racial colonialism inaugurated in the mid-to-late fifteenth century. And again it must be said that in the middle of it all was theological discourse, mainly of a Thomist-Aristotelian sort, coupled with the discourse of canon and civil law, which also functioned in relationship to theology. I was unable to engage these important pre-Enlightenment matters here without ballooning even further an already big book. (5–6)

I build on his suggestions here in taking up the medieval theological discourses of canon law on Jews.

18. My work follows Jennings's in tracing how the subjection of Jews into inferiority is a supersessionary act insofar as it removes Jews as God's elect and replaces them with, while placing them beneath, Christians. The imposition of servitude operates to subordinate not only Jews, but Muslims and Africans as well.

19. A similar trend in the scholarship of early modernity considers the intersection of religion and race: see the work of Kidd, Britton, Loomba (2002), Loomba and Burton, Adelman, Shapiro, Harrison, Bartels, and Lampert (2004b). The study of early modern race is too large for me to cover here, but some important works include Erickson and Hall; Hall; Hendricks and Parker; Feerick; Akhimie; MacDonald; Floyd-Wilson; Royster; Ian Smith; Thompson (2006, 2008); Little; Chapman; Coles et al.; Iyengar; and Spiller.

20. Numerous scholars have rejected religious identity as racial on the basis of its mutability. In his recent analysis of race in fourteenth- and fifteenth-century English literary and physiognomy texts, Whitaker continues this line of thought. While he contends that "racial ideology emerges from and competes with religion in medieval English literature," he maintains the longstanding distinction that religious identity, because of its mutability, does not constitute race (2009, iv):

When blackness persists despite the black figure's spiritual state, racial discourse is shown to be a separate entity from religion, even though blackness may not be entirely dissociated from its negative metaphorical and spiritual implications. When blackness does not survive a black figure's conversion to Christianity, then racial discourse is shown to be at the service of religious discourse. In the latter case, race supports the suppositions of religious inferiority and superiority but by no means is it the same thing. (227–28)

Ultimately, for Whitaker, racial discourse differs from religious ideas of inferiority.

21. She argues that while modern conceptions of ethnicity and race imagine them as fixed, they are also marked by a fluidity that contributes to their efficacy (7). Isaac similarly allows that some ideas about hereditary characteristics include notions of change (38). However, in his definition of racism, he ultimately insists on immutability as a necessary element.

22. Although she emphasizes how discourses of on color draw upon a nexus of faith and biology, she also considers the similar functioning of blood purity laws in an argument akin to that of Martínez (Loomba 2009, 506). For an important recent contribution to the debate over fluidity and fixity, see Akhimie.

23. As Loomba argues:

While such transformations can be legitimately interpreted as the sign of a somewhat fluid notion of identity, at another level they can also be seen to tighten the association of particular skin color and bodily attributes with particular faiths or moral qualities, which is a central feature of racial ideologies. The equation between a particular kind of body and a particular kind of religious belief is underlined when a black Muslim is depicted as being transformed into a white Christian. (2009, 504)

See also Kinoshita and de Weever on whitened Muslim women.

24. Sapir Abulafia offers an important exception in her excellent discussion of the role of Jewish *service* as well as *servitude* in a synchronic historical analysis across a number of communities in Western Europe of this medieval Jewish–Christian dynamic (2011; see also 2013).

25. Strikingly, the rulings of popes and ecclesiastical councils redeploy figures of Jewish servitude in their anachronistic application to Muslims, rendering the latter as similarly subordinated to Christians. See chapter 5.

26. See Loomba's analysis of early modern racism in which she demonstrates the ways in which it draws on other discourses of social hierarchy, including class, gender, and sexuality (2002, 22–44); see also Stepan.

27. Isaac makes this point his analysis of racism in classical antiquity: "This work is not concerned with the actual treatment of foreigners in Greece and Rome, but with opinions and concepts encountered in the literature. It traces the history of discriminatory ideas rather than acts, although [it also] traces the impact such ideas may have had in the sphere of action" (2).

28. Eliav-Feldon, Isaac, and Ziegler make a similar statement in the coauthored introduction to their collection *The Origins of Racism in the West*: "It is intellectually sound and morally justified to study racism as a topic in the history of ideas . . . to study its conceptual development over time, rather than its practical application or the social relationships which lay at the root of the phenomenon" (2009, 4). Bethencourt flatly disagrees: "Racism . . . cannot be understood within the confines of intellectual history. Instead, political and social practices are crucial" (2). The necessity and value of both approaches seems obvious to me.

29. For differing opinions on the comparison of negative ideas toward Jews in late medieval Iberia and Nazi Germany see Tal and Yerushalmi. For intellectual histories on ideas about Jews, see Nirenberg (2013) and Baker.

30. However, persisting claims of Jewish enslavement continue to circulate in early modernity, as I demonstrate in chapter 4. See also Trubowitz.

31. Other religions also develop racist discourses in their theological texts; for considerations of racist ideas developed in Judaism and Islam see Schorsch (2004, 16–49) and Goldenberg (1999).

CHAPTER 1

1. The term *servitus Judaeorum* variously denotes Jews as slaves, servants or serfs (Kisch 428, n. 48). Scholars addressing this question concur for the most part that it emerges initially in theological contexts. A representation of slavery as punishment for the Jews' sins first appears in the Hebrew Bible in the books relating the destruction of the First Temple, such as Jeremiah: 2:14–17 as well as in subsequent rabbinic texts (Baron 1952, 9 136). For a fuller consideration of metaphors of Jews as slaves in biblical, rabbinic and Jewish political texts, see Herzser (449–52)

2. Interestingly, the status of Jews as citizens in civil law persisted through to the early modern period, where it existed in uneasy tension with canon law attempts to enforce Jewish subordination to Christians. See Stow (1977) for a discussion of the status of the Jew in canon and civil law in early modern Catholic thought. Simonsohn provides an excellent discussion of the canon law development of Jewish inferiority in his multivolume compendium of medieval and early modern papal texts on the Jews (7, 94–156). For studies of Jews in medieval canon law, see also Brundage (1988), Czerwinski, Freidenreich (2014), Gilchrist, Grayzel, Linder, Pakter, Simonsohn, and Watt (1991, 1992). No one analyzes in depth the role that biblical figures play in the transmission of this theological idea into canon law or its development into a concept of hereditary inferiority.

3. Pope Alexander III called for and presided over this Council. Additionally, canon 26 prohibits Jews from employing domestic Christian slaves or servants in their homes, and requires that Jewish converts to Christianity be able to retain their property, because "converts ought to be in better circumstances [melioris conditionis]"

as Christians than they had been as Jews (Grayzel 1966, 296–97 #1). We see the idea of preventing Jewish superiority to Christians influencing all parts of this canon.
The concept of *melior conditio*, a better position, is "a phrase used throughout the canons to indicate the relative status of Jews and Christians" (Grayzel 1989, 278 n. 1). See also canon 10 of the 1195 Council of Montpelier, which similarly orders that new Christians be allowed to keep their property "since it is right for converts to the faith to be in better circumstances [melioris conditionis] than they had been before" (Grayzel 1966, 299, slightly amended). Stow provides a list of ecclesiastical laws ordering that converts be ensured a better status (1977, 387–89).

4. And yet the concept did have material consequences for Jews living in medieval Europe:

> The special status was a mixture of protection and dependency, of discrimination in favour of and against the Jews. What is clear, however, is that it paved the way for the almost total elimination of the Jews from Christian society. Theological formulas, although not legal in character, had a substantial influence on the emergence of this special Jewish status. (Simonsohn, 7, 99)

5. Mary Nyquist uses the term "figurative slavery," as distinguished from literal chattel slavery, to denote a type of political slavery.

> Greek, and later Roman, antityranny ideology represents the tyrant's subjects as figuratively enslaved—enslavement that seeks to dishonor and disenfranchise citizens who are meant to be "free." Such figurative, political slavery can be either internally or externally imposed and has numerous significations. . . . Figurative slavery—ethical, psychological, or spiritual as well as political—appears in countless cultural and historical contexts. (1, 4)

6. Furthermore, the ecclesiastical legal system was much better organized and more effective than the secular law systems (Pakter, 31).

7. Auerbach's influential analysis of *figura* emerged in the mid-twentieth century, a period which saw a renewed interest in typology. Some other important contemporary works include Daniélou's *Sacramentum futuri; études sur les origines de la typologie biblique*, Lubac's *Exégèse médiéval* and *Lampe and Woollcombe's Essays on Typology*. I rely primarily on Auerbach's formulation of *figura* because his thinking has proved central for subsequent scholarship, not only as evidenced in Lerer's edited volume, but particularly in recent studies that reconsider figures and the place of the Jew in Christian exegesis: Robbins (1991, 1999); Lupton; Freinkel; Biddick; Lampert (2004b); and Librett.

8. The relationship of figure to the terms "allegory" and "type" has been the subject of much analysis. While Auerbach "adamantly distinguished typology from allegory" in his book *Mimesis* on the basis that only the former "retains characteristics of concrete historical reality" (see Lupton's discussion, 20), he posits a looser association between the terms in "Figura":

> *Figura* is not the only Latin word used for historic prefiguration; often we find the
> Greek terms *allegoria* and still more frequently *typus*; *allegoria* generally refers to
> any deeper meaning and not only to phenomenal prophecy, but the boundary
> is fluid, for *figura* and *figuraliter* often extend beyond figural prophecy. . . . But
> *allegoria* could not be used synonymously with *figura* in all contexts, for it did not
> have the same implication of "form" [its sense in early classical Latin use]. . . . As
> for *typus*, the only reason why it fell behind *figura* is that it was a foreign word.
> But this consideration was far from negligible, for in anyone who spoke Latin
> (or later a Romance language), *figura* more or less consciously evoked all the
> notions involved in its history, while *typus* remained an imported lifeless sign.
> (47–48).

I follow this "fluid" understanding of the figure and allegory, in seeing the figure
as a specific kind of allegory applied to readings of the Hebrew Bible in terms
of the New Testament. I use type and figure interchangeably, contra Auerbach's
dictum here, especially as he elsewhere translates the Greek *typoi* as "figures"
(49). The etymology of the Greek *typos*, like that of *figura*, carries a sense of form
(Lampe and Woollcombe 60–1). Scholars who have sought to distinguish and
define figure, type and allegory include Lampe and Woollcombe, Lubac (1947),
and Daniélou. More recently Daniel Boyarin subordinates typology to the term
"allegory," which Paul uses in Galatians 4, arguing the latter is the "key to his
discourse" (32; see 13–38 for the full account of his reasoning). Lisa Freinkel
examines, and ultimately rejects, the debates over the distinctions between allegory and typology (4). Biddick observes that the "anxious insistence on a sharp
divide between typology and allegory is, I think, a way of warding off anxiety
about the excess of typology" (106, n. 4). She cites Young's *Biblical Exegesis and
the Formation of Christian Culture* as refusing a separation between allegory and
typology in its reconsideration of early Christian hermeneutics.

9. While Auerbach traces the development of the term *figura* in pre-Christian Latin
   sources, he does not consider the tradition of allegory in classical Greek literature, in the Hebrew Bible or in Jewish exegesis, all of which influenced the
   texts of the early Jesus movement. Woollcombe offers a brief account of what he
   calls Greek allegorism in early Christian texts (Lampe and Woollcombe 50–60);
   see also Lubac (1947) and Smalley's discussion in *The Study of the Bible in the
   Middle Ages* (1–26). Daniel Boyarin shows the important place of allegory in first-
   century Hellenistic Judaism in his consideration of the works of Philo and Paul,
   in contrast to another Jewish interpretive practice, midrash (13–38). Robbins
   gives a brief overview of midrash and notes important studies (1991, 12–16, especially in the notes to these pages, 147–49, nn. 24–34).

10. Auerbach's characterization of the Pauline figure must be re-evaluated in light of
    the scholarly revision of Paul, which has situated the apostle as operating within
    the context of, rather than attacking first-century Jewish beliefs. The scope of my
    current project prevents me from accounting for the extensive scholarship on

Paul that postdates Auerbach's work: some important publications include: W. D. Davies, *Paul and Rabbinic Judaism*; E. P. Sanders, *Paul and Palestinian Judaism*; Daniel Boyarin, *A Radical Jew*; John Gager, *Reinventing Paul* and *Who Made Early Christianity?*; Paula Fredricksen, "How Later Contexts Affect Pauline Content, or: Retrospect is the Mother of Anachronism," in *Jews and Christians in the First and Second Centuries*; and recently Matthew Thiessen, *Paul and the Gentile Problem*.

11. Boyarin argues that while Paul writings are neither antisemitic nor anti-Judaic, they are supersessionist:

> This brings us to the question of supersession. Richard Hays denies that Pauline theology is supersessionist (Hays 1989, 98–102). For Paul the Christian community stands in continuity with and not against the historical Israel. There has been, moreover, no rejection of Israel owing to the faults or flaws, as in some other New Testament theologies, nor finally are the Christian believers free of either ethical or moral requirements or unsusceptible to sin (as the Corinthians apparently thought). Hays's reading then defangs Paul of his 'anti-Semitism' without, however, as in the case of some modern liberal apologists for Paul, removing the teeth of Paul's critique. I would argue, however (and here, I think, the different hermeneutical perspectives of a self-identified Jew and a self-identified Christian show up): If there has been no rejection of Israel, there has indeed been a supersession of the historical Israel's hermeneutic of self-understanding as a community constituted by physical genealogy and observances and the covenantal exclusiveness that such a self-understanding entails. . . .What will appear from the Christian perspective as tolerance, namely Paul's willingness—indeed insistence—that within the Christian community all cultural practice is equally to be tolerated, from the rabbinic Jewish perspective is simply an eradication of the entire value system which insists that our cultural practice is our task and calling in the world and must not be abandoned or reduced to a matter of taste. The call to human Oneness, at the same time that it is a stirring call to equality, constitutes a threat as well to Jewish (or any other) difference. While it is not anti-Semitic (or even anti-Judaic) in intent, it nevertheless has had the effect of depriving continued Jewish existence of any reality or significance in the Christian economies of history. (31–2)

12. However, patristic opinion was not univocal; for example, Tertullian (c. 2nd–3rd c. CE):

> expressly denied that the literal and historical validity of the Old Testament was diminished by the figural interpretation. He . . . refused to consider the Old Testament as mere allegory; according to him, it had real, literal meaning throughout, and even where there was figural prophecy, the figure had just as much historical reality as what it prophesied. The prophetic figure, he believed, is a concrete historical fact, and it is fulfilled by concrete historical facts. (Auerbach, 30)

13. Robbins anticipates this perspective in her discussion of Paul's citation of Jewish Scripture; though she does not take into account revisionist views of the apostle:

> In this interpretive gesture, the Old Testament does not simply prefigure the events of the New. It prefigures the figural relationship itself. The Old Testament prefigures specifically its own supersession by the New Testament. The Old Testament is thus cited as an authority to discredit the Old Testament. (1991, 5)

Freinkel makes a similar argument in her discussion of Paul's use of allegory or figure (11). Like Boyarin, she notes the supersessionary displacement effected by the figure:

> Thus the appropriation of Scripture involves a transfer of property—a theft, or a vindication, depending on whose ground one stands; the Hebrew Bible is repossessed as Christian Old Testament. Through figural interpretation the Christian believer quite literally takes the place of the Jew in Scripture, displacing a Jewish meaning and a Jewish reference. (55)

See also Robbins in her analysis of Emmanuel Levinas's ethical critique of the figure in the contemporary poetry of Paul Claudel in which "the Old Testament is said to prefigure, and thus to charge itself with, deicide" (1999 49, 39–54 passim). Biddick devotes an entire book to the "captivating bundle of supersessionary fantasies about temporality [that she terms] the *Christian typological* imaginary" (2). The temporal logic of supersession resulted in the subordination of the Hebrew Bible to Christian meaning:

> Christians subsumed the Hebrew Bible into an "Old Testament" and conceived of this Old Testament as a text anterior to their New Testament. "Christian-ness" was thus affirmed by the repetitive cutting off of the old Jewish time from the new Christian time. Even though Christians shared literary genres and rhetorical conventions with pagan and Jewish contemporaries, their notion of supersession came to distinguish their reading and writing. (1)

Lampert also discusses supersession (2004b, 10–11, 24–9). An interesting phenomenon of the hierarchy of figural reading is its capacity for reversal. Chenu provides fascinating examples of "instances in which theologians of the period did not treat the Old Testament as a bygone and defunct stage in the divine plan but on the contrary resorted to the Old Covenant somehow to illuminate or elaborate elements in the New by recourse to what had gone before," a practice he deplores (147, 148, 157–59). A number of more recent works have explored the theoretical implications of this reversal, notably Lupton, who considers typology and supersession not only in terms of Jewish/Christian dialectic, but a Christian/secular one as well (xxvii–xxix). Robbins (1991), Freinkel, and Biddick make similar moves in their arguments.

14. Some scholars would disagree with the claim that Paul creates a hierarchy here. For example, Gaston and Gager argue "that Paul never intended to replace 'the

Law' as the means of salvation and justification for Jews but only to add Christ as a means of salvation for ethnic gentiles" (summarized in Boyarin 42). Fredriksen has recently argued that Paul's rejection of circumcision for gentiles tells us nothing about his view of Jewish observance of the Law: "Since Paul expects the Parousia in his own lifetime, he is utterly unconcerned with what coming generations are to do" (2014, 36, 31–9 passim). Nevertheless, by emphasizing the master/slave element of these fraternal figures, Paul clearly privileges some aspect of the Jesus movement over another Jewish position.

15. All quotations of the Bible in Hebrew are taken from the Koren edition; Greek, Latin, and English quotations of the Bible are taken from the Greek New Testament, the Vulgate and the Douay Rheims translation.

16. Henceforth, I will translate "יעבד" (*ya'avod*) as "he will be a slave to" rather than use the more neutral translation "he will serve" or "he will work," since the Greek term used in the Septuagint and the New Testament, "*douleusei*," is a future tense of a verb based on the word "*doúlos*," slave. The Latin term *servus* can denote either servant or slave.

17. Gershon Cohen discusses the concept of Jewish servitude in Christian theology as developed through the biblical narrative of Jacob and Esau (31–8).

18. As Boyarin contends in a discussion of Romans 11 and 14:

> Jews who did not accept allegiance to Christ were considered by Paul to be lopped-off and abandoned branches of the People of God. Keeping the Law was for Paul adiaphora; faith in Jesus was most certainly not! Romans 14, especially if the "weak" and the "strong" are the law-abiding and the not-law-abiding, supports both halves of this proposition eloquently. (42)

Other scholars would disagree. For example, Gager alternatively argues that what appear to be attacks on Jewish law in fact refer to fellow members of the Jesus movement who oppose Paul in requiring Gentiles members to follow Jewish law (including circumcision) in addition to having faith. Furthermore, "Just as [Paul] no longer thinks of salvation for Gentiles within the Mosaic covenant, so he does not imagine salvation for Jews as happening through their acceptance of Christ" (2015, 26, 28)

19. Boyarin argues that Galatians 4:21–31 provides the key to Paul's allegory, but considers the question of slavery only in passing (32–36). Thiessen has recently argued that "Paul could use Ishmael to show that gentile circumcision resulted in slavery, not covenantal sonship" (100). Rather than derogating Jews or their practice of the Law here, Galatians may instead be arguing that a gentile inappropriately adhering to Jewish Law produces servitude.

20. The Greek follows the Hebrew closely here; the Hebrew text of Genesis uses the term "אמה" (*amah*) "maid" to describe Hagar, parallel with the Septuagint and Galatians word *paidiskes* (maid). However, Paul's allegorical reading introduces the concept of slavery here in employing the terms *douleian*, (slavery), and *douleuei*, (she is a slave), to describe the status of both Hagar and her children (Gal

4:24–5). The Society of Biblical Literature English text of the New Testament reflects Paul's contrast of the *eleutheras* (free woman) to the "maid" by translating *paidiskes* as "female slave" (4:23). Furthermore, the Latin term *ancilla*, employed in the Vulgate translation of the Bible, denotes an enslaved woman in the terminology of Roman law (Buckland, 399). Henceforth, I will render the terms *amah*, *paidiskes*, and *ancilla* as "slave-woman" when used in the Galatians context.

21. For example, Paul himself is termed "a slave/servant (doulos) of Jesus Christ" at the beginning of Romans (1:1). The master served determines the goodness or evil of the service; servants of righteousness serve God, servants of iniquity, sin (Rom 6:12–23). The choice to serve good or evil here is apparently open to all; see Garnsey on Paul.

22. This is an odd claim for Jews to make, given the evidence of Exodus and the requirement to remember being slaves in Egypt that runs through the Pentateuch.

23. Lieu contrasts the way in which this passage has traditionally been understood with more recent contextualized readings, while noting a continuing lack of consensus:

> In the Fourth Gospel Jesus declares the Jews to be children of a father who is the devil and who was a murderer from the beginning (John 8:44; there is probably a covert reference to Cain). With its "evangelical" authority that charge has had a long legacy—it is taken up by many later church writers—and, together with the overall presentation of the Jews in the Gospel, has earned John the label 'the father of the anti-Semitism of the Christians'. Recent study has proposed conflicting interpretations of the gospel's attitudes toward the Jews [e.g., as reflecting a sharp break between those inside and outside the Jesus movement or as instead referring to a split within the community of believers]. (81–2)

Given Augustine's later use of this verse in his elaboration of Cain as a figure for the Jews, he may have perceived John's suppressed citation of this same figure. See Freyne on anti-Jewish polemic in Matthew and John.

24. A similar concept of hereditary guilt, lasting to the third and fourth generations, appears in the Hebrew Bible; see for example Exodus 34:7 and Numbers 15:18. Fredriksen shows how a "trail of blood" motif, articulated in Second Temple Jewish legends about the deaths suffered by the prophets at the hands of the Jews, enters into the texts of the New Testament, such as Matthew 23; he includes this idea again in chapter 27 (2010, 91). Fredriksen quotes the relevant passage:

> Therefore I send you prophets and wise men and scribes, some of whom you will kill and crucify, and some you will scourge in your synagogues and persecute from town to town, that upon you may come all the righteous blood shed on earth, from the blood of the innocent Abel to the blood of Zechariah son of Barachiah, whom you murdered between the sanctuary and the altar. Matthew 23:29–35 (RSV)

> This "trail of blood" motif, as Matthew deploys it, inculpates every generation of Jews since the second generation of humanity, associating the Jewish people with Cain. In this view, the Jews killed the prophets, and finally they killed even Christ himself. (Fredriksen 2010, 91–2)

While again not developing Cain as an explicit figure for the Jews as murderers of Jesus, Matthew does make this connection available for subsequent interpreters, including Augustine.

25. Fredriksen reflects on the tensions of reading this verse with a double awareness of its sense in its original context and subsequent destructive interpretations:

> "Matthew," a Greek-speaking Jew of the late first century CE, set his story about Jesus some six decades earlier, about forty years before Rome's war with Jerusalem. The fires of the Temple's destruction illumine his tale of Christ's passion. "All the people" of Jerusalem, in his narrative year 30, curse their own generation and the next: "our children" would grow to be the adults cut down in the Roman siege of 70 CE. Matthew, looking backwards from his vantage c. 90, links these events causally: Jerusalem's rejection of Jesus c. 30 "caused" the fires of 70. The narrative characters of 30 in effect cursed themselves. . . .[Matthew] could not know the violence that these words would eventually unleash as they reverberated in the long echo chamber of Christian anti-Judaism, reinterpreted as a standing curse across generations. (Fredriksen, 2013)

26. Fredriksen explains in her wide-ranging account of Augustine's cultural influences:

> Ancient empires, in other words, accommodated as a matter of course a wide range of religious practices. To see this accommodation as "religious tolerance" is to misunderstand it. Ancient society was not liberal in the sense that modern civil societies tend (or try) to be. But it was, of practical necessity, pluralistic. Religious differences were a normal fact of life. (2010, 10, 3–102)

27. Although Augustine's teaching on the Jews is "original and distinctive," it draws from a number of traditional *adversus Judaeos* ideas (Fredriksen 2010, 321–24).

28. Fredriksen distinguishes between "rhetorical" and "historical Jews," explaining that the former are a polemical construct (2010, 226–27, 273, 307). She surveys evidence of cordial Christian–Jewish relations in the period in stark contrast to contemporary anti-Jewish rhetoric:

> True, church leaders routinely condemned Judaism along with paganism and with heresy, and their rhetoric *adversus Iudaeos* defined Jews in particular as the ultimate "other" against which to calibrate orthodox Christian belief and practice. It would be a mistake, however, in light of all this other evidence, to see their condemnations as a reliable measure of the actual separation of these communities or as an accurate index of a more general hostility. On the contrary: The vitality of habitual contacts, both social and religious, between Christians and Jews— as among Christians of all various sorts, Jews, and pagans— probably

accounts for much of the shrillness and the obsessive repetitiveness of patristic invective. (2010, 101, 93–102 passim)

She also considers the contexts for Augustine's contacts with his Jewish neighbors, noting that the evidence, though minimal, does not suggest his negative writings against Jews influenced his dealings with Jewish people (2010, 307–14). Cohen anticipates Fredriksen's "rhetorical Jew" in his development of the " 'hermeneutical Jew'—that is, the Jew as constructed in the discourse of Christian theology, and above all in Christian theologians' interpretation of Scripture" (1999, 2–3).

29. Hezser explains that in the context of imperial Rome, the status of the conquered was likened to enslavement. This applied to the

> Jews [who] were subdued by the Romans and victims of Roman colonialism. . . .The discourse on slavery was closely interlinked with colonialist discourse in antiquity: the conquest by foreign rulers was considered 'enslavement', and the actual enslavement of at least a part of the native population was a common aspect of military defeat. (453)

30. Saperstein, Haynes, and Jeremy Cohen all consider Augustine's writings on Jews and demonstrate their importance for medieval Christianity. Fredriksen and Unterseher focus on the development of Augustine's ideas about Jews within his own historical context. Folliet focuses on Augustine's idea of the Jews as book carrier/custodian/slave to explain the positive role they play in Christian society.

31. See also Sapir Abulafia's discussion of Augustine's Psalm commentaries in which he reads Cain in as a figure for Jewish service to Christianity (2011, 6–7).

32. It is precisely through the failure to understand the Christological significance of their own texts that Jews act as servants or slaves to the Church in proving its truth, and not their own: "Augustine constructs his idea of the Jews as wandering book slaves who witness to Christian truth. . . . The *books* refer to scripture, the (misunderstood) script for the Jews' visible practices, whose deepest meanings had to await the messiah's crucifixion and resurrection before they could be retroactively understood by others" (Fredriksen 2010, 320, 276–77). See also Unterseher on Jewish subjection (141–42) and Sapir Abulafia on Jewish service (2011, 7–8).

33. I organize the following discussion by considering Augustine's use of figures initially developed by Paul, before turning to the addition of Cain and Ham. This method does not follow the exposition of figures of Jewish servitude as they appear in the chronology of Augustine's works, but as Cohen, Unterseher, and Fredriksen demonstrate, this strategy and perspective are already present in the *Contra Faustum* (397 C.E) one of his earlier writings on Jews (Cohen 1999, 41).

34. The Latin reads:

> Haec forma intellegendi . . . quem ad modum scripturas duorum testamentorum, veteris et novi, accipere debeamus. Pars enim quaedam terrenae civitatis

imago caelestis civitatis effecta est, non se significando, sed alteram, et ideo serviens. (*Civitate Dei* 15. 2, 418)

35. The Latin reads: "Quod autem dictum est: *Maior serviet minori*, nemo fere nostrorum aliter intellexit, quam maiorem populum Iudaeorum minori Christiano populo serviturum. . . . Christus . . . est dominus fratris sui quia populus eius dominatur Iudaeis" (Book 16. Chapters 35, 164 and 37 172).

36. Unterseher reviews prior Jewish and Christian interpretations of the significance of Cain. Amongst earlier church fathers Justin Martyr, Irenaeus and Tertullian briefly associate Cain with the Jews (72–6). Jerome extends this identification, and understands Cain's dwelling in the land of Nod as signifying the wandering suffered by the Jews as punishment for deicide, thus connecting the figure to the *adversus Judaeos* trope that Augustine also adopts (76–7). None of the earlier exegetes suggest that Cain figures Jewish servitude.

37. The Latin reads:

> Judaei . . . infidelitatis . . . sunt, quia Christo veniente . . . Qui [Cain] si obtemperasset Deo . . . ipse peccato suo dominaretur; non illo sibi dominante servus peccati, fratrem occideret innocentem. . . . Sic et Judaei, in quorum haec figura gerebantur, si . . .tempus salutis per gratiam in peccatorum remissionem agnoscentes, . . .eidem peccato, quamdiu esset adhuc in eorum mortali corpore, per spem gratiae liberi dominarentur. Nunc autem . . .regnante peccato in eorum mortali corpore . . .exarserunt odio adversus eum [Jesus]. . . . Itaque occiditur Abel minor natu a fratre majore natu: occiditur Christus caput populi minoris natu a populo Judaeorum majore natu. . . . (*Contra Faustum, Patrologia Latina* vol. 42 12.9, cols. 258–59)

38. The connection between these two stories might have been suggested to Augustine by Hyppolytos's allegory, cited by Jerome, which connects Esau's plot to kill Jacob (Genesis 27:41) with Cain's murder of Abel.

> Quia igitur iniquitas est inimica justitiae, Esau in discordiam concitatur, et necem fraudulentus excogitat, dicens in corde suo: *Appropinquent dies passionis patris mei, et occidam Jacob fratrem meum* (Gen. 27, 41). Diabolus fratricidas Judaeos in Cain ante praemeditans, in Esau manifestissime confitetur: tempus quoque interfectionis ostendens: *Appropinquent*, inquit, *dies passionis patris, ut interficiam fratrem meum.*
>
> [Since, therefore, violence is the enemy of justice, deceitful Esau, agitated about the quarrel, and devising murder, says in his heart: "the days of the passion {the Christological term "passion" substitutes for the word *luctus* (mourning) of the Vulgate text} of my father draw near, and I will kill my brother Jacob." The devil, considering in advance the fratricidal Jews in Cain, openly acknowledges in Esau, showing the time of the murder. He says: *the days of the passion of the father draw near so that I can murder my brother.*] (*Epistola XXXVI. Seu rescriptum Hieronymi ad Damasum, Patrologia Latina* vol. 22 16, cols. 460–61, my translation)

Similarly, in his treatise *De Cain et Abel*, Ambrose cites Genesis 25:23 regarding Jacob and Esau in his discussion of Abel and Cain as figures for the Church and the Synagogue, respectively; he also references the Jews as parricides for killing their Lord (qtd. in Unterseher, 77).

39. Augustine includes verses from John in this passage:

> So also the Jews, of whom all these things are a figure, if they had been content, instead of being turbulent, and had acknowledged the time of salvation through the pardon of sins by grace, and heard Christ saying, "They that are whole need not a physician, but they that are sick; I came not to call the righteous, but sinners to repentance;" Matthew 9:12–13 and, "Every one that commits sin is the [slave] of sin;" and, "If the Son make you free, you shall be free indeed," John 8:34, 36 (*Contra Faustum* 12.9, 186)

I have cut it to focus the discussion on Cain and servitude.

40. The Latin reads:

> *Gemens et tremens eris in terra.* [Gen. 4:12] Nunc ecce quis non videat, quis non agnoscat in tota terra, quacumque dispersus est ille populus, quomodo gemat moerore amissi regni, et tremat timore sub innumerabilibus populis Christianis? . . . . Ut hoc toto tempore quod septenario dierum numero volvitur, quia non interit gens Judaea, satis appareat fidelibus Christianis, quam subjectionem meruerint, qui superbo regno Dominum interfecerunt. (*Patrologia Latina Contra Faustum*, vol. 42 12 12, cols. 260–61)

41. The guilt, though unintentional, of even contemporary Jews is made clear in an earlier passage:

> And what answer can the Jews give at this day, when we ask them with the voice of God, that is, of the sacred Scriptures, about Christ, except that they do not know the Christ that we speak of? Cain's ignorance was pretended, and the Jews are deceived in their refusal of Christ. (*Contra Faustum*, 12.10, 186)

Here he makes a distinction between Cain's feigned ignorance in contrast to the Jews who are deceived; they did not recognize Jesus as the messiah. Nevertheless, they and their descendants are guilty of Jesus's death.

42. The Latin reads:

> Judaei tamen manent cum signo; nec sic victi sunt, ut a victoribus absorberentur. Non sine causa Cain ille est, qui . . . posuit in eo Deus signum, ne quis eum occideret. . . . Sunt ergo Judaei, non sunt occisi, necessarii sunt credentibus Gentibus. . . . per omnes gentes dispersi sunt Judaei, testes iniquitatis suae et veritatis nostrae (*Ennartiones in Psalmos Patrologia Latina* vol. 36 58:12, part one 21–2 col. 705).

43. Fredriksen argues correctly that the mark of the Jews is their continued observance of their Law. She contends that this is a mark of God's protection rather than a "mark of shame" (2010, 271). However, Jews misunderstand the Hebrew

Bible in this observance; they in fact preserve Scripture as slaves to Christian truth. Thus the adherence to the Law operates as a symbol of their servitude as much as their preservation. Furthermore Fredriksen admits that "the one who bears [the mark] is a murderer" (271); his crime is part of Cain's mark as well: "They make visible to the Christian faithful the subjection they merited because they, in the pride of their kingdom, put the Lord to death" (*Contra Faustum*, qtd. in Fredriksen, 271).

44. Fredriksen coins this term to refer to the Jews' role:

> The whole nation (*gens*), carrying the Law and the prophets, is a librarian who ports a chest full of books (*scriniaria*, feminine of *scriniarius* because of the feminine *gens*; *Against Faustus* 12.23).

> From Cain to Ham to slaves to servile book caretakers. Out of this congested set of images and episodes Augustine constructs his idea of the Jews as wandering book slaves who witness to Christian truth. The *wandering* part and the part about *obvious Jewish identity* (conveyed to outsiders by visible, physical behaviors) come from Genesis 4: Cain, the exiled, divinely marked, divinely protected fratricide. The *slave serving the church* comes from Noah's curse to Ham, who becomes a slave to his brothers in Genesis 9. The books refer to scripture, the (misunderstood) script for the Jews' visible practices, whose deepest meanings had to await the messiah's crucifixion and resurrection before they could be (retrospectively) understood by others. (emphasis in original 2010, 320)

45. The Latin reads:

> Medius autem filius, id est, populus Judaeorum, ideo medius, quia nec primatum Apostolorum tenuit, nec ultimus in Gentibus credidit, vidit nuditatem patris, quia consensit in necem Christi; . . .ideoque fit servus fratrum suorum. Quid est enim aliud hodieque gens ipsa, nisi quaedam scriniaria Christianorum, bajulans Legem et Prophetas ad testimonium assertionis Ecclesiae, ut nos honoremus per sacramentum, quod nuntiat illa per litteram. (*Patrologia Latina* vol. 42 12. 23 col. 266)

The Schaff edition translates "assertionis" as doctrine, but as Fredriksen notes, the term emphasizes the freedom of the Church in contrast to Jewish servitude:

> The Jews carry their books around *ad testimonium adsertionis ecclesiae*, "to testify to the *adsertio* of the church." . . . An *adsertio* is a formal declaration of freedom, a public, legal act by which a slave becomes a freedman. The Law and the prophets, borne by the slave-Jews, testify to the divine manumission of the church. (2010, 320–21)

I will emend all subsequent quotations of this passage to follow Fredriksen's suggestions regarding both *scriniaria* (bookslave) and *adsertionis* (manumission).

46. Augustine does not develop a racialized concept of Jewish inferiority here. His articulation of Jewish servitude serves rhetorical purposes in theological

arguments rather than describing the status of late fourth-century Jews under Christian rule. Nevertheless, religious identity in the period does serve as a marker of ethnicity that verges on race (Fredriksen 2010, 6–7, 3–10 passim).

47. Chapter 4 provides a fuller consideration of Augustine's writings on Noah's curse in addition to the substantial exegetical tradition that understood the servitude inflicted on Ham's children as figuring the enslavement of the Jews.

48. In addition to her discussion of *adsertio* as emphasizing Christian freedom against Jewish enslavement noted above, see Fredriksen's fascinating discussion of the epistolary controversy over the apostles' adherence to the law in which Jerome accuses Augustine of Judaizing in presenting too positive a view of Jewish observance. The fact that Jerome himself had been the recipient of similar charges might have contributed to his attack on Augustine (2010, 290–302).

49. As Fredriksen affirms:

> Augustine's theological legacy had a fundamental effect on subsequent Latin Christianity. In the changed social context of later periods, his teachings on Jews and Judaism came to be interpreted literally, both for good and for ill. Thus his reference to Psalm 59:12, "Slay them not"—for Augustine a metaphor against impeding Jewish religious practice —was eventually taken as counsel to spare Jewish lives. However, his reference to Psalm 66:23, "Bend down their backs forever"— for Augustine a metaphor for the Jews' "earthly" orientation when reading Scripture— was eventually taken as prescribing active Christian oppression. Augustine deserves neither blame in the second instance nor praise in the first. No author can be responsible for the ways that later generations put his work to use. (2010, 374–75)

50. In addition to editing the *Decretales*, Raymond served as papal confessor from 1230 until 1238, when he became Master-General of the Dominicans:

> But most of all, Raymond's zealousness manifested itself in his efforts to uphold orthodoxy within Christendom by fighting heresy and to expand the dominion of the Roman Church by converting the infidel. . . . Toward the end of his life, Raymond prevailed upon Thomas Aquinas to compose his *Summa contra gentiles* as a means of attracting converts to Christianity. (Cohen 1982, 105)

51. Although ecclesiastical law develops with some independence from civil law, the two codes do share areas of overlap:

> One particularly significant development during the generations following Gratian was the fast-growing interdependence between canon law and the revived Roman civil law. Gratian apparently included few, if any, references to Roman law in the original version of the *Decretum*, but early in its history anonymous interpolators added almost 150 further canons to his book, including substantial numbers of Roman law texts. Canonists in the late twelfth century habitually borrowed terms, ideas, concepts, and institutions

from the civilians, while civilian writers frequently compared canonical institutions and practices with those that they found in Roman legal texts. By the early thirteenth century the symbiotic relationship between the two. . . had grown so close and pervasive that scholars sometimes speak of a "reception" of Roman law by the canonists. "Reception" in this context means that canonists accepted the law of Justinian's *Corpus* as a supplementary source of canon law. Thus when canonical sources failed to supply answers to a question or solutions to a problem, canonists sometimes drew the information and legal rules that they needed from Roman law sources. (Brundage 1995, 59–60)

52. As stated in Justinian's sixth-century *Institutes*:

> Slaves (*servi*) are so called because commanders generally sell the people they capture and thereby save (*servare*) them instead of killing them. The word for property in slaves (*mancipia*) is derived from the fact that they are captured from the enemy by force of arms (*manu capiantur*).

(Digest 1,5: 'On the Status of Persons': 4: Florentinus, from *Institutes*, book 9; reprinted in Wiedemann, 13)

53. The Latin reads: "Origo autem vocabuli servorum in Latina lingua inde creditur ducta, quod hi qui iure belli possent occidi, a victoribus cum servabantur servi fiebant, a servando appellati" (19.15, 186).

54. While few scholars go as far as to follow the assessment of Graetz, who styled the pope "an embittered enemy of the Jews and Judaism" (vol. 3, 496, 496–520 passim) some have viewed Innocent's policies as especially antagonistic to the Jews. One exception is Synan, who situates the pope's policies within the context of his other, more pressing concerns, while also showing a range of both negative and positive pronouncements on the Jews role in Christian society (83–102). He does acknowledge the pope's attempt to instantiate Jewish subordination with recourse to figures, but Synan views this status as temporary because of the anticipated fulfilment of the prophecy that all Jews will convert (92–3). Chazan and Tolan view Innocent's Jewish pronouncements in isolation from the pope's other goals, which result in harsher assessments. Chazan argues that "the central thrust of Innocent's policies vis-á-vis the Jews was to identify more boldly avenues of Jewish harmfulness and to legislate limitations that would diminish [it]" but this conclusion derives from a failure to recognize the extent to which the pope's writings emphasize Augustine's protective doctrine regarding Jews (1999, 203, 195–97). Tolan surveys Innocent's "theology of Jewish slavery [and] his fear of the consequence of . . .Jews who do not accept their subservient place in Christian society," but he sees these as "fairly standard in writing and legislation in the late twelfth or early thirteenth centuries" (2012b, 6, 10). He argues that Innocent innovates "a preoccupation with purity and with the dangers of pollution that close daily contact with Jews represent to the body of Christendom" (10,

11–12 passim). I would argue that Innocent's new contribution lies precisely in introjecting the theology of Jewish slavery into the discourse of canon law via figures. Furthermore, I think this doctrine provides a better rationale for explaining his attitudes toward Jews within the larger context of other more troubling concerns. For a more positive recent evaluation of medieval papal policy toward the Jews that also includes Jewish attitudes toward the popes, see Rist; she considers Jewish servitude only in passing.

55. Grayzel cites Oliver Emerson's essay, which refers to Peter Comestor's description of Cain's mark: "et posuit Deus signum in Cain, tremorem capitis." Peter Comester might have been a teacher of Innocent III (Grayzel 1966 126, n. 2). The Latin rendering of the Septuagint describes Cain as "gemens et tremens [moaning and shaking]." The Vulgate, more closely following the Hebrew, renders Genesis 4:12: "vagus et profugus eris super terram" [a fugitive and a vagabond shalt thou be upon the earth]. On Cain's trembling see Mellinkoff (1981, 41) and Resnick (2012, 206–12, 248). See chapter 2 for further discussion of Cain's punishment in relation to Jewish bodies.

56. The Vulgate reads: "Imple facies eorum ignominia et quaerent nomen tuum Domine." In his *Summa Abel*, under the rubric of *Jews*, Peter the Chanter (d. 1197) explains the preservation of the Jews so that they might be punished, and cites the verse "the elder shall serve the younger"; he continues "a remnant of the Jews will be saved (Romans 9:27, cf. Isaiah 10:22), on account of their conversion which [will] happen through distress," also quoting Psalm 82:17 for support (qtd. in Sapir Abulafia, 2011 195). Peter the Chanter has also been identified as possibly a teacher of Innocent III (Clarke, 1–20).

57. Compare the Vulgate version of Lamentations 1:8 "peccatum peccavit Hierusalem propterea instabilis facta est" [Jerusalem hath grievously sinned, therefore is she become unstable] with Clement's "Peccatum peccavit populus Judeorum propterea est factus instabilis."

58. In a subsequent letter to the King of Aragon (1267), Clement mentions Cain in reference to the Jews when condemning the Talmud and ordering its confiscation. The language echoes that of the letter sent to Poland, but omits any mention of Jewish servitude as punishment for the crucifixion. The text of the letter reads in part:

> Because the reprehensible Jewish lack of faith was long ago deservedly rejected because of its vice of ingratitude,. . . this. . . sinful people . . . has been made to wander over the earth like the fratricide Cain, who was driven from the face of God because his crime was too great for forgiveness. This miserable people likewise denied the Son of the Eternal Father . . . they . . . felled him, and flogged him, and impiously killed the Crucified One, calling His blood down upon themselves and their children. To this day the dispersed Jews do not want to understand . . . that sufficient humaneness is accorded them when they are

permitted to dwell among the faithful without burdensome disgrace. (Grayzel 1989, 97–8)

59. The earliest example of this citation does not address the improper status of Jews relative to Christians, but appears in a letter regarding the conversion of a synagogue to a church in France (1204). The example of Hagar and Sarah invokes the principle that Jews should not be allowed a higher status than Christians to ensure that the newly founded Christian institution is treated at least as well as the previous Jewish institution.

> All places freed for the worship of God deserve to be . . .endowed with the gift of eternal liberty; but such places deserve this especially which are divested of the blind Jewish perversion of Faith,. . . since it is clear that they who have chosen to worship God there in freedom of the spirit, deserve no longer to be called the children of a slave but rather the children of a free mother (filios ancille, sed libere) . . .We decree that just as the clergy of the nearby churches took nothing out of this place while it was in Jewish possession, so they shall not, hereafter, impose upon the church here established any condition or burdens in prejudice of its liberty, so that the status of the church shall not be made worse, lest in those respects in which it was free (libera) while the Jews inhabited it, it become a slave (ancilla) through observing Christian piety. (Grayzel 1966, 104–5)

Innocent writes to order that neighboring clergy place no impositions upon the Christians that were not required of the Jews. He alludes to the comparative *deterior/melior conditio*, worse or better condition; Christians should always inhabit the latter in relation to Jews. See note 3 on the idea of *melior conditio*.

60. One of Innocent's complaints concerns the practice of Jews who "by means of their vicious usury . . .appropriate ecclesiastical goods and Christian possessions. Thus seems to be fulfilled among the Christians that which the prophet bewailed in the case of the Jews, saying 'Our heritage has been turned over to strangers, our houses to outsiders.'" He quotes here from Lamentations 5:2 (Hereditas nostra versa est ad alienos, domus nostrae ad extraneos), the book mourning the destruction of the first Temple and the Jews' dispersion into captivity. This proof-text paradoxically serves to represent Jews as the conquerors and despoilers of Christians and their property, and implicitly argues that this constitutes a profane challenge to Christian notions of order and history.

61. Compare Innocent's phrase "sanguis clamat in Patris auribus" with the Vulgate's rendering of Genesis 4:10: "vox sanguinis fratris tui clamat ad me de terra."

62. The use of Galatians to reprimand the improper domination of Christians by Jews also appears in the language of subsequent popes. For example, in a 1244 decretal, Innocent IV includes this proof-text in an admonition that Jews not employ Christian servants:

Lest the children of the [free-woman/libere] serve the children of the [slave/ancille], but since they were condemned to slavery by the Lord for whose death they sinfully plotted, they shall recognize themselves, as a result of this act, as slaves of those whom the death of Christ set free while condemning them to slavery. (Grayzel 1966, 253)

This language repeats the text of Innocent III's 1205 decretal *Etsi Judaeos*, which I consider in a subsequent section. Innocent III's use of this figure also influences conciliar rulings, such as the one that Council of Oxford decrees in 1222:

Since it is absurd that the children of a free woman shall be slaves to the children of a bondswoman, (filii libere ancille filiis famulentur) and since no little scandal in the case of many regularly arises in the Church of God from Jews and Christians living under the same roof, we decree that in the future Jews shall not possess Christian slaves. (Grayzel 1966, 315)

Similarly, the 1287 Synod of Exeter 1287 cites Galatians in support of its prohibiting Jews from employing Christians as domestic servants:

The kingdom of God is passed from the Jews and given to the people doing justice, as is discovered written in Scripture. [paraphrase of Matt. 21:43] Through which it pleased him that Christians be given liberty, and Jews placed under them in perpetual servitude. As it is therefore written: "Send away the slave woman and her son, for the son of the slave woman shall not be heir with the son of the free woman" [Gal. 4:30]. (Grayzel 1989, 257, my transl.)

Canon law texts and commentaries sometimes include Muslims in the Galatians trope of the free and slave woman; see chapter 5 for a full discussion of this phenomenon and its implications.

63. For some recent discussions of medieval Jewish counternarratives on Jesus and Christianity see Cuffel, Meerson et al., Rowe (2012, 133–42, and references in n. 11).

64. The anxiety over the status of Christian antecedents relative to that of Jews also registers in the linguistic transformation of the definition of "gentile." In classical Latin *gentilis* has neutral meanings "Of or belonging to the same clan (gens), stock, or race" as well as negative ones: "Of slaves who bore the name of their masters... In opp to Roman, ... foreigners." It also signifies a heathen or pagan as distinguished from a Jew or Christian (Andrews et al.). However, in the medieval European context, where the majority of Christians descended from Gentile and not Jewish converts to Christianity, more positive meanings emerge. Blaise defines *gentilis* as "noble . . . beau, élégant, cultivé" (noble, handsome, elegant, cultivated) while Du Cange et al. includes both negative and positive definitions: "Gentiles. . . Barbaros;" "Gentilis. . . Nobilis, ingenuus [freeborn];" "Gentilitas: Paganismus;" "Gentilia: Nobilitas." Langland explicitly describes how their rejection of Jesus results in the Jews' transformation from "gentil men" to "lowe cherlis":

The iuwes, þat were gentil men, ihesu þei dispised,
Bothe his lore & his lawe; now ar þei lowe cherlis.
As wyde as þe worlde is, wonyeth þere none
But vnder tribut & taillage as tykes & cherles. (*Piers Plowman* B. xix. 37, qtd. in
the *Medieval English Dictionary* under "tike")

In a fascinating inversion, the pre-Christian Jews have the elevated status of gentlemen, but in rejecting Jesus, have been subordinated to serfs or low-born people.

65. The term also appears in two sermons ascribed to Augustine. The first follows very closely Cassian's text:

3. *Adam vendidit libertatem. Inde posteri nascuntur servi.* Quod, rogo, istud, cujusve peccatum est? Sine dubio Adae, cujus praevaricatione, atque, ut ita dicam, negotiatione damnosa, fraudulentoque commercio venditi sumus. Omnem enim prolem suam, serpentis persuasione seductus illiciti cibi perceptione distractam, jugo perpetuae servitutis addixit. Hic namque mos solet inter vendentem ementemque servari, ut is qui se alieno cupit dominio mancipare, aliquid pretii pro jactura propriae libertatis et addictione perpetuae servitutis a suo consequatur emptore. Quod etiam inter Adam atque serpentem manifestissime videmus impletum. Ille enim a serpente pretium libertatis suae esu interdictae arboris capiens, a naturali libertate discessit: illique maluit semetipsum perpetua vendere servitute, a quo vetiti pomi lethale pretium fuerat assecutus: qua deinceps conditione constrictus, non immerito omnem posteritatis suae progeniem, perpetuo eidem, cujus effectus est servus, subdidit famulatu. Quid enim aliud servile conjugium potest procreare, quam servos? (Pseudo-Augustine, *Patrologia Latina* vol. 39 *S. Augustini Complectens Sermones Supposititios. Classis Prima. De Veteri et Novo Testamento. Sermo CIII. De verbis Apostoli, Rom. cap. VII, 24, 25,* cols. 1944–1945)

The second sermon introduces the term in the context of explaining Noah as a type of Jesus; the curse of perpetual servitude that Noah imposes, while mentioned, is not explained in the analysis of the figure (*Complectens Sermones Supposititios Classis II. Sermones De Tempore. Sermo CLXIV. In Pascha*, VI. 3. *Patrologia Latina* vol. 39 col. 2067).

66. For the Latin text see *Patrologia Latina*, vol. 49 23.12 col. 1254A–1266A.

67. His discussion follows very closely the sermon on the same topic attributed to Augustine:

Noe quoque vir agricola cum plantasset vineam, et inebriatus vino obdormisset, discoopertus jaceret in tabernaculo suo, et expergefactus a somno, filio suo verecundiam suam non celanti maledictum perpetuae servitutis imponens, Christum significavit . . . (*Patrologia Latina* vol. 57 col. 596A–B). See note 65.

68. See under "Procopius of Gaza" in Cross and Livingstone.

69. The Latin reads: "Noachus nudatus est in domo sua: sic Christus crucifixus est a Judaeis. Chamus typus est populi Judaiei, qui illusit Christo e cruce pendenti: . . . Verum Judaeos perpetuae adjudicavit Christus servituti" (*Commentarii in Genesin*, IX, *Patrologiæ Græcæ* vol. 87a IX col. 306–7).

70. Salo Baron argues that the first legal application of the theological concept of *servitus Judaeorum* appears in the Seventeenth Council of Toledo's decree, following the order of King Egica that Jewish converts to Christianity who had relapsed and devised a conspiracy against the king be "subjected to perpetual servitude" [perpetuae servituti subactae] (Baron, 9 136; Linder, 536–37). While this decree does mention that the Jews are "known to be defiled with the vilest strain of sacrilege, stained with the blood of Christ" there is no mention of their being subjected to slavery as a *result* of this crime. In fact, the tenor of the decree does not assume that the Jews' role in the crucifixion has already accomplished their subjection, but instead requires that offending Jews be subjected to perpetual slavery, "granted to those people whom [the king] shall order them to serve" (537). It appears that the language of perpetual servitude enters into this decree from the secular Laws of the Visigoths, which contain a number of examples of this phrase (Linder, 273–83). King Egica, the convener of the Toledan Council, also promulgated a novel, or new secular law, ordering that those who converted to Christianity motivated by a desire to avoid a tax upon the Jews rather than by true faith should be "perpetually subjected . . . to the fisc [the royal treasury]." Similarly, converts persisting in the observance of Judaism who tried to conduct business with Christians "would become a slave of the fisc for life" (Linder, 283). These codes specify a permanent enslavement of a particular subset of people to a ruler or royal institution, rather than delineate a spiritual status of perpetual servitude imposed upon all Jews. Contra Baron, Innocent III, not the Seventeenth Council of Toledo, introduces this theological concept into law.

71. As Czerwinski observes, "A drastic change takes place during the pontificate of Innocent III. Up to this time the Jews were regarded as a protected people. The canon Dispar and the frequently issued statements of protection, Sicut Iudeis, indicate this. Innocent III also issued Sicut Iudeis but with some changes indicating a greater hostility toward the Jews" (306). We see the influence of *Etsi* here as it transforms the Jews' vulnerable reliance on the protective power of the papacy into a position of punitive servility.

72. The text reads in part:

> The Jews, . . .who [only] out of mercy are . . .admitted into intimacy with us, and who ought to [acknowledge] the yoke of perpetual enslavement because of their guilt. . . .Since. . . it is a crime that one reborn in the baptismal font should be defiled by the rites or familiarity of an unbeliever and that the Christian religion should be oppressed by the dominion of the unfaithful when a blasphemer holds in [slavery] an unfortunate man redeemed by the blood of Christ,

therefore we order . . . that . . . the. . . excesses of the Jews . . . be completely suppressed. . . in order that they should not again dare to straighten their neck bent under the yoke of perpetual slavery in insult against the Redeemer. (Grayzel 1966, 199–201)

73. This status of the Jews becomes the example of the nadir to which Christians should never be demeaned, as expressed in a 1234 letter Gregory writes complaining to the Abbot of Cluny regarding the interdict decreed against Cistercian monks. In taking this action, the French prelacy put their fellow Christians "into worse condition than even the perfidious Jews, who are by their own guilt condemned to perpetual slavery . . . for these friars are cut off from communion with the faithful from which even Jews are not shut out" (Grayzel 1966, 211). The palpable error of placing Christians in a "deterioris conditionis" than that of Jews need not be condemned, but merely stated.

   Incongruously enough, Urban IV applies the concept not only to Jews, but to Muslims as well. In a 1263 letter, he asks the King of Hungary to appoint Christian, rather than Jewish and Muslim tax collectors, to prevent the latter from occupying public offices: "It is neither convenient nor honest that these same Jews and Muslims, whose proper guilt submitted them to perpetual servitude, should exercise strength of power in regard to Christians" [quod non est conveniens vel honestum, ut eisdem iudeis et sarracenis, quos propria culpa *submisit perpetue servituti*, exercendi vim potestatis in christianos] (Grayzel 1989, 78–9, my translation). Chapter 5 considers the expansion of this concept to Muslims.

74. Pakter claims that out of all of his letters on the Jews, Innocent includes *Etsi* alone in his *Compilatio III* (136). However Simonsohn documents that seven of Innocent's letters make it into the definitive collection of canon law, the *Corpus Juris Canonici*, and at least one other of them, *Post miserabilem*, a letter granting crusaders remission of interest owed to Jews, appears in the *Compilatio III*. See the marginal commentary that cites this decretal with reference to Innocent's collection (*Corpus Juris Canonici* II, Lib. V, tit. XIX, c. 12)

75. "The official collection of canon law which superceded [sic] all previous collections was the *Decretales* of Gregory IX. The collection was made by Raymond of Penaforte who drew upon the previous compilations and the letters of Gregory IX" (Czerwinski, 27).

76. "'*Etsi Iudaeos*' prohibited Jews from hiring Christians and Christians from working for Jews. Though cohabitation was the greatest evil envisioned by Innocent, '*Etsi Iudaeos*' was not limited to servants living with Jews; his text spoke only of servants. Later interpreters read the text as applying to any labor for Jews" (Pakter, 135).

77. As Pakter explains, "One reason for this volume is that the canonists had inherited a large number of texts from Roman law, early councils and Gregory I. In sheer numbers, there was more source material on slaves than on any other

issue which the canonists had to deal with" (84). As early as the sixth century, Justinian's Code proscribed Jews (along with heretics and pagans) from owning Christian slaves: "Ne Christianum mancipium haereticus vel paganus vel Iudaeus habeat vel possideat vel circumcidat [No heretic, or pagan or Jew should have, or possess or circumcise a Christian]" (Code: I, X., qtd. in Czerwinski 38, n. 25, my translation). Note the emphasis in the placement of "Christian" in the syntax of the sentence; even though it is the object of the verb, it preceded the subjects.

78. This interest in Jewish property in slaves was anomalous in canon law: "Medieval canon law was not concerned with the property rights of Jews in general; as far as the canonists were concerned, Jews were as free to inherit, purchase and otherwise acquire property, as any Christian would be. The one exception was the ownership of slaves" (Pakter, 84).

79. Twelfth-century canonists did not object to the very idea of Jews employing Christian servants:

> Huguccio saw no degradation in working for Jews; a presumption of social equality between Jews and Christians underlies his work. [Other] Italian canonists had occasionally spoken of Jews as being theologically inferior to Christians. It was in this sense that Alexander II urged protection of Jews because "they are always willing to serve" [Dispar nimirum]. . . . While Huguccio implied that Jews were inferior before God, he did not advocate inferiority as a social program. He never claimed Jews were personally inferior, or that it was demeaning or inappropriate to work for them. (Patker, 135)

However:

> Thirteenth century canonists were more critical of Jews employing free Christians. Opposition was first registered in northern Europe. The French *Summa "Antiquitate,"* which opposed free Christians serving Jews, reports that Jews bribed the Bishop of Paris in order to employ Christians. Alanus extended the prohibition against owning Christian slaves to hiring free Christians. Huguccio's views were supplanted in Italy. Laurentius Hispanus opposed Jews' employing free Christians for the same reason he opposed Jews' serving in public office: to prevent them from appearing as masters of Christians. (Pakter, 134)

80. He addresses this issue in his *Glossa Ordinaria* on the *Decretum* (c. 1215). (GL. Ord. Di.54. c.13 s.v. <u>ad libertatem</u> inf 17 q.4). "Sed nunquid Christianus potest emere Iudaeum mancipium? Sic tamen ut cum illo non moretur" (Czerwinski, 124; Winroth, 145). Pope Gregory I had established that Jews could not employ free Christians as domestic servants in his decretal, *Multorum ad nos* (594): "You should leave no opportunity for the simple in mind to serve in a certain manner the Jewish superstition, not so much out of persuasion as of the right of power over them" (Linder, 427; Pakter, 92–3). Johannes assumes that cohabitation between Christians and Jews should be eschewed, regardless of the power

dynamic. Canon law sought to prevent familiarity between Jews and Christians in a number of contexts: for example, Lateran IV's canon 68 orders that Jews and Christians wear distinguishing clothing to avoid mixing together, a rule subsequently taken up by local councils and secular rulers (Grayzel 1966, 309).

81. Originally entitled *Summa de paenitentia*, Raymond's text was an influential manual of laws for confessors (Goering, 419).

82. "Quid de Christiano, numquid potest emere, vel habere Judaeum vel Paganum mancipium? Utique 23 q. 8 c. Dispar [C. 23 q.8 c. 11]. Extra, de Judaeis, Et si Judaeos [X, V, 6, c. 13]. Ubi dicitur, quod Judaei servi sunt christianorum. Non tamen debet cum illo morari, ita quod eum habeat familiarem. . . Si autem voluerit ille fieri christianus, potest; nec debet dominus prohibere, nec poetest: nam Spiritus sancti vocatio omnia vincula solvit" (Czerwinski 126, n. 68).

83. Czerwinski aptly registers the significance of citing these two decretals together: "Etsi iudeos served as a basis for the reinterpretation of Dispar. There is a considerable difference between being 'ready to serve' and being 'condemned to perpetual servitude,' but Raymond of Peñafort joined them in his works to indicate the lowly status of the Jews" (307).

84. According to the canon law, slaves of Jews who convert to Christianity must be freed, but Christians were permitted to own Christian slaves (Pakter 93). In this instance, "The reason for the objections of the master seems to be to prevent the liberation of the convert. What apparently has happened was a literal interpretation of the spirit making one free" (Czerwinski, 125–26).

85. "Nunquid Christianus potest paganum mancipium vel iudaeum emere. Respondeo sic . . . sed iudaeum secum in familia non habebit. . . Sed si voluerit effici Christianus sibi prohibere non potest nec debet. Quia ubi spiritus ibi libertas" (Czerwinski 128, n. 70). In addition to *Dispar* and *Etsi*, he also cites *Fraternitatem* Di. 54 c. 15, which requires Jews to sell or free non-Christian slaves who wish to convert to Christianity. An English translation of the original text of this law, Gregory I's 596 dectretal, can be found in Linder (430–31). For a detailed account of the history of canon law on the slaves and servants of Jews, see Pakter (84–140).

86. The text reads:

> Those who desire in a sincere effort to bring aliens to the Christian religion— to the right faith—should strive toward it with allurements, not harshness (asperitatibus), lest those whose mind might be attracted by clear reason should be driven back by hostility; for those who act otherwise and wish, under this pretext, to keep them away from the accustomed observation of their rite, prove that they are acting for themselves and not for the sake of God. (Linder, 443)

87. As Linder explains:

> Toledo IV dealt with the entirely new situation created by the forced baptism imposed on the Jews of Spain by Sisebut (612–621), that is the existence of

crypto-Jews, formally baptized and recognized as Christians, alongside communities of non-baptized and openly practicing Jews. The council condemned on principle any forced baptism [but] refused, on strong theological grounds, any compromise on the indelible nature of baptism once it had been duly performed. (Linder, 485)

88. Goering notes the influence of both texts: "William of Rennes composed an 'apparatus' or gloss to Raymond's *Summa* (c. 1245), and both became standard texts in the Dominican schools for the duration of the thirteenth century" (422).

89. Pakter provides the reference:

Guilelmus Redonensis, *Apparatus* to *Summa de Casibus* (c. 1241–1245). Printed as marginal gloss to Raymundus de Pennaforte's *Summa* (Rome 1603) 33:

Asperitatibus, Sed numquid possent auferri eis filij eorum ad baptizandum? Respondeo: adulti non debent, nisi consenserint sponte baptizari, nec etiam paruuli per illos, qui non sunt domini eorum. Sed si vere dominis serui Iudaei sunt, sicut credo, ut extra eod. Et si Iudaeos (X 5.6.13) et 23 q.8 Dispar (c.11), et Gen. 9 maledictus Chanaan, seruus seruorum erit fratribus suis, credo, quod Principes, quorum sunt serui Iudaei, possunt eis auferre filios paruulos absque omni iniuria; cum illi in filiis non habeant potestatem tanquam serui. Et sicut ijdem Principes possent eosdem paruulos tanquam mancipia sua aliis dare, vel vendere in servitutem, inuitis parentibus, ita possent eos offerre ad baptismum; et in hoc mererentur; dum tamen non facerent propter compellendos hoc modo parentes ad fidem sed propter seluandos pueros per fidei sacramentum. . . . (322, n. 295)

90. In a discussion of whether a parent's sin can be transferred to an offspring, Raymond also uses the person of Canaan to figure Jewish hereditary servitude as punishment for the crime of deicide:

Item Cham peccante, Chanaan filius ejus maledicitur: Giezi delinquente, lepra transmittitur ad posteros, Judaeis clamantibus: Sanguis ejus supernos & super filios nostros. Etiam reliquiae eorum poenae mortis Christi addictae sunt. (Similarly, Ham sinning, his son Canaan is cursed; Gehazi offending, leprosy is passed to [his] offspring; the Jews crying: "His blood upon us and upon our children," likewise the remnants of them are enslaved as punishment for the death of Jesus.) (*Summa de paenitentia*, III, 32, 5, p 374, my translation. See also Czerwinski 45,n. 44, although he introduces some errors into his transcription)

The reference to Gehazi derives from 2 Kings 5:20–27 in which the fraudulent servant and his offspring are cursed by Elisha with perpetual leprosy. Irven Resnick notes that this verse is used as a proof-text to link Jews and leprosy:

Although leprosy became a medieval metaphor for sin and heresy, it is equally true that it became a metaphor for Judaism. . . . In addition, the figure of Elisha's acquisitive servant Gehazi, who sought payment for the miraculous cure after his master had refused Naaman's every gift, for which Gehazi and all of his descendents were cursed with leprosy (2 Kgs. 5:20–27), became a symbol for all the Jews. According to Caesarius of Arles (d. 542), Gehazi represents the whole of the Jewish people that is afflicted with the sin of leprosy, but from which the Gentiles have been freed. (122, 128)

The Jewish polemical association of Gehazi with Jesus predates the Christian interpretations (Cuffel 53, 37). In chapter 4 I will consider at greater length in the association of Jewish servitude with the figure of Ham.

91. He refers to *Etsi* as "& sic," which follows the reference to *Dispar*. (Pakter, 328; Rowan, 18; Francesco Zabarella 169v).

92. His proof, however, does not depend on the servitude of the Jews (Rowan, 22ff). He does cite *Dispar* in a screed that he inserts in the midst of his argument. In this digression, he uses the decretal to demonstrate that the Jews have forfeited their right to be tolerated in Christian society.

> The Jews are most ungrateful to Christians, whom they curse daily with public curses and public execrations, they despoil with their usuries, they deny their servile dues, they deride our most immaculate faith and proceed to defile it with the blackest blasphemies against our Savior, even in public. . . . (qtd. in Rowan, 16)

In challenging Christianity, Jews fail to inhabit their proper subordinated position and are no longer deserving of protection (Rowan, 15–16).

93. However, Innocent IV elsewhere does make use of the doctrine of *servitus Judaeorum*; in a 1244 decretal forbidding Jews to employ Christian servants, he echoes the language of *Etsi*, citing Galatians to denounce the impropriety of Jews, the children of the slave woman, employing free Christians (Grayzel 1966, 253).

94. As Simonsohn notes,

> This papal perception of the status of the Jews [as slaves] in no way inhibited papal avowal of the status of Roman Jewry, which was that:
> > All Jews and Jewesses who live in Roman and dwell there with their families, are to be treated as and are understood to be Roman citizens in everything, and are so considered by everybody, and may enjoy the privileges of Roman citizens. (7, 101)

Boniface IX made this affirmation in a 1402 decretal; Martin V confirmed it again in 1430 (Simonsohn 7 101 n.20; 1 539–44). In a different context, Gregory IX, writing to the Archbishops and bishops of France in 1233 and Innocent IV, writing to the Archbishop of Vienne in 1247, request the release of wrongfully imprisoned Jews, ordering that they be restored "to their former liberty [Judeis libertati pristine restitutis/ Judeos pristine restituant libertati]" (Grayzel 1966, 201, 265). However, this probably refers to their liberty prior to imprisonment and not to the status of free person versus slave.

95. However, Czerwinski argues:

> Hostiensis personally approved of kidnapping of Jewish children and their baptism, although it was illegal. This is the case if the children were more

than seven years old. If they children were less than seven, they remained
Christians, but this conversion of children under seven years of age, whose
parents were both Jewish, should not be done as it is a form of unwilling
baptism. (198)

96. Pakter notes: "By 1270, involuntary baptism of Jewish children had become so
topical among Parisian theologians that St Thomas Aquinas (1225–74) picked it
for his Christmas Quodlibet." The text of this quodlibet is identical with *Summa
Theologica* II.2.q.10.a.12 ff (Pakter 324, n. 299).

97. As Aquinas reasons:

> The custom of the Church enjoys the greatest authority and ought to be jealously
> maintained in all matters. . . . Now never was it the usage of the Church to bap-
> tize Jewish children against their parents' will, though in past times there have
> been many very powerful Catholic princes like Constantine and Theodosius
> with whom most holy bishops were on most friendly terms, as Sylvester with
> Constantine and Ambrose with Theodosius, who would not have hesitated to
> claim that this should be done had it been at all reasonable. So therefore it
> seems hazardous to assert, against the Church's custom observed up till now,
> that Jewish children should be baptized despite the unwillingness of their par-
> ents. (2.2.10.12 reply to 1 77)

98. The Latin reads: "ut iura dicunt, Iudaei merito culpae suae sint vel essent perpetuae servituti addicti, et sic eorum res terrarum domini possint accipere
tanquam suas" (*De regimine Iudaeorum (Epistula ad ducissam Brabantiae)* art.
1, resp. ad argumentum, numerus 727, linea 5, pag. 249). See Simonsohn's
discussion, 7, 98.

99. R. W. Dyson, in his notes on *De Regimine Iudaeorum*, also suggests a connection
to *Etsi*: "What St Thomas probably has in mind here is the canon X. 5:6:13: *Esti
Judaeos* (CIC 2:775f)" (Dyson 233, n. 82).

Emperor Frederick II also incorporated the term perpetual servitude in a
1237 law for the city of Vienna excluding Jews from serving in public office,
"so they will not abuse official power for the oppression of Christians; for of
old, imperial authority has imposed perpetual servitude upon the Jews, as punishment for their crime" (qtd. in Kisch, 149) "ab officiorum prefecrura Judeos
excipimus. ne sub pretextu prefecture opprimant Christianos: cum imperialis
auctoritas a priscis temporibus ad perpetrati judaici sceleris ultionem eisdem
Judeis indixerit perpetuam servitutem" (Kisch 431, n. 64). Frederick also relied
on *Etsi* in formulating his law; see Kisch, 150–51. Pakter concurs on this point,
136. However, Aquinas's text is much closer to the wording of *Etsi* than to the
language of Frederick's law.

100. Pakter emphasizes the influence of theological contexts on Aquinas's thinking
regarding the conversion of Jewish children: "The involuntary baptism of
Jewish children had become so topical among Parisian *theologians* that St

Thomas Aquinas (1225–74) picked it for his Christmas Quodlibet. . . .Some of [his] grounds were borrowed from canonists or civilians. Yet on the whole, *St Thomas embraced most of the theologians premises, including the servile status of Jews*" (324, emphasis mine). Pakter does not consider *De Regimine Judaeorum*, but even in the *Summa* Aquinas emphasizes the civil nature of the Jews' servitude to secular rulers in discussing the conversion question.

101. In addition to its impact on canon law:

"Jewish servitude" as expressed in "*Etsi iudaeos*" [also] signified a change in public . . .law. In public law, Innocent's doctrine of the "servitude of the Jews" provided a new rationale for tax assessments. Guido Kisch correctly saw "*Etsi*" as a bridge between the theological notion of Jewish servitude and Frederick II's 1237 proclamation of Jews as the "serf of the chamber" . . .in order to justify taxing them. It was no longer necessary to sell privileges to Jews or to fine them on trumped-up charges as had been done in England or France. The mere fact that they were Jews rendered them vulnerable to levies. (Pakter, 136)

102. Coincidentally, almost exactly to the day: Innocent III writes his letter on 15 July 1205, while Paul composes his in 1555 on "the day before the Ides of July" (Stow, 298).

103. While decreasingly necessary with regard to Jews, however, the concept of perpetual servitude (again secured with recourse to biblical figures) reappears in a form that attaches to infidels and pagans in canonical writings and papal bulls of the fourteenth and fifteenth century; a phenomenon I discuss in chapter 5.

104. For example, see the discussion in chapter 2 of Jacques de Vitry.

CHAPTER 2

1. From Cecco d'Ascoli's commentary on Sacrobosco's *De sphaera*, written shortly before 1324 (qtd. in Biller 1992, 199 and 2001, 141).

2. Although this idea has received renewed interest in the last 25 years, earlier authors, including Poliakov (vol. 1, 143), Trachtenberg (50–2, 149) and Gilman (1986, 74–5) have noted it as well.

3. While Johnson has argued that Jewish bleeding begins as anal bleeding and does not originate as a type of male menstruation, Resnick cites other evidence to argue in favor of understanding the condition as menstrual. Biller notes the disagreement without adjudicating it (2001, 138). Cuffel tracks how gender inflects interreligious polemic (117–55). On the ascription of bleeding to Jews, she observes:

Sometimes the parallel between the sickly, oozing religious other and menstruating women was made explicit. At other times it was not, yet gender was a continual thread in this thirteenth-century polemical theme. . . . Thirteenth-century Christian tales of special Jewish ailments, menstrual or otherwise, were directed specifically at Jewish men. (156)

I argue that the flow of blood supernaturally imposed on Jewish bodies signifies a humiliating, inferior difference, which either menstruation or bleeding hemorrhoids could indicate.

4. Ingested food was thought to produce these different substances (Klibansky et al., 5). Later refinements of this doctrine explained that the stomach, in the course of digestion, transformed food into chyle, which was carried to the liver where it was concocted or cooked into the humors. The substance of blood was understood to be a combination of the humor blood mixed with lesser amounts of the other humors; yellow and black bile ostensibly functioned to purify and strengthen the blood. The humors combined as blood served in turn to nourish the body (Siraisi, 105–6).

5. Sexual difference also influenced one's humoral make-up, as women were thought as a rule to have colder, moister complexions than men, though individuals could vary on the spectrum. Additionally, climate and geographical region purportedly altered human complexions; peoples living in cold northern lands possessed similarly cold, moist bodies, in contrast to the hot, dry constitutions of peoples inhabiting warmer areas (Siraisi, 102–3). The climate conditions of different locations were thought to produce various geographical or ethnic characters. On the question of the relationship of humoral discourse to the construction of race, see Ziegler; Floyd-Wilson; Isaac; and Akbari.

6. As articulated in the third-century BCE treatise *Of the Constitution of the Universe and of Man*:

> For those governed by the purest blood. . . are agreeable, laugh, joke and have rosy, well-coloured bodies; those governed by yellow bile are irritable, violent, bold and have fair, yellowish bodies; those governed by black bile are indolent, timid, ailing, and, with regard to body, swarthy and black-haired; but those governed by phlegm are sad, forgetful, and, with regard to the body, very pale. (qtd. in Klibansky et al., 59)

7. Classical Greek natural philosophy and medicine associate the melancholy humor with a wide range of symptoms and behaviors. My discussion of melancholy and its manifestations focuses only on those elements that will be significant for the analysis of Jewish melancholic bleeding later in this chapter. For a fuller consideration, see Klibansky et al.

8. Blood, while sometimes linked to disease, was normally associated with a temperate or healthy complexion (Klibansky et al., 13). Phlegm, black and yellow bile were all initially understood as "excretions, 'humores vitiosi,' causing illness . . . ; one could only speak of true health when all the humors were present in the right combination, so that each harmful influence neutralized the other" (11). Paradoxically, these humors could refer to disease states or normal complexions (12).

9. The text is attributed to and most likely composed by Hippocrates, circa 415 B.C.E. It famously opens "Life is short, the Art long," and is the most highly

regarded and widely known of the author's works, with more Greek manuscripts than any other Hippocratic book, in addition to translations into Hebrew, Arabic, Syriac, and Latin (*Hippocrates*, I.i.99, xxxiii–xxxvi). The *Aphorisms* were included in the *Articella*, a twelfth-century collection of medical treatises that was used as a basic text in medical education (Biller 1992, 206 n. 3).

10. Pseudo-Aristotle, in his *Problemata*, identifies two types of melancholy humor: in addition to a "hot" black bile, there is a colder type that he also associates with sadness: "When the temperament caused by admixture of black bile is colder, it gives rise, as has been already remarked, to despondency of various kinds, but when it is hotter to cheerfulness. Hence the young are more cheerful, the old more despondent, the former being hot and the latter cold; for old age is a process of cooling" (Book XXX. I, 955a 31–4). The *Problemata* also connects melancholy with insanity, but gives it a positive nuance in designating it as a divine frenzy (Klibansky et al. 14, 18, 23–4, 38–4). Klibansky et. al. note the influence of this text on later medieval and early modern views of melancholy in relation to insanity, genius or intellectual endeavors.

11. Generally, Hippocrates's statements and sections lack an apparent organizing principle, which makes evaluation of any of his terse pronouncements difficult (I xxxiii).

12. The editor's note to VI.xi states that "Hemorrhoids were supposed to be one of Nature's ways of removing impurities," (n. 2, 183) but offers no support for this claim.

13. The Latin text reads:

> Hemorrhoidæ sunt quinque venæ exeuntes in ano, ex quibus diversæ passions fiunt, scilicet inflatio, retentio, fluxus. Quandoque, autem superfluitates vi nature transmittuntur ad partes & ruptis venis illis, emittuntur, & corpus ab diversis ægritudinibus liberator. Sed si fuerit fluxus immoderatus, varies efficiuntur passiones. Quando vero propter consuetudinarie retinentur, maximæ ægritudines consequuntur, vt, hydropisis; phthisis, mania, & melancholia, &c. (7.54, 337; I have silently extended all contractions in the original)

14. Müller argues that the *Breviarium* is misattributed to Arnold of Villanova, proposing instead that Arnold of Naples authored the work around 1320 (162).

15. Resnick identifies an additional source: "A similar view is found in the Middle English translation of the *compendium medicinae* of Gilbert the Englishman, whom Theodorich often cites" (2012, 204 n. 116). Gilbert states: "Moche flowing of pes veines comep eipirwhilis in certeyn tymes, as pe flowing of blode pat comep to women ones in a monepe" (Getz, 279). The translation dates from the early fifteenth century, but the Latin original was composed in the thirteenth century.

16. Resnick corroborates the point that the classical discussion of melancholy omits mention of Jews (2000, 252).

17. Representations of Judas with his intestines spilling out of his body as he hangs himself appear in medieval illuminated manuscripts; for example, the Lewis Psalter at the Free Library of Philadelphia includes one (Lewis E 185 fol. 13r). This psalter is digitized and easily viewed online. Anthony Bale analyzes the significance of medieval visual representations of Judas's ruptured bowels (2010, 86–9).

18. Trachtenberg and Resnick link a subsequent iteration of mythical Jewish murderousness, the blood libel, with the fiction of periodic Jewish bleeding (149; 2000, 244).

19. In his analysis of the text, Gavin Langmuir argues that Thomas intentionally emphasizes the connections between William and Jesus in order to transform the boy into a saint and bring glory to his monastery (Langmuir, 235).

20. The Latin reads: "per posteriora eius sanguis guttatim profluere inchoauit. Adeoque diuina circa eum claruit ultio, ut reuera cum iudeis dicere et ipse possit: *Sanguis innocens super nos et super filios nostros*" (111).

21. The Vulgate text reads: "sanguis eius super nos et super filios nostros [his blood {be} upon us and upon our children]." Thomas replaces "eius" with "innocens," "the innocent blood be upon us," thus opening up the applicability of the statement to any martyr and more closely drawing the connection between Jesus and William, the Jews of the New Testament with the Jewish behavior of Sheriff Chesney.

22. The trope of divine punishment employed to "explain" Jewish bleeding is used by Thomas here to establish a comparison; because of his "Jewish" actions, the Christian sheriff's body is punished by being transformed into a Jewish one. Johnson makes a similar point:

> And the full implications of the story in which the Sheriff is punished when he becomes Jew-like are only evident to one who has a specific notion of what it means to be a Jew. This is a vivid example of the discursive construction of the Jewish body, a body whose true Jewishness is irrespective of parentage. (286)

Bale also notes Thomas's linking of Judas's punishment with Chesney's (2010, 56–7).

23. The Latin reads: "Quorum primi sunt Judei. homines obstinati. plus quam mulieres imbelles. ubique serui. singulis lunationibus fluxum sanguinis. patientes. vetus testamentum ad literam seruant. et literam habent hebream" (qtd. in Biller 2001, 158).

24. He may be qualifying the truth of this claim by his double use of the passive form of the verb "dico," to call or say, indicating that he is passing along the words of others. Biller suggests that Caesarius uses this word to indicate that he is introducing an oral tradition into his text (1992, 196).

25. The Latin reads: "in nocte sextae feria, quae Pascha . . .praecedit. Tunc enim Judaei laborare dicuntur quadam infirmitate, quae fluxus sanguinis dicitur, circa quam occupati aliis tunc minus intendere possunt" (*Dialogus*, II.xxiii. vol. 1 92).

26. Jacques was born sometime around 1160–1170 and died in 1240. Like Innocent III, he studied preaching with Peter the Chanter at the University of Paris. An ordained priest and Augustinian canon, he served outside the monastery, preaching against the Albigensian heresy and in support of the fifth crusade for the Holy Land. He was elected bishop of Acre, during which time he wrote the *Historia*. Upon his return he was named cardinal bishop of Tusculum and served in the papal curia until his death (Jacques 1972, 4–7). As Hinnebusch explains in the introduction to the second book of the *Historia Hierosolimintana Abbreviata*, "Jerusalem is incorporated into the title, for the recovery and the defense of the Holy City and Places were the central purpose of the crusades and crusader states" (Jacques 1972, 10). The volume is divided into three books: the *Historia Orientalis*, which provides a background of earlier crusades, discusses Muhammad and Islam, describes the land, plants, animals, and different peoples living in the Holy Land; the *Historia Occidentalis*, book two, focuses on the recent religious and moral history of the West; the third book, which he may not have written, focuses on events in Holy Land from time of Lateran Council to capture of Damietta (10).

27. Bolton argues for a linkage between the goals of the papacy and Jacques's own vocation:

> The call to crusade—the recovery of the Holy Land lost since 1187—was one of the specific causes which Jacques de Vitry preached and which sprang from his concern to achieve the *vita apostolica* in his day, both in the West and in Christ's own patrimony in the East. This was a view shared by Innocent III and his friends.
>
> When Innocent, smarting from the twin blows of disaster and disgrace inflicted by the Fourth Crusade of 1204, embarked on his revitalizing plans for a fifth, he had no more enthusiastic a supporter than Jacques de Vitry, particularly so in France. To both men, the crusading ideals of liberation of the Holy Land and mission amongst the infidel were tasks of faith which could not be brushed aside, no matter how seemingly impossible their nature. (57)

28. Since canon law strictly prohibits this practice, Jacques may instead refer to servants, not slaves, as Innocent mentions in *Etsi*.

29. Innocent protests that

> princes . . .receive Jews . . .and appoint them their agents for the collection of usury; and they are not afraid to . . .oppress the poor of Christ. Moreover, when the Christians, who had taken a loan from the Jews, have paid them back the principal and more besides, it often happens that these appointees (of the princes). . . after seizing the pledges, and after casting these Christians into prison, compel them to pay most exorbitant usury. (Grayzel 1966, 127)

30. The Latin text reads:

> Alii autem Iudaei de quibus patres eorum clamaverunt: "Sanguis eius super nos et super filios nostros" per universum fere mundum and in omnem

ventum dispersi, vbique sunt servi, vbique tributarii fortitudo eorum vt ait
Isaias propheta, conversa est in favillam. Imbelles enim et imbecilles facti
sunt quasi mulieres. Unde singulis lunationibus, ut dicitur, fluxum sanguinis patiuntur. Percussit enim eos Deus in posteriora et opprobrium sempiternum dedit illis. Postquam enim fratrem suum verum Abel acciderunt
facti sunt vagi et profugi super terram, sicut maledictus Cain, habentes caput
tremulum, id est, cor pavidum, die ac nocte timentes, vite sue non credentes.
(qtd. in Biller 2001, 158)

31. Although Jacques does not mention it, there is a tradition in Hebrew scripture,
    picked up by Christian exegetes, in which the Jews are likened to a menstruating
    woman, especially in the context of the destruction of the First Temple. Rupert of
    Deutz comments on Isaiah 64:6: "And we are all become like one unclean and all
    our righteous deeds are like the garment of a menstruating woman" in support
    of the claim that only Jesus can remove the defilement of Israel (cited in Resnick
    2000, 248–49). More pointedly, Paschasius Radbertus (d. 860) cites Jeremiah's
    prophecy of the destruction of the Temple, Lamentations 1:17, "Jerusalem is like
    a menstruating woman," to argue that as a menstruating woman is an abomina-
    tion, so the Jews were and are today (cited in Resnick 2000, 249).

32. Jerome's Vulgate includes two translations of the Psalms, one that follows the
    Hebrew Bible, another that follows the Greek Septuagint. The translation of
    the Hebrew reads "et percussit hostes suos retrorsum obprobrium sempiter-
    num dedit eos [And {God} beat his enemies back, he consigned them to eternal
    shame]" (my transl). The Septuagint version offers Jacques a text that locates
    punishment in the body.

33. The Vulgate text reads: "dabit enim tibi Dominus ibi cor pavidum . . .te timebis
    nocte et die et non credes vitae tuae." For Cain's trembling head, see n. 55 in
    chapter 1.

34. Compare:

    Ut esset Cain vagus et profugus super terram, nec interficeretur a quoquam,
    tremorem capitis signum Dominus imposuit super eum [paraphrase of
    Gen 4]; quare Judei, contra quos clamat vox sanguinis Jesu Christi, etsi occidi
    non debeant, ne divine legis obliviscatur populus Christianus, dispergi tamen
    debent super terram ut vagi, quatenus facies ipsorum ignomnie repleatur, et
    querant nomen Domini Jesu Christi. . . .sed [debent] comprimi servitute, qua se
    dignes merito reddiderunt cum in illum manus injecere sacrilegas qui veram
    eis conferre venerat libertatem, super eos et filios suos esse ipsius sanguinem
    conclamantes. (Grayzel 1966, 126)

35. "The text was widely read and copied in the Middle Ages: 124 manuscripts of the
    Latin texts are extant, as is a 13th-century translation into French" (Tolan, 2010).
    Biller notes Jacques's influence on Dominicans (2001, 143); Bird traces the ex-
    tensive reception of his text by the order:

The eastern history also quickly became a favored source for members of the Dominican order, including Vincent of Beauvais, who used it for his *Speculum historiale*, and Thomas of Cantimpré, who wove many of James's depictions of natural wonders into his *De natura rerum*. Both works were intended as pastoral sourcebooks for Dominican preachers and James's entire history was also copied by Dominicans. (58–9)

Johnson briefly addresses the significance of the Dominican circulation of the idea of Jewish bleeding (290–91). As Jeremy Cohen demonstrates, the Dominicans, along with the Franciscans, actively eroded the protected status of the Jews in Christian society articulated by Augustine:

> From the establishment of these first and most important mendicant orders in the Roman Church early in the thirteenth century, until the end of the medieval period and even beyond, Dominican and Franciscan friars directed and oversaw virtually all the anti-Jewish activities of the Christian clergy in the West. As inquisitors, missionaries, disputants, polemicists, scholars, and itinerant preachers, mendicants engaged in a concerted effort to undermine the religious freedom and physical security of the medieval Jewish community. . . .
> The Dominicans and Franciscans developed, refined, and sought to implement a new Christian ideology with regard to the Jews, one that allotted the Jews no legitimate right to exist in European society. (1982, 13–14)

Given their hostile stance toward Jews, it is not surprising to find Dominicans in the forefront of those circulating accounts of the humiliating Jewish bleeding disease.

36. The Latin text reads: "*Et percussit inimicos suos in posteriora [obprobrium sempiternum dedit illis].* . . . Opprobrium sempiternum fuit, quia vilissima fuit huiusmodi infirmitas. Et dicunt quidam quod hoc opprobrium sustinent Judaei, quia in vindictam Dominicae Passionis patiuntur fluxum sanguinis, et ideo sunt ita pallidi" (qtd. in Johnson 281, n. 26).

37. In Thomas of Monmouth's account, the loss of blood over a two-year period "weakened [Chesney's] bodily powers and made him grow pale [uultui pallorem induxit]" (Johnson, 111). An extended period of bleeding here seems to cause pallor in complexion.

38. As mentioned in note 35, Thomas of Cantimpré was familiar with Jacques's work; he wrote a supplement to de Vitry's hagiography of Marie of Oignies (Jacques 2012).

39. The Latin text reads:

> Constat quidem ex sancto Euangelio, quod Pilato lauante manus, and [*sic*] dicente: Mundus ego sum a sanguine iusti huius Iudaei impiissimi clamauerunt: Sangnis [*sic*] eius super nos, and [*sic*] super filios nostros. Super quo beatissimus Augustinus in sermone quodam, qui incipit: In cruce, innuere videtur,. . . quod ex maledictione parentum currat adhuc in filios vena facinoris, per maculam sanguinis: Vt per hanc importune fluidam proles impia inexpiabiliter

crucietur, quousque se ream sanguinis Christi recognosact poenitens, & sane-
tur. (qtd. in Johnson 288, n. 46)

40. Most of the contemporary scholars who write on this idea of Jewish male
bleeding assume that the theological trope influences this new medical knowledge; as Johnson argues, a "literalization of an exegetical motif" occurs when the
idea of Jewish bleeding developed in Christian discourse engenders the "fact"
of Jewish bodily difference in texts on medicine and natural philosophy (286).
Biller advances the view that "a myth about Jews having a flux of blood," circulating prior to Caesarius of Heisterbach's redaction of the tale in the first quarter
of the thirteenth century, pre-exists and serves as a source for the medical explanation of "Jewish" hemorrhoids (1992, 196). While he argues in a later essay
that this belief is "scientific" and free from theological influence, he suggests
that de Vitry's account of Jewish bleeding, which cites Matthew 27:25, Psalms
77:66, and refers to Cain's murder of Abel, probably influenced Albert's non-
theological account (2001, 153, 158, 143). Resnick, who first identified Jacques's
account, affirms that "it was Christian natural philosophers who identified hemorrhoids as a Jewish disease, bringing natural science into the service of theology" (Resnick 2000, 252).

41. Albert the Great was also the teacher of Thomas of Cantimpré (Resnick 2013,
727, 729, 735).

42. The Latin text reads:

> Praeterea, haermorroidae causanter ex superfluitate sanguinis grossi, quia
> quando talis sanguis abundant in corpore, descendit ad inferius. . . et tunc fre-
> quenter rumpitur una vena vel duae, et tunc fluit sanguis. . . . Unde illus maxim
> accidit viventibus ex nurtimento grosso et salso, sicut Iudaeis, per naturam.
> (qtd. in Biller 2001, 159–60.)

43. Although, as we saw above, Albert refers to hemorrhoidal bleeding as menstruation in terms of its function, here he distinguishes the two conditions with
regard to timing: "And because this blood is thick and has an earthy nature,
the moon does not have dominion over its flow the way it does over menses"
(Albertus, 310).

44. While no particular evidence links the Dominicans to the authors of this quodlibet, the former had a strong presence at the University of Paris, albeit in the
faculty of theology rather than arts and sciences where this debate took place
(Cohen 1982, 40). The Dominican order sent Albert the Great to study at the
University of Paris (c. 1240), and subsequently named him as Dominican chair
in theology at the university around 1245 (Resnick 2013, 6–7).

45. The Latin text reads:

> Queritur utrum iudei paciuntur fluxum. Arguitur quod non, quia xpistiani
> et aliqui iudei sunt euisdem complexionis. . . Oppositum patet ex veritate
> quia illi leccatores paciuntur fluxum ut in pluribus. . . .iudei habent fluxum

sanguinis hemoreidarum. Et causa est prima quia dicunt medici quod fluxus sanguinis causatur ex sanguine grosso indigesto quem natura purgat. Sed iste magis habundat in iudeis quia ipse sunt melancolici ut in pluribus. . . sed iudei naturaliter retrahunt se a societate et coniuncti cum aliis ut patet, ergo sunt melancolici. Item, pallidi sunt, ergo sunt melancolice complexionis. Item, timidi sunt naturaliter et hec tria sunt accidencia propria melancolicorum, ut dicit Ipocras. Sed ille qui multum est melancolicus multum habet de sanguine melancolico, et inde debet habere fluxum sanguinis, sed iudei sunt huiusmodi (qtd. in Biller 1992, 205–6).

46. The failure to mention a source does not preclude readers, or listeners, from recognizing its influence, as Cuffel explains in her discussion of Brian Stock's scholarship on the transmission of ideas in eleventh- and twelfth-century Europe:

> Textual knowledge and modes of allegorization could be and were transmitted orally. Indeed, for Stock, one of the surest signs of a community's having passed into true "textuality" was the point at which the "organizing text" no longer needed to be 'spelt out, interpreted, or reiterated. . . .Interaction by word of mouth could take place as a superstructure of an agreed meaning, the textual foundation of behavior having been entirely internalized.' . . .Derogatory epithets, stories, or pictorial representations frequently functioned as abbreviations for more complex sets of polemical associations. Such agreed upon associations within a group may be said to be the foundation of a 'textual community of polemic' in which the full narrative and its meaning no longer needs to be spelled out. (Cuffel, 105)

47. While the main text was probably composed by a student of Albert's in the late thirteenth or early fourteenth century, the date of the commentary is probably later and its country of origin unknown. (Lemay, 1–2)

48. The Latin text reads:

> Advertendum quod Iudei ut plurimum patiuntur fluxum emorroydarum prop-ter tria: et quia communiter sunt in ocio, et ideo aggregantur sibi fluiditates melancholicae; secundo, quia communiter sunt in timore et anxietate, et ideo multiplicatur sanguis melancholicus, iuxta illud Ypocratis, *Timor et pusillanimitas si multum tempus habuerint, melancholicum faciunt*; tercio quod hoc est ex ulcione divina, iuxta, *Et percussit eos in posteriore dorsi, opprobrium sempiternum dedit illis*. (qtd. in Biller 2001, 163)

49. Biller and Lawn believe the text was compiled sometime after the second half of the thirteenth century (Biller 1992, 198–99; Lawn, 99–102). The text is also ascribed to Aristotle under the title *Problemata varia anatomica*; it circulates in the early modern period as *The Problems of Aristotle* (Kaplan 2015, 119–20).

50. The Latin text reads:

> primum quare aliqui uiri patiuntur fluxum emoroidarum? Respondetur quod tales sunt melanchonici [*sic*]; ideo autem multem generator in eis melancholia,

quia frigidi sunt, quae primo mittitur ad splenem ad primam sedem melanconie [*sic*] et ibi propter sui multitudinem non potest retineri et ideo emittitur ad
spinam dorsi ubi sunt predicte quinque uene que terminant in collo, et quando
ille uene ualde replunentur sanguine malanconico [*sic*] tunc iste uene aperiuntur ui nature et exit iste sanguis semel in mense et menstruum semel fluit in
mulieribus, et tales uiri per talem fluxum praeseruantur a magnis infirmitatibus, ut ydropesi, lepra, et huiusmodi. (38)

51. The Latin text reads:

Quare Judei patiuntur indifferenter hunc fluxum? Respondetur primo theologice ipse tempore passionis Christi clamabant, *Sanguis eius super nos et super
filios nostros.* Ideo dicitur in psalmo: *Percussit eos in posteriora dorsi. . . .*Sed quia
Judei non sunt in labore neque in motu neque in conuersatione hominium et
etiam quia sunt in magno timore quia nos ulciscantur [ulsciscamur] passionem
Christi redemptoris nostri, haec omnia faciunt frigiditatem et impediunt digestionem. Ideo in eis generatur multus sanguis melanconicus [*sic*] qui in ipsis
tempore menstruali expellitur seu expurgatur. (qtd. in Biller 2001, 164)

The author of this text uses the same emendation of the Psalm text that appears
in Bernard of Gordon's *Lilium medicinae*.

52. Biller identifies two other works that explain Jewish bleeding as a punishment for
crucifying Jesus. The first provides the epigraph of this chapter, Cecco d'Ascoli's
commentary on Sacrobosco's *De sphaera*, written shortly before 1324. In a discussion of eclipses, d'Ascoli includes this observation: "Because of sin Jews
never contemplate the heavens and after the death of Christ all Jewish men, like
women, suffer menstruation" (my translation; cited in Biller 1992, 99 and 2001,
141). Two later manuscripts of Michael Scot's *Liber introductorius*—an expansive cosmology that considers heaven, earthly phenomena, geography, human
society, animals, plants and minerals—contain a similar statement. Scot spent
time at the University of Paris shortly before his death in 1235. The later manuscripts of his work contain material added up to 1320. In the context of a survey
of human difference based on region that considers Lombards, Slavs, Germans,
Greeks, Tartars, Muslims, Scots, Jews, and Egyptians, these later manuscripts
state "that Jews emit blood *per virgam* [through the penis] every lunar month because they told Pontius Pilate that 'His blood be upon our heads' [paraphrase of
Matt. 27:25]" (Thorndike, 80). As discussed earlier, the claim that Christian men
bleed through the penis appears in the commentary on *De secretis mulierum* (qtd.
in Lemay, 71).

53. Biller notes the very wide circulation of the *Lilium medicinae*, "which is known
in over fifty later medieval Latin manuscripts, leaving aside those of the French,
German, Spanish, and Irish translations, and had six printed editions. It was
a prescribed text in medical faculties—at the University of Montpellier after
1400, at the University of Vienna in 1520" (Biller 1992, 201). The *Omnes homines*

appears to have had a smaller circulation in Latin manuscripts, but "a quite extraordinary circulation in the early modern period: fifty-six Latin editions before 1668, at least thirty-one German ones before 1668. This has continued in modern times, for example, with at least twenty-five English editions between 1684 and 1930" (201–2; see also Biller 2001, 163). I have found at least thirteen editions printed in London and Edinburgh between 1583 and 1684, the first in Latin, the rest in English. For a discussion of the early modern English reception of Jewish bleeding, see Kaplan 2015, 119–22.

54. Even though the Christian texts considered above found their primary audience within the faith, their messages would be perceived by religious opponents:

> As late antique Jews, Pagans, and Christians increasingly adopted and adapted one another's values and scientific lore, the somatic language of each group became increasingly similar and thus comprehensible to members of other faiths. [All three] . . .capitalized on these shared meanings in their polemics, creating invectives that not only warned members of their own communities but that also would have made sense and been deeply insulting to those against whom they were polemicizing. . . .The threads connecting these shared assumptions were strengthened beginning around the twelfth century not only by increased familiarity with one another's written texts but also by personal contact through missionizing, war, and pilgrimage and the resulting familiarity with one another through oral exchanges. (Cuffel, 241)

CHAPTER 3

1. The Latin reads:

> Non uult enim deus prorsus occidi, non omnino extingui, sed ad maius tormentum et maiorem ignominiam, ut fratricidam Cain, uita morte deteriore seruari. . . . Sic de dampnatis dampnandisque Iudaeis ab ipso passionis mortisque Christi tempore iustissima dei seueritas facit, et usque ad ipsius mundi terminum factura est. Qui quoniam Christi sanguinem utique iusta carnem fratris sui fuderunt, serui, miseri, timidi, gementes, ac profugi sunt super terram. . . (*Letters* 1:328–29)

Peter concludes the sentence by quoting the prophetic texts of Isaiah and Paul to confirm the final conversion and salvation of the Jews. However, until that moment, the Jews' punishment perdures.

2. For Augustine's protective doctrine, see Cohen (1999, 245–70). The theme of Cain and Jewish subjection operate as leitmotifs in Peter's writings on the Jews, as he reverts to them on several other occasions. In the *Adversus Iudeorum*, Peter employs Cain to emphasize the humiliating element of the Jews' punishment, likening it again to a life worse than death that extends even into the afterlife, in which demons will mock them in hell: "Thus are you cursed, . . . in what is

worse than death, for the duration of the present age you are made a reproach among men, while for the future forevermore you will be a mockery among the demons" (Peter 2013, 232). See also his sermon, *De laude dominici sepulchri* (In Praise of the Lord's Grave), preached in the pope's presence, c. 1146–1147, in which he compares God's rejection of the Jews with his rejection of Cain's offering (qtd. in Cohen 1999, 252). Cohen notes that Peter "made repeated reference to the divinely ordained subjection of the Jews by other nations," citing several examples (1999, 265 n. 135).

3. Relevant to the example of Cain, see especially Bernstein's discussion of exile as punishment in which the convict may be lawfully killed by anyone (116–17).

4. See Strickland (2003); Mellinkoff (1993); Blumenkranz; and Lipton; though Lipton does not focus on psalter illustrations of dark Jews (2014, 171–99) she does consider how *Bibles moralisées* variously represent the fate of the Jews in Christian eschatology (1999, 112–135). Petzold has noted the portrayal of dark attackers in the English context: "It would be interesting to look at the question of skin colour in connection with some of the christological illustrations in a group of early and mid-thirteenth-century English manuscripts where certain of the miscreants are singled out by having blackened faces" (127, n. 8).

5. See the foundational work by Bindman et. al.; Mellinkoff (1993); Strickland (2003); and Verkerk on the negative values associated with Africans in visual portrayals.

6. The Latin terms *infernus* and *inferior* share the root *inferus*, which denotes: "below, beneath, underneath, lower," as well as the inhabitants of the lower world, and the lower world itself (Andrews et al., *infernus, inferior* and *inferus*).

7. "Indeed, monks had been the first to see in the Psalter an exemplary book of Christian prayer. . . [embracing] the *entire* text of the Psalter both for personal prayer and for use in their liturgical synaxes" (Dyer, 66). Until the fourteenth century, "the psalter was the most commonly used book for private devotions" (Calkins, 207). In his *Letter to Marcellinus*, which considers the nature of the Psalms, Athanasius, fourth-century Bishop of Alexandria, writes: "He who takes up this book—the Psalter—goes through prophecies about the Saviour, as is customary in the other Scriptures, with admiration and adoration, but the other psalms he recognizes as being his own words" (qtd. in Holladay, 165).

8. See also Bestul, who describes this period as experiencing a "theological reinterpretation of the meaning of the incarnation and nature of Christ's redemption [which] led to a sharper focus on Christi's humanity and. . . suffering" (34).

9. As Bestul argues:

"From the point of view of a stylistic development, the culmination of these tendencies is in the works inspired by the techniques of visual meditation advocated by the Franciscans of the thirteenth century, notably by Bonaventure. The expanded role of the Jews, in other words, is a symptom of the growth of

Franciscan realism in the thirteenth century, part of a larger hypothesis about the development of medieval realism in general. (72)

10. For scholars who consider this transformation in more detail, see Rohrbacher on the charge of Jewish deicide in medieval art, Jordan on the Jewish sponge-bearer, and Hourihane on the shift to representing Pontius Pilate as a Jew. For visual representations of Jews as enemies of Jesus, see also Mellinkoff (1993, 41–3, 65–9, 76, 92), Strickland (2003, 107–22), and Bale (2006, 149–68 passim). Other important works on the Passion include Marrow (1977, 1979), Kupfer's collection, and Jeremy Cohen (2007).

11. For some important scholarship on the association of blackness with evil in the Christian tradition, see Bindman et al.; Kelly; Mellinkoff (1993); Strickland (2003); Verkerk; Morrow; Hunter; Mayerson; Byron; and Goldenberg (2009). It should be noted that cultures other than Christianity contribute to the detrimental significance of blackness (Schorsch 2004; Goldenberg 1999, 2003). Furthermore, not all of the Church Fathers' discussions of blackness and black people represented them as evil and inferior; another trend positively identifies Ethiopians as a figure for the Gentile Church whose faith in Jesus contrasts them to the sinful, unbelieving Jews (Courtès). We need to be cautious of reifying negative ideas of blackness by repeating them. For some scholarship on positive representations of blackness in medieval texts and images, see Keita (2006, 2011a, 2011b), Paul Kaplan (1985), introduction in Bindman, and Heng (2015). Nevertheless, the adverse view of blackness is strong and has enduring consequences; the Christian context is the most relevant for the current study.

12. In a separate essay on the Winchester Psalter (c. 1161) I consider the introduction of dark "African" Muslims in representations of the Passion, an iconographic context that initially included only Jewish enemies of Jesus. This innovation should also be considered as possibly contributing to the trend in subsequent English psalters of depicting Jews with dark skin. See Arjana, who reads dark tormentors as a Muslim–Jewish hybrid.

13. The Hebrew prophets Jeremiah (13:23) and Amos (9:7) both link Jews with Ethiopians. For a discussion of patristic sources linking Ethiopians and Jews see Courtès (204–13 passim). See my discussion of this phenomenon (Kaplan, 2013). Morrow briefly notes the "comparison of obstinate Jews with sinful Ethiopians" in biblical exegesis (84–5). However, as in the case of Ethiopians, there are also some positive interpretations of Jews as the Ethiopian bride of Jesus in commentaries on the *Song of Songs*. See for example those offered by Isidore of Seville in his *Allegories of Scripture* or Justus of Urgel (6th c. Spain), who explains that she represents the first Church of Jerusalem, that is, converted Jews, "black by confession of sins, beautiful by grace of sacrament" (Courtès, 210). Nevertheless, while patristic authors do not present damnation and blackness as permanent states for either Ethiopians or Jews, they nevertheless essentialize blackness as the marker of evil, sin, and damnation.

14. Palmer also notes the range of colors that medieval images use to portray devils, and suggests another reason for the employment of black: "Although usually pictured as black to signify their deprivation from light, red, blue, yellow
or green devils occur as cultural norms dictate" (24). See also Jeffrey Russell's
discussions of the range of colors in which the devil is depicted, including black,
blue, brown, gray, green, red, white, pallid and yellow (24, 68–9, 129–33, 186,
209–11, 232–33, 243, 297, 324).

15. John Trevisa's Middle English translation of Bartholomaeus's *De Proprietatibus*
describes Ethiopia as "bloo mennes londe" (qtd. in Kelly, 38). As Kelly
explains: "The compound *blo* + *mon* is used to denote various dark-skinned peoples, including Ethiopians, Indians, and Saracens" (41). As Kelly demonstrates,
the Middle English romance, *The King of Tars*, describes Muslims as

> "Sarrazins bote blo & blac" (1226). In the *Cursor Mundi*, "Four sarȝins wit [David]
> can mete,/ Blac and bla als led [lead] þai war. . . . (8072–73)" In the *Sowdone of
> Babylone* Laban's army is made up of "Thre hundred thousand of Sarsyn felle,/
> Some bloo, some yolowe, some blake as more [Moor/African],/ Some horrible
> and strange as devel of helle" (1004–06). . . .In *Sir Tristrem*, the hero defeats a
> giant, 'Balliagog al blo' (2976). (Kelly, 44–5)

Descriptions of the appearance of Muslims and Africans offer a range of colors—
yellow, blue and black—some associated with lead, that dark-pale substance.
Similarly, as suggested in the quotation from the *Sowdone of Babylone*, Christian
authors from the twelfth century onward employ similar colors to describe the
complexion of devils:

> In Middle English, in fact, "blue" devils are almost as common as black devils.
> In the [thirteenth-century] *Ancrene Wisse*, the author rails against "þe acursede
> gast . . . blac as blamon." In the legend of St. Bartholomew in the earliest text
> of the *South English Legendary* (late twelfth century), the devil is described as
> "swattore þane euere blouȝman." In *Seinte Marherete*, the devil is "an unsehen
> [strange] unwiht [fiend/devil], much deale blackne þen eauer eani blaman."
> (Kelly, 43)

16. *Lividus* derives from *liveo*, which classical Latin defines as " a bluish color, black
and blue, livid,. . . II. A. . . . lead-colored" (*liveo*, in Andrews et al.). The medieval definition of *lividus* lists "subniger, fuscus, pallidus " [blackish, dark, pallid]
(Andrews et al.). The etymology of *liveo* connects it to the Greek "πελιός πελλός
[*pelios, pellos*], dark-blue," and relates it to the Latin terms *pullus*, "Dark-colored,
blackish-gray, dusky, blackish" and *pallidus*, "pale, pallid" (*liveo, pullus, pallidus,*
in Andrews et al.). Pastoureau notes that in antiquity, mourning clothes are
described with the term "*pullus*, . . . a dark, drab wool, its color somewhere between gray and brown" that is sometimes also synonymous with another term
for blackness, *ater*: "laden with many pejorative figurative meanings [in imperial
Rome]: dirty, sad, gloomy, malevolent, deceitful, cruel, harmful, deathly" (35). In
an early Scandinavian context, the colors black and pallid are used to describe

the Hel, goddess of the realm of the dead: "Not only are her features hideous and her hair a disheveled tangle, but her skin is two-tone: black on one side, 'pallid' (*blass*) on the other" (36).

17. The Latin reads:

> De Colore Livido:
>
> Color liuidus . . .in rebus habentibus humorem grossum & frigidum generatur, vt patet in . . .plumbo. Plumbum tamen naturaliter est album quamuis superficialiter sit liuidum. . . Vnde color liuidus signum est frigiditatis dominantis, quia liuidus color in vrina est signum extinctionis naturalis caloris, & mortificationis animalis. (Book 19, chapter 19, 1156)

18. The Latin reads:

> De Colore Livido:
>
> Color ergo liuidus est malus in animatis corporibus, nam vel signat dominium frigoris calorem natrualem extinguentis, & naturam mortificare inchoantis, vel superabundantiam melancholici sanguinis, colorē omnino & cutis superficiem vitiantis, vel cordis angustiam, calorem sanguinis ad interiora reuocantis, vt patet in inuidus, vel dolorem casus siue concussionis sanguinem intercutaneum corrumpentis, vt patet in fustigatis. (Book 19, chapter 20, 1156–57)

19. As McVaugh summarizes: "According to the Aristotelian works, life is humid and warm in temperament, and (all other things being equal) the more moisture possessed by a living thing, the longer its life, since it will take longer to dry out. If an organism is not fed, its natural heat (envisioned as a flame) will consume the moisture of the body which, lacking replacement, will bring about death" (271). McVaugh cites Aristotle's *De longitudine et brevitate vitae* (*Aristotelis Opera VI* Venice 1562 fols 144–48v), and *De iuventute et senectute* (ibid. fols. 148–59) as particularly relevant.

20. Kelly offers additional support for these claims:

> There are many literary instances of the colours blue and black used to describe bruises and/or the colour of death, and two examples will suffice. In the Harley lyric 'I Syke When Y Singe,' Christ's body is cold, and his 'ble [skin color] waxeth blo' (23–24). In Chaucer's *Knight's Tale*, the mortally injured Arcite is described thus: 'As blak he lay as any cole or crowe/So was the blood yronnen in his face' (2692–93). (41, 46)

21. Bibliothèque municipale de Valenciennes, Ms.99, 37r. Palmer notes that representations of devils do not appear in Christian art until the seventh or eighth centuries (22–4).

22. As Augustine explains, the first death comprises two parts: "It is the death of a soul when God abandons it, just as it is the death of a body when its soul abandons it. Hence the death of both combined, that is, of the whole human being, occurs when a soul abandoned by God abandons a body" (*Civitate Dei* 13.2, 137). The first death includes both the initial death of the soul, followed

by the death of the body. These constitute the one death of "the whole human being." Original sin constitutes a type of the first part of this death: "For when in the flesh of the unruly soul there arose an unruly movement, on account of which our first parents covered up their shameful members, one death was experienced, that in which the soul was forsaken by God" (13.15, 183). However, this initial death does not kill the human being:

> When, however, the soul itself forsook the body, now broken down with length of years and worn out by old age, man experienced another death. . . . Thus these two deaths made up that first death, which is that of the whole man; it is followed ultimately by the second death unless the man should be set free by grace. (13.15, 185)

The second death afflicts those infidels who are not freed by grace.

23. The Latin reads: "Ubi angelus Domini alligavit diabulum serpentem antiqum et cum illo pseudopropheta, qui fecit signa coram ipso, et misit eum in abyssum et clausit, et signavit super illum donec consummentur mille anni" (36r). Omont transcribes the lines and suggests that they paraphrase Rev 19:20, 20:1–3 (72, 81).

24. The Vulgate reads: "Et adprehensa est bestia, et cum illo pseudopropheta: qui fecit signa coram ipso. . . . Vivi missi sunt hii duo in stagnum ignis ardentis sulphure" (Rev 19:20).

25. The Latin text reads: "haec mors secunda est: hic est stagnus ignis et sulforis ubi est missus diabulus et infernus" (37r).

26. The Latin reads: "Miseria ad dolorem pertinet, tenebrae ad caecitatem. . . foris dolor cruciat quos diuisos a uero lumine intus caecitas obscurat" (qtd. in Bernstein, 57).

27. The Latin translation of the Greek reads:

> impii quique qui in hac vita errorum tenebras et noctem ignorantiae dilexerunt, obscuris et atris post resurrectionem coporibus induantur, ut ea ipsa caligo ignorantiae quae in hoc mundo interiores eorum mentes obsederat in futuro per exterius corporis appareat indumentum. (*Peri Archon* II.10.8 *Patrologiæ Græcæa* vol. 11)

Courtès refers to this passage from Origen in his discussion of the color of the damned (201).

28. For an analysis of Gregory's development of this concept in the monastic context, see Bernstein (33–98).

29. As Bernstein concludes:

> The pains of the damned, including darkness, chains, dismemberment, and torture, were very similar to those imposed on slaves. The rhetoric of religious devotion as slavery to God and sin as slavery to the devil perpetuated this arrangement. . . . the fact that slavery was familiar enough to serve as a metaphor assured hell a constant resonance with real-world experience. Slavery made hell plausible. (357)

30. For dates and probable influences among these psalters and the Munich Psalter, see Morgan (1982, 68–73, 75–6).

31. Art historians have been unable to determine definitively the relative chronology between these two psalters. I first examine the Royal Psalter, with its slightly more positive representations of Jews, since the general chronological trend in the period moves from a more neutral representation of Jews to a more hostile one (Blumenkranz, 96–104, Lipton, 2014).

32. The various narratives of Jesus before the Jewish and Roman authorities appear in Matthew 26–7, Mark 14–15, Luke 22–5 and John 18–19. In this psalter, someone has written "22 Luke" in the margin next to both the image of the betrayal and the image of the trial. Although this inscription was probably added after the illustration was made, the directive to Luke is apt.

33. Similarly shaped red locks of hair appear in the Royal Psalter's depiction of the Massacre of the Innocents (fol. 3r) and the Last Supper (fol. 5r) but none of the Jews has dark skin.

34. Red hair is a trait regularly used in disparaging depictions of Cain, Judas, and enemies of the faith in general (Mellinkoff 1993, I.147–59). Depiction in profile served as another negative signifier (1993, I.211–12). Mellinkoff discusses the significance and variety of "misshapen" features to denote evil figures, including Jews (1993, I.121–26). For other discussions of the significance of deformed features and portrayals of the Jews, see Strickland (2003, 61–78; 108–55), Bale (2010, 65–75), and Lipton (2014, 171–99).

35. See also Matthew's account: "Then did they spit in his face, and buffeted him: and others struck his face with the palms of their hands, / Saying: Prophesy unto us, O Christ, who is he that struck thee?" (Matt. 26: 67–8).

36. Although Pilate orders this torture, according to John (19:1), no official appears in this picture.

37. The text of Matthew reads: "Then Judas, who betrayed him, seeing that he was condemned, repenting himself, brought back the thirty pieces of silver to the chief priests and ancients, /Saying: I have sinned in betraying innocent blood. But they said: What is that to us? look thou to it. /And casting down the pieces of silver in the temple, he departed: and went and hanged himself with an halter" (27:3–5).

38. Of images of the betrayal I have viewed that include dark Jews, the majority depict Judas with white skin; see Mellinkoff vol. II image I.30 for one exception. Other reasons for Judas's whiteness might be that he distinguishes himself from his fellow Jews insofar as, in repenting his betrayal, he implicitly recognizes Jesus's status as Messiah. Furthermore, as Judas is one of the apostles it might be problematic to represent him as dark and damned. Mellinkoff also notes that he is sometimes depicted with a halo, including, paradoxically, the image in which he appears with dark skin (1993, 59, 135, 232).

39. Matthew's text reads:

> But the chief priests having taken the pieces of silver, said: It is not lawful to put
> them into the corbona, because it is the price of blood.
> And after they had consulted together, they bought with them the potter' s field,
> to be a burying place for strangers.
> For this cause the field was called Haceldama, that is, "The field of blood, even
> to this day." (Matt. 27:6–8)

"Corbona" is a Latin term derived from the Hebrew *qorban*, an offering presented at the Temple; it refers here to "The treasury of the temple at Jerusalem,
where such offerings, when made in money, were placed; also transf. Church-
treasury" ("corban, n." *Oxford English Dictionary*).

40. Class may also influence the decision to portray the priests and judges as white
and the mob as brown; see Freedman on depictions of peasants with dark skin
(139). In discussing images that represent Muslims with dark and light skin
color, Patton similarly refers to a "traditional association of light skin color with
higher rank" (116). Additionally, the gospels make distinctions in rank in variously allocating blame for the crucifixion sometimes to the elders, sometimes
to the crowd, which may account for the contrast in skin tones. See also Cohen's
discussion of the traditions in Christian exegesis that differ in according blame
for Jesus's death to the people or the elders (1983). Strickland also considers vari-
ation in skin color in visual representations of Jews as well as Muslims (2003, 111,
173–82). While I have moved away from its reading in this current project, see my
earlier consideration of Jews depicted with dark and light skin (Kaplan, 2013).

41. The visceral impact of this threat may register in the fact that these figures
are somewhat damaged by rubbing; psalter users often touched the figures
depicted, either to venerate or attack them, and their engagement still marks
this page. Similarly, in the corresponding image of the mocking in the Royal MS,
the tormentor on the left also shows damage that may be the result of rubbing.
Strickland likewise speculates about the rubbing of an image in another medieval English psalter (2003, 114).

42. Like the psalter, the book of hours included the Psalms and prayers, but the texts
were "arranged by their liturgical rather than biblical order" (van Liere, 30).

43. As Lisa Lampert argues, "the Jews' motivation for attacking Mary is tied directly
to the Incarnation and to the Crucifixion. The attack reaffirms the Jews' treachery
against Christ" (2004a, 133).

44. As Bale explains: "The *Transitus Mariae* of Pseudo-Melito of Sardis, the prototype
and template of all subsequent Latin and English versions of the story, describes
the death, funeral and assumption of the Virgin; similar accounts. . . held that a
Jew or group of Jews attacked the bier, and that Mary's death was accompanied by
miracles" (2010, 93). For discussions of various medieval representations of this
narrative, see Bale (2010, 90–117) and Lampert (2004a, 134, 225 n. 110). See also
Rubin's extensive exploration of medieval ideas of Mary in relation to the Jews.

45. Even the "white" figures depicted in this manuscript, such as the nimbed saints who attend on Mary's body in the illumination of her death, funeral and burial (fol 61r), have pale brown skin.

46. The trope of Jewish blindness as figuring their misbelief is common in Christian exegesis; see Lampert (2004b, 28, 43–6, 121–22, and 147; Lipton 2014).

47. This image recalls Ambrose's commentary on the *Song of Songs* in which the Jews' "blackness, like that of the Ethiopians, is due to the Sun, but this time to the lack of it in the darkness of abandonment: 'I am black because of the Sun of Justice which shone upon me in the past, has abandoned me; my face has lost its color; the keenness of my eyes is dulled . . . I wander in the darkness'" (qtd. in Courtès, 204).

48. Contemporary canon lawyers confirm this claim; Johannes Teutonicus's commentary on Lateran Canon 68 explains that a Jew is distinguished from Christian by clothing: "Just as a free person is distinguished from a slave by a hat, . . . and a prostitute from a wife by clothing, and a man from a woman by hair and clothing" (Garcia y Garcia, 267–68). As Vincent argues regarding the derogatory force of this canon:

> The parallels drawn here between Jews, slaves and prostitutes suggest from the outset it was realized that Jews were to be disparaged as a result of the statute of 1215. Like prostitutes, Jews were coming increasingly to be seen . . .as a distinct social group, of lower social and legal status than Christians. (214)

The English history of badge enforcement—in its numerous ecclesiastical and royal enactments, the application to both Jewish women and men, the extension of the requirement to children, and the increasing size of the badge—reveals a persistent concern to make visible and to disparage the Jewish community. For some recent discussions of the badge, see Heng (2011a & b), Vincent, and Tolan (2015a).

49. Camille powerfully argues for a similar process in the visual representations of Jews in the period:

> The stigma the Jews had to bear in thirteenth-century Christian societies was often a visual sign and can be seen as part of the new emphasis on visual organization and order of society. The most extreme form that visual control of the Other took in this period was making the Jews themselves into images, into spectacles of alterity. (180)

For other important recent monographs that explore the cultural work hostile images of Jews perform in medieval culture, see Bale (2006 and 2010) and Rowe (2011 and 2008).

50. This trend registers in "high Gothic artworks[, which] reproduced the proportions and anatomical details of the human face and body. . . with new accuracy and care" (2014, 173–74). She cites a mid-thirteenth-century treatise on the Virgin Mary that claims Jews have dark hair, based apparently on contemporary empirical evidence (175).

51. Vincent makes a similar point, drawing on the earlier work of Lipton (1999) and Mellinkoff:

> At much the same time, Christian artists were refining the iconography by which Jews and heretics were to be represented, and often confused with one another in pictorial terms. Like the papacy, artists sought to devise a distinctive outward symbol for Jews. As with the papal legislation, iconography at first sought merely to distinguish Jews from Christians. Distinction, however, led rapidly to segregation and to the attachment of shame and ridicule to the outward symbols of Jewish identity (213).

52. She concludes: "If so, then its purpose would be to engender revulsion toward vices endemic among Christians as well as Jews, by giving sin an imaginary and constructed but nonetheless convincing 'Jewish' face" (2014, 175–76). Lipton is at pains to prove that hostile visual representations of Jews, such as the representation of Isaac of Norwich in a 1233 English exchequer tax receipt, regularly implicate Christians as well, and thus do not advance a racial view of Jews:

> In spite of its caricatures of Jewish faces, then, this cartoon does *not* forward an argument about an essentialist, somatically grounded, or outwardly visible Jewish perfidy or difference. Instead, the sketch acknowledges that Christians and Jews are considerably less different from one another than the Jews' exaggerated profiles initially seemed to suggest and that appearance is a guide to very little. (182)

However, in reifying evil as "Jewish," even if Christians can participate in the behavior, these images nevertheless identify Jews and Judaism as a source of sin to be eschewed. Lipton does not consider the images, absent Christian assailants, of dark, menacing Jewish attackers of Jesus in thirteenth-century English psalters that I analyze here.

53. The Paris quodlibit describes their appearance in relation to their predominant humor: "Jews. . . are pallid, therefore they are of melancholic complexion" (qtd. in Biller 1992, 192–93). Hugh of St. Cher's account implies that paleness results from the blood loss the Jews suffer in their cursed illness: "they suffer a flux of blood. And that is why they are so pale (pallidi)" (qtd. in Johnson, 281). Similarly, in Thomas of Monmouth's account of anal bleeding, the loss of blood over a two-year period ""diminished [Sheriff Chesney's] strength of body and induced pallor in his face (uirtutem corporis . . . imminuit, uultui pallorem induxit)" (ed. Jessop 111, my translation). An extended period of bleeding here results in pallid complexion. Cuffel discusses representations of Jews with a dark complexion in a variety of contexts including illness (162–64). See also Resnick's analysis of a dark-skinned Jews in a "scientific" context (2012, 249, 268–319).

54. The person in question was the brother of Anaclet, a twelfth-century candidate for the papacy who was challenged in part on the basis of his persisting Jewishness. For a recent analysis, see Resnick (2013b). We might also consider

the tantalizingly vague suggestion of a distinctive Jewish appearance in the name of a Norwich Jew, Hak le Blo, Yitzchak/Isaac the Blue/Black (Roth, 24–25). While the color could refer to some other defining quality of Hak, we can surmise, as Roth does, that it may indicate something about the perceived shade of his skin (25). See also Richardson's mention of Moses, son of "Le Brun" (179, 287). Although he does not comment on their appearance, Chaucer associates the Jews with the dark/light substance of lead through their connection to Saturn. The *House of Fame* describes the "The Ebrayk Josephus," "of secte saturnyn," standing on a pillar of "led, withouten faille/ . . . the metal of Saturne" (295–96, ll.1432–33, 1448–49). Josephus, and by extension the whole Jewish people who are the subject of his chronicles, belong to the sect of Saturn, who is also associated with lead. I am grateful to Steven Kruger for bringing this quotation to my attention. Arabic texts on astrology (ca. ninth- and tenth-century) connect Saturn with melancholy and the Jews (Biller 2001, 140–41, 154–56; see also Klibansky et al., 127–28, 130–31 who omit this connection). These works are translated into Latin in the early to mid-twelfth century; Hermann of Carinthia made use of them in his 1143 *De Essentiis*: "Belonging to Saturn are melancholy, fraud, wickedness, envy, perfidy and obdurateness, which old writings argue are in the Jews and the experience of today proves" (qtd. in Biller 2001, 156, 141).

55. The life-saving significance of Jesus's death is emphasized in representations of the cross in Christian liturgy and visual images. Kauffmann notes that

> In most thirteenth-century Crucifixions the cross is shown as a tree, either lopped or flowering. This is the *lignum vitae*, the living cross identified with the tree of life which had its origin at the Creation (Genesis 2:9; 3:24). The identification of this tree with the cross had its source in Early Christian Commentary and particularly in the liturgy. The antiphon *In exaltatio s. crucis* [In exaltation of the holy cross] identifies the cross with the tree of life in the words *lignum vitae crux tuae domine* [Lord, your cross is the tree of life]. (2003, 179–80)

56. As discussed in chapter 1, in a 1205 letter to the King of France complaining about numerous instances of impious Jewish exercise of authority over Christians, Innocent articulates—and challenges—the assumption that methods of execution correlate to status:

> What is even worse, blaspheming against God's name, they publicly insult Christians by saying that they (Christians) believe in a peasant (*rusticum*) who had been hung by the Jewish people. Indeed, we do not doubt that He was hung for us, since He carried our sins in his body on the cross, but we do not admit that He was a peasant either in manners or in race. Forsooth, they themselves cannot deny that physically He was descended from priestly and royal stock, and that His manners were distinguished and proper. (Grayzel 1966, 107–9)

He appears to respond to contemporary Jewish polemics against Jesus, some of which mention the shameful manner of his death (Cuffel, 132–33, 142).

57. Paul succinctly explains the consequences as well as the absolution of this transgression: "For the wages of sin is death. But the grace of God, life everlasting in Christ Jesus our Lord" (Rom 6:23). John makes clear the saving effect of faith: "Jesus said . . . : I am the resurrection and the life: he that believeth in me, although he be dead, shall live: And every one that liveth and believeth in me shall not die for ever" (11:25–6).

58. Original sin resulted not only in death, but, as explained in chapter 1, perpetual servitude.

CHAPTER 4

1. Some important contributions to this discussion include Aaron; Blackburn; Braude; David Brion Davis (1984); Stacy Davis; Evans; Fredrickson; Freedman; John Block Friedman; Goldenberg (2003); Hannaford; Haynes; Sylvester Johnson; Winthrop Jordan; Lewis; Schorsch (2004); Washington; and Whitford. The scope of my argument does not permit me to address in detail these numerous and wide-ranging discussions of Ham.

2. I rely on Fredriksen's dating of Augustine's works (2010, 383–84). A number of patristic exegetes, including Origen (mid-third century), Basil (late fourth century), and Ambrose (late fourth century) anticipate and possibly influence Augustine's formulation. See Garnsey's discussion of their opinions as well as of the innovation of Augustine's formulation (44–5, 195, 204–5, 206–19). Interestingly, Origen's *Homily on Genesis* describes Ham's enslaved offspring, the Egyptians, as dark-skinned: "Not without merit, therefore, does the discoloured posterity imitate the ignobility of the race" (qtd. in Garnsey, 44). See the discussion of the Latin *decolor* as "dark" and of Origen's elaboration, with recourse to Pharoah, of darkness as a sign of sin in Verkerk (59, 66–7, 69–70).

3. In his *Literal Meaning of Genesis* Augustine does describe Eve's subordination to Adam delineated in Genesis 3:16 as a servitude resulting from her sin (XI.37). However, neither the original Hebrew, Septuagint, nor the Latin Bible text uses the term "slavery" to describe this status.

4. Garnsey explains that Augustine also develops the association of original sin with slavery (215–29).

5. Many English translations render *servus* as "servant" rather than "slave." For example, the Geneva Bible renders the terms *eved avadim* or *servus servorum* as "servant of servants." However, the note on this phrase states: "That is, a most vile slave" (Genesis 9:25, The Bible). As in chapter 1, in my translations from the Latin I will render *servus* as "slave"; in other translations from Latin to English that use "servant," I will replace the term with "slave" and put it in brackets to indicate the alteration.

6. On the level of prophecy, the Hebrew text makes sense, as it predicts the future subordination of the Canaanites by the descendants of Shem, Israel. Augustine suggests this reading:

How is it that Ham, sinning in offending his father, is not cursed in himself but in his son Chanaan; unless because this in a certain way prophesies the land of Chanaan, from whence the Chanaanites will be taken, expelled and vanquished by the children of Israel, who come in the name of Sem? [*Quare peccans Cham in patris offensa, non in seipso, sed in filio suo Chanaan maledicitur; nisi quia prophetatum est quodammodo terram Chanaan, ejectis inde Chananaeis et debellatis, accepturos fuisse filios Israel, qui venirent de semine Sem?*] (*Quaestiones in Heptateuchum.* Book 1 *Quaestiones in Genesim*, XVII. [Gen 9:25] *Patrologia Latina* vol. 34) col. 551, my translation)

However, as an etiology of slavery, the cursing of Canaan for Ham's transgression raises a number of problems, which have been addressed over the centuries by many exegetes and scholars.

7. Garnsey seems to suggest that Augustine's general formulation of slavery to sin was a

handy [weapon] in his polemic against Jews. . . . Jews in Augustine as in Paul are slaves to the Law through fear. Then, the supersession of the Jews by the Christians is a regularly recurring motif in Augustine. Apart from the use of the Esau/Jacob story as a paradigm for this, Augustine has an extravagant image of the Jews as slaves employed as custodians and carriers of books (the Old Testament) which are for their Christian masters to read, comprehend and profit from. (220).

However, given the consistent iteration of Jews as slaves to sin that predates the account of slavery's origin and runs through Augustine's corpus, it seems more likely that the general theory of slavery presented in *Civitate Dei* derives from the template firmly established with regard to Jewish servitude.

8. Jerome's *Dialogue Against the Luciferians* establishes Noah's drunkenness as a figure for the passion of Jesus and might have influenced Augustine's choice:

When Noah left the ark he planted a vineyard, drank thereof, and was drunken. Christ also, born in the flesh, planted the Church and suffered. The elder son made sport of his father's nakedness, the younger covered it: and the Jews mocked God crucified, the Gentiles honoured Him. (22, 331)

Jerome, as translator of the Bible, certainly knew how the text specified the number and order of Noah's three sons: "Shem, Ham and Japhet" (Gen. 6:10; 7:13; 9:18; 10:1). Yet here he reduces Noah's sons to two. Although he doesn't name him, Jerome implicitly identifies the oldest son as Ham, the one who viewed his father's nakedness. Ham figures the Jews, while the younger son who covered Noah, a conflation of Shem and Japhet, represents the Gentiles. The alteration of birth order and reduction of the sons from three to two creates an elder/younger dichotomy of Jews and Gentiles characterized by Paul's discussion of Esau's replacement by Jacob; Jerome applies a supersessionary logic in his reading of this episode. Although not explicitly named, Ham becomes a type for the Jews who mocked Jesus during the crucifixion.

9. Augustine also considers Genesis 9 episode in *Civitate Dei*, absent a discussion of servitude. This reading again represents Shem and Japhet as the Jewish and Gentile followers of Jesus, but offers another account of Ham's significance:

> Ham, whose name means 'Hot', . . . what does he signify but the hot breed of heretics? For heretical hearts are wont to be fired not by the spirit of wisdom, but by that of impatience, and thus to disturb the peace of the saints. (16.2, 7)

While reading Ham as a figure for heretics, he also interprets the larger story as adumbrating the Jews, guilt for Jesus's death. Yet here Augustine suppresses a direct identification of Ham and the Jews, explaining that Shem and Japhet had "learned, no matter how, of their father's nakedness, which symbolized the Saviour's passion," omitting the text's description of Ham as the one who tells his brothers of Noah's nakedness (16.2, 9). Augustine, as always, a careful reader of the text, notes that the expression " 'in his house,' [is] a neat turn of phrase to indicate that Christ was to endure death on the cross at the hands of people of his own flesh, those of his own household and bloody [sic] namely the Jews" (16.2 11). Even while maintaining their guilt, Augustine here de-emphasizes the association of Jews with Ham and omits discussion of the curse of slavery visited upon Canaan. Fredriksen notes that in *Civitate Dei* he similarly drops the association of Jews with Cain, reformulating him as the founder of the earthly city and a model for of Christian identity (2010, 346–47). In both cases, Augustine wanted to use figures of Ham and Cain to explain another aspect of Christian history. However, *Civitate Dei* does not discard the concept of Jewish servitude, but relies on Paul's figures of Esau (Book 16 chapter 35, 37) and Hagar (Book 15 chapter 2), as I discuss in chapter 1.

10. The Latin translation of the original Greek reads:

> Nunc paululum allegoriae immoremur. Agricola Nocahus plantavit et instruxit vincam pulcherrimam, nempe populum suum in Christo. Primus ex vino bibit Noachus: sic Christus, cujus ille typus erat, passus est. Inebriatus est Noachus: sic Christus passion consummatus est. Noachus nudatus est in domo sua: sic Christus crucifixus est a Judaeis. Chamus typus est populi Judaiei, qui illusit Christo e cruce pendenti: . . . Verum Judaeos perpetuae adjudicavit Christus servituti, dicens: "Omnis, qui facit peccatum, servus est peccati. At servus non manet in domo ia aeternum. Si igitur Filius vos in liberate asseruit ex servitude, liberi estis." [John 8:34–6] . . . "Et fiat Chanaan servus eius," etc. Ecquid cernis Noachum fatidico ore illa insonuisse. Etenim Madian, id est, Medus, quem genuit Japhet, pulcherrima tabernacula et aedificia occupavit Sem, scilicet Median, quae non minima Persidis pars est. Potest hoc loco praedici imperium Romanum, quod invasit tabernacula Sem et Chanaan. Itaque Noachi oracula, quae in modum benedictionis profatur, abiere in maledictionem. Siquidem

Persis et Romanis servierunt Judaei: et adhuc Chanaan servituti subjectus est. (*Patrologiæ Græcæ* vol. 87a, IX col. 306–7)

11. "Exile, Babylonian" (Porten, 609).

12. The Latin reads:

Jam vero illud quod post diluvium de vinea quam plantavit, inebriatus est Noe, et nudatus in domo sua, cui non appareat Christi esse figuram? qui inebriatus est, dum passus est; nudatus est, dum crucifixus est; in domo sua, id est, in gente sua, et in domesticis sui, utique Judaeis. (*Mysticorum, Patrologia Latina* vol. 83 8 col. 235A–B))

13. The Latin reads:

Quam nuditatem, id est, passionem Christi, videns Cham derisit, et Judaei Christi mortem videntes subsannaverunt. . . .Medius autem frater Cham, id est, populus impius Judaeorum (ideo medius, quia nec primatum apostolorum tenuit, nec ultimus in gentibus credidit) vidit nuditatem patris, quia consensit in necem Domini Salvatoris. Post haec nuntiavit foras fratribus. Per eum quippe manifestatum est, et quodammodo publicatum, quod erat in prophetia secretum. Ideoque fit servus fratrum suorum.

Quid est enim hodie aliud gens ipsa, nisi quaedam scriniaria Christianorum, bajulans legem et prophetas ad testimonium assertionis Ecclesiae, ut nos honoremus per sacramentum, quod nuntiat illa per litteram? (*Mysticorum, Patrologia Latina* vol. 83 8 col. 235C–236A)

14. Isidore also draws from both the *Contra Faustum* and the *Civitate Dei* to harmonize the two types represented by Ham—Jews and heretics—that Augustine mentions; here the text acknowledges explicitly that Ham represents both groups.

And Ham, whose name means hot, the middle son, separated, as it were, from both sides, remaining neither among the nobles of Israel, nor among the fullness of the gentiles, signifies not only the tribe of the Jews but that of the heretics, hot, not with the spirit of wisdom, but of impatience, with which the hearts of heretic are accustomed to burn, and to disturb the peace of the saints.

[Cham porro, qui interpretatur calidus, medius filius, tanquam ab utroque discretus, nec in primitiis Israelitarum, nec in plenitudine gentium permanens, significat non solum Judaeorum, sed etiam haereticorum genus calidum, non spiritu sapientiae, sed impatientiae, quo solent haereticorum fervere praecordia, et pacem perturbare sanctorum.] (*Mysticorum, Patrologia Latina* vol.83 8 col. 236C, my translation)

15. The Latin text reads:

Item quod, Cham peccante, posteritas ejus damnatur, significat quod reprobi hic quidem delinquunt, sed in posterum, id est, in futurum, sententiam damnationis excipiunt. Sicut et plebs Judaea, quae Dominum crucifixit, etiam in filiis poenam damnationis suae transmisit. Dixerunt enim: Sanguis ejus super nos et super filios nostros (Matth. XXVII, 25). (*Patrologia Latina*, vol. 83 8 col. 237A)

16. Isidore repeats this association of Jews with Ham and their damned descendants with Canaan in his *Allegoriae Quaedam Sacrae Scripturae* in the section *Ex Veteri Testamento*

> Ham signifies the Jews, who make fun of Christ incarnated and dead. Canaan, his son, who, for his father's sin, was damned with a curse (Gen. 9), indicates the posterity of the Jews, who in the Passion of the Lord received the sentence of condemnation, when the Jews cried out: His blood be upon us and upon our children. [Cham Judaeos significat, qui Christum incarnatum atque mortuum derident. Chanaam, filius ejus, qui pro patris delicto maledictione damnatur (Genes. IX), posteritatem indicat Judaeorum, qui in passione Domini damnationis sententiam, clamantibus Judaeis: Sanguis ejus super nos, et super filios nostros.] (*Patrologia Latina* vol. 83 col. 103A, my translation).

While he does not emphasize the idea of servitude here, he links Ham exclusively with the Jews and brings in Matthew 27 again as a proof-text for the hereditary nature of their curse.

17. As Sabrina Longland writes, "Isidore's writings were very influential and widely read by other medieval authors; every monastic library would have wanted to own copies of his works." Citing N. R. Ker's *Medieval Libraries of Great Britain*, she notes that "lists of surviving books known to have come from English medieval libraries mention an *Isidorus* again and again" (53).

18. The Latin text reads:

> Per filium minorem populus Judaeorum designatur. "Maledictus Cham" [for Chanaan]: vindictam super Judaeos praefigurare videtur. Dicitur autem Cham [for Chanaan] quod esset servus Sem et Japheth; per quod intelligitur malam partem Judaeorum curvandam esse ad bonam partem Judaeorum et populi gentium. Etenim Cham populum Judaeorum, et Sem bonam partem populi Judaeorum, et Japheth populum gentium. (*Expositio In Primum Librum Mosis, Patrologia Latina* vol. 91 9 col. 228A)

19. The Latin text reads:

> Benedictus Dominus Deus Sem; sit Cham [for Canaan] servus illius." Quid enim aliud est populus Judaeorum, nisi quidam servus populi Christiani, bajulans legem et prophetas, ut nos honoremus per sacramentum quod illi nuntiant per litteram? (*Patrologia Latina* vol. 91 9 col. 228C)

20. The Latin reads: "Peccante autem Cham, posteritas illius damnatur, quia reprobi hic quidem delinquunt, sed in futuro damnationem excipiunt. Sed et Judaei in posteros damnationem transmiserunt, dicentes: 'Sanguis ejus super nos, et super filios nostros.'" (*Patrologia Latina* vol. 91 9 col. 228D)

21. Longland notes this influence:

The great theologian and abbot of Fulda, Rabanus Maurus (766 or 784–856), repeats entire passages on the subject from Isidore's *Quaestiones* in his *Commentaria in Genesim*, and particularly in the *De universo*, where he includes the sentence quoted above [Cham laughed {*derisit*} on seeing the nakedness, which is the passion of Christ, and the Jews mocked {subsannaverunt} on seeing the death of Christ.] (53).

22. As Rabanus iterates:

> After this he announced to his two brothers outside: Through them it is obviously clear what was in the secret prophecy: and for that reason he was made a slave to the brothers.
>
> For what else indeed is this same nation today, but a bookslave for the Christians, bearing the law and prophets and testifying to the manumission of the Church, so that we can honor in the sacrament what they disclose in the letter? [Post haec nuntiavit foras fratribus. Per eum quippe manifestum est, quod erat in prophetia secretum; ideoque fit servus fratrum suorum. Quid est enim aliud hodie gens ipsa, nisi quaedam scriniaria Christianorum, bajulans legem et prophetas, ad testimonium assertionis Ecclesiae, ut nos honoremus per sacramentum quod nuntiant illi per litteram? (*Commentariorum in Genesim, Patrologia Latina* vol. 107 9 col. 525D, my translation following the English translation of Augustine)

23. Again, closely following Isidore:

> Also with respect to which, Ham sinning, his offspring were damned, it signifies insofar as the reprobates here offend, but in the posterity, that is, in the future, they receive the sentence of condemnation. And though [it is] the mob of Jews who crucified the Lord, even now they transmit the penalty of their damnation to their children. For they said: His blood be upon us and upon our children (Mt 27, 25). [Item quod Cham peccante posteritas ejus damnatur, significat quod reprobi hic delinquunt, sed in posterum, id est, in futurum, sententiam damnationis excipiunt. Sed et plebs Judaea quae Dominum crucifixit, etiam in filiis poenam damnationis suae transmisit. Dixerunt enim: Sanguis ejus super nos et super filios nostros (Matth. XXVII).] (*Commentariorum in Genesim, Patrologia Latina* vol. 107 9 col. 526B, my translation)

24. Longland explains that the *Allegoriae in Vetus Testamentum* was printed as a doubtful work in the Appendix in Migne under the name of Hugh of St. Victor, Richard's teacher, but has since been verified as Richard's work (54).

25. The Latin text reads:

> Quem infelix Cham, id est incredulus Judaeorum populus derisit,. . . . Unde et Chanaan filius Cham maledictione punitur, quia Judaeorum progenies Judaeorum maledictione damnatur. . . .Et Chanaan filius Cham fit servus servorum, quia infideles successores Judaeorum servi sunt Christianorum, quia

Christiani servi sunt Christi, cui servire regnare est. . . . maledictio Chanaam filii Cham damnatio est et dispersio Judaicae gentis. (*Allegoriae in Vetus Testamentum, Patrologia Latina* vol. 175 col. 643C–644B)

26. The marginal commentary loosely quotes Isidore's *Mysticorum expositiones sacramentorum seu quaestiones in vetus testamentum*, which in turn quotes Augustine. The comments on Ham as a figure for the Jews respond to Genesis 9:22:

> Is[idore] *Quod cum [Cham] vidisset etc.* Iudei Christi mortem videntes subsannauerunt. . . . *Cham vidit* quia in necem domini consensit. . . . *Ideo fit seruus seruorum fratrum suorum*: Quia gens illa christianorum scriniaria baiulat legem et prophetas in testimonium ecclesiae: ut honoremus per sacramentum quod illa nunciat per litteram. [Isidore. "Which when Ham had seen etc." The Jews mocked, seeing the death of Christ. . . . "Ham saw" because assented in the murder of the Lord. . . . "Therefore he was made a slave of slaves to his brothers": Because that people, the bookslave of Christians, carries the law and prophets in witness of the Church: so that we honor in the sacrament what that [people] announces in the letter.] (*Genesis et Exodus cum glossa ordinaria*, BSB Clm 14132, fol 40r image 83, my translation; contractions silently expanded)

This text derives from a digitized image of a thirteenth-century French manuscript of the *Glossa*; I also consulted the Raush incunabula (1480–81) and a digitized version of the 1603 Venetian edition. The texts from all three are nearly identical.

27. The Latin text reads:

> Cham [Quia neci Christi consensit. Medius frater, id est, populus Iudaeorum, qui nec primatum Apostolorum tenuit, nec ultimus in gentibus credidit. Israel secumdem carnem.] (40r image 83, contractions silently expanded)

28. Paul's distinction makes the contrast between flesh and spirit in Romans 8:4–6. Augustine distinguishes between carnal and spiritual Israel, Jews and Christians, in *De Doctrina Christiana*, Book 3, chapter 34, sections 48–9.

29. The Latin text reads:

> Noe . . .ait: Maledictus Chanaan [Plebs Iudaica, quae dum {Christum} crucifixit penam in filios transmisit dicens: Sanguis eius super nos & super filios nostros, {Matt. 27:25}] puer, seruus seruorum erit fratribus suis. Dixitque: Benedictus Dominus Deus Sem, [Ex quo Iudaei] sit Chanaan seruus eius. Dilatet Deus Iapheth [Ex quo gentes] et habitet [Conuenientibus in ecclesia Iudeis & gentibus.] in tabernaculis Sem. [Ecclesiis quas construxerunt apostoli Prophetarum filii.] Sit Chanaan [Israel secundum carnem] servus eius. [Scriniarius diuinorum librorum.] (40v image 84, contractions silently expanded)

30. Thirteen manuscripts of this text have been identified by James, all English in origin, ranging in date from the beginning of the thirteenth century to the

fourteenth century; eleven were produced in the thirteenth century (144). James opines that in late twelfth-century England "the pursuit and collection of types for artistic purposes was actively prosecuted" (146).

31. James does not identify all the sources this manuscript might have drawn from, though he notes that the text makes mention of Augustine and Jerome, among others. He states that "There lay ready to [the author's] hand a digest of the principal comments on the whole Bible in the shape of the *Glossa Ordinaria*. All monastic libraries of any consideration contained it." (147)

32. Parker and Little mention the *Pictor in Carmine* in their discussion of the section of the Cloisters Cross that links Ham to the Jews at the time of the crucifixion (56).

33. The other verse, also written on the long side of the crucifix, reads:

    TERRA TREMIT MORS VICTA GEMIT SVRGENTE SEPVLTO
    VITA CLVIT SYNAGOGA RVIT MOLIMINE STVLT[O]
    (The earth trembles, Death defeated groans with the buried one rising.
    Life has been called, Synagogue has collapsed with great foolish effort). (Parker
    and Little, 52)

34. Longland states that Bury St. Edmunds cross is the only surviving work of art on which this couplet appears (45).

35. The earliest surviving manuscript, dated 1324, was probably produced "in Southwestern Germany or Northern Italy; the compiler is anonymous, but may have been a Dominican." Scott puts the number of surviving manuscripts and block-book copies at over 380 (178).

36. As noted in chapter 3, medieval English psalters also represent the mocking before a "Jewish" judge—either Caiaphas, Herod, or Pilate.

37. The Vulgate reads: tunc expuerunt in faciem eius et colaphis eum ceciderunt alii autem palmas in faciem ei dederunt / dicentes prophetiza nobis Christe quis est qui te percussit." The account in Mark describes a similar scene: "And some began to spit on him, and to cover his face, and to buffet him, and to say unto him: Prophesy: and the servants struck him with the palms their hands. [et coeperunt quidam conspuere eum et velare faciem eius et colaphis eum caedere et dicere ei prophetiza et ministri alapis eum caedebant]" (14:65). Luke 22 also describes the mocking and veiling Jesus: "And the men that held him, mocked him, and struck him. / And they blindfolded him, and smote his face. And they asked him, saying: Prophesy, who is it that struck thee? [et viri qui tenebant illum inludebant ei caedentes / et velaverunt eum et percutiebant faciem eius et interrogabant eum dicentes prophetiza quis est qui te percussit]" (22:63–4).

38. As Morrow explains, figures depicted with crossed hands reference the crucifixion (82).

39. While the scene draws on biblical persons, this event does not actually occur in the text of the Bible. Originally formulated in rabbinic bible commentary, the story appears in Peter Comestor's late twelfth-century *Historia Scholastica* in

the section on Exodus 32, which tells the story of the creation of the golden calf (Sarna and Sperling, "Hur"). When Aaron and Hur refused to participate, "the angry people, spitting gobs in Hur's face, as it is related, smothered him. [Aaron vero, et Hur restiterunt. Sed indignatus populus, spuens in faciem Hur, sputis, ut traditur, eum suffocavit]" (*Historia Libri Exodi, Patrologia Latina* vol. 198 73 col. 1189D, my translation).

40. Not all of the texts of the *Speculum* included pictures. An unillustrated fifteenth-century English translation, *The mirour of mans saluacioun*, following the pattern established in the earliest Latin versions, identifies Ham as a figure for the Jews as mockers of Jesus (Henry, 117, ll 2169–84). The text distinguishes Noah's humiliation by Ham from that of Jews derision of Jesus, who was "bejaped more vileynsly" in front of hostile spectators at the house of the high priest, Caiaphas. One sixteenth-century continuation of the *Speculum* tradition can be found in Ulrich Pinder's *Speculum passionis Domini Nostri [The Mirror of the Passion of Our Lord]* (1507). It offers a more faithful account of New Testament's portrayal of the Passion in which both Jews and Roman soldiers attack Jesus. In the section describing how the Roman soldiers, carrying out Pilate's orders, mock, beat, and spit upon Jesus, Pinder includes biblical figures for this event: "The soldier's mocking is figured in Genesis 9 when Noah is sleeping in his tent, because Noah signifies Christ whom the Jews derided" (Pinder II.35 fol 44v, my translation). He also cites the mocking of the prophet Elisha by the children (2 Kings 2:23–4), as well as verses from Psalms and Isaiah. *The myrrour or glasse of Christes passion* (1534), John Fewterer's English translation of Pinder's text, emphasizes the Jews' role in the soldiers' actions.

> Also these saugiours [soldiers] dyd these thynges to Christe . . . and though the gentyles dyd thus mocke Christe: yet it is imputed to the Iues for they were the autours and the cause of this illusion [mocking]. . . . This . . . mockynge of Christe was figured in Noe when he slepte in his tabernacle: his sonne Cham dyd laughe hym to scorne. Noe dothe signyfye Christe whome the Iues his owne chyldren dyd mocke and scorne. (Pinder and Fewterer article 35 fol 97v)

While acknowledging the Roman role in Jesus's death, the text focuses on the Jews' culpability as the "autours and cause of this illusion." As proof, the figure of Ham mocking Noah appears here; while Pinder omits mention of Ham and emphasizes the identification of Noah with Jesus, Fewterer brings Ham's mocking of Noah into the text to establish its anticipation of the anti-type in which the Jews mock Jesus. While typological interpretation lost its dominance with the advent of the Protestant Reformation, resulting in the decreased production of the intensely figural *Speculum*, its influence did not entirely disappear (Wilson and Wilson, 11, 215). As I will discuss in the section on early modern considerations of Ham, the connection that Pinder establishes among the Jews' mocking of Jesus, Ham's mocking of Noah and the boys' mocking of Elisha reappears in the work of Richard Day.

41. The text of Genesis delineates the family of Ham:

> And the sons of Cham: Chus, and Mesram, and Phuth, and Chanaan. And the
> sons of Chus: Saba, and Hevila, and Sabatha, and Regma, and Sabatacha. The
> sons of Regma: Saba and Dadan. Now Chus begot Nemrod: he began to be
> mighty on the earth. And he was a stout hunter before the Lord. Hence came
> a proverb: Even as Nemrod the stout hunter before the Lord. And the begin-
> ning of his kingdom was Babylon, and Arach, and Achad, and Chalanne in the
> land of Sennaar. Out of that land came forth Assur, and built Ninive, and the
> streets of the city, and Chale. Resen also between Ninive and Chale: this is the
> great city. And Mesraim begot Ludim, and Anamim, and Laabim, Nepthuim,
> And Phetrusim, and Chasluim; of whom came forth the Philistines, and the
> Capthorim. And Chanaan begot Sidon, his firstborn, the Hethite, And the
> Jebusite, and the Amorrhite, and the Gergesite, The Hevite and the Aracite: the
> Sinite, And the Aradian, the Samarite, and the Hamathite: and afterwards the
> families of the Chanaanites were spread abroad. And the limits of Chanaan
> were from Sidon as one comes to Gerara even to Gaza, until thou enter Sodom
> and Gomorrha, and Adama, and Seboim even to Lesa. These are the children of
> Cham in their kindreds, and tongues, and generations, and lands, and nations.
> (10: 6–20)

42. Braude queries a stable association of Ham with Africa prior to the early modern
    period, arguing that the Bible itself and commentators from Josephus onward
    do not consistently associate Ham with Africa. Furthermore, he states that no
    consensus regarding the location and boundaries of Africa existed prior to the
    fifteenth-century European exploration of sub-Saharan Africa (1997, 103–15
    passim). Granted, the biblical text names offspring of Ham who settle in modern
    day Iraq, Israel and Palestine. However, Genesis locates other of Ham's descen-
    dants in northern and southern Africa—Mitzraim/Egypt and Cush/Ethiopia, for
    example—thus establishing his identification with this continent.

43. The Latin text reads: "Quomodo divisus est orbis a filiis et nepotibus Noe? Sem,
    ut aestimatur, Asiam, Cham, Africam, Japhet Europam sortitus est" (Alcuin, 95).

44. The Latin text reads:

> CHAM, calidus, et ipse ex praesagio futuri cognominatus est. Posteritas enim
> ejus eam terrae partem possedit, quae vicino sole calentior est. Unde et Aegyptus
> usque hodie Aegyptiorum lingua Cham dicitur. . . Chanaan, filius Cham, inter-
> pretatur motus eorum. Quod quid est aliud, nisi opus eorum? Pro motu enim
> patris, id est, pro opere ejus, maledictus est. (*Patrologia Latina* vol. 82 7.6, col.
> 276A–B)

45. His offers a more gentle, though still supersessionst, treatment of the Jews in
    this same context: "Heber (i.e. Eber) means "passage." His etymology is mys-
    tical, because God passed away from his stock, nor would God remain among
    them when his grace was transferred to the gentiles—for from Heber rose the
    Hebrews" (163).

46. The Latin text reads:

> Filii Cham quatuor, a quibus ortae sunt gentes hae. Chus, a quo Aethiopes pro-
> geniti. Mesraim, a quo Aegyptii perhibentur exorti. Phut, a quo Lybii; unde et
> Mauritaniae fluvius usque in praesens dicitur Phut, omnisque circa eum regio
> Phuthensis. Chanaam, a quo Afri, et Phoenices, et Chananaeorum decem
> gentes. . . . Filii Chanaam undecim, ex quo Chananaeorum decem gentes,
> quorum terram, iis expulsis, Judaei possederunt. . . .Hae sunt gentes de stirpe
> Cham, quae a Sidone usque ad Gaditanum fretum omnem meridianam partem
> tenent. (*Patrologia Latina* vol. 82, 9.2, col. 329A–330B)

47. In the medieval period, the term Africa usually designated the northern portion
    of the continent: "Affrik(e (n.) (North) Africa, or the Roman province of Africa"
    (*Medieval English Dictionary*).

48. The Latin text reads:

> Filii autem filiorum Noe qui commemorantur creduntur singuli singularum
> gentium progenitores exstitisse, qui ita inter se orbem diviserunt, ut Sem
> primogenitus Asiam obtineret, et Cham secundus Africam, Japheth ultimus
> Europam; ita duntaxat ut, quia major/large est multo Asia terrarum situ quam
> Europa vel Lybia, progenies Cham et Japheth etiam nonnullam in Asia portio-
> nem teneret (*Patrologia Latina* vol. 91, 3 col. 115B)

49. The Latin text reads:

> CAPUT X. Generationes filiorum Noe.
>
> Filii autem Cham, Chus, et Mesraim et Phuth et Chanaan. Chus usque
> hodie ab Hebraeis Aethiopia nuncupatur, Mesraim Aegyptus, Pluth Lybies, a
> quo et Mauritaniae fluvius usque in praesens Phuth dicitur, omnisque circa
> eum regio Phutensis. Multi scriptores tam Graeci quam Latini, hujus rei testes
> sunt. Quare autem in una tantum climatis parte, antiquum Lybiae nomen
> resederit, et reliqua terra vocata sit Africa, non hujus loci nec temporis est. Porro
> Chanaan obtinuit terram quam Judaei deinceps obsederunt ejectis Chananaeis.
> (*Patrologia Latina* vol. 107 9 col. 527C)

50. The Latin text reads:

> Cham calidus interpretatur. Et ipse ex praesagio futuri cognominatus. Posteritas
> enim ejus eam terrae partem possedit, quae vicino sole calentior est. Unde et
> Aegyptus usque hodie Aegyptiorum lingua Cham dicitur. Hic Judaeorum des-
> ignat imaginem, qui Christi carnem atque mortem derident. . . . In his ergo
> tribus filiis Noe secunda origo saeculi surrexit, ut tres partes mundi a trium
> generatione implerentur. Porro Sem in filiis suis Asiam, et Cham Libyam,
> et Japhet Europam possederunt. In quibus etiam Ecclesia Christi, sanctae
> Trinitatis fide plantanda, praemonstrabatur. (*Patrologia Latina* vol. 111 2.1 col.
> 34C–34D)

51. The Latin text reads:

Chanaan, filius Cham, interpretatur motus eorum. Quod quid est aliud, nisi opus eorum? Pro motu enim patris, id est, pro opere ejus maledictus est. Unde de sedibus suis ejectus, filiis fratrum suorum terram possessionis suae reliquit, posteritatem indicans Judaeorum, qui in passione Domini damnationis sententiam exceperunt, clamantes: Sanguis ejus super nos et super filios nostros (Matth. XXVII). Ob quod a patria quasi ingrati per Romanos in ultionem sanguinis Christi expulsi, locum sanctae Ecclesiae dederunt, in qua verus cultus unius Dei perseverat in aeternum. (*Patrologia Latina* vol. III 2.1, col. 34D–35A)

52. Devisse and Mellinkoff both discuss this image briefly (2010b, 131–32; 1993, I 203, 310 n. 45).

53. See Hill; Johnstone; Scribner (278–98 passim); Kaplan (2002 244–45, 270–80); and Guibbory (60–88 passim, 186–95).

54. See Shuger (11–54) and Pelikan (23–39). However, see Stacy Davis, who demonstrates the persistence in early modern Catholic exegesis of Ham as figuring the Jews (109–22).

55. For a detailed discussion of the illustrations and their alterations through various editions, see Chew. See also the analysis in Luborsky and Ingram (I 315–24).

56. The Genesis caption reads: "When Cham the father of Chanaan saw the nakednes of his father, he tolde his two brethren etc. Gen. 10." The image misattributes this verse to Genesis 10. The 2 Kings 2:23 caption reads: "Heliseus is mocked of little children crying vnto him: Come vp thou baldhead, etc. 2 Reg. 2." See note 40 for discussion of Pinder, who cites these two texts as figures for the mocking of Jesus.

57. While these images clearly associate Jews with Ham, his transgression also supports a different homiletical subject: the impious disrespect for superiors, whether parents or clergy. Patristic exegesis first develops this approach. In his *Commonitory for the Antiquity and Universality of the Catholic Faith*, Vincent of Lérins (d. 450) condemns the disrespect of both holy men and parents (28–9). He likely influenced Odo of Cheriton's handling of the Ham in the *Sermones Dominicales de tempore*, in which Odo denounces lay criticism of the clergy (qtd. in Longland, 56, 58). While he brings in the parallel between Ham's action and the mocking of Jesus, the Jews operate here as another example of spiritual and filial impiety, rather than a people cursed with inferiority. This interpretation anticipates later Protestant commentaries, which understand Ham as violating the fifth commandment, honoring one's parents. The Geneva Bible (1599) glosses on this episode evacuate the association of Jews with Ham to focus on his status as a son who acted: "In derision and contemt of his father" (*Bible* 1599 4r, image 6). The commentary on Genesis 9:24–5, the verses which include Noah's pronouncement of the curse on Canaan, explains: "He pronounceth as a Prophet the curse of God against all of them, that honour not their parents; for Ham and his posteritie were accursed" (4v, image 7). Although the gloss describes Canaan's status as "a most vile slave," it does not elaborate on

this servitude, either to link the curse to those who dishonor parents or to any other group.

58. After the 1569 edition, the collection was published under the title *A booke of Christian praiers*.

59. See entry for Alexander Ross, *Oxford Dictionary of National Biography (DNB)*.

60. The text reads:

> The Church is drunke with gall and wormewood
> & thou hast made proud Rome to drinke her blood
> But now Lord bring her, vnto thy Wine seller
> Stay her with Flagons, and with new wine fill her:
> Giue her of thy best graces a good measure,
> And let Rome drinke the dreggs of thy displeasure. (1630 4 image 6)

61. Creative exegetes also find new biblical prooftexts for Jewish servitude. When early modern approaches to Bible geography remove Jews from the lineage of Ham, they return them to the line of Shem, the peoples of Asia whom classical sources associate with slavery. See Milton's *The Tenure of Kings and Magistrates*: "generally the people of Asia, and with them the Jews also, especially since the time they chose a King against the advice and counsel of God, are noted by wise Authors much inclinable to slavery" (756). The notes to this quotation include references to the doctrine of Asian slavery as expressed in Aristotle, *Politics*, VII, vi, and in Hippocrates, *On Airs, Waters, and Places*, lxxvi ("the Asiatic race is feeble"; "since monarchy prevails in the greater part of Asia, men are not their own masters nor independent, but are the slaves of others"). See also Trubowitz. I am very grateful to Jason Rosenblatt for these references. Braude traces the trend, beginning in early modernity, that not only associates Shem with Jews, Asia, and Muslims, but also represents Noah's curse falling on Shem as the progenitor of Jews and Africans (138–42).

62. This identification of Cain with Ham, however, only appears in the 1482 edition. In addition to the Higden example, Friedman notes other texts that connect or conflate Cain and Ham, including texts as diverse as *Beowulf* and an early sixteenth-century Flemish image of a tree of vices (100, 104–5). He seems entirely unaware of the exegetical tradition that reads Cain and Ham as figuring the Jews' crime and punishment with servitude. Freedman considers Cain and Ham in the context of Noah's curse as an explanation for the servile status of serfs. His argument anticipates mine in demonstrating the extent to which these typological figures helped formulate an inherently inferior status, but he does not attend to the exegetical tradition that formulates this status with recourse to Jewish deicidal sin (86–104). Harrison discusses the early modern deployment of Cain and Ham to figure religious nonconformists, including idolators, Jews and Muslims (105–12).

63. However, Boys directs his exhortations not to the Jews, but to his fellow Christians who fail to be edified by these examples: "Hee that reads and beleeues these things, and yet is an obstinate despiser of prophecie, killing, crucifying, scourging, persecuting the messengers of the Lord from City to City: shall receiue greater damnation then either Cain or Ierusalem, as hauing neglected greater meanes of saluation" (189).

64. Like Boys, Wither addresses a Christian audience, for whom the examples of Cain and the Jews will serve "to warne vs, that wee resist not God's grace once offred" (109).

65. Trained abroad in the civil law and serving as Regius professor of civil law at Cambridge University, Smith most likely encountered the canon law development of Jewish servitude in his studies (*DNB*; see entry for Sir Thomas Smith (1513–77).

66. In an early seventeenth-century account of his own enslavement in Muslim lands, William Davies gives an "empirical" description of Jews as "a slaue to the world . . . dispersed throughout most parts of the world, liuing in extreame slauery" (D4v, E1r, images 16–17).

67. The *DNB* notes that "*De republica Anglorum* enjoyed great popularity, going through eleven English editions by 1640; a Latin edition appeared around 1610, and there were further Latin editions printed on the continent in 1625, 1630, and 1641."

CHAPTER 5

1. It would be more accurate to state that this type is applied to multiple anti-types. Morris demonstrates how exegetes such as Pope Gregory VII (1073–1085) "used the image of the *ancilla* to describe the Holy Mother Church, oppressed by temporal interests, contrasting it to the reforming idea of the *libertas ecclesiae*" (179). In a number of different texts, Innocent III employs the figure of the *ancilla* to refer to Jews, Muslims, and the captured city of Jerusalem. He links the crusades with ecclesiastical reform in a sermon preached at the Fourth Lateran Council, in which Jerusalem is personified: "Come over to me, then, all you who love me, to free me from such misery. For I who used to be mistress of the nations have been made tributary. . . What disgrace that the sons of the bondwoman, those most vile offspring of Hagar, hold captive our mother, the enslaved mother of all the faithful" (qtd. in Morris, 186). Innocent both references and collapses the contrast between free Christian and enslaved Muslim in protesting the deep impropriety of Muslims ruling over Jerusalem, the holy city of Christians. As Morris explains: "The Pauline distinction between the sons of the *ancilla* and the sons of the 'free mother' was present and applied to Muslims and Christians respectively. However, both images were brought together with the subjugation of the holy city. Jerusalem became '*matrem nostrum ancillatam*'" (186).

2. For discussion of Muslims and Jews in canon law, see Herde; Gilles; Zacour; Kedar; Czerwinski; Freidenreich; and Tolan (2013, 2015b). Freidenreich charts the change over time in the canon law treatment of Muslims. While the earlier literature (c. 650–1000), with a few exceptions, does "not equate Muslims and Jews directly" (Freidenreich 2009, 97), this changes after 1000 when Western canon law compilations begin to place Jews and Muslims in the same category (Freidenreich 2011, 53–68). Although the law on Muslims in this period addresses a range of concerns, "A major objective of [the later] canons addressing Jews and Saracens is to ensure that Christians do not find themselves in any way subservient to non-Christians" (Freidenreich 2011, 42).

3. The Latin heading reads: "Iudaeos non debemus persequi, sed Sarracenos" (C.23 c.8 c.11 *Corpus Juris Canonici*).
   For canon law views of Muslims as bearers of power and as more threatening than Jews, see Freidenreich (2009, 86–90; 2011, 45–53).

4. Sapir Abulafia discusses the First Crusade context of this ruling (2011, 139–40).

5. This opinion runs counter to Jeremy Cohen's argument that the theologically valuable position of the Jews' witness to Christian truth, defined by Augustine, was degraded in their comparison to Muslims as both came to be seen as heretics (1999, 147–66; 317–63).

6. As noted in chapter 1, what infuriated popes like Innocent was the Jews' refusal to occupy their proper position of inferiority in Christian society.

7. The Latin reads: "Code: I, X. Ne Christianum mancipium haereticus vel paganus vel Iudaeus habeat vel possideat vel circumcidat."

8. The logic of servile, that is, inferior, infidels usurping a position of superiority relative to free Christians, animates all of these complaints. For example the Council of Montpelier (1195) echoes the language of the Third Lateran Council in forbidding the preference of Jews and Muslims over Christians: "Jews or Muslims should have no power over Christians, nor should any presume to prefer them over Christians" (my translation, Grayzel 1966, 299). The council also forbids Christians from acting as domestic servants to Jews and Muslims and rules that converts should keep their property so that they will be in a *melioris conditionis* than that which they enjoyed as infidels.

   In Hungary, the threat of Muslims as well as Jews not only ruling over but converting Christians horrified and vexed several popes; the free/slave inversion operates here as well, insofar as Christian converts to Islam disturbingly improve their condition, contrary to the doctrine of Christian liberty. See for example Honorius III's 1225 letter to the Archbishop of Colosza (Hungary):

   > For although it was decided in the Council of Toledo, and afterward reaffirmed in the General Council, that a blasphemer of Christ should not be given preferment in public office, since it is quite absurd that any such should exercise power over Christians, you, so we understand, have permitted this statute to be violated under your very eyes by Jews and pagans [Muslims],

although publicly in your synods you hurled the sentence of excommunication against all who give preferment to infidels in these offices. . . Moreover, we have heard that Saracens do . . . hold many Christian slaves. Since they purchase them freely whenever they wish, they rule over them at will, (even) compelling them to live in accordance with their rites. Furthermore, what is most pitiful of all, many Christian country folk (rustici) of their own free will transferring themselves to them and following their rites, publicly profess themselves Saracens, because in many ways the condition of Saracens is easier than that of Christians. . . .For it is a crime that those who were reborn in the baptismal font should associate in the rites and conversation of infidels, or that the Christian religion should be polluted by being subjected to infidels, or that a blasphemer should retain in servitude one redeemed by the blood of the Lord Christ. (Grayzel 1966, 171–73)

In a 1231 letter, similarly complaining of transgressions in Hungary that invert the proper categories of slave and free, Gregory IX protests:

On account of the oppression of the Christian poor and the dominion of Saracens and Jews over the faithful Christians, and because these Christians are weighted down by intolerable exactions, and because they see the Saracens enjoying the prerogative of a better status (melioris conditionis) and greater freedom, many Christians openly transfer themselves to the former, and observe their rites in order to enjoy freedom like theirs. . . . Furthermore, Saracens buy Christian slaves, and after satisfying their will and their passion upon them as if they were of their own people, they compel them to apostasize, and do not permit them to baptize their children. The poor among the Christians are so afflicted with burdens and exactions, that they are forced to sell their sons and daughters to Saracens, and thus the free become the slaves, and those who were once Christians become Saracens. (Grayzel 1966, 185)

See also Gregory's 1233 letter to the King of Hungary, which virtually repeats the complaints articulated in the 1231 letter (Grayzel 1966, 209).

9. "Twelve sons in all were born to Ishmael. . . .and it is these who conferred their names on the Arabian nation and its tribes in honour both of their own prowess and of the fame of Abraham." (Josephus I.12.3–4, 106–9). Others who follow this approach in identifying Ishmael with Arabia in a historical and geographical context are: Eusebius, Jerome, Isidore, Bede, and Peter Comestor in his *Historia scholastica* (c. 1170) (Zacour, 18; Tolan, 2012; Morey, 6). For Jewish biblical, early midrashic, and Talmudic associations of Ishmael with Arabs or Muslims, see Bakhos (67–84).

10. The Latin reads: "Ismaelitas et Agarenos, qui nunc Sarraceni appellantur, assumentes sibi falso nomen Sarae, quo scilicet de ingenua et domina videantur esse generati." (*Commentariorum in Ezechielem Prophetam Patrologia Latina* vol. 25 8.25, col. 233C, my translation). However, Jerome's commentary on Galatians

4: 25–6 follows Paul and other exegetes in identifying Hagar with the Jews: "Pene cunctorum super hoc loco ista est explanatio, ut Agar ancillam, interpretentur in Lege, et in populo Judaeorum. [Nearly all of the commentators on this passage interpret it to mean that the slave woman Hagar represents the Law and the Jewish people]" (*Commentariorum in epistolam ad Galatas Patrologia Latina* vol. 26 2 cols. 390B–390C; *Commentary on Galatians*, 187).

11. Tolan explains that Saracen "was originally a term used by Greek and Roman geographical and ethnographical authors to refer to certain peoples of the Arabian peninsula," noting that Ptolemy's *Geography* (c. 150 C.E.) provides the first recorded use of the word (2012, 513). Tolan reviews the scholarship on the origins of the term (513–14). His essay offers a detailed consideration of the treatment of Ishmael and the Saracens in the works of Jerome, Isidore, and Bede.

12. *De fide et legibus* is part of William's larger opus, the *Magisterium divinale et sapientale*, in which he attempts to synthesize philosophy and Christianity (Teske 17–19).

13. The Latin reads:

> gens Arabum & gens Sarracenorum, sed nomen Saracenorum falsò sibi usurpant à Sarra, tanquàm filii Sarrae per Ismahelem, cùm tamen nihil cognationes, sed solam adoptionem ad Sarram habent, sicut legitur Genes. 16. . . . Verè autem Agareni sunt, quia ex Agar per Ismahelem descenderunt. (chapter 18 50r)

14. The Latin reads: "Licet ergo propria culpa Iudaeos servituti subiecerit: ipsos tamen tolerat pietas Christiana" (Liber V. col. 1518. 3b).

15. The Latin reads:

> De Sarracenis . . .Et unde dicantur. A Sara uxore Abrahae, voluerunt nuncupari: & . . . ab ea nati non sunt, nec originem habuerunt, imo ab Agar ancilla Sarae quasi Agareni, vel Agarieni deberent potius nuncupari . . . unde competentius dicimur filii Sare, quae fuit legitima, quia in Sara firmata est ecclesia, and ideo Pagani, vel Iudaei, non debent sub se Christianos habere, ne filii liberae. i. Sar[a]e, hoc est Christiani filiis.f.extra fidem catholicae positis famulentur. Ancillae. f. Agar, . . .e. & si Iudaeos. (Liber V. col. 1523. 2)

16. Simonsohn notes this conflation: "In 1263 Urban IV repeated the complaints of his predecessors about conditions in Hungary, where Jews and Moslems were alleged to hold sway over Christians. He consigned both Jews and Moslems to 'perpetual servitude'" (vol. 7, 100). Cohen does as well: "In 1263 Urban IV instructed that guilt had condemned the Saracens as well as the Jews to perpetual servitude" (1999, 163 and note).

17. The figure also appears in Alfonso X of Castile's thirteenth-century secular legal code, the *Siete partidas*, which offers a succinct articulation of the relationship of Islam to Hagar. In the section on "the Moors, "a people who believe that Mohammed was the Prophet and Messenger of God," the first law offers to explain the derivation of the word "moor": "Sarracenus, in Latin, means Moor, in Castilian, and this name is derived from Sarah, the free wife of Abraham,

although the lineage of the Moors is not traced to her, but to Hagar, who was Abraham's servant" (Part 7, Title 25, law 1, qtd. in Muldoon 1977, 94). The author merely asserts, rather than explains the connection between Saracen and Moor, offering instead the familiar derivation of Saracen from Sarah. The Muslims falsely claim their lineage from the "free wife" of Abraham, when in fact they are descendants of the slave Hagar.

18. Rowan considers this text in an essay on Ulrich Zasius's early sixteenth-century treatise on the baptism of Jewish children. Unaware of the ways in which typological figures could signify both Jews and Muslims, Rowan rejects the application of Ham to both faith groups on ethnological grounds:

> If this had been taken literally, then the Arabs and the Jews would have been seen not as Semites but Hamites, an eccentric anthropology. The children of the Jews were thought by Stephen to be capable of being bought and sold, and once out of the parental household they could then be baptized, since the Institutes of Justinian had recognized no true paternal power for slaves. It is significant that Zasius tacitly dropped the Ham argument, though he had encountered it in three texts he is known to have read. Perhaps its lack of support in tradition, or its racist tinge, bothered a man who strongly asserted the curative powers of baptism for all Jewish debilities (18).

However, I have shown the development of a tradition that reads both Jews and Muslims as infidels who deserve to be enslaved by Christians. Rowan's anachronistic reference suggests the influence of later readings of Ham as an inferior African, but ignores the very widespread application of the figure of Ham to represent Jewish servitude.

19. Henri Gilles notes another commentator who, on the question of involuntary baptism, includes Muslims along with Jews in the category of slaves who do not have power over their children. In his commentary on *Clementines* 5.2.un., Cardinal-bishop Pierre d'Estaing (d. 1377) argues that Muslims, like Jews, are slaves to the prince. Henri Gilles paraphrases his argument: "Parents, as slaves, do not exercise any paternal power over their children. The master, like the prince, may baptize them, just as he may give or sell them, against the will of their parents. But he may not do it to push the parents to convert, only the eternal salvation of the children should be taken into consideration" (205, my translation of the French). Gilles does not mention if d'Estaing includes references to other decretals, such as *Etsi*, or to the figure of Ham/Canaan. I have not been able to examine a copy of d'Estaing's text, but he appears to follow the influential opinion of William of Rennes, which does include these references. See the discussion in chapter 1.

20. Oldradus's collection of consilia is one of the earliest and most important; its frequent reproduction in manuscripts and in print testifies to its popularity. Zacour defines consilia thus:

> A medieval lawyer's consilium was usually his certified opinion about a case being heard or about to be heard by a court of law. The client for whom it was prepared might be a litigant but more often was the court itself, seeking help in settling a difficult case. The consilium took a certain form, naming the main parties to the case, reciting the facts, reviewing the relevant laws and their apparent contradictions, and bearing the name and seal of the advocate (or advocates) who wrote it. . . . The fact that consilia were also called other things—*responsa, allegationes, quaestiones*—reminds us that they sometimes had nothing to do with court cases. (Zacour, ix, 3,5)

21. On the question of whether Jews owe tithes, Pakter explains: "While it was generally accepted that Jews did not owe personal tithes, it was universally agreed that they owed tithes on land, even if not every Christian did" (138). Sapir Abulafia discusses the history of Jews owing, and not paying, tithes (2011, 114–15). See also Freidenreich's discussion (2011, 58).
22. For "tributary slave" Du Cange explains: "Servi Tributarii . . . Qui praeter operam manualem, ad certas res sub annui census nomine praestandas tenebantur {Tributary slaves are held, who besides manual labor, are responsible for an annual stipulated tax on a certain property}."
23. As Forsythe explains:

> Perhaps the single most important and lasting innovation in the Roman state around the middle of the fifth century B.C. was the Law of the Twelve Tables, so-called because this first major codification of law was initially engraved on twelve bronze tablets and was displayed in public. Even though many of this early lawcode's specific provisions eventually became obsolete, it nevertheless continued to be of significance, as it was the precondition for all the subsequent development of Roman law. (201)

24. Aristotle's theory of natural slavery circulated in the eleventh and twelfth centuries; while it gained some acceptance, "the general medieval conception of slavery was that slavery was not a consequence of biological inferiority, but rather the result of the fall of man and a consequence of sin" (Muldoon 2005, 74).
25. See Freedman's discussion of the problem of justifying peasant servitude in the medieval European context which considered all Christians as free; he briefly notes the capacity of this idea for constructing Jewish inferiority (239–56, esp 256).
26. While slavery as an institution declined in Europe during the medieval period, it continued to be practiced in areas where Christians and Muslims had prolonged contact. (Muldoon 2005, 77; see also Phillips 51, 88, cited by Muldoon)
27. The Talmud destroys Augustine's idea that Jews are bookslaves to Christians insofar as it asserts a Jewish interpretation of Hebrew Bible contrary to a Christian

one. Cohen traces the thirteenth-century erosion of the Augustinian justification for Jews within Christian society (1999, 317–63).

28. As he explains:

> The late thirteenth century saw a blurring of the lines distinguishing Jews and Moslems. Christians saw them as joined by common opposition to the Christian faith and overlooked the religious and other differences between them. This blurring of distinctions between various non-Christians seems part of a general process of reducing the world to two classes of people, those within the Church and those outside of it. (Muldoon 1979, 52)

29. The Latin reads: "ut iura dicunt, Iudaei merito culpae suae sint vel essent perpetuae servituti addicti, et sic eorum res terrarum domini possint accipere tanquam suas." (art.: 1, resp. ad argumentum, numerus: 727, linea: 5, pag. 249). See Simonsohn vol. 7, 98 and the discussion in chapter 1.

30. As Muldoon argues:

> For the next century and a half, the defenders and the opponents of European expansion drew upon the thirteenth-century legal materials concerning the rights of infidels to define the relationship that ought to exist between such people and Christians. For the first time, canonistic thinking about the rights of infidels was applied directly to specific situations involving existing infidel societies. (1979, 107)

31. The Latin reads: "Omnia enim subiecta fuerunt Christo, oues et boues et uniuersa pecora campi, ut habetur in psalmo" (qtd. in Muldoon 1976, 475). The actual Psalm text reads: "Omnia subjecisti sub pedibus eius oves et boves universas insuper et pecora campi [Thou hast subjected all things under his feet, all sheep and oxen: moreover the beasts also of the fields]." The biblical text describes how the animals are subjected to humans, not Jesus.

32. The Latin reads: "per boues autem et pecora . . . intelligimus Saracenos quo tanquam bestie ratione carentes spreto Deo uero idola colunt. Modo etsi ad pascendum Petro isti a Christo non sunt commendati, sunt tamen sub pedibus Petri subiecti quo ad dominium diuinam et potestatem" (qtd. in Muldoon 1976, 475).

33. The Latin reads:

> Set per Saram significatur sancta mater ecclesia, et per Agar amcillam [sic] significatur illa amcilla [sic] maledicta in qua secta Macomecti que ab ea traxit originem significatur. . . . Et ideo sancta ecclesia que per Saram ut dixi significatur iurisdictionem habet in hanc amcillam [sic] et sectam paganorum, non quidem eos ad fidem compellendo set exortando . . . (qtd. in Muldoon 1976, 475)

34. The ability to enslave was a collateral result of these opinions, but as interest in gaining control over African lands increased, so did interest in trading enslaved peoples. As Saunders explains: "The possibility of acquiring slaves first brought the Infante D. Henrique popular support for his voyages to the south and his

desire to find new suppliers of slaves was undoubtedly a major reason for the continued exploration of the African littoral" (Saunders, 2).

35. The misrepresentation of African peoples as uncivilized and thus animal-istic provides another justification for the construction of an inferior condi-tion conducive to slavery: "Finally, to justify the enslavement of the blacks and Idzāgen, the Portuguese crown's official propagandists declared that these West Africans were primitive peoples whose enslavement in Portugal brought them the inestimable benefits of Christianity and European material civilization" (Saunders, 35).

36. The bull was issued by Eugenius IV from Florence in 1442 (Jordão and Barreto, vol. 1, 21).

37. The Latin reads:

> . . . tibi Sarracenos, et Paganos, aliosque infideles, et Christi inimicos quos-cunque, et ubicunque constitutos Regna, Ducatus, Comitatus, Principatus, aliaque Dominia, Terras, Loca, Villas, Castra, et quaecunque alia possesiones, bona mobilia, et immobilia . . .fuerint, invadendi, conquerendi, expugnandi, et subjugandi, illorum personas in perpetuam servitutam redigendi, regna quo-que, Ducatus, Comitatus, Principatus, aliaque Dominia, possesiones, et bona hujusmodi, tibi et succesoribus tuis Regibus Portugalliae, perpetuo applicandi, et appropriandi, ac in tuos et eorundum successorum usus, et utilitates conver-tendi plenam, et liberam, auctoritate Apostolica, tenore praesentium concedi-mus facultatem. (Jordão and Barreto vol. 1, 22)

38. The Latin reads: "Multi Guinei, et alii Nigri vi capti, quidam etiam non pro-hibitarum rerum permutatione, seu alio legitimo contractu emptionis . . .in copioso numero ad Catholicam fidem conversi extiterunt." The bull also settled an ongoing dispute between Spain and Portugal over control of an area of north-western Africa, and territories to the south, in granting exclusive rights to the Portuguese (Jordão and Barreto vol. 1, 32; Davenport vol. I, 12).

39. The Latin reads:

> . . . quod cum olim praefato Alfonso Regi, quoscumque Sarracenos, et Paganos, aliosque Christi inimicos ubicumque constitutos, ac regna, ducatus, principa-tus, dominia, possessions, et mobilia, et immobilia bona quaecumque per eos detenta, ac possessa invadendi, conquirendi, expugnandi, debellandi, et subju-gandi, illorumque personas in perpetuam servitutem redigendi . . . aliis nostris litteris plenam et liberam inter caetera concessimus facultatem. . . .(Jordão and Barreto vol. 1, 32)

40. In the printed text of the nineteenth-century edition, the editor instructs the reader that articles 2–17 follow the tenor of the letter of Nicholas V, *Romanus Pontifex* (1454 [o.s.]) and directs the reader to the page where that document appears in the volume (Jordão and Barreto vol. I, 36).

41. The language of perpetual servitude initially developed to subordinate Jews, and then applied to Muslims and Africans, also enters into papal documents on the Spanish expropriation of the Americas.

> After the discovery of America in 1492, Ferdinand and Isabella of Spain were foresighted enough to see that if Spain did not receive from the Pope in regard to the American "Indies" the same authority and permissions which Portugal had received in regard to West Africa, then Spain would be at an disadvantage with making use of her newly discovered territories. . . .Pope Alexander VI was approached and already on May 3, 1493, he issued two Bulls . . . in both of which he extended the identical favours, permissions, etc. granted to the monarchy of Portugal in respect of West Africa to the Monarchy of Spain in respect of America. . . .They received "full and free permission to invade, search out, capture and subjugate the Saracens and pagans and any other unbelievers and enemies of Christ wherever they may be, as well as their kingdoms, duchies, counties, principalities and other property. . . and to reduce their persons into perpetual slavery." In other words, it would appear that, in effect, Portugal and Spain were understood by the Holy See to be at war with the enemies of Christendom—the Negroes [*sic*] of West Africa and the "Indians" [*sic*] of America—wherever they may be. (Maxwell, 55–6)

For a consideration of how the medieval Jewish context influences constructions of race and identity in the New World, see Martínez and Jonathan Boyarin.
42. "The Slavonic population in parts of central Europe having been reduced to a servile condition by conquest . . . " "slave, n.1 (and adj.)." *OED Online*.
43. While alternative defenses of the trade in enslaved people developed, awareness of the just war rationalization persisted, cropping up in critics' attacks on slavery. In his 1555 *Arte da Guerra no Mar*, Fernão de Oliveira questioned whether

> slaves purchased by the Portuguese had been reduced to slavery legally according to Roman and canon law. He asserted, correctly, that this was not so: rather, the vendors of slaves. . . acquired them by robbery, rapine and other unjust means. . . . He saw very clearly that . . . the trade by its very existence engendered the deplorable slave hunts which African wars had become. (Saunders, 43)

44. The original reads: "en sos fijos e en sus generaciones e los dio en su maldición por siervos a Sem e a Jafet" (90).
45. The original reads: "E los moros vienen principalmente de Cam, que pobló a África, . . .que por el falso predicamiento de Mahomat se tornassen moros" (91).
46. The orginal reads: "Ca pues que moros son, todos son de Cam, e si pudiéremos algo levar d'ellos por batalla o por cualquier fuerça, e aun prender a ellos e ferlos nuestros siervos, que non fazemos ý pecado nin tuerto nin yerro ninguno" (91).

47. As Saunders explains:

> Zurara was the main Portuguese exponent of the idea that West Africans were
> slaves because of sin. In one passage he noted that the blacks were slaves of the
> Idzāgen because the blacks were of the sinful race of Ham, who had been cursed
> by his father Noah. Ham had committed the sin of looking upon his father's
> nakedness while the latter was drunk, for which Noah condemned Ham's son
> Canaan and his descendants to be slaves forever (Gen. xi. 22–5). (The belief that
> Ham's descendants and been cursed with blackness as well as servitude was,
> interestingly enough, not a Christian tradition, but part of Portugal's Jewish and
> Muslim inheritance.) Elsewhere the chronicler followed scholastic philosophers
> in asserting that the sinfulness which reduced men to the status of natural slaves
> was a matter of conduct. Aquinas, commenting on Aristotle, had observed that
> man was free because he was reasonable, but sin fettered freedom and, by sin-
> ning, man could fall into the "slavish state of the beasts" (Saunders, 38).

Sanders parenthetical remark relies on Jordan's work (2012), which has since
been challenged.

48. As discussed in chapter 4.
49. *Contra Faustum* 12, 9–13, 23. See discussion in chapters 1 and 4.
50. See the discussion of alternative interpretations of Ham in chapter 4; Stacy Davis
    explores the range of exegetical traditions of Ham.
51. The text does not portray any discord, or even a conversation, between Cain
    and Adam.
52. See Davis (1966, 100–1).
53. The continued servile or inferior status of converts to Christianity, whether
    they be Africans, conversos or moriscos offers another point of comparison be-
    tween Africans, Jews, and Muslims (see Jennings, 33–36). See also Martínez for
    how *limpieza di sangre* operates in the New World context. Chapter 1 considers
    debates between canonists on the hypothetical question of whether conversion
    would free Jews purchased as slaves by Christians.

References

Aaron, David H. "Early Rabbinic Exegesis on Noah's Son Ham and the So-Called 'Hamitic Myth.'" *Journal of the American Academy of Religion* 63.4 (1995): 721–59.

Abulafia, David. "The Servitude of Jews and Muslims in the Medieval Mediterranean: Origins and Diffusion." Roma: École francaise de Rome, 2000 *Mefrim: Melanges de L'Ecole francaise de Rome: moyen-age* 112.2 (2000): 1–27. http://www.torrossa.it/resources/an/2206612.

Adelman, Janet. *Blood Relations: Christian and Jew in the Merchant of Venice*. Chicago: University of Chicago Press, 2008.

Akbari, Suzanne Conklin. *Idols in the East: European Representations of Islam and the Orient, 1100–1450*. Ithaca, NY: Cornell University Press, 2009.

Akhimie, Patricia. *Shakespeare and the Cultivation of Difference: Race and Conduct in the Early Modern World*. New York: Routledge, 2018.

Albertus Magnus. *Questions Concerning Aristotle's On Animals*, transl. Irven M. Resnick and Kenneth F. Kitchell, Jr. Washington, DC: Catholic University Press, 2008.

Alcuin. *Aelfric's Anglo-Saxon Version of Alcuini Interrogationes Sigeuulfi Presbyteri in Genesin*, ed. George Edwin MacLean. Halle: E. Karras, Printer, 1883. http://archive.org/stream/lfricsanglosaxooomaclgoog#page/n100/mode/2up.

Alfonso X. *General Estoria*, ed. Pedro Sánchez-Prieto Borja. Madrid: Fundación José Antonio de Castro, 2009.

Altschul, Nadia. "Saracens and Race in Roman de la Rose Iconography: The Case of Dangier in Bodleian Douce 195." *Digital Philology* 2.1 (2013): 1–15.

Andrews, E. A., William Freund, Charlton T. Lewis, and Charles Short. *A Latin Dictionary Founded on Andrews' Edition of Freund's Latin Dictionary*. New York: Oxford University Press, 2002.

Anidjar, Gil. *The Jew, the Arab: A History of the Enemy*. Redwood City, CA: Stanford University Press, 2003.

Anidjar, Gil. *Semites: Race, Religion, Literature*. Redwood City, CA: Stanford University Press, 2008.

Annales Bertiniani, ed. G. Waitz. Hanover: Impensis Bibliopolii Hahniani, 1883. http://www.mgh.de/dmgh/resolving/MGH_SS_rer._Germ._5_S._43.

Annals of St-Bertin, transl. and annotated by Janet L. Nelson. Manchester: Manchester University Press; New York: St. Martin's Press, 1991.

Appiah, Kwame Anthony. "Race," in *Critical Terms for Literary Study*, ed. Frank Lentricchia and Thomas McLaughlin. Chicago: University of Chicago Press, 1990, 274–87.

Aquinas, Thomas. *De regimine Iudaeorum (Epistula ad ducissam Brabantiae)*, in *Library of Latin Texts—Series A*. Turnhout, Belgium: Brepols Publishers, 2013. http://clt.brepolis.net.proxy.library.georgetown.edu/LLTA/pages/TextSearch.aspx?key=MTHAQORI__.

Aquinas, Thomas. *Summa Theologiae: Latin Text and English Translation, Introductions, Notes, Appendices, and Glossaries*, ed. Thomas Gilby. New York: McGraw-Hill, 1964.

Arjana, Sophia R. *Muslims in the Western Imagination*. New York: Oxford University Press, 2015.

Auerbach, Erich. "Figura," in *Scenes from the Drama of European Literature*. Minneapolis: University of Minnesota Press, 1984, 11–76.

Augustine. *Contra Faustum*, in *Nicene and Post-Nicene Fathers: First Series*. Vol. 4. Peabody, MA: Hendrickson Publishers, 1994a, 151–345.

Augustine. *Ennarationes in Psalmos* in *Nicene and Post-Nicene Fathers: First Series*. Vol. 8. Peabody, MA: Hendrickson Publishers, 1994b.

Augustine. *City of God*. Cambridge, MA: Harvard University Press, 2014.

Augustine. *Quaestionum in Heptateuchum*. Patrologia Latina Online. Vol. 34. http://gateway.proquest.com.proxy.library.georgetown.edu/openurl?url_ver=Z39.88-2004&res_dat=xri:pld-us&rft_dat=xri:pld:ft:all:Z400059561.

Baker, Cynthia M. *Jew*. New Brunswick, NJ: Rutgers University Press, 2017.

Bakhos, Carol. *Ishmael on the Border: Rabbinic Portrayals of the First Arab*. Albany: State University of New York Press, 2006.

Bale, Anthony. *The Jew in the Medieval Book: English Antisemitisms, 1350–1500*. Cambridge: Cambridge University Press, 2006.

Bale, Anthony. *Feeling Persecuted: Christians, Jews and Images of Violence in the Middle Ages*. London: Reaktion, 2010.

Balibar, Étienne. "Is There a 'Neo-Racism'?" in, *Race, Nation, Class: Ambiguous Identities*, ed. Étienne Balibar and Immanuel Wallerstein. New York: Verso, 1991, 17–28.

Baron, Roger de. *Practica maior*, in *Cyrurgia Guidonis De Cauliaco, Et Cyrurgia Bruni, Teodorici, Rolandi, Lanfranci, Rogerii, Bertapalie*. Venice, 1519. http://digital.onb.ac.at/OnbViewer/viewer.faces?doc=ABO_%2BZ196711908.

Baron, Salo Wittmayer. *A Social and Religious Sistory of the Jews*. 18 vols. ed., rev. and enl. New York: Columbia University Press, 1952–.

Baron, Salo Wittmayer. "Medieval Nationalism and Jewish Serfdom," in *Ancient and Medieval Jewish History: Essays*, ed. Leon A. Feldman. New Brunswick, NJ: Rutgers University Press, 1972a, 308–22.

Baron, Salo Wittmayer. "'Plenitude of Apostolic Powers' and Medieval 'Jewish Serfdom,'" in *Ancient and Medieval Jewish History: Essays*, ed. Leon A. Feldman. New Brunswick, NJ: Rutgers University Press, 1972b, 284–307.

Bartels, Emily C. "Othello and Africa: Postcolonialism Reconsidered." *William and Mary Quarterly* 54.1 (1997): 45–64.

Bartels, Emily C. *Speaking of the Moor: From Alcazar to Othello*. Philadelphia: University of Pennsylvania Press, 2008.

Bartholomaeus Angelicus [*sic*]. *De Rerum Proprietatibus*. Frankfurt: Minerva, 1964.

Bassett, Molly H., and Vincent W. Lloyd, eds. *Sainthood and Race: Marked Flesh, Holy Flesh*. London: Routledge, 2015.

Beckett, Katherine Scarfe. *Anglo-Saxon Perceptions of the Islamic World*. Cambridge: Cambridge University Press, 2003.

Bede. *In Pentateuchum Commentarii. Patrologia Latina Online*. Vol. 91. http://gateway. proquest.com.proxy.library.georgetown.edu/openurl?url_ver=Z39.88-2004&res_ dat=xri:pld-us&rft_dat=xri:pld:ft:all:Z300007189.

Bede. *Hexaemeron, sive libri quatuor in principium genesis, usque ad nativitatem isaac et electionem ismaelis. Patrologa Latina Online*. Vol. 91. http://gateway.proquest.com. proxy.library.georgetown.edu/openurl?url_ver=Z39.88-2004&res_dat=xri:pld- us&rft_dat=xri:pld:ft:all:Z300007183.

Bernstein, Alan E. *Hell and Its Rivals: Death and Retribution Among Christians, Jews, and Muslims in the Early Middle Ages*. Ithaca, NY: Cornell University Press, 2017.

Bestul, Thomas H. *Texts of the Passion: Latin Devotional Literature and Medieval Society*. Philadelphia: University of Pennsylvania Press, 1996.

Bethencourt, Francisco. *Racisms: From the Crusades to the Twentieth Century*. Princeton, NJ: Princeton University Press, 2013.

Biblia latina. With the Glossa Ordinaria of pseudo-Walafrid Strabo and interlinear glosses of Anselmus Laudunensis. Strasbourg: Adolf Rusch, 1480.

Biblia sacra iuxta Uulgatam uersionem. Library of Latin Texts. Centre Traditio Litterarum Occidentalium Turnhout. Belgium: Brepols, 2002–2005. http://clt. brepolis.net/llta/pages/Toc.aspx.

The Bible. [Geneva Bible] London, 1599. *Early English Books Online*. http://gateway. proquest.com.proxy.library.georgetown.edu/openurl?ctx_ver=Z39.88-2003&res_ id=xri:eebo&rft_id=xri:eebo:citation:23244196.

Bibliorum sacrorum cum glossa ordinaria, ed. Fulgensis Strabus; Nicholas of Lyra; Paul Burgensus; Matthias Toringus; François Feuardent; Jean Dadré, Jacques de Cuilly. Venetiis, 1603. https://archive.org/details/bibliorumsacroruo1strauoft.

Biddick, Kathleen. *The Typological Imaginary: Circumcision, Technology, History*. Philadelphia: University of Pennsylvania Press, 2003.

Bildhauer, Bettina, and Robert Mills. *The Monstrous Middle Ages*. Toronto: University of Toronto Press, 2003.

Biller, Peter. "Views of Jews from Paris around 1300: Christian or 'Scientific'?" in *Christianity and Judaism: Studies in Church History* 29, ed. Diana Wood. Cambridge: Blackwell, 1992, 187–297.

Biller, Peter. "A 'Scientific' View of Jews from Paris around 1300." *Micrologus* 9 (2001): 137–68.

Bindman, David, Henry Louis Gates, Jr. and Karen C. C. Dalton, eds. *The Image of the Black in Western Art.* Cambridge, MA: Belknap Press of Harvard University Press, in collaboration with the W. E. B. Du Bois Institute for African and African American Research; Houston: Menil Collection, 2010.

Bird, Jessalynn. "The Historia Orientalis of Jacques de Vitry: Visual and Written Commentaries as Evidence of a Text's Audience, Reception, and Utilization." *Essays in Medieval Studies* 20 (2003): 56–74.

Blackburn, Robin. "The Old World Background to European Colonial Slavery." *William and Mary Quarterly* 54.1 (1997): 65–102.

Blaise, Albert. *Dictionnaire latin-français des auteurs chrétiens.* Turnhout, Belgium: Brepols, 1975.

Blumenkranz, Bernhard. *Le Juif médiéval au miroir de l'art chrétien.* Paris: Études augustiniennes, 1966.

Blurton, Heather, and Hannah Johnson. "Virtual Jews and Figural Criticism: Some Recent Scholarship on the Idea of the Jew in Western Culture." *Philological Quarterly* 92.1 (2014): 115–30.

Bolton, Brenda. "Faithful to Whom? Jacques de Vitry and the French Bishops." *Revue Mabillon* n.s. 9 (1998): 53–72.

Bonet, Honoré. *The Tree of Battles*, transl. G. W. Coopland. Cambridge, MA: Harvard University Press, 1949.

Bonnassie, Pierre. *From Slavery to Feudalism in South-Western Europe.* Cambridge: Cambridge University Press; Paris: Editions de la Maison des Sciences de l'homme, 1991.

Boyarin, Daniel. *A Radical Jew: Paul and the Politics of Identity.* Berkeley: University of California Press, 1994.

Boyarin, Jonathan. *The Unconverted Self: Jews, Indians, and the Identity of Christian Europe.* Chicago: University of Chicago Press, 2009.

Boys, John. *An exposition of the festiuall epistles and gospels vsed in our English liturgie.* London, 1615. *Early English Books Online.* http://gateway.proquest.com/openurl?ctx_ver=Z39.88-2003&res_id=xri:eebo&rft_id=xri:eebo:citation:23292433.

Braude, Benjamin. "The Sons of Noah and the Construction of Ethnic and Geographical Identities in the Medieval and Early Modern Periods." *William and Mary Quarterly* 54.1 (1997): 103–42.

Britton, Dennis Austin. *Becoming Christian: Race, Reformation, and Early Modern English Romance.* New York: Fordham University Press, 2014.

Brooks, Douglas A. *Milton and the Jews.* Cambridge: Cambridge University Press, 2008.

Brown, George. "The Psalms as the Foundation of Anglo-Saxon Learning," in *The Place of the Psalms in the Intellectual Culture of the Middle Ages*, ed. Nancy van Deusen. Albany: State University of New York, 1999, 15–42.

Bruder, Edith, and Tudor Parfitt. *African Zion: Studies in Black Judaism.* Newcastle upon Tyne: Cambridge Scholars Publishing, 2012.

Brundage, James A. "Intermarriage between Christians and Jews in Medieval Canon Law." *Jewish History* 3.1 (1988): 25–40.

Brundage, James A. *Medieval Canon Law.* New York: Longman, 1995.

Brunotte, Ulrike, Anna-Dorothea Ludewig, and Axel Stähler, eds. *Orientalism, Gender, and the Jews: Literary and Artistic Transformations of European National Discourses.* Berlin: Walter De Gruyter Oldenbourg, 2015.

Buckland, W. W. *The Roman Law of Slavery: The Condition of the Slave in Private Law from Augustus to Justinian.* New York: AMS Press, 1969.

Buell, Denise Kimber. *Why This New Race: Ethnic Reasoning in Early Christianity.* New York: Columbia University Press, 2005.

Burk, Rachel. "Salus erat in sanguine: Limpieza de sangre and Other Discourses of Blood in Early Modern Spain." PhD diss., University of Pennsylvania, 2010.

Burton, Jonathan. *Traffic and Turning: Islam and English Drama, 1579–1624.* Newark: University of Delaware Press, 2005.

Byron, Gay. *Symbolic Blackness and Ethnic Difference in Early Christian Literature* New York: Routledge, 2002.

Caesarius of Heisterbach. *Dialogus Miraculorum,* ed. Joseph Strange. 2 vols. Cologne: J. M. Heberle, H. Lempertz & Company, 1851.

Caesarius of Heisterbach. *The Dialogue on Miracles,* transl. H. von E. Scott and C. C. Swinton Bland. 2 vols. London: G. Routledge & Sons, Ltd., 1929.

Calkin, Siobhain Bly. "Marking Religion on the Body: Saracens, Categorization, and the King of Tars." *Journal of English and Germanic Philology* 104.2 (2005): 219–38.

Calkins, Robert G. *Illuminated Books of the Middle Ages.* Ithaca, NY: Cornell University Press, 1983.

Camille, Michael. *Mirror in Parchment: The Luttrell Psalter and the Making of Medieval England.* Chicago: University of Chicago Press, 1998.

Carter, J. Kameron. *Race: A Theological Account.* New York: Oxford University Press, 2008.

Cassian, John. *John Cassian, The Conferences,* ed. Boniface Ramsey. New York: Paulist Press, 1997.

Cassian, John. *Collationum. Patrologia Latina Online.* Vol. 49. http://gateway.proquest.com/openurl?url_ver=Z39.88-2004&res_dat=xri:pld-us&rft_dat=xri:pld:ft:all:Z300047328.

Cawsey, Kathy. "Disorienting Orientalism: Finding Saracens in Strange Places in Late Medieval English Manuscripts." *Exemplaria* 21.4 (2009): 380–97.

Chapman, Matthieu. *Anti-Black Racism in Early Modern English Drama: The Other "Other."* New York: Routledge, 2016.

Chaucer, Geoffrey. *The Works of Geoffrey Chaucer,* ed. F. N. Robinson. Boston: Houghton Mifflin, 1961.

Chazan, Robert. *European Jewry and the First Crusade*. Berkeley: University of California Press, 1987.

Chazan, Robert. *In the Year 1096: The First Crusade and the Jews*. Philadelphia: Jewish Publication Society, 1996a.

Chazan, Robert. "Twelfth-Century Perceptions of the Jews: A Case Study of Bernard of Clairvaux and Peter the Venerable," in *From Witness to Witchcraft: Jews and Judaism in Medieval Christian Thought*, ed. Jeremy Cohen. Wiesbaden: Harrassowitz, 1996b, 187–201.

Chazan, Robert. "Pope Innocent III and the Jews," in *Pope Innocent III and His World*, ed. John C. Moore and Brenda Bolton. Brookfield, VT: Ashgate, 1999, 187–204.

Chenu, Marie-Dominique. "The Old Testament in Twelfth-Century Theology," in *Nature, Man and Society in the Twelfth Century*, ed. and transl. Lester K. Little and Jerome Taylor. Toronto: University of Toronto Press, 1997, 146–61.

Chew, Samuel. "The Iconography of *A Book of Christian Prayers* (1578) Illustrated." *Huntington Library Quarterly* 8.3 (May 1945): 293–305.

Clarke, P. D. "Peter the Chanter, Innocent III and Theological Views on Collective Guilt and Punishment." *The Journal of Ecclesiastical History* 52.1 (2001): 1–20.

Cohen, Gerson. "Esau as Symbol in Early Medieval Thought," in *Jewish Medieval and Renaissance Studies*, ed. Alexander Altmann. Cambridge, MA: Harvard University Press, 1967, 19–48.

Cohen, Jeffrey Jerome. *Of Giants: Sex, Monsters, and the Middle Ages*. Minneapolis: University of Minnesota Press, 1999.

Cohen, Jeffrey Jerome. "On Saracen Enjoyment: Some Fantasies of Race in Late Medieval France and England." *Journal of Medieval and Early Modern Studies* 31.1 (2001): 113–46.

Cohen, Jeffrey Jerome. *Medieval Identity Machines*. Minneapolis: University of Minnesota Press, 2003.

Cohen, Jeffrey Jerome. *Hybridity, Identity, and Monstrosity in Medieval Britain: On Difficult Middles*. New York: Palgrave Macmillan, 2006.

Cohen, Jeffrey Jerome, ed. *Cultural Diversity in the British Middle Ages: Archipelago, Island, England*. Basingstoke: Palgrave Macmillan, 2008.

Cohen, Jeffrey Jerome. "Race," in *A Handbook of Middle English Studies*, ed. Marion Turner. Malden, MA: Wiley-Blackwell, 2013a, 109–22.

Cohen, Jeffrey Jerome. "The Future of the Jews of York," in *Christians and Jews in Medieval England: Narratives and Contexts for the York 1190 Massacre*, ed. Sarah Rees Jones and Sethina Watson. Suffolk: Boydell and Brewer, 2013b, 278–93.

Cohen, Jeremy. *The Friars and the Jews: The Evolution of Medieval Anti-Judaism*. Ithaca, NY: Cornell University Press, 1982.

Cohen, Jeremy. "The Jews as the Killers of Christ in the Latin Tradition, from Augustine to the Friars." *Traditio* 39 (1983): 1–27.

Cohen, Jeremy. "The Muslim Connection or On the Changing Role of the Jew in High Medieval Theology," in *From Witness to Witchcraft: Jews and Judaism in Medieval Christian Thought*, ed. Jeremy Cohen. Wiesbaden: Harrassowitz, 1996, 141–62.

Cohen, Jeremy. *Living Letters of the Law: Ideas of the Jew in Medieval Christianity.* Berkeley: University of California Press, 1999.

Cohen, Jeremy. *Christ Killers: The Jews and the Passion from the Bible to the Big Screen.* Oxford: Oxford University Press, 2007.

Coles, Kimberly Anne, Ralph Bauer, Zita Nunes, and Carla L. Peterson, eds. *The Cultural Politics of Blood, 1500–1900.* New York: Palgrave Macmillan, 2015.

Corpus Juris Canonici. Rome, 1582. http://digital.library.ucla.edu/canonlaw/index.html.

Courtès, Jean Marie. "The Theme of 'Ethiopia' and 'Ethiopians' in Patristic Literature," in *The Image of the Black in Western Art*, vol. 2, part 1, ed. David Bindman, Henry Louis Gates, Jr., and Karen C. C. Dalton. Cambridge, MA: Belknap Press of Harvard University Press, in collaboration with the W. E. B. Du Bois Institute for African and African American Research; Houston: Menil Collection, 2010–, 199–214.

Cross, F. L., and Elizabeth A. Livingstone. *The Oxford Dictionary of the Christian Church.* Oxford: Oxford University Press, 2005.

Cuffel, Alexandra. *Gendering Disgust in Medieval Religious Polemic.* Notre Dame, IN: University of Notre Dame Press, 2007.

Cutler, Allan H., and Helen E. Cutler. *The Jew as Ally of the Muslim: Medieval Roots of Anti-Semitism.* Notre Dame, IN: University of Notre Dame Press, 1986.

Czerwinski, Francis Richard. "The Teachings of the Twelfth and Thirteenth Century Canonists about the Jews." PhD diss., Cornell University, 1972.

Dagenais, John, and Margaret R. Greer, eds. "Decolonizing the Middle Ages," Special Issue, *Journal of Medieval and Early Modern Studies* 30.3 (2000).

Daniélou, Jean. *Sacramentum futuri; études sur les origines de la typologie biblique.* Paris: Beauchesne, 1950.

Davenport, Frances G., and Charles Oscar Paullin, eds. *European Treaties Bearing on the History of the United States and Its Dependencies*, 4 vols. Washington, DC: Carnegie Institution of Washington, 1917–37.

Davies, William. *A true relation of the travailes and most miserable captiuitie of William Dauies.* London: 1614. *Early English Books Online.* http://gateway.proquest.com/openurl?ctx_ver=Z39.88-2003&res_id=xri:eebo&rft_id=xri:eebo:citation:99845034.

Davies, W. D. *Paul and Rabbinic Judaism: Some Rabbinic Elements in Pauline Theology.* London: Society for Promoting Christian Knowledge, 1955.

Davis, David Brion. *The Problem of Slavery in Western Culture.* Ithaca, NY: Cornell University Press, 1966.

Davis, David Brion. *Slavery and Human Progress.* New York: Oxford University Press, 1984.

Davis, David Brion. "Constructing Race: A Reflection." *William and Mary Quarterly* 54.1 (1997): 7–18.

Davis, Stacy Nicole. *This Strange Story: Jewish and Christian Interpretation of the Curse of Canaan from Antiquity to 1865.* Lanham, MD: University Press of America, 2008.

Day, Richard. *Christian prayers and meditations in English French, Italian, Spanish, Greeke, and Latine*. London, 1569. *Early English Books Online*. http://gateway.proquest.com/openurl?ctx_ver=Z39.88-2003&res_id=xri:eebo&rft_id=xri:eebo:image:5495:15.

Devisse, Jean. "Christian and Black," in *The Image of the Black in Western Art*, ed. David Bindman, Henry Louis Gates, Jr., and Karen C. C. Dalton, vol. 2, part 1. Cambridge, MA: Belknap Press of Harvard University Press, in collaboration with the W. E. B. Du Bois Institute for African and African American Research; Houston: Menil Collection, 2010a, 31–72.

Devisse, Jean. "The Black and His Color: From Symbols to Realities," in *The Image of the Black in Western Art*, ed. David Bindman, Henry Louis Gates, Jr., and Karen C. C. Dalton, vol. 2, part 1. Cambridge, MA: Belknap Press of Harvard University Press, in collaboration with the W. E. B. Du Bois Institute for African and African American Research; Houston: Menil Collection, 2010b, 73–137.

de Weever, Jacqueline. *Sheba's Daughters: Whitening and Demonizing the Saracen Woman in Medieval French Epic*. New York: Garland Publishing, 1998.

Du Cange, Charles, Henschel Du Fresne, G. A. Louis, P. Carpentier, Johann Christoph Adelung, and Léopold Favre. *Glossarium Mediae Et Infimae Latinitatis*. Niort: L. Favre, 1883.

Dyer, Joseph. "The Psalms in Monastic Prayer," in *The Place of the Psalms in the Intellectual Culture of the Middle Ages*, ed. Nancy Van Deusen. Albany: State University of New York, 1999, 59–90.

Dyson, R. W., ed. *Aquinas: Political Writings*. Cambridge: Cambridge University Press, 2002. http://proxy.library.georgetown.edu/login?url=http://search.ebsco-host.com/login.aspx?direct=true&AuthType=ip,uid&db=eooxna&AN=112334&site=ehost-live&scope=site.

Eliav-Feldon, Miriam, Benjamin H. Issac, and Joseph Ziegler, eds. *The Origins of Racism in the West*. Cambridge: Cambridge University Press, 2009.

Elukin, Jonathan. "The Eternal Jew in Medieval Europe: Christian Perceptions of Jewish Anachronism and Racial Identity." PhD diss., Princeton University, 1994.

Elukin, Jonathan. "The Discovery of the Self: Jews and Conversion in the Twelfth Century," in *Varieties of Religious Conversion in the Middle Ages*, ed. James Muldoon. Gainesville: University Press of Florida, 1997, 63–76.

Elukin, Jonathan. "From Jew to Christian? Conversion and Immutability in Medieval Europe," in *Jews and Christians in Twelfth-Century Europe*, ed. Michael A. Signer and J. H. Van Engen. Notre Dame, IN: University of Notre Dame Press, 2001, 171–89.

Emerson, Oliver F. "Legends of Cain, Especially in Old and Middle English." *PMLA*, 21.4 (1906): 831–929.

Encyclopaedia Judaica Online, 22 vols. Ed. Michael Berenbaum and Fred Skolnik. 2nd ed. Detroit: Macmillan Reference, 2007. *Gale Virtual Reference Library*, http://link.galegroup.com/apps/pub/9780028660974/GVRL?u=wash43584&sid=GVRL.

Epstein, Steven A. *Purity Lost: Transgressing Boundaries in the Eastern Mediterranean: 1000–1400.* Baltimore: Johns Hopkins University Press, 2006.

Erickson, Peter, and Kim F. Hall. "'A New Scholarly Song': Rereading Early Modern Race." *Shakespeare Quarterly* 67.1 (2016): 1–13.

Evans, William McKee. "From the Land of Canaan to the Land of Guinea: The Strange Odyssey of the 'Sons of Ham.'" *American Historical Review* 85.1 (1980): 15–43.

Feerick, Jean. *Strangers in Blood: Relocating Race in the Renaissance.* Toronto: University of Toronto Press, 2010.

Floyd-Wilson, Mary. *English Ethnicity and Race in Early Modern Drama.* Cambridge: Cambridge University Press, 2003.

Folliet, Georges. "'Iudaei tamquam capsarii nostri sunt' Augustin, Enarratio in Ps. 40,14." *Augustiniantum* 44 (2004): 443–67.

Forsythe, Gary. *A Critical History of Early Rome: From Prehistory to the First Punic War.* Berkeley: University of California Press, 2005.

Frakes, Jerold C., ed. *Contextualizing the Muslim Other in Medieval Christian Discourse* New York: Palgrave Macmillan, 2011.

Frassetto, Michael. "Historiarum libri quinque," in *Christian–Muslim Relations 600–1500,* ed. David Thomas, Barbara Roggema, Sala J. P. Monferrer, and John Chesworth. Leiden: Brill, 2009a. http://dx.doi.org/10.1163/1877-8054_cmri_COM_23194.

Frassetto, Michael. "Sermons," in *Christian–Muslim Relations 600–1500,* ed. David Thomas, Barbara Roggema, Sala J. P. Monferrer, and John Chesworth. Leiden: Brill, 2009b. http://dx.doi.org/10.1163/1877-8054_cmri_COM_23192.

Fredrickson, George M. *Racism: A Short History.* Princeton, NJ: Princeton University Press, 2002.

Fredriksen, Paula. *Augustine and the Jews: A Christian Defense of Jews and Judaism.* New Haven, CT: Yale University Press, 2010. http://ebookcentral.proquest.com/lib/georgetown/detail.action?docID=3420730.

Fredricksen, Paula. "Anti-Judaism and Early Christianity: Paula Fredriksen on David Nirenberg's *Anti-Judaism: The Western Tradition.*" *Marginalia Review of Books.* December 9, 2013. http://marinalia.lareviewofbooks.org/anti-judaism-and-early-christianity/.

Fredricksen, Paula. "How Later Contexts Affect Pauline Content, or: Retrospect is the Mother of Anachronism," in *Jews and Christians in the First and Second Centuries: How to Write Their History,* ed. Peter J. Tomson and Joshua Schwartz. Leiden: Brill, 2014, 17–51.

Freedman, Paul. *Images of the Medieval Peasant.* Redwood City, CA: Stanford University Press, 1999.

Freidenreich, David M. "Muslims in Canon Law, 650–1000," in *Christian–Muslim Relations: A Bibliographical History, Volume 1 (600–900),* ed. David Thomas, Barbara Roggema, Sala J. P. Monferrer, and John Chesworth. Leiden: Brill, 2009, 83–98. http://referenceworks.brillonline.com/browse/christian-muslim-relations-i

Freidenreich, David M. "Muslims in Western Canon Law, 1000–1500," in *Christian–Muslim Relations: A Bibliographical History, Volume 3 (1050–1200)*, ed. David Thomas, Barbara Roggema, Sala J. P. Monferrer, and John Chesworth. Leiden: Brill, 2011, 41–68. http://referenceworks.brillonline.com/browse/christian-muslim-relations-i

Freidenreich, David M. "Jews, Pagans, and Heretics in Early Medieval Canon Law," in *Jews in Early Christian Law: Byzantium and the Latin West, 6th–11th Centuries*, ed. John V. Tolan, N. R. M. De Lange, Laurence Foschia, and Capucine Nemo-Pekelman. Turnhout, Belgium: Brepols, 2014, 73–91.

Freinkel, Lisa. *Reading Shakespeare's Will: The Theology of Figure from Augustine to the Sonnets*. New York: Columbia University Press, 2002.

Freyne, Sean. "Vilifying the Other and Defining the Self: Matthew's and John's Anti-Jewish Polemic in Focus," in *"To See Ourselves as Others See Us": Christians, Jews, and "Others" in Late Antiquity*, ed. Jacob Neusner, Ernest S. Frerichs, and Caroline McCracken-Flesher. Chico, CA: Scholars Press, 1985, 118–43.

Friedman, Jerome. "Jewish Conversion, the Spanish Pure Blood Laws and Reformation: A Revisionist View of Racial and Religious Antisemitism." *Sixteenth Century Journal* 18.1 (1987): 3–29.

Friedman, John Block. *The Monstrous Races in Medieval Art and Thought*. Cambridge, MA: Harvard University Press, 1981.

Frojmovic, Eva, and Catherine E. Karkov, eds. *Postcolonising the Medieval Image*. New York: Routledge, 2017.

Fuchs, Barbara. "Conquering Islands: Contextualizing The Tempest." *Shakespeare Quarterly* 48.1 (1997): 45–62. www.jstor.org/stable/2871400.

Fulton, Rachel. *From Judgment to Passion: Devotion to Christ and the Virgin Mary, 800–1200*. New York: Columbia University Press, 2002.

Gager, John G. *Reinventing Paul*. Oxford: Oxford University Press, 2000.

Gager, John G. *Who Made Early Christianity?: The Jewish Lives of the Apostle Paul*. New York: Columbia University Press, 2015.

García y García, Antonio. *Constitutiones Concilii Quarti Lateranensis Una Cum Commentariis Glossatorum. Monumenta iuris canonici. Series A., Corpus glossatorum*, v. 2 Città del Vaticano: Biblioteca apostolica vaticana, 1981.

Garnsey, Peter. *Ideas of Slavery from Aristotle to Augustine*. Cambridge: Cambridge University Press, 1996.

Genesis et Exodus cum glossa ordinaria. Bavarian State Library MS 14132. http://daten.digitale-sammlungen.de/~db/0003/bsb00034372/images/index.html.

Getz, Faye Marie, ed. *Healing and Society in Medieval England: A Middle English Translation of the Pharmaceutical Writings of Gilbertus Anglicus*. Madison: University of Wisconsin Press, 1991.

Gilles, Henri. "Législation et doctrine canoniques sur les Sarrasins," in *Islam et chrétiens du Midi (XIIe–XIVe s.). Cahiers de Fanjeaux*, 18. Toulouse: E. Privât, 1983, 195–213.

Gilman, Sander L. *Jewish Self-Hatred: Anti-Semitism and the Hidden Language of the Jews*. Baltimore: Johns Hopkins University Press, 1986.

Gilman, Sander L. *The Jew's Body*. New York: Routledge, 1991.

Glancy, Jennifer A. *Slavery in Early Christianity*. Oxford: Oxford University Press, 2002.

Goering, Joseph. "The Internal Forum and the Literature of Penance and Confession," in *The History of Medieval Canon Law in the Classical Period, 1140–1234: From Gratian to the Decretals of Pope Gregory IX*, ed. Wilfried Hartmann and Kenneth Pennington. Washington, DC: Catholic University of America Press, 2008, 379–428.

Goldenberg, David M. "The Development of the Idea of Race: Classical Paradigms and Medieval Elaborations." *International Journal of the Classical Tradition* 5.4 (1999): 561–70. www.jstor.org/stable/30222480.

Goldenberg, David M. *The Curse of Ham: Race and Slavery in Early Judaism, Christianity, and Islam*. Princeton, NJ: Princeton University Press, 2003.

Goldenberg, David M. "Racism, Color Symbolism, and Color Prejudice," in *The Origins of Racism in the West*, ed. Miraim Eliav-Feldon, Benjamin H. Isaac, and Joseph Ziegler. Cambridge: Cambridge University Press, 2009, 88–108.

Graetz, Heinrich, *History of the Jews*. 6 vols. Philadelphia: Jewish Publication Society of America, 1891–98.

Grayzel, Solomon. *The Church and the Jews in the XIIIth Century*. Volume 1. New York: Hermon Press, 1966.

Grayzel, Solomon, and Kenneth R Stow. *The Church and the Jews in the XIIIth Century*. Volume 2. New York: Jewish Theological Seminary in America; Detroit: Wayne State University Press, 1989.

Green, Monica H. "Bodily Essences: Bodies as Categories of Difference," in *A Cultural History of the Human Body in the Middle Ages*, ed. Linda Kalof. Vol. 2. Oxford: Berg, 2010, 141–62, notes, 248–51.

Gregory I. *Moralia in Iob*. *Library of Latin Texts. Series A*. http://clt.brepolis.net/LLTA/pages/TextSearch.aspx?key=QGREG1708.

Guibbory, Achsah. *Christian Identity, Jews, and Israel in Seventeenth-Century England*. Oxford: Oxford University Press, 2010.

Hahn, Thomas. "The Difference the Middle Ages Makes: Color and Race before the Modern World." *Journal of Medieval and Early Modern Studies* 31.1 (2001): 1–37.

Hall, Kim F. *Things of Darkness: Economies of Race and Gender in Early Modern England*. Ithaca, NY: Cornell University Press, 1995.

Hall, Kim F., ed. *Othello, the Moor of Venice: Texts and Contexts*. Boston: Bedford/St. Martin's, 2007.

Hannaford, Ivan. *Race: The History of an Idea in the West*. Washington, DC: Woodrow Wilson Center Press; Baltimore: Johns Hopkins University Press, 1996.

Harrison, Peter. *Religion and the Religions in the English Enlightenment*. Cambridge: Cambridge University Press, 1990.

Harrison-Kahan, Lori. *The White Negress: Literature, Minstrelsy, and the Black-Jewish Imaginary*. New Brunswick, NJ: Rutgers University Press, 2011.

Havercamp, Alfred. "Baptised Jews in German Lands during the Twelfth Century," in *Jews and Christians in Twelfth-Century Europe*, ed. Michael A. Signer and J. H. Van Engen. Notre Dame, IN: University of Notre Dame Press, 2001, 255–310.

Haynes, Stephen R. *Noah's Curse: The Biblical Justification of American Slavery*. Oxford: Oxford University Press, 2002.

Hearn, M. F. *Romanesque Sculpture: The Revival of Monumental Stone Sculpture in the Eleventh and Twelfth Centuries*. Ithaca, NY: Cornell University Press, 1981.

Hendricks, Margo, and Patricia A. Parker, eds. *Women, "Race," and Writing in the Early Modern Period*. New York: Routledge, 1994.

Heng, Geraldine. *Empire of Magic: Medieval Romance and the Politics of Cultural Fantasy*. New York: Columbia University Press, 2003.

Heng, Geraldine. "Jews, Saracens, Black Men, Tartars: England in a World of Difference," in *A Companion to English Literature and Culture c. 1350–c. 1500*, ed. Peter Brown. Oxford: Wiley-Blackwell, 2007, 247–69.

Heng, Geraldine. "The Invention of Race in the European Middle Ages I: Race Studies, Modernity, and the Middle Ages." *Literature Compass* 8.5 (2011a): 258–74.

Heng, Geraldine. "The Invention of Race in the European Middle Ages II: Locations of Medieval Race." *Literature Compass* 8.5 (2011b): 275–93.

Heng, Geraldine. "Reinventing Race, Colonizations, and Globalisms Across Deep Time: Lessons from the *Longue Durée*." *PMLA* 130.2 (2015a): 358–66.

Heng, Geraldine. "An African Saint in Medieval Europe: The Black Saint Maurice and the Enigma of Racial Sanctity," in *Sainthood and Race: Marked Flesh, Holy Flesh*, ed. Molly H. Bassett and Vincent W. Lloyd. New York: Routledge, 2015b, 18–44.

Heng, Geraldine. *The Invention of Race in the European Middle Ages*. Cambridge: Cambridge University Press, 2018.

Henry, Avril, ed. *The Mirour of Mans Saluacioun[e]: A Middle English Translation of Speculum Humanae Salvationis*. Aldershot: Scolar, 1986.

Herde, Peter. "Christians and Saracens at the Time of the Crusades: Some Comments of Contemporary Medieval Canonists." *Studia Gratiana* 12 (1967): 361–76.

Hess, Andre. *The Forgotten Frontier: A History of the Sixteenth Century Ibero–African Frontier* Chicago: University of Chicago Press, 1978.

Hezser, Catherine. "Slavery and the Jews," in *The Cambridge World History of Slavery*, ed. by Keith Bradley and Paul Cartledge, Vol. 1. Cambridge: Cambridge University Press, 2011, 438–55.

Higden, Ranulf. *Prolicionycion [sic]*. Westminster: 1482. *Early English Books Online*. http://gateway.proquest.com/openurl?ctx_ver=Z39.88-2003&res_id=xri: eebo&rft_id=xri:eebo:citation:99842300.

Hill, Christopher. *Antichrist in Seventeenth-Century England*. New York: Oxford University Press, 1971.

Hippocrates. *Hippocrates*, transl. W. H. S. Jones, 6 vols. Cambridge, MA: Harvard University Press, 1959–1967.

Hirschman, Charles. "The Origins and Demise of the Concept of Race." *Population and Development Review* 30.2 (2004): 385–421.

Holladay, William L. *The Psalms through Three Thousand Years*. Minneapolis: Fortress Press, 1993.

The Holy Bible, translated from the Latin Vulgate. [Douay Rheims]. Turnhout, Belgium: Brepols; New York: Wildermann, 1938.

The Holy Scriptures, ed. Harold Fisch. Jerusalem: Koren Publishers, 1992.

Hostiensis (Henry of Susa). *Summa Aurea*. Venice: 1574. *The Medieval Canon Law Virtual Library*, http://web.colby.edu/canonlaw/tag/gregory-ix/.

Hourihane, Colum. *Pontius Pilate, Anti-Semitism, and the Passion in Medieval Art*. Princeton, NJ: Princeton University Press, 2009.

Hunter, G. K. "Othello and Colour Prejudice." *Proceedings of the British Academy* 53 (1968): 139–63.

Iogna-Prat, Dominique. *Order & Exclusion: Cluny and Christendom Face Heresy, Judaism, and Islam (1000–1150)*. Ithaca, NY: Cornell University Press, 2002.

Isaac, Benjamin H. *The Invention of Racism in Classical Antiquity*. Princeton, NJ: Princeton University Press, 2004.

Isidore of Seville. *Allegoriae Quaedam Sacrae Scripturae Ex Veteri Testamento*. *Patrologia Latina Online*. Vol. 83. http://gateway.proquest.com/openurl?url_ver=Z39.88-2004&res_dat=xri:pld-us&rft_dat=xri:pld:ft:all:Z300017102.

Isidore of Seville. *Etymologiarum*. *Patrologia Latina Online*. Vol. 82. http://gateway.proquest.com/openurl?url_ver=Z39.88-2004&res_dat=xri:pld-us&rft_dat=xri:pld:ft:all:Z500018503.

Isidore of Seville. *Etymologies*, ed. Stephen A. Barney, Jennifer A. Beach, and Oliver Berghof. New York: Cambridge University Press, 2006.

Isidore of Seville. *Mysticorum Expositiones Sacramentorum Seu Quaestiones In Vetus Testamentum*. *Patrologia Latina Online*. Vol. 83. http://gateway.proquest.com/openurl?url_ver=Z39.88-2004&res_dat=xri:pld-us&rft_dat=xri:pld:ft:all:Z300017310.

Isidore of Seville. *Sententiae*. *Library of Latin Texts*. Series A. http://clt.brepolis.net/LLTA/pages/TextSearch.aspx?key=QISIDSENT.

Iyengar, Sujata. *Shades of Difference: Mythologies of Skin Color in Early Modern England*. Philadelphia: University of Pennsylvania Press, 2005.

Jacques de Vitry, *The History of Jerusalem. A.D. 1180*, transl. Aubrey Stewart. *Palestine Pilgrims' Text Society* 11.2 (1896).

Jacques de Vitry. *The Historia Occidentalis of Jacques de Vitry. A Critical Edition*, ed. John Frederick Hinnebusch. Fribourg: The University Press, 1972.

Jacques de Vitry. *Histoire orientale (Historia orientalis)*, ed. and transl. Jean Donnadieu. Turhout, Belgium: Brepols, 2008.

Jacques de Vitry. *Vita Marie de Oegnies / Iacobus de Vitriaco. Supplementum / Thomas Cantipratensis*, ed. R. B. C. Huygens. Turnhout, Belgium: Brepols, 2012.

James, Montague R. "Pictor in Carmine," in *Archaeologia or Miscellaneous Tracts Relating to Antiquity*. London: Society of Antiquaries, 1951, 141–66.

Jennings, Willie J. *The Christian Imagination: Theology and the Origins of Race*. New Haven, CT: Yale University Press, 2010.

Jerome, Saint. *Commentariorum in epistolam ad Galatas. Patrologia Latina Online*. vol. 26. http://gateway.proquest.com/openurl?url_ver=Z39.88-2004&res_dat=xri:pld-us&rft_dat=xri:pld:ft:all:Z300067326.

Jerome, Saint. *Commentariorum in Ezechielem Prophetam Libri Quatuordecim. Patrologia Latina Online*. Vol. 25. http://gateway.proquest.com.proxy.library.georgetown.edu/openurl?url_ver=Z39.88-2004&res_dat=xri:pld-us&rft_dat=xri:pld:ft:all:Z400067606.

Jerome, Saint. *Epistola XXXVI. Seu rescriptum Hieronymi ad Damasum, Patrilogia Latina Online*. Vol. 22. http://gateway.proquest.com/openurl?url_ver=Z39.88-2004&res_dat=xri:pld-us&rft_dat=xri:pld:ft:all:Z500069382.

Jerome, Saint. *The Dialogue against the Luciferians*, in *Nicene and Post-Nicene Fathers: Second Series*. Vol. 6, ed. Philip Schaff and Henry Wace. Peabody, MA: Hendrickson Publishers, 1994, 319–334.

Jerome, Saint, *Commentary on Galatians*. transl. Andrew Cain. Washington, DC: Catholic University of America Press, 2010.

Jestice, Phyllis. "A Great Jewish Conspiracy? Worsening Jewish–Christian Relations and the Destruction of the Holy Sepulcher," in *Christian Attitudes Toward the Jews in the Middle Age: A Casebook*, ed. Michael Frassetto. New York: Routledge, 2007, 25–42.

John of Imola (Ioannes De Imola). *Super Clementinis . . . Co[m]mentaria*. Lyon, 1525. http://catalog.hathitrust.org/Record/011359840.

Johnson, Sylvester A. *The Myth of Ham in Nineteenth-century American Christianity: Race, Heathens, and the People of God*. New York: Palgrave Macmillan, 2004.

Johnson, Willis. "The Myth of Jewish Male Menses." *Journal of Medieval History* 24.3 (1998): 273–95.

Johnstone, Nathan. *The Devil and Demonism in Early Modern England*. Cambridge: Cambridge University Press, 2006.

Jordan, W. C. "The Last Tormentor of Christ: An Image of the Jew in Ancient and Medieval Exegesis, Art, and Drama." *Jewish Quarterly Review* 78.1/2 (1987): 21–47.

Jordan, W. C. "Why 'Race'?" *Journal of Medieval and Early Modern Studies* 31.1 (2001): 165–73.

Jordan, Winthrop D. *White over Black: American Attitudes toward the Negro, 1550–1812*. 2nd ed. Chapel Hill: University of North Carolina Press, 2012. https://heinonline.org/HOL/Index?collection=slavery&index=slavery/whiovblak.

Jordão, L. M., and Barreto I. A. da Graça, eds. *Bullarium patronatus Portugalliæ regum in Ecclesiis Africæ, Asiæ atque Oceaniæ*. 3 vols. Lisbon: Typographia Nationali, 1868–1879.

Josephus, Flavius. *Jewish Antiquities*. 9 vols. transl. H. St. J. Thackeray. Loeb Classical Library 242. Cambridge, MA: Harvard University Press, 1930, 2014.

Kalmar, Ivan D, and Derek J. Penslar, eds. *Orientalism and the Jews*. Waltham, MA: Brandeis University Press, 2005.

Kaplan, M. Lindsay, ed. *The Merchant of Venice: Texts and Contexts*. Boston: Bedford/ St. Martin's, 2002.

Kaplan, M. Lindsay. "Jessica's Mother: Medieval Constructions of Jewish Race and Gender in *The Merchant of Venice*." *Shakespeare Quarterly* 58.1 (2007): 1–30.

Kaplan, M. Lindsay. "The Jewish Body in Black and White in Medieval and Early Modern England," in "Image of the Jew in Britain," Special Issue. *Philological Quarterly* 92.1 (2013): 41–65.

Kaplan, M. Lindsay. "'His blood be upon us and upon our children:' Medieval Theology and the Inferior Jewish Body," in *The Cultural Politics of Blood, 1500–1900*, ed. Ralph Bauer, Kim Coles, Zita Nunes, and Carla Peterson. New York: Palgrave Macmillan, 2015, 107–26.

Kaplan, Paul H. D. *The Rise of the Black Magus in Western Art*. Ann Arbor: University of Michigan Research Press, 1985.

Kaplan, Paul H. D. "Introduction to the New Edition," in *The Image of the Black in Western Art*, vol. 2, part 1, ed. David Bindman, Henry Louis Gates, Jr., and Karen C. C. Dalton. Cambridge, MA: Belknap Press of Harvard University Press, in collaboration with the W. E. B. Du Bois Institute for African and African American Research; Houston: Menil Collection, 2010–, 1–30.

Karp, Jonathan. "Ethnic Role Models and Chosen Peoples: Philosemitism in African American Culture," in *Philosemitism in History*, ed. Jonathan Karp and Adam Sutcliffe. New York: Cambridge University Press, 2011.

Kauffmann, C. M. *Romanesque Manuscripts, 1066–1190*. London: H. Miller, 1975.

Kauffmann, C. M. *Biblical Imagery in Medieval England, 700–1550*. London: H. Miller, 2003.

Kaye/Kantrowitz, Melanie. *The Colors of Jews: Racial Politics and Radical Diasporism*. Bloomington: Indiana University Press, 2007.

Kedar, Benjamin. "De Iudeis et Sarracenis: On the Categorization of Muslims in Medieval Canon Law," in *Studia in Honorem Eminentissimi Cardinalis Alphonsi M. Stickler. Studia et textus historiae juris canonici* 7, ed. Alphonso M. Stickler and R. J. Castillo Lara. Rome: LAS, 1992, 207–13.

Keen, Maurice Hugh. *The Laws of War in the Late Middle Ages*. London: Routledge & Kegan Paul, 1965.

Keita, Maghan. "Saracens and Black Knights." *Arthuriana* 16.4 (2006): 65–77.

Keita, Maghan. "Race: What the Bookstore Hid," in *Why the Middle Ages Matter: Medieval Light on Modern Injustice*, ed. Celia Chazelle, Simon Doubleday, Felice Lifshitz, and Amy G. Remensnyder. London: Routledge, 2011a, 130–40.

Keita, Maghan. "Power and Beauty: The Pleasures and Dangers of Blackness in Medieval and Renaissance Representations." Unpublished paper circulated at the George Washington University Medieval and Early Modern Studies Institute, February 11, 2011b. http://www.gwmemsi.com/2011/01.

Kellett, Edward. *Miscellanies of divinitie*. Cambridge, 1635. *Early English Books Online*. http://gateway.proquest.com/openurl?ctx_ver=Z39.88-2003&res_id=xri: eebo&rft_id=xri:eebo:citation:99842271.

Kelly, Kathleen Ann. "'Blue' Indians, Ethiopians, and Saracens in Middle English Narrative Texts." *Parergon* 11.1 (June 1993): 35–52.

Kelsey, George. "The Racist Search for the Self." *Journal of Religious Ethics* 6.2 (1978): 240–56.

Kidd, Colin. *The Forging of Races: Race and Scripture in the Protestant Atlantic World, 1600–2000*. Cambridge: Cambridge University Press, 2006.

Kim, Dorothy. "Reframing Race and Jewish/Christian Relations in the Middle Ages." *transversal* 13.1 (2015): 52–64.

Kinoshita, Sharon. "'Pagans Are Wrong and Christians Are Right': Alterity, Gender, and Nation in the Chanson de Roland." *Journal of Medieval and Early Modern Studies* 31.1 (2001): 79–111.

Kisch, Guido. *The Jews in Medieval Germany; A Study of their Legal and Social Status*. Chicago: University of Chicago Press, 1949.

Klibansky, Raymond, Erwin Panofsky, and Fritz Saxl. *Saturn and Melancholy; Studies in the History of Natural Philosophy, Religion, and Art*. New York: Basic Books, 1964.

Kruger, Steven F. "Medieval Christian (Dis)identifications: Muslims and Jews in Guibert of Nogent." *New Literary History* 28. 2, *Medieval Studies* (Spring 1997): 185–203.

Kruger, Steven F. *The Spectral Jew: Conversion and Embodiment in Medieval Europe*. Minneapolis: University of Minnesota Press, 2006.

Krummel, Miriamne Ara. *Crafting Jewishness in Medieval England: Legally Absent, Virtually Present*. New York: Palgrave Macmillan, 2011.

Kupfer, Marcia, ed. *The Passion Story: From Visual Representation to Social Drama*. University Park: Pennsylvania State University Press, 2008.

Lampe, G. W. H., and K. J. Woollcombe. Essays on Typology. Napierville, IL: A.R. Allenson, 1957.

Lampert, Lisa. "Race, Periodicity, and the (Neo-)Middle Ages." *Modern Language Quarterly* 65.3 (September 2004a): 391–421.

Lampert, Lisa. *Gender and Jewish Difference from Paul to Shakespeare*. Philadelphia: University of Pennsylvania Press, 2004b.

Langmuir, Gavin. *Toward a Definition of Antisemitism*. Berkeley: University of California Press, 1990.

Lavezzo, Kathy. "Complex Identities: Selves and Others," in *The Oxford Handbook of Medieval English Literature*, ed. Elaine Treharne and Greg Walker. Oxford: Oxford University Press, 2010, 434–57.

Lavezzo, Kathy, ed. "Jews in Britain-Medieval to Modern." Special Issue, *Philological Quarterly* 92.1 (2013).

Lavezzo, Kathy. *The Accommodated Jew: English Antisemitism from Bede to Milton*. Ithaca, NY: Cornell University Press, 2016.

Lawn, Brian. *The Salernitan Questions; An Introduction to the History of Medieval and Renaissance Problem Literature*. Oxford: Clarendon Press, 1963.

Lemay, Helen Rodnite. *Women's Secrets: A Translation of Pseudo-Albertus Magnus's De secretis mulierum with Commentaries*. Albany: State University of New York Press, 1992.

Lerer, Seth, ed. *Literary History and the Challenge of Philology: The Legacy of Erich Auerbach*. Redwood City, CA: Stanford University Press, 1996.

Lerner, Michael, and Cornel West. *Jews and Blacks: Let the Healing Begin*. New York: G. P. Putnam's Sons, 1995.

Lester, Julius. *Lovesong: Becoming a Jew*. New York: Arcade Publishing, 1991.

Lewis, Jack P. *A Study of the Interpretation of Noah and the Flood in Jewish and Christian Literature*. Leiden: E.J. Brill, 1968.

Librett, Jeffrey S. *Orientalism and the Figure of the Jew*. New York: Fordham University Press, 2014.

Liere, Frans van. *An Introduction to the Medieval Bible New York*. Cambridge: Cambridge University Press, 2014.

Lieu, Judith. "History and Theology in Christian Views of Judaism," in *The Jews Among Pagans and Christians in the Roman Empire*, ed. Judith Lieu, John North, and Tessa Rajak. London: Routledge, 1992, 79–96.

Linder, Amnon. *The Jews in the Legal Sources of the Early Middle Ages*. Detroit: Wayne State University Press, 1997.

Lipton, Sara. *Images of Intolerance: The Representation of Jews and Judaism in the Bible Moralisée*. Berkeley: University of California Press, 1999.

Lipton, Sara. *Dark Mirror: The Medieval Origins of Anti-Jewish Iconography*. New York: Metropolitan Books/Henry Holt and Company, 2014.

Little, Arthur L. *Shakespeare Jungle Fever: National-Imperial Re-Visions of Race, Rape, and Sacrifice*. Redwood City, CA: Stanford University Press, 2000.

Lobrichon, Guy. "Making Sense of the Bible," in *The Cambridge History of Christianity Volume 3: Early Medieval Christianities, c. 600–c. 1100*, ed. Thomas F. X. Noble and Julia M. H. Smith. Cambridge: Cambridge University Press, 2010, 531–53. https://doi.org/10.1017/CHOL9780521817752.

Lomperis, L. "Medieval Travel Writing and the Question of Race." *Journal of Medieval and Early Modern Studies* 31.1 (2001): 147–64.

Longland, Sabrina. "A Literary Aspect of the Bury St. Edmunds Cross." *Metropolitan Museum Journal* 2 (1969): 45–74.

Loomba, Ania. *Shakespeare, Race, and Colonialism*. Oxford: Oxford University Press, 2002.

Loomba, Ania. "Periodization, Race, and Global Contact." *Journal of Medieval and Early Modern Studies* 37.3 (Fall 2007): 595–620. doi:10.1215/10829636-2007-015.

Loomba, Ania. "Race and the Possibilities of Comparative Critique." *New Literary History* 40.3 (Summer 2009): 501–22.

Loomba, Ania, and Jonathan Burton. *Race in Early Modern England: A Documentary Companion*. New York: Palgrave Macmillan, 2007.

Lubac, Henri de. "'Typologie' et 'Allégorisme,'" *Recherches de Science Religieuse* 34 (1947): 180–226.

Lubac, Henri de. *Exégèse médiéval: Les quatres sens de l'écriture*. 2 vols. Paris: Aubier, 1959.

Lupton, Julia Reinhard. *Afterlives of the Saints: Hagiography, Typology, and Renaissance Literature*. Redwood City, CA: Stanford University Press, 1996.

Luborsky, Ruth S., and Elizabeth M. Ingram. *A Guide to English Illustrated Books, 1536–1603*. Tempe, AZ: Medieval & Renaissance Texts & Studies, 1998.

MacDonald, Joyce G. *Race, Ethnicity, and Power in the Renaissance*. Madison, NJ: Fairleigh Dickinson University Press, 1997.

MacDonald, Joyce G. *Women and Race in Early Modern Texts*. Cambridge: Cambridge University Press, 2002.

Majid, Anouar. *We Are All Moors: Ending Centuries of Crusades against Muslims and Other Minorities*. Minneapolis: University of Minnesota Press, 2009.

Mariscal, George. "The Role of Spain in Contemporary Race Theory." *Arizona Journal of Hispanic Cultural Studies* 2 (1998): 7–23.

Marrow, James H. "*Circumdederunt me canes multi*: Christ's Tormentors in Northern European Art of the Late Middle Ages and Early Renaissance." *Art Bulletin* 59.2 (1977): 167–81.

Marrow, James H. *Passion Iconography in Northern European Art of the Late Middle Ages and Early Renaissance: A Study of the Transformation of Sacred Metaphor into Descriptive Narrative*. Kortrijk: Van Ghemmert, 1979.

Martínez, María E. *Genealogical Fictions: Limpieza De Sangre, Religion, and Gender in Colonial Mexico*. Redwood City, CA: Stanford University Press, 2008.

Martínez, María E., David Nirenberg, and Max-Sebastián Hering Torres. *Race and Blood in the Iberian World*. Zürich, Berlin: LIT Verlag, 2012.

Matar, N. I. *Turks, Moors, and Englishmen in the Age of Discovery*. New York: Columbia University Press, 1999.

Mathisen, Ralph W. "The Citizenship and Legal Status of Jews in Roman Law during Late Antiquity (ca. 300–540 CE)," in *Jews in Early Christian Law: Byzantium and the Latin West, 6th–11th Centuries*, ed. John Tolan, Nicholas de Lange, Laurence Foschia, and Capucine Nemo-Pekelman. Turnhout. Belgium: Brepols, 2014, 35–54.

Maximus, St. *Sermones. Patrologia Latina Online*. Vol. 57. http://gateway.proquest.com/openurl?url_ver=Z39.88-2004&res_dat=xri:pld-us&rft_dat=xri:pld:ft:al l:Z400040744.

Maxwell, John Francis. *Slavery and the Catholic Church: The History of Catholic Teaching Concerning the Moral Legitimacy of the Institution of Slavery*. London: Barry Rose Publishers, in association with the Anti-Slavery Society for the Protection of Human Rights, 1975.

Mayerson, Philip. "Anti-Black Sentiment in the 'Vitae Patrum.'" *Harvard Theological Review* 71.3/4 (1978): 304–11.

McNamer, Sarah. *Affective Meditation and the Invention of Medieval Compassion*. Philadelphia: University of Pennsylvania Press, 2010.

McVaugh, Michael R. "The '*Humidum Radicale*' in Thirteenth-Century Medicine." *Traditio* 30 (1974): 259–83.

Medieval English Dictionary in the *Middle English Compendium* Ann Arbor: University of Michigan, 1998–. http://quod.lib.umich.edu/m/med.

Meerson, Michael, Peter Schafer, and Yaacov Deutsch, eds. *Toledot Yeshu ("The Life Story of Jesus") Revisited*. Tuebingen: Mohr Siebeck, 2011.

Mellinkoff, Ruth. "Cain and the Jews." *Journal of Jewish Art* 6 (1979): 16–38.

Mellinkoff, Ruth. *The Mark of Cain*. Berkeley: University of California Press, 1981.

Mellinkoff, Ruth. "Demonic Winged Headgear." *Viator* 16 (1985): 367–405.

Mellinkoff, Ruth. *Outcasts: Signs of Otherness in Northern European Art of the Late Middle Ages*. 2 vols. Berkeley: University of California Press, 1993.

Michaelis, Beatrice, and Elahe Haschemi Yekani. "Queering Archives of Race and Slavery—Or, on Being Wilfully Untimely and Unhappy," in *Postcoloniality—Decoloniality—Black Critique: Joints and Fissures*, ed. Sabine Broeck and Carsten Junker. Frankfurt am Main: Campus, 2014, 269–83.

Mignolo, Walter D. "Afterword: What Does the Black Legend Have to Do with Race?" in *Rereading the Black Legend*, ed. Margaret R. Greer, Walter D. Mignolo, and Maureen Quilligan. Chicago: University of Chicago Press, 2007.

Milton, John. *Complete Poems and Major Prose*, ed. Merritt Y. Hughes. New York: Odyssey Press, 1975.

Mirrer, Louise. *Women, Jews, and Muslims in the Texts of Reconquest Castile*. Ann Arbor: University of Michigan Press, 1996.

Mittman, Asa S. *Maps and Monsters in Medieval England*. New York: Routledge, 2006.

Monteira Arias, Ines. "Seeking the Origins of Christian Representation of Islam: Anti-Muslim Images in Romanesque Art." *Islamophobia Studies Yearbook Jahrbuch für Islamophobieforschung* 7 (2016): 86–112.

Moore, J. C. *Pope Innocent III (1160/61–1216): To Root Up and to Plant*. Leiden: Brill, 2003.

Morey, James H. "Peter Comestor, Biblical Paraphrase, and the Medieval Popular Bible." *Speculum* 68.1 (1993): 6–35.

Morgan, Nigel J. *Early Gothic Manuscripts*. London: H. Miller, 1982.

Morris, David. "The Servile Mother: Jerusalem as Woman in the Era of the Crusades," in *Remembering the Crusades: Myth, Image, and Identity*, ed. Nicholas Paul and Suzanne Yeager. Baltimore: Johns Hopkins University Press, 2012, 174–194.

Morrow, Kara Ann. "Disputation in Stone: Jews Imagined on the Saint Stephen Portal of Paris Cathedral," in *Beyond the Yellow Badge: Anti-Judaism and Antisemitism in Medieval and Early Modern Visual Culture*, ed. Mitchell B. Merback. Leiden: Brill, 2008, 63–86, 443–53.

Muldoon, James. "'*Extra ecclesiam non est imperium:*' The Canonists and the Legitimacy of Secular Power." *Studia Gratiana* 9 (1966): 551–80.

Muldoon, James. "A Fifteenth-Century Application of the Canonistic Theory of the Just War," in *Proceedings of the Fourth International Congress of Medieval Canon Law, Toronto, 21–25, August, 1972*, ed. Stephan Kuttner. Città del Vaticano: Biblioteca Apostolica Vaticana, 1976, 467–80.

Muldoon, James, ed. *The Expansion of Europe: The First Phase*. Philadelphia: University of Pennsylvania Press, 1977.

Muldoon, James. *Popes, Lawyers, and Infidels: The Church and the Non-Christian World, 1250–1550*. Philadelphia: University of Pennsylvania Press, 1979.

Muldoon, James. *Varieties of Religious Conversion in the Middle Ages*. Gainesville: University Press of Florida, 1997.

Muldoon, James. "Spiritual Freedom—Physical Slavery: The Medieval Church and Slavery." *Ave Maria Law Review* 3.1 (2005): 69–94.

Müller, Wolfgang P. *Criminalization of Abortion in the West: Its Origins in Medieval Law*. Ithaca, NY: Cornell University Press, 2012.

Nadhiri, Aman Y. *Saracens and Franks in the 12th–15th Century European and Near Eastern Literature: Perceptions of Self and Other*. London: Routledge, 2017.

Nirenberg, David. "Love Between Muslim and Jew in Medieval Spain: A Triangular Affair," in *Jews, Muslims, and Christians in and around the Crown of Aragon: Essays in Honour of Professor Elena Lourie*, ed. Harvey J. Hames. Leiden: Brill, 2004, 127–55.

Nirenberg, David. "Was There Race Before Modernity? The Example of 'Jewish' Blood in Late Medieval Spain," in *The Origins of Racism in the West*, ed. Miraim Eliav-Feldon, Benjamin H. Isaac, and Joseph Ziegler. Cambridge: Cambridge University Press, 2009, 232–64.

Nirenberg, David. *Anti-Judaism: The Western Tradition*. New York: Norton, 2013.

Nyquist, Mary. *Arbitrary Rule : Slavery, Tyranny, and the Power of Life and Death*. Chicago: University of Chicago Press, 2013.

Omont, Henri. "Manuscrits illustrés de l'Apocalypse aux IXe et Xe siècles." *Bulletin de la Société française de reproductions de manuscrits á pientures* 6 (1922): 64–93.

Origen. *Peri Archon. Patrologiæ Græcæ Online*. vol. 11. http://phoenix.reltech.org/cgi-bin/Ebind2html/Migne/Gko11.

Oxford Dictionary of National Biography in Association with the British Academy: From the Earliest Times to the Year 2000, ed. H. C. G. Matthew and Brian Harrison. Oxford: Oxford University Press, 2004. http://www.oxforddnb.com/ Abbrev. *DNB*.

Oxford English Dictionary. 2nd ed. prepared by J. A. Simpson and E. S. C. Weiner. Oxford: Oxford University Press, 1989. http://www.oed.com/Abbrev. *OED*.

Pagden, Anthony. "The Peopling of the New World: Ethnos, Race and Empire in the Early-Modern World," in *The Origins of Racism in the West*, ed. Miraim Eliav-Feldon, Benjamin H. Isaac, and Joseph Ziegler. Cambridge: Cambridge University Press, 2009, 292–312.

Pakter, Walter. *Medieval Canon Law and the Jews*. Ebelsbach: Gremler, 1988.

Palmer, Barbara. "The Inhabitants of Hell: Devils," in *The Iconography of Hell*, ed. Clifford Davidson and Thomas H. Seiler. Kalamazoo, MI: Medieval Institute Publications, Western Michigan University, 1992, 20–40.

Parfitt, Tudor. *Black Jews in Africa and the Americas*. Cambridge, MA: Harvard University Press, 2012.

Parker, Elizabeth C., and Charles T. Little. *The Cloisters Cross: Its Art and Meaning*. New York: Metropolitan Museum of Art, 1994.

Pastoureau, Michel. *Black: The History of a Color*. Princeton, NJ: Princeton University Press, 2009.

Patrologia Graeca Online. http://proxy.library.georgetown.edu/login?url=http://purl. org/reltech/Migne.

Patrologia Latina Online. http://proxy.library.georgetown.edu/login?url=http://pld. chadwyck.com/.

Patterson, Orlando. *Slavery and Social Death: A Comparative Study*. Cambridge, MA: Harvard University Press, 1982.

Patton, Pamela Anne. *Art of Estrangement: Redefining Jews in Reconquest Spain* University Park: Pennsylvania State University Press, 2012.

Pelikan, Jaroslav. "Exegesis and Hermeneutics," in *The Reformation of the Bible, the Bible of the Reformation*, ed. Jaroslav Pelikan, Valerie R. Hotchkiss, and David Price. New Haven, CT: Yale University Press, 1996, 23–39.

Peter of Cluny, see Peter the Venerable.

Peter Comestor. *Historia Scholastica*. *Patrologia Latina Online*. Vol. 198. http:// gateway.proquest.com/openurl?url_ver=Z39.88-2004&res_dat=xri:pld-us&rft_ dat=xri:pld:ft:all:Z300091821.

Peter the Venerable. *The Letters of Peter the Venerable*, ed. Giles Constable. 2 vols. Cambridge, MA: Harvard University Press, 1967.

Peter the Venerable, and Irven Resnick. *Against the Inveterate Obduracy of the Jews*. Washington, DC: Catholic University of America Press, 2013. www.jstor.org/ stable/j.ctt3fgnx7.

Peter the Venerable, and Irven Resnick. *Writings Against the Saracens*. Washington, DC: Catholic University of America Press, 2016. www.jstor.org/stable/ j.ctt1d8hbmo.

Petzold, Andreas. "'Of the Significance of Colours': The Iconography of Colour in Romanesque and Early Gothic Book Illumination," in *Image and Belief: Studies in Celebration of the Eightieth Anniversary of the Index of Christian Art*, ed. Colum Hourihane. Princeton, NJ: Princeton University Press, 1999, 125–34.

Phillips, William D. *Slavery from Roman Times to the Early Transatlantic Trade*. Minneapolis: University of Minnesota Press, 1985.

Pinder, Ulrich. *Speculum passionis Domini Nostri Ihesu Christi*. Nuremberg, 1507. https://opacplus.bsb-muenchen.de/metaopac/search?documentid=6353479.

Pinder, Ulrich, and John Fewterer. *The myrrour or glasse of Christes passion*. London, 1534. *Early English Books Online*. http://gateway.proquest.com.proxy.library. georgetown.edu/openurl?ctx_ver=Z39.88-2003&res_id=xri:eebo&rft_id=xri:eebo :citation:99843440.

Poliakov, Leon. *The History of Anti-Semitism*. 3 vols. New York: Vanguard Press, 1965–.

Porten, Bezalel. "Exile, Babylonian," in *Encyclopaedia Judaica*, ed. Michael Berenbaum and Fred Skolnik. Vol. 6. 2nd ed. Detroit: Macmillan Reference, 2007, 608–11. http://link.galegroup.com/apps/doc/CX2587506183/GVRL?u=wash43584&sid =GVRL&xid=8786cd52.

Procopius of Gaza. *Commentarii in Genesin. Patrologia Graeca Online.* Vol. 87a. http:// phoenix.reltech.org/cgi-bin/Ebind2html/Migne/Gk086a.

Pseudo-Aristotle. *Problemata varia anatomica after University of Bologna MS 1165 (2327),* ed. L. R. Lind. Lawrence: University of Kansas Publications, 1968.

Pseudo-Augustine. *S. Augustini Complectens Sermones Supposititios. Classis Prima. De Veteri et Novo Testamento. Patrologia Latina Online.* Vol. 39. http://gateway.pro-quest.com/openurl?url_ver=Z39.88-2004&res_dat=xri:pld-us&rft_dat=xri:pld:ft:all:Z500055443.

Pseudo-Augustine. *S. Augustini Complectens Sermones Supposititios. Classis II. Sermones De Tempore. Patrologia Latina Online.* Vol. 39. http://gateway.proquest.com/openurl?url_ver=Z39.88-2004&res_dat=xri:pld-us&rft_dat=xri:pld:ft:all:Z500055558.

Purchas, Samuel. *Purchas his pilgrims.* London, 1625. *Early English Books Online.* http://gateway.proquest.com/openurl?ctx_ver=Z39.88-2003&res_id=xri:eebo&rft_id=xri:eebo:citation:29.

Rabanus Maurus. *Commentariorum in Genesim. Patrologia Latina Online.* Vol. 107. http://gateway.proquest.com/openurl?url_ver=Z39.88-2004&res_dat=xri:pld-us&rft_dat=xri:pld:ft:all:Z500173592.

Rabanus Maurus. *De universo libri viginti duo. Patrologia Latina Online.* Vol 111. http://gateway.proquest.com/openurl?url_ver=Z39.88-2004&res_dat=xri:pld-us&rft_dat=xri:pld:ft:all:Z400170939.

Raleigh, Sir Walter. *The History of the World.* London, 1614 [i.e., 1617]. *Early English Books Online.* http://gateway.proquest.com/openurl?ctx_ver=Z39.88-2003&res_id=xri:eebo&rft_id=xri:eebo:citation:99848201.

Ramey, Lynn T. *Black Legacies: Race and the European Middle Ages.* Gainesville: University Press of Florida, 2014.

Raymond of Peñafort. *Summa de paenitentia.* Verona, 1744.

Resnick, Irven M. "Medieval Roots of the Myth of Jewish Male Menses." *The Harvard Theological Review* 93. 3 (2000): 241–63.

Resnick, Irven M. *Marks of Distinction: Christian Perceptions of Jews in the High Middle Ages.* Washington, DC: Catholic University of America Press, 2012.

Resnick, Irven M. ed. *A Companion to Albert the Great: Theology, Philosophy, and the Sciences.* Leiden: Brill, 2013a.

Resnick, Irven M. "Race, Anti-Jewish Polemic, Arnulf of Seéz, and the Contested Papal Election of Anaclet II (A.D. 1130)," in *Jews in Medieval Christendom,* ed. Kristine T. Utterback and Merrall L. Price. Leiden: Brill, 2013b, 45–70.

Richard of St. Victor. *Allegoriae in Vetus Testamentum. Patrologia Latina Online.* Vol. 175. http://gateway.proquest.com/openurl?url_ver=Z39.88-2004&res_dat=xri:pld-us&rft_dat=xri:pld:ft:all:Z600113516.

Rist, Rebecca. *Popes and Jews, 1095–1291.* Oxford: Oxford University Press, 2016.

Robbins, Jill. *Prodigal Son/Older Brother: Interpretation and Alterity in Augustine, Petrarch, Kafka, Levinas.* Chicago: University of Chicago Press, 1991.

Robbins, Jill. *Altered Reading: Levinas and Literature*. Chicago: University of Chicago Press, 1999.

Robinson, Henry. *John the Baptist, forerunner of Christ Iesvs: or, A necessity for liberty of conscience*, London?: s.n., 1644. *Early English Books Online*. http://gateway.proquest.com/openurl?ctx_ver=Z39.88-2003&res_id=xri:eebo&rft_id=xri:eebo:citation:11926175.

Rohrbacher, Stefan. "The Charge of Deicide. An Anti-Jewish Motif in Medieval Christian Art." *Journal of Medieval History* 17.4 (December 1991): 297–321.

Root, Deborah. "Speaking Christian: Orthodoxy and Difference in Sixteenth-Century Spain." *Representations* 23 (Summer 1998): 118–34.

Rosner, Fred, and Suessman Munter, transl. and ed. *Treatise on Hemorrhoids. Medical Answers (Responsa)*. Philadelphia: Lippincott, 1969.

Ross, Alexander. *An exposition on the fourteene first chapters of Genesis*. London, 1626. *Early English Books Online*. http://gateway.proquest.com/openurl?ctx_ver=Z39.88-2003&res_id=xri:eebo&rft_id=xri:eebo:citation:99851398.

Ross, Alexander. *Three decads of diuine meditations*. London, 1630. *Early English Books Online*. http://gateway.proquest.com/openurl?ctx_ver=Z39.88-2003&res_id=xri:eebo&rft_id=xri:eebo:citation:99851458.

Roth, Cecil. "Portraits and Caricatures of Medieval English Jews," in *Essays and Portraits in Ango-Jewish History*. Philadelphia: Jewish Publication Society of America, 1962, 22–25.

Rowan, Steven W. "Ulrich Zasius and the Baptism of Jewish Children." *The Sixteenth Century Journal* 6.2 (1975): 3–25.

Rowe, Nina. "Idealization and Subjection at the South Porch of Strasbourg Cathedral," in *Beyond the Yellow Badge: Anti-Judaism and Anti-Semitism in Medieval and Early Modern Visual Culture*, ed. Mitchell Merback. Leiden: Brill, 2008, 179–202.

Rowe, Nina. *The Jew, the Cathedral and the Medieval City: Synagoga and Ecclesia in the Thirteenth Century*. Cambridge: Cambridge University Press, 2011.

Rowe, Nina. "Other." *Studies in Iconography* 33 (2012): 131–144.

Roye, Gui de. *Thus endeth the doctrinal of sapyence the whyche is ryght vtile and prouffytable to alle crysten men*. Westminster, 1489. *Early English Books Online*. http://gateway.proquest.com/openurl?ctx_ver=Z39.88-2003&res_id=xri:eebo&rft_id=xri:eebo:citation:99844823.

Royster, Francesca T. *Becoming Cleopatra: The Shifting Image of an Icon*. New York: Palgrave Macmillan, 2003.

Rubiés, Joan-Pau, ed. *Medieval Ethnographies: European Perceptions of the World Beyond*. Burlington, VT: Ashgate Variorum, 2009.

Rubin, Miri. *Mother of God: A History of the Virgin Mary*. New Haven, CT: Yale University Press, 2009.

Russell, Frederick H. *The Just War in the Middle Ages*. Cambridge: Cambridge University Press, 1975.

Russell, Jeffrey B. *Lucifer, the Devil in the Middle Ages*. Ithaca, NY: Cornell University Press, 1984.

Sanders, E. P. *Paul and Palestinian Judaism: A Comparison of Patterns of Religion.* Philadelphia: Fortress Press, 1977.

Sandoval, Alonso de. *Treatise on Slavery,* ed. Nicole von Germeten. Indianpolis: Hackett Publishing, 2008.

Sandoval, Alonso de. *Un tratado sobre la esclavitud,* ed. Enriqueta Vila Vilar. Madrid: Alianza Universidad, 1987.

Saperstein, Marc. *Moments of Crisis in Jewish–Christian Relations.* London: SCM Press; Philadelphia: Trinity Press International, 1989.

Sapir Abulafia, Anna. *Christian–Jewish Relations, 1000–1300: Jews in the Service of Medieval Christendom.* New York: Pearson Education, 2011.

Sapir Abulafia, Anna, "Notions of Jewish Service in Twelfth- and Thirteenth-Century England," in *Christians and Jews in Angevin England: The York Massacre of 1190, Narratives and Contexts,* ed. Sarah Rees Jones and Sethina Watson. Woodbridge: York Medieval Press; Rochester, NY: Boydell Press, 2013, 204–21.

Sarna, Nahum M., and S. David Sperling. "Hur," in *Encyclopaedia Judaica,* ed. Michael Berenbaum and Fred Skolnik, 2nd ed., Vol. 9. Macmillan Reference USA, 2007, 622–23. *Series,* http://link.galegroup.com/apps/doc/CX2587509323/GVRL?u=w ash43584&sid=GVRL&xid=f9216368.

Saunders, A. C. de C. M. *A Social History of Black Slaves and Freedmen in Portugal, 1441–1555.* Cambridge: Cambridge University Press, 1982.

Scott, Kathleen L. "Four Early Fifteenth-Century English Manuscripts of the Speculum humanae salvationis and a Fourteenth-Century Exemplar," in *Decoration and Illustration in Medieval English Manuscripts, English Manuscript Studies 1100–1700,* ed. A. S. G. Edwards. Vol. 10. London: British Library, 2002, 177–203.

Schorsch, Jonathan. *Jews and Blacks in the Early Modern World.* New York: Cambridge University Press, 2004.

Schorsch, Jonathan. *Swimming the Christian Atlantic: Judeoconversos, Afroiberians and Amerindians in the Seventeenth Century.* Leiden: Brill, 2009.

Scribner, Robert W. *Popular Culture and Popular Movements in Reformation Germany.* London: Hambledon Press, 1987.

Shapiro, James. *Shakespeare and the Jews.* New York: Columbia University Press, 1996.

Shell, Marc. "Marranos (Pigs), or from Coexistence to Toleration." *Critical Inquiry* 17:2 (1991): 306–35.

Shuger, Debora K. *The Renaissance Bible: Scholarship, Sacrifice, and Subjectivity.* Berkeley: University of California Press, 1994.

Simonsohn, Shlomo. *The Apostolic See and the Jews.* 8 vols. Toronto: Pontifical Institute of Mediaeval Studies, 1988–1991.

Siraisi, Nancy G. *Medieval & Early Renaissance Medicine: An Introduction to Knowledge and Practice.* Chicago: University of Chicago Press, 1990.

Smalley, Beryl. *The Study of the Bible in the Middle Ages,* 3rd ed. Oxford: Blackwell, 1983.

Smith, Anna Deavere. *Fires in the Mirror: Crown Heights, Brooklyn, and Other Identities.* New York: Anchor Books/Doubleday, 1993.

Smith, Ian. *Race and Rhetoric in the Renaissance: Barbarian Errors.* New York: Palgrave Macmillan, 2009.

Smith, Lesley. *The Glossa Ordinaria: The Making of a Medieval Bible Commentary.* Leiden: Brill, 2009.

Smith, Sir Thomas. *De republica Anglorum.* London, 1583. *Early English Books Online.* http://gateway.proquest.com/openurl?ctx_ver=Z39.88-2003&res_id=xri: eebo&rft_id=xri:eebo:citation:99852840.

Society of Biblical Literature Greek New Testament. http://sblgnt.com.

Spiller, Elizabeth. *Reading and the History of Race in the Renaissance.* Cambridge: Cambridge University Press, 2011.

Stacey, Robert C. "The Conversion of Jews to Christianity in Thirteenth-Century England." *Speculum* 67.2 (1992): 263–83. www.jstor.org/stable/2864373.

Stacey, Robert C. "Crusades, Martyrdoms and the Jews of Norman England, 1096– 1190," in *Juden und Christen zur Zeit der Kreuzzüge,* ed. Alfred Haverkamp. Sigmaringen: Jan Thorbecke Verlag, 1999, 233–51.

Stepan, Nancy Leys. "Race and Gender: The Role of Analogy in Science," in *Anatomy of Racism,* ed. David T. Goldberg. Minneapolis: University of Minnesota Press, 1990, 38–57.

Stoler, Ann Laura. "Racial Histories and their Regimes of Truth." *Political Power and Social Theory* 11 (1997): 183–206.

Stow, Kenneth R. *Catholic Thought and Papal Jewry Policy, 1555–1593.* New York: Jewish Theological Seminary of America, 1977.

Strickland, Debra Higgs. *Saracens, Demons, and Jews: Making Monsters in Medieval Art.* Princeton, NJ: Princeton University Press, 2003.

Strickland, Debra Higgs. "Monstrosity and Race in the Late Middle Ages," in *The Ashgate Research Companion to Monsters and the Monstrous,* ed. Asa Simon Mittman with Peter J. Dendle. Burlington, VT: Ashgate, 2012, 365–86.

Strickland, Debra Higgs. "Meanings of Muhammad in Later Medieval Art," in *The Image of the Prophet between Ideal and Ideology,* ed. Christiane Gruber and Avinoam Shalem. Berlin: De Gruyter, 2014, 126–38.

Stroll, Mary. *The Jewish Pope: Ideology and Politics in the Papal Schism of 1130.* Leiden: Brill, 1987.

Sweet, James H. "The Iberian Roots of American Racist Thought." *William and Mary Quarterly* 54.1 (1997): 143–66.

Synan, Edward A. *The Popes and the Jews in the Middle Ages.* New York, Macmillan, 1965.

Tal, Uriel. "Religious and Anti-Religious Roots of Modern Anti-Semitism." Leo Baeck Memorial Lecture. New York: Leo Baeck Institute, 1971.

Tartakoff, Paola. *Between Christian and Jew: Conversion and Inquisition in the Crown of Aragon, 1250–1391.* Philadelphia: University of Pennsylvania Press, 2012.

Thiessen, Matthew. *Paul and the Gentile Problem*. New York: Oxford University Press, 2016.

Thomas of Monmouth. *The Life And Miracles of St. William of Norwich*, ed. Augustus Jessopp and Montague Rhodes James. Cambridge: Cambridge University Press, 1896.

Thomas, James M. "The Racial Formation of Medieval Jews: A Challenge to the Field." *Ethnic and Racial Studies* 30.10 (2010): 1737–55.

Thompson, Ayanna, ed. *Colorblind Shakespeare: New Perspectives on Race and Performance*. London: Routledge, 2006.

Thompson, Ayanna, ed. *Performing Race and Torture on the Early Modern Stage*. London: Routledge, 2008.

Thorndike, Lynn. *Michael Scot*. London: Nelson, 1965.

Tolan, John V. *Saracens: Islam in the Medieval European Imagination*. New York: Columbia University Press, 2002.

Tolan, John V. "Jacques de Vitry," in *Christian–Muslim Relations 600–1500*, ed. David Thomas. 2010. http://dx.doi.org/10.1163/1877-8054_cmri_COM_24582.

Tolan, John V. "'A wild man, whose hand will be against all': Saracens and Ishmaelites in Latin Ethnological Traditions from Jerome to Bede," in *Visions of Community in the Post-Roman World: The West, Byzantium and the Islamic World, 300–1100*, ed. Walter Pohl, Clemens Gantner, and Richard E. Payne. Farnham, UK: Ashgate, 2012a.

Tolan, John V. "Of Milk and Blood: Innocent III and the Jews, revisited." 2012b. https://hal.archives-ouvertes.fr/hal-00726485.

Tolan, John V. "The Legal Status of the Jews and Muslims in the Christian States," in *A History of Jewish–Muslim Relations: From the Origins to the Present Day*, ed. Abselwahab Meddeb and Benjamin Stora. Princeton, NJ: Princeton University Press, 2013, 145–50.

Tolan, John V. "The First Imposition of a Badge on European Jews: The English Royal Mandate of 1218," in *The Character of Christian–Muslim Encounter: Essays in Honour of David Thomas*, ed. Douglas Pratt, Jon Hoover, John Davies, and John Chesworth. Leiden: Brill, 2015a, 145–66.

Tolan, John V. "Jews and Muslims in Christian Law and History," in *The Oxford Handbook of Abrahamic Religions*, ed. Adam J. Silverstein, Guy G. Stroumsa, and Moshe Blidstein. Oxford: Oxford University Press, 2015b, 166–88.

Trachtenberg, Joshua. *The Devil and the Jews: The Medieval Conception of the Jew and its Relation to Modern Antisemitism*. 2nd ed. Philadelphia: Jewish Publication Society, 1983.

Trubowitz, Rachel. "The People of Asia and With Them the Jews: Israel, Asia, and England in Milton's Writings," in *Milton and the Jews*, ed. Douglas A. Brooks. Cambridge: Cambridge University Press, 2008, 151–77.

Unterseher, Lisa. *The Mark of Cain and the Jews: Augustine's Theology of Jews and Judaism*. Piscataway, NJ: Gorgias Press, 2009.

Verkerk, D. H. "Black Servant, Black Demon: Color Ideology in the Ashburnham Pentateuch." *Journal of Medieval and Early Modern Studies* 31.1 (2001): 57–77.

Vincent of Lérins. *The Commonitorium of Vincentius of Lerins*, ed. Reginald Stewart Moxon. Cambridge: Cambridge University Press, 1915.

Vincent, Nicholas. "Two Papal Letters on the Wearing of the Jewish Badge, 1221 and 1229." *Jewish Historical Studies* 34 (1994): 209–24.

Washington, Joseph R. *Anti-blackness in English Religion, 1500–1800*. New York: E. Mellen Press, 1984.

Watt, John. "The Jews, the Law, and the Church: The Concept of Jewish Serfdom in Thirteenth-Century England," in *The Church and Sovereignty c. 590–1918: Essays in Honour of Michael Wilks*, ed. Diana Wood. Oxford: Blackwell, 1991, 153–72.

Watt, John. "Jews and Christians in the Gregorian Decretals," in *Christianity and Judaism: Papers Read at the 1991 Summer Meeting and the 1992 Winter Meeting of the Ecclesiastical History Society*, ed. Diana Wood. Cambridge, MA: Published for the Ecclesiastical History Society by Blackwell Publishers, 1992, 93–105.

Whitaker, Cord. "Race and Conversion in Late Medieval England." PhD diss., Duke University, 2009.

Whitaker, Cord. "Black Metaphors in the King of Tars." *Journal of English and Germanic Philology* 112.2 (2013): 169–93.

Whitaker, Cord, ed. "Making Race Matter in the Middle Ages." Special Issue. *postmedieval* 6.1 (2015).

Whitford, David M. *The Curse of Ham in the Early Modern Era: The Bible and the Justifications for Slavery*. Farnham, England: Ashgate, 2009.

Wiedemann, Thomas E. J., ed. *Greek and Roman Slavery*. London: Routledge, 1988.

Wilson, Adrian, and Joyce Lancaster Wilson. *A Medieval Mirror*. Berkeley: University of California Press, 1984. http://ark.cdlib.org/ark:/13030/ft7v19p1w6/.

William of Auvergne. *Opera omnia*. Paris, 1674 Facsimile. Frankfurt am Main: Minerva, 1963.

Winroth, Anders. *The Making of Gratian's Decretum*. Cambridge: Cambridge University Press, 2000.

Wither, George. *The Psalmes of David translated into lyrick-verse, according to the scope, of the original*. [Amsterdam?], 1632. *Early English Books Online*. http://gateway.proquest.com/openurl?ctx_ver=Z39.88-2003&res_id=xri:eebo&rft_id=xri:eebo:citation:99838122.

Yerushalmi Y. H. "Assimilation and Racial Anti-Semitism: The Iberian and German Models." Leo Baeck Memorial Lecture. New York: Leo Baeck Institute, 1982.

Young, Frances. *Biblical Exegesis and the Formation of Christian Culture*. Cambridge: Cambridge University Press, 1997.

Zabarellae, Francesco. *In Clementinarum Volumen Commentaria. Hac in editione . . . ab innumeris erroris repurgata*. Venice, 1602.

Zacour, Norman P. *Jews and Saracens in the Consilia of Oldradus de Ponte*. Toronto: Pontifical Institute of Mediaeval Studies, 1990.

Ziegler, Joseph. "Physiognomy, Science and Proto-Racism, 1200–1500," in *The Origins of Racism in the West*, ed. Miraim Eliav-Feldon, Benjamin H. Isaac, and Joseph Ziegler. Cambridge: Cambridge University Press, 2009, 181–99.

Zurara, Gomes Eanes de. *The Chronicle of the Discovery and Conquest of Guinea*, ed. and transl. Charles Raymond Beazley and Edgar Prestage. 2 vols. London: Hakluyt Society, 1896–99.

Zurara, Gomes Eanes de. *Cronica dos feitos notaveis que se passaram na conquista de guine por mandado do infant D. Henrique*, ed. Torquato de Sousa Soares. 2 vols. Lisbon: Academia Portuguesa da História, 1978.

Index